# HENRY VII

England's famous Tudor dynasty was established only through the determined struggles of its first monarch, Henry VII. This original biography examines how Henry VII balanced his own inexperience against his overriding aim to preserve Tudor kingship and establish the roots of a dynasty.

The reign of Henry VII (1485–1509) was vitally important in stabilising English monarchy and providing the sound financial and institutional basis for later developments in government. But until now the details of Henry as a person, his court, household and subjects have remained relatively unknown.

*Henry VII* illuminates the life of the man himself, how he ran his government, and the nature of the country over which he ruled since he first claimed the throne in 1485. Covering important themes in the political history of this period such as kingship and the development of government, response to rebellion, foreign policy and the Church, Sean Cunningham analyses how Henry VII redefined institutions and procedures to maintain his power, setting the benchmark for the personal power of later Tudor monarchs.

This highly readable new study uses up-to-date research to throw fresh light on the role of Henry VII's personality in the establishment and preservation of England's Tudor regime.

**Sean Cunningham** is an Assistant Keeper of Public Records at the National Archives. He is author of *Richard III: A Royal Enigma* (2003).

# ROUTLEDGE HISTORICAL BIOGRAPHIES

SERIES EDITOR: ROBERT PEARCE

*Routledge Historical Biographies* provide engaging, readable and academically credible biographies written from an explicitly historical perspective. These concise and accessible accounts will bring important historical figures to life for students and general readers alike.

In the same series:

*Bismarck* by Edgar Feuchtwanger
*Neville Chamberlain* by Nick Smart
*Oliver Cromwell* by Martyn Bennett
*Churchill* by Robert Pearce
*Edward IV* by Hannes Kleineke
*Gladstone* by Michael Partridge
*Henry VII* by Sean Cunningham
*Henry VIII* by Lucy Wooding
*Hitler* by Martyn Housden
*Jinnah* by Sikander Hayat
*Lenin* by Christopher Read
*Louis XIV* by Richard Wilkinson
*Martin Luther King Jr.* by Peter J. Ling
*Martin Luther* by Michael Mullet
*Mary Queen of Scots* by Retha M. Warnicke
*Mao* by Michael Lynch
*Mussolini* by Peter Neville
*Nehru* by Ben Zachariah
*Emmeline Pankhurst* by Paula Bartley
*Richard III* by Ann Kettle
*Franklin D. Roosevelt* by Stuart Kidd
*Stalin* by Geoffrey Roberts
*Trotsky* by Ian Thatcher
*Mary Tudor* by Judith Richards

# HENRY VII

Sean Cunningham

Routledge
Taylor & Francis Group

LONDON AND NEW YORK

First published 2007
by Routledge
2 Park Square, Milton Park, Abingdon, Oxon, OX14 4RN

Simultaneously published in the USA and Canada
by Routledge
270 Madison Avenue, New York, NY 10016

*Routledge is an imprint of the Taylor & Francis Group, an informa business*

© 2007 Sean Cunningham

Typeset in Garamond by Saxon Graphics Ltd
Printed and bound in Great Britain by
Antony Rowe Ltd, Chippenham, Wiltshire

*British Library Cataloguing in Publication Data*
A catalogue record for this book is available from the British Library

*Library of Congress Cataloging in Publication Data*
Cunningham, Sean, 1967–
    Henry VII / Sean Cunningham.
        p. cm. — (Routledge historical biographies)
    Includes bibliographical references and index.
1. Henry VII, King of England, 1457-1509. 2. Great Britain—History—Henry
VII, 1485-1509. 3. Great Britain—Kings and rulers—Biography. I. Title.
II. Title: Henry 7th. III. Title: Henry the seventh.
    DA330.C86 2007
    942.05'1092—dc22

                                                                2006030860

ISBN 978-0-415-26620-8 (hbk)
ISBN 978-0-415-26621-5 (pbk)

# DEDICATION

To Kate, Kathy and Katherine – three of a kind

# Contents

# ILLUSTRATIONS

## PLATES (BETWEEN PP. 150 AND 151)

## MAPS

# Acknowledgements

I wish to thank Margaret Condon, Steve Gunn and DeLloyd Guth for great kindness, expert criticism, and encouragement over a number of years.

Steve Gunn, Bob Pearce, Vicky Peters and Liz Gooster have read the entire text in manuscript, saving me from many errors and greatly improving the book. They have also proved enduringly patient as the project became delayed. James Ross and Matthew Davies have also commented on various sections. Thanks also to Jane Blackwell, Philippa Grand, Emma Langley and Katherine Davey for their work on this book.

This book would not have been written without the support and encouragement of Sandy Grant and Tony Pollard. Sandy sparked my enduring interest in late medieval history, while both he and Tony have done their best to ensure that this book has not slipped from the radar.

Ian Arthurson, John Currin and Ralph Griffiths have proved inspirational – both in their detailed work on Henry VII's reign, and in their personal generosity. I am very grateful also to Rowena Archer, John Austin, Michael Bennett, Jim Bolton, Paul Brand, Clive Burgess, Paul Cavill, Linda Clark, David Crook, Cliff Davies, Rees Davies, Lisa Ford, Sandy Grant, David Grummitt, Michael Hicks, Rosemary Horrox, Susannah Humble, Adrian Jobson, Michael Jones, Maureen Jurkowski, Hannes Kleineke, Malcolm Mercer, Cath Nall, Jenni Nuttall, Stephen O'Connor, Simon Payling, Sarah Peverley, Tony Pollard, Colin Richmond, James Ross, David Santiuste, David Starkey, Livia Visser-Fuchs and John Watts for document references, advice, and discussion offered during the long preparation of this book.

I am grateful to members of the Late Medieval Seminar at the Institute of Historical Research for comment and discussion of several research papers over many years. Jim Bolton deserves great credit for his commitment, through this seminar, to medieval scholarship in London. I and several other scholars have benefited immensely from his guidance and expertise. I must also express my thanks to Doug Biggs, Jeff Hamilton, and the affiliates of the White Hart Society for several recent opportunities to present my ideas at the International Congress on Medieval Studies.

Current and former colleagues at the PRO/National Archives have endured my struggles with this book for longer than they might have hoped. To Nick Barratt, Amanda Bevan, Liz Hallam-Smith and James Travers, especially, I wish to express my thanks for their support and interest.

Without the encouragement of my parents I would not have been in a position to write this book. I hope the end product compensates for the time spent away from my wife Kate and sons Sam and Dan. Above all, Kate seems to have suffered Henry Tudor for far longer than Elizabeth of York had to. For that I can only apologise with deep gratitude.

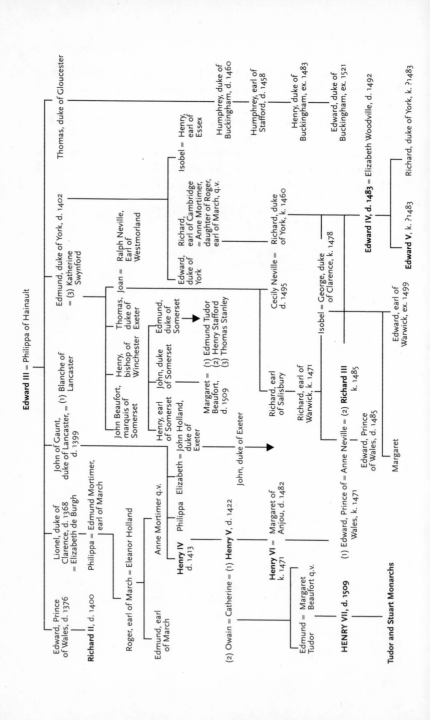

# 1

# INTRODUCTION

## OVERVIEW OF THE BOOK

In Shakespeare's *King Richard III* the victorious Henry Tudor, earl of Richmond, has a surprisingly undeveloped role as the saviour of England from Richard's tyranny and the Wars of the Roses at the battle of Bosworth on 22 August 1485. Looking back from 1597, Shakespeare saw the fruits of the Tudor triumph, and he captured the significance of the battle with the lines:

> All that divided York and Lancaster
> United in their dire division.
> O now let Richmond and Elizabeth,
> The true succeeders of each House,
> By God's fair ordinance conjoin together,
> And let their heirs – God, if his will be so -
> Enrich the time to come with smooth-faced peace ...¹

Henry Tudor would unite the contending nobles of England through his marriage to Princess Elizabeth of York. Shakespeare was asking his audience to recognise that Henry's triumph ended civil war and initiated the development of the prosperity that later Elizabethans were enjoying. Despite that achievement, the above speech was just about Henry's only

appearance in Shakespeare's works. And therein lies the root of the problem of how his reign has been interpreted.

Generations of historians and writers agreed that Henry's seizure of
the throne heralded a new period of English kingship. The overmighty
nobles and private armies of the fifteenth century were put under the
king's control. The monarchy broke away from a reliance on parliament
for money. The crown by-passed the local influence of noble landholders
and placed power in the hands of the king's new-made men, lawyers, and
professional administrators, to begin a revolution in the way the country was ruled. Henry VII's reign was seen as the first step in this period
of rapid change in crown government. The ruthless grip on power he
achieved was the key factor in creating conditions for later sixteenth century developments to thrive.

The great administrative and institutional changes that Henry
brought about were important and worthy, but a little uninspiring and
unexciting for readers of medieval history. His reputation has suffered as
historians have struggled to free Henry from the labels of great legislator
and administrator. The period 1985 to 2009 marks the half-millennium
since Henry VII ruled England. Yet the beginning and end of Henry's
reign have been, and will be, marked only in terms of the monarchs who
came before and after him.

Of all the rulers of the Tudor century, Henry is most frequently overlooked because he remains firmly sandwiched between two of the most
notorious, monstrous, and intriguing monarchs to have ruled England
– Richard III and Henry VIII. These two kings now have a grotesque
and magnified reputation that extends beyond the known facts of their
lives. It also permeates deep into popular culture to the extent that they
both exist almost as caricatures of kingship: Richard as the archetypal
medieval villain, and Henry as the model of royal gluttony, excess, and
extravagance.

Henry VII remains in their shadows and over time his reputation has
paled against these two giants of popular English history. They have such
notoriety only because writers have devoted a great deal of imagination
to the task of creating the popular image we now know so well. Whether
they are represented accurately is still a matter of great discussion. For a
monarch such as Richard III especially, alleged literary misrepresentation
of the king by writers such as Polydore Vergil, Thomas More, Edward
Hall and William Shakespeare, has meant that there is a body of work that

has dominated the popular view of the king. This literature-as-history has provided orthodoxy against which Richard's modern supporters have been able to struggle and counteract. Henry VII, whose reputation to a great extent remains constrained by the same body of Tudor and Stuart writers, has generated no such curious fascination.

Henry is still one of the most enigmatic and apparently inaccessible of English monarchs, despite the prominent fascination with the Tudor dynasty in studies of British history and popular culture. This book intends to show that the fifty-two years of Henry's life from 28 January 1457 to 21 April 1509 not only incorporated a crucial period in the development of the power of centralised crown government but also represents a fascinating story of transition from obscurity to royal status, and the mastery of all the skills of monarchy as he struggled constantly to hold onto the crown reputedly plucked from a battlefield thorn bush.

For many years, history books regarded 1485 as a key event in English history – a turning point, the beginning of a Tudor revolution in government.[2] Some academics disregarded this, and argued that Henry VII was very much a product of his age and could not have initiated anything new in government without a heavy reliance upon the institutions, personnel, and practices that had been in place before he gained the throne. From the 1970s this argument over Henry as the continuator of medieval practice or innovator of more modern Renaissance ideas has raged between academics without anyone really tackling the king and his reign in depth: the areas to investigate have been identified, but a full and balanced investigation is still awaited.

This was perhaps because the sources for Henry's reign were wholly the same as for any other fifteenth-century king – scattered, more difficult to access, and harder to interpret – and Tudor historians were reluctant to adopt the methods of medievalists. Henry VII is doubly unlucky in that much of the material that does exist for his immediate predecessors has not survived from his reign. Returns of MPs to the House of Commons, most of the assessments for taxation, and financial material on annuities and other payments are missing. Furthermore, many of the chronicle sources that provide valuable personal insights into events during the Wars of the Roses were not continued after Henry took the crown.

We have two schools of historians, strictly divided by the boundary of scholarship represented by 1485, neither being willing to move away from their own familiar sources and historiographical traditions. The last major study of Henry VII – by S.B. Chrimes in 1972 – was written by a medievalist, but used Tudor historians as source material. Chrimes was also a great constitutional authority, so his own expertise helped to create a work that focused on the administrative history of Henry's reign. This study underlined the power of the crown as an institution, but offered very little on politics and personalities, not least the character of the king himself.

Henry VII's reign now occupies an inconvenient position in the chronology of English rulers and their contribution to the development of the modern nation. Even if we disregard that, Henry has always been a difficult king to make glamorous. As the monarch who ended the Wars of the Roses, his reign at first sight does not provide the stereotypical medieval evidence of battle, turmoil, murder and revenge that is found under Henry VI, Edward IV and Richard III. Nor does the period 1485–1509 contain the seismic events that were to change the fabric of English society during the reign of Henry VIII.

As the conqueror of Richard III, we might expect Henry VII to have been more warmly studied by historians, but his reputation has suffered as 'collateral damage' in the campaign to rehabilitate Richard III. Indeed, it was the Tudor manipulation of Richard III's reputation that has prompted some historians to label Henry as a propagandist. What is clear was that once he had won the crown, Henry did everything in his power to hold onto it. After a century of noble squabbling over the authority of the crown, this was perhaps a wholly reasonable attitude to hold.

Henry was unique among medieval monarchs. No king since William the Conqueror had less knowledge of or familiarity with England than did Henry when he took the throne in 1485. No king was more successful at resisting rebellion than Henry, yet none of his predecessors had faced such numerous, protracted, and complex conspiracies. No king mastered the practical demands of ruling the country to the same extent as Henry, yet few saw their initiatives and efforts in government overturned and disregarded so rapidly by successors. No king since 1066 had a greater inheritance than Henry, yet none had a smaller royal family or close circle of allies among whom it could be distributed. As a result, he did not distribute it very widely at all. No king had such a strong reliance upon the influence of the main women in his life – his mother and his wife – both for his very claim to the throne and also as a means of exercising royal power. All of this makes Henry VII an intriguing figure, but one who is very difficult to understand, even within the context of his age.

There are very many aspects of Henry VII's rule that conform to broader ideas, but just as Henry existed within the framework of institutions and ideas that he inherited and absorbed, the circumstances of his personal life before he became king had a very powerful and direct influence upon the way he ruled the country and the techniques he developed to maintain power. Of course, all monarchs start their reigns by drawing on the experience, awareness, education and loyalties of their childhood, upbringing, and adult life spent in preparation for rule. But Henry Tudor's life into his mid-twenties was almost devoid of any prospect of even the most basic or fleeting contact with noble, let alone royal, responsibility.

When he did become king there is an almost perceptible struggle between the established practices of the ancient institutions of government and Henry's wish to create effective rule on his own terms, using servants and officials that he could maintain and control. Because he had no practical experience of running his life as a nobleman within England, he brought a distinctly personal and uncluttered attitude to the rigours of kingship.

Even if Henry's ruling ethos can be boiled down to 'preservation of the Tudor dynasty at all costs', there remains very much more to the first Tudor monarch than the overriding image of a dour accountant king who sacrificed normal royal pleasures for state-building and dynastic security. Ralph Griffiths neatly summed up popular apathy towards Henry VII in the introduction to his book *The Making of the Tudor Dynasty*. He commented that, although Richard III was a king strongly suspected by contemporaries of murdering his own nephews and of poisoning his wife, few visitors asked for a souvenir of Henry from the Bosworth battlefield visitor centre. This could be because the English love the story of heroic failure that Richard III represents. However, since the 1920s, Richard III has been the focus of a society actively promoting a revision of the defamatory reputation given to him. Henry VII has had no such champion, and assessments of his character and achievements have languished as a result.

## HENRY VII: THE MAN AND HIS REPUTATION AS KING

As with most medieval kings, little easily accessible biographical detail survives for Henry VII. His actions and motives often have to be reconstructed from evidence of his decision-making through grants, accounts, or legal records. In his study of Henry VII in 1972,[3] Stanley Chrimes pleaded for more work to be done on the scores of records from Henry's reign unused in the Public Record Office and elsewhere. He particularly valued the books recording payments and receipts of Henry's personal chamber, a collection that has not survived from earlier reigns yet remains to be analysed in detail for Henry's. These volumes are a wonderful resource, since they record daily expenditure on everything from a few pennies for church offerings, alms, or boat hire, to major building works or the financing of armies. What they can't provide is fly-on-the-wall evidence of the private life of the royal family. We can know the relative value of some of the objects he brought into his palaces and apartments. It is rare, however, that the entries indicate the thoughts and intentions behind Henry's purchases.

If we look back 500 years we see Henry giving the queen £40 in loose change, paying 66s to his Breton godson Henry Pynago, and offering 6s to a servant for a branch of oranges. The man portrayed in these accounts promoted lavish state occasions, festivals and feasts; he sponsored and enthusiastically judged jousts and tournaments, paying large sums to upgrade the tiltyards at the palaces of Westminster and Kennington; we know the names of all the king's musicians, who were paid very well, and the generous New Year's gifts offered to the grooms and pages of the king's and queen's households. Henry's court was frequently entertained by tumblers, jugglers, a 'long Fleming' and a Scottish fool. He lost money at cards, tennis, chess and dice. He was typical of medieval nobles in his love of hunting with hawks and hounds, and supplied regular money to maintain Queen Elizabeth's obsessive interest in horses. There are also entries like the extra rewards for those servants who were on duty and missed New Year's Eve celebrations, or excessive generosity such as 40s to a servant who brought some figs, 12d for a gift of apples, or 6s for one of his falconers who gave Henry a prize lamprey.

A snapshot from 1502–03, during the rebuilding (as Richmond Palace) of the fire-damaged medieval royal residence at Sheen, gives some indication of the king's private arrangements. Henry provided various sums to the grooms of the chamber, who by the end of 1502 had travelled throughout the country to find red deer, hinds and fawns suitable for the new deer park; the village blacksmith was paid 66s for a little clock for the palace in November 1502. Building works were far from complete, since scaffolding was paid for and over £10 spent to complete a new entrance gate that same month. By January 1503 Henry was decorating his apartments. Tabernacles were newly painted by Master Thomas Starre; boatloads of Henry's treasure and plate were moved from the less hospitable Tower of London; two organs were transferred from Westminster palace, as was a birdcage that cost over £2. By the spring of 1503 a new gallery had been built at the palace, costing £50, and the master craftsman Bernard Flower had spent almost £64 in glazing the royal apartments.

The payments at that time varied considerably: an entry for 10s for the gardener at the Tower in December 1502 is followed by the enormous sum of £30,000 spent in purchasing land for the endowment of the king's chapel at Westminster. The depth of the evidence is great but untapped. A full understanding of Henry's reign requires comprehensive investigation of these and other unique sources. Lists of such evidence prove that Henry VII was a real person enjoying normal human concerns and pleasures, and not simply an abstract or stereotypical figure of a particular type of kingship. This fact is often hard to remember when reading academic studies.

The evidence of Henry's most affectionate feelings relate not to his relationship with his wife, but his mother. Modern readers might draw immediate conclusions from this fact alone. In 1501 Henry acceded to her request for a licence with all his heart, not only in that particular matter but also in all things that should be to her honour and pleasure. He also begged forgiveness for writing so infrequently, but his failing eyesight made this very difficult. It was a mark of his determination to please her that he struggled over several days to finish the letter in his own hand.[4]

Their relationship was immensely strong, despite little more than a few weeks together before Henry became king at the age of 28. Margaret made up for lost time and became a domineering presence behind his personal rule from 1485. The evidence of Henry's relationship with Queen Elizabeth, on the other hand, suggests that she was a matrimonial prize to bind her Yorkist relatives to the Tudor crown. Elizabeth was denied the type of political role that other powerful women like Margaret Beaufort, Queen Elizabeth Woodville, and Cecily, duchess of York, had earlier enjoyed, and had employed in the struggle for the crown from 1483 to 1485. It has been difficult for historians to get behind this official downplaying of Elizabeth's role in the Tudor state to discover her real relationship with Henry.

Images of Henry give little indication of his personality. The formal and idealised views in late medieval portraiture make it dangerous to suggest any insight into character. Most surviving images of Henry were intended as iconography for official purposes. There is no surviving contemporary portrait of Henry before 1500. A representation of Henry as a young man exists in the Library of Arras in northern France, but is probably a sixteenth-century copy. Only two pictures are believed by experts to have been painted in his lifetime. Perhaps the earliest exists at Hever Castle in Kent, and accompanies a life portrait of Prince Arthur completed before his marriage to Catherine of Aragon in 1501. The famous image of the king in the National Portrait Gallery was commissioned in 1505 as Henry contemplated a second marriage. With his uneven eyes, straight nose and thin lips, it perhaps provides the clearest view of Henry in later life.

Although early sixteenth-century copies, two portraits at the London Society of Antiquaries might come closest to capturing the essence of Henry VII and the transformation that his reign wrought on his appearance. The picture of a youthful king (Scharf XXII) shares the same nose, lips, chin and sunken eyes as the image of the much-older man (Scharf XXIV). That grey-haired king has a shrewd, gaunt face, and looks troubled at being distracted from something more important. Two other representations of Henry emphasise yet further the decline in Henry's last years. The terracotta portrait bust by Pietro Torrigiano in the Victoria and Albert Museum is perhaps the most famous image of the king. It captures Henry's strong features and imposing presence. Although it was created in 1508–09 it contrasts strongly with Henry's death mask in Westminster Abbey. This object was expertly made, but has suffered damage, especially to the nose, and no longer shares common features with other portraiture. Nevertheless, it has the same drawn quality about the cheeks and eyes, and suggests that the king was wasted by his final illness.

Some modern works on Henry still enforce the view that he was only painstaking and meticulous, parsimonious, obsessed with accumulating cash, shadowy and remote, ruthless, inscrutable and severe. It becomes tempting to view images of the king with these adjectives in mind. Many of these descriptions are found in John Guy's *Tudor England*. But even a closer look at contemporary sources offers some contradictions that suggest that complex research is needed to understand Henry VII. Within Vergil there is ample evidence that Henry's court was lavish, that he was generous to guests, warm, friendly and accessible. Aspects of austere and accessible descriptions of Henry are found in letters of Venetian, Florentine, Milanese and Spanish ambassadors, which offer snapshots at different periods within the reign.

Henry's avarice apparently risked rebellion on the one hand, yet after the last serious uprising of the reign was crushed in 1497 he was described as more relaxed and free to count his treasure. In 1496 a Florentine merchant could comment that should the English nobility rise up against their king, Henry would receive little support since his avaricious policies had caused his people to abandon him. Later in the reign, the Venetian ambassador claimed that had Henry attempted to change the established traditions of the country, every Englishman would have given the impression of being deprived of his life – clearly suggesting that he attempted nothing of the sort. Confusing evidence comes from the descriptions of Henry and his court in contemporary accounts. A deeper reading of all of these sources, however, does get closer to the real reasons for the contradictions in Henry's behaviour and the increasing harshness of his rule: that the recurring crises of the reign prevented any kind of long-term consolidation of authority.

Henry remains something of a tragic figure. There is a great gulf between our understanding of the public monarch and the private man, yet more evidence exists to unite the two distinct sides to Henry's personality than can be presented here. His life as king was only just longer than the wasted years of his childhood and exile, and he was relatively old when he won the crown. Although he successfully established our most famous ruling dynasty, this was only achieved through constant vigilance. His fear of deposition prevented him from relaxing and he was probably too ill to enjoy fully the fruits of his policies once his enemies had been undermined. He is a far more colourful, dynamic, sympathetic and fascinating figure than almost all the sources suggest in isolation – which is largely how they have been used.

# 2

## GAINING THE CROWN

### CHILDHOOD, YOUTH AND EXILE, 1457–1483

Henry Tudor's route to the throne of England is a remarkable story of triumph over disaster, obscurity and isolation. Once he became king, the unconventional experience of his youthful years made his retention of the crown all the more impressive, especially as the previous four kings had been deposed violently. Henry's background was unusual. His grandfather, Owain Tudor, had married Henry V's widow, Katherine of Valois, probably in 1431–2. Later writers romanticised the origins of this relationship with stories of how the queen had fallen in love with Owain when he was swimming in a river near the court, but the marriage was kept secret until Katherine was dead in 1437.

While it must have been a startling relationship, the marriage was certainly based in genuine passion. Owain and Katherine's four children, including three sons – Edmund, Jasper and Owain – all shared a direct blood connection to the kings of France. The ruling English Lancastrian regency for Henry VI was more concerned that this half-blood line should not undermine the status of the crown. Owain was initially viewed with suspicion, and Edmund and Jasper were sent to live at Barking Abbey in Essex. As Henry VI assumed more personal responsibility, Owain Tudor was restored to favour by the end of 1439. In the early 1440s his two eldest sons joined him in the royal social circle. In 1447, the death of his last uncle allowed Henry VI to pay more attention to his Tudor kinsmen. Jasper and Edmund became, respectively, earls of Pembroke and Richmond in 1452 and they were given grants of land appropriate to their rapid rise in status.

In March 1453 the Tudor brothers also received the joint wardship of Margaret, daughter of John Beaufort, duke of Somerset (d. 1444). She was heiress to the powerful Beaufort family. Henry VI probably had dynastic reasons for bringing his Tudor and Beaufort relatives together. He also seems to have been directly involved in ensuring that Edmund and Margaret eventually married by 1455, when Margaret was only 11 years old. The Beauforts were legitimated offspring of Edward III's son John of Gaunt, and this connection further strengthened Tudor claims to royal blood.

Once given their elevated status, Jasper and Edmund Tudor played a full part in the political crisis that developed during the 1450s. When Henry VI fell into a first period of mental incapacity in 1453, both Tudor brothers seem to have backed Duke Richard of York's claim to be Protector. Having served York's regime they were placed in an impossible position when Henry VI recovered his sanity at the close of 1454. Jasper was far-sighted enough to join the search for a compromise between York's royal claims and the rejuvenated followers of the king. His support for mediation probably continued after the brief but bloody street battle at St Albans on 1 May 1455. Although the Tudor earls swore allegiance to the king in parliament later that month, they were part of a broad group of lords seeking to repair the political damage done by the outbreak of violence. Slow progress, however, probably caused Edmund and Jasper to commit to the king's cause by the end of the year.

Edmund Tudor was soon the king's leading agent in south Wales. He worked hard to overcome initial opposition and to establish personal authority. This responsibility made Edmund a target for the Yorkists as the hostility between Richard, duke of York, and the king's supporters heightened in the second half of the 1450s. York's allies in his Welsh Marcher lordships, Sir William Herbert and Sir Walter Devereux, raised a force of 2,000 troops and attacked Edmund at Carmarthen castle in August 1456. Edmund was captured and imprisoned. By 1 November he was dead: most probably from disease. Henry Tudor was born three months later on 28 January 1457.

Margaret Beaufort became Henry's mother when only just 14 years of age. Not surprisingly, it was a very difficult birth in which both mother and baby were close to death. Since Margaret had no further children we can speculate that she suffered lasting physical damage as a result of this early pregnancy. The bond between Henry and his mother was formed in circumstances we today find difficult to comprehend. Their relationship was the basis for almost all of Henry's actions as king, and became the steadfast foundation of the Tudor dynasty. At the start of 1457, however, no one would have accepted Henry Tudor's place in the royal succession, let alone the possibility that he might one day become king. Deprived of a father, and with a mother who would have been distressed even without the tragedy of her husband's death, Henry was immediately reliant upon others for his safety. Much of the tenacity and stubbornness Henry later showed perhaps grew from the example of his protector – the dynamic and singularly determined figure of his uncle Jasper, earl of Pembroke.

Jasper probably blamed the Yorkists for his brother's death, since he became openly hostile towards them from that time. His first concern was for his widowed sister-in-law and her infant son. The sympathetic Humphrey Stafford, duke of Buckingham, took them into his care at Pembroke castle. This connection resulted in the marriage of Margaret to Buckingham's son, Henry, at the start of April 1457.

Jasper then took over his brother's role and stepped up his efforts to secure south Wales for the Lancastrian crown. Through careful management of his followers he established a sound reputation as a noble leader. The descent into civil war in 1459 saw Jasper secure his region against York's supporters. He swore an oath to uphold Henry VI's authority and to maintain the rights of Edward, Prince of Wales, in parliament at Coventry in October 1459. His closeness to the crown brought Jasper and his father Owain many estates forfeited by the king's opponents.

By that date the Yorkist lords were exiled in Ireland and Calais. Jasper's main role was to secure the south and west of the principality against their possible return. This defensive role meant that the Tudors were able only to make one major contribution to the military conflict before Henry VI was deposed. In February 1461 Jasper and his father Owain recruited a major part of the Welsh Lancastrian force that confronted a Yorkist army at Mortimer's Cross near Leominster. The battle was a disaster for the Tudors. Owain was captured and mercilessly executed afterwards. Jasper beat a hasty retreat to south Wales. He evaded the forces of Edward IV and remained around Tenby, even after the decisive Yorkist victory at Towton in Yorkshire on 29 March drove surviving Lancastrian leaders into exile. By the end of the year Jasper had joined the Lancastrian royal family in Scotland. He was attainted and deprived of his estates in Edward IV's first parliament of November 1461. Without allies or resources he could no longer continue the struggle against the Yorkist crown as King Edward's servants quickly recovered power in Wales.

In May 1461, 4-year-old Henry Tudor was with his mother and her second husband at Pembroke castle when Sir William Herbert (soon Lord Herbert of Raglan) took over Jasper Tudor's authority in south Wales. Herbert formally acquired the wardship and marriage[1] of Henry Tudor for the enormous sum of £1,000 in 1462. Henry was removed from his mother's care and went to live in the Herbert household at Raglan castle. Margaret followed her husband into England. She was allowed some contact with Henry, and did visit him at Raglan, but this was infrequent. Instead of breaking the bond between them, each year of separation seems to have strengthened the basis of their future relationship.

Young Henry was in the care of William Herbert's wife, Anne Devereaux. She was rewarded once Henry came to the throne, so there was some element of gratefulness in his later treatment of the people who had brought him up. Henry shared his youthful years with Herbert's heir, also named William Herbert, and Henry Percy, who would become 4th earl of Northumberland in March 1470. Both of these boys were just a few years older than Henry, and as far as the evidence shows they were his only childhood companions of equal rank. Their connection with Henry eased their passage into Tudor favour after 1485.

Henry received some formal and suitable education as a young member of the peerage. He retained the title of earl of Richmond, even though Edward IV had regranted his father's lands. While Edward tried to track down and eliminate the Lancastrians who threatened his crown, surviving documents provide little evidence of how Henry lived through his first decade. Despite his blood connection to Henry VI, Henry Tudor had done nothing to offend Edward IV, and we can only assume that he resided quietly and untroubled at Raglan.

The memory of Jasper's strong leadership in Wales gave him a prominent part in the Lancastrian plans to topple Edward IV. Henry VI and Queen Margaret had suffered many military and political setbacks by

1464, but in February that year Brittany provided ships and allowed a Lancastrian force to head for Wales. Although this expedition came to nothing, the garrison at Harlech castle was inspired to continue to hold out for Henry VI. This last outpost of resistance became a focus for broader Lancastrian efforts. The Welsh dimension also placed greater responsibility on Jasper Tudor's shoulders. He exploited his status as a Welshman near the top of the English peerage. Once his nephew was king, Welsh writers championed Jasper's struggle and developed the heroic Welsh dimension to his leadership during the 1460s. But for much of the decade, the attainted earl of Pembroke was an emissary, messenger, and diplomatic beggar on behalf of Henry VI. Since Lord Herbert could not be everywhere at once, Jasper was able to visit Harlech frequently by sea. His lingering presence in a region that remained unsympathetic towards the Yorkist king gave at least a chance to the Lancastrian cause if the political tide could be made to turn against Edward IV.

Interest in the Lancastrians' position grew once again in parts of Europe from the mid-1460s. Edward IV's inappropriate marriage to Elizabeth Woodville and his mishandling of the kingmaking Richard Neville, earl of Warwick, brought about a shift in England's foreign relations. By June 1468 the French king Louis XI, alarmed at England's alliance with his enemy Duke Charles of Burgundy, supplied Jasper with the resources for a military expedition. He certainly made the most of them. After landing near Harlech he raided throughout north Wales. Lord Herbert achieved the surrender of Harlech castle in August 1468 but Jasper once again slipped away by sea. If nothing else, this event demonstrated that Jasper Tudor's belief in the almost-lost Lancastrian cause could still carry the fight to Edward IV – a lesson that Henry was to learn well by 1483.

Jasper's earldom of Pembroke was granted to Lord Herbert at the start of September 1468. But only ten months later, on 26 July 1469, Herbert was defeated and executed at the battle of Edgecote near Banbury, during a rising in favour of the earl of Warwick. This disaster for Yorkist power in Wales marked the beginning of a collapse in Edward IV's national authority. Warwick and the king's brother George, duke of Clarence, joined the Lancastrian party then gathering strength in France. A combination of French backing and Warwick's manpower drew together a large force that sailed from Normandy to Devon in September 1470. The arrival of an invading enemy when King Edward was away from

Westminster prompted him to flee to the Netherlands. The longed-for restoration of Henry VI took place at the start of October. A reunion of the 13-year-old Henry with his mother and uncle could occur in the happiest of circumstances – a vindication of family tenacity and dynastic perseverance.

Jasper made straight for south Wales with the intent of reviving his personal power. Henry remained at Raglan, but was soon transferred to the Devereaux seat at Weobley castle in Herefordshire. During the crisis of Edward IV's deposition, Henry was passed to the custody of the Herefordshire knight Sir Richard Corbet, who made sure that Henry and Jasper were reunited at Hereford during the first week of October 1470. Later that month Henry met his mother for the first time in many years in what must have been emotional circumstances. The family spent almost two weeks together in London and on a journey along the Thames valley. By 12 November, Margaret departed from her teenage son and Henry returned to London with his uncle. This was almost certainly the last time mother and son were together until Henry seized the crown over fifteen years later.

Jasper Tudor naturally recovered his dominance in Wales, but the lands of Henry's earldom of Richmond could not be prised from the hands of the king's grasping ally, George, duke of Clarence. Clarence remained the key to the regime's success: his and Warwick's defection from the Yorkists gave Henry VI a chance of converting others who had prospered under Edward IV. Edward seized the initiative and landed unopposed in Yorkshire on 12 March 1471. He was soon welcomed in London at the head of a growing army. On 14 April Clarence switched sides and the earl of Warwick died as his army was massacred in the fog at the battle of Barnet. Jasper was raising forces in Wales when Queen Margaret and the Lancastrian Prince of Wales landed in Dorset with another army. With Warwick already dead, Edward regrouped in London and was quickly on the trail of the queen's force into Gloucestershire. At Tewkesbury on 4 May, and with Jasper Tudor still approaching from south Wales, the Lancastrian cause suffered a final, disastrous defeat. In another vicious encounter, Prince Edward was killed and the duke of Somerset captured and executed two days later. Crucially, Henry VI died (most probably murdered on Edward IV's orders), in the Tower on the night of 21 May.

Without their king or his heir, the Lancastrian cause almost fell apart. It was only then that Henry Tudor's blood connection both to the

Beauforts and Henry VI propelled him into the spotlight as a Lancastrian figurehead. Once the news of Tewkesbury reached them, Jasper and Henry reversed their route and headed back to Chepstow castle. From there, Jasper captured and callously beheaded Sir Roger Vaughan who had been sent from the battlefield by Edward IV to intercept the Tudors. Jasper and Henry were then besieged in Pembroke castle but rescued by men who remembered the good lordship Jasper had shown earlier in his haphazard career. Further attempts were made to seize the Tudors, but they evaded all efforts to track them down and sailed from Tenby to Brittany in October 1471.

The threat from his enemies had receded considerably, but Edward IV realised that he could not be entirely sure of his security until all threads of the Lancastrian opposition were tied up. With the Tudors and Edward's other obstinate opponent, John de Vere, 13th earl of Oxford, on French territory, the Lancastrian struggle now became a more direct extension of the internal politics of France. Duke Francis II of Brittany sought to attract England's soldiers and cash to boost his struggle to preserve Breton independence from Louis XI. When the Tudor fugitives became his guests they were also important assets in the diplomatic bargaining that developed between Brittany, England, and France. Edward IV sent troops to Brittany in the spring of 1472. They helped to resist French attacks on the border and further plans for a stronger alliance were made in Brittany, and also by Breton ambassadors in London the following November.

Displaying an honourable stubbornness that thwarted the Yorkist kings to 1485, Duke Francis refused to tie the fate of Jasper and Henry Tudor into any of these agreements. Edward knew that he could not force Francis's hand since Brittany was an important part of the Yorkist crown's network of alliances against France. The best Edward could hope for was closer confinement of two of his principal rebels. By 1474, Louis XI also accepted this situation. Henry and Jasper probably moved around with the Duke's court. Demands that Jasper should be returned to French soil were rejected by Francis in several carefully argued diplomatic exchanges. In 1474, however, rumours that they could be kidnapped or even murdered by English (or French) agents caused Jasper and Henry to be housed in more secure and more remote Breton castles. They were sent to separate locations in this year as Edward IV and Louis XI headed towards war.

England and France avoided conflict with what many lords viewed as a disappointing agreement at Picquingy in August 1475. Edward IV received a French pension but very little prestige. He did, however, secure a new level of understanding with the French that brought limited security to the Breton frontier. As a result, Edward also tried a bolder strategy to persuade Duke Francis to hand the Tudors over. Margaret Beaufort and her husband had already made their peace with Edward after Tewkesbury. After such a disheartening defeat it is likely that she started to look for ways to bring her son back into the fold of the Yorkist aristocracy. It was proposed that a suitable bride for Henry should be found among the noble elite and that he should have a grant of lands to match his status as earl of Richmond.

Duke Francis was now frequently ill and temporarily deprived of his ablest councillors. He was eventually persuaded of the honesty of Edward IV's proposal to marry Henry into his family. Francis agreed to hand Henry over to English ambassadors at the end of 1476. When on the point of boarding ship at St Malo, Henry probably pretended to be ill and caused a delay to his repatriation. This was enough time for Francis to reverse his decision and send officials to intercept Henry's party. While discussions were ongoing, Henry escaped to sanctuary in St Malo and was eventually returned to the Duke's court. Edward IV was furious, but could do little else other than try to exert further pressure.

As his continued protection of the Tudors frustrated both England and France, Francis brought uncle and nephew together at Vannes in 1476. Further English promises of troops to counteract more aggressive French policy attempted to force Brittany into a decision on the return of Henry and Jasper. The uneasy situation continued into the 1480s. Edward IV attempted to lure Henry with new arrangements over the inheritance of his mother's lands and clearer marriage proposals. Henry's position was still unresolved when Edward died suddenly on 9 April 1483.

While Duke Francis and his leading councillors treated Henry and his uncle honourably, they were still prisoners. Breton accounts provide a reasonable guide to where the Tudors lived, but very little is known about Henry's personal life and physical health before he became king. Henry had a restricted but active upbringing in Brittany. Fragments of accounts show some of the castles he stayed in, and gifts such as horses, but nothing to suggest an unusually inactive upbringing. He must have received conventional martial training and been possessed of some personal courage since he was prepared to risk his safety on the battle-field when he had very little to lose but his life. In his late teenage years Henry did spend part of his exile with Brittany's elite professional soldiers, such as Bertran du Parc. It is probable that he received as normal a noble education as possible, and this included physically demanding training in the techniques and tactics of warfare. So Polydore Vergil's assertion that Henry was lean, muscular and strong suggests a man who was not in physical decline until his final few years of life.

Jasper probably remained at Vannes after 1475. Henry is found in various locations with lower-ranking guardians. This might suggest that Jasper was considered the more important figure, even after the death, in 1475, of Henry Holland, duke of Exeter, further reduced the direct descendants of the Lancastrian kings. Duke Francis paid for horses and personal servants for the Tudors and they lived as eminent noble guests of the court. But by 1481 Henry's expenses had become far greater than Jasper's.

As an active young man in his mid-twenties, Henry might have placed more demands on Duke Francis's purse. It is more likely, however, that a shift in the value of Henry's presence in Brittany had come about. The struggle against French dominion was more intense by then. Francis was also struggling to cope with more frequent bouts of illness, during which his councillors jostled for influence over policy. Edward IV's death heightened this problem to even greater levels. Henry's status had developed slowly during his exile so far. In the twenty-eight months that were to follow, Henry would progress from the status of a prisoner dependent on the goodwill of others to become king of England. This startling transformation compensated for the long years of abandonment, disappointment, and false hope that had marked the twenty-six years of his life since 1457.

## THE TRANSFORMATION OF THE TUDOR THREAT

During Richard III's reign, Henry Tudor's status as a claimant for the English crown was positively transformed from the bleak isolation of exile. After the close of 1483 especially, his prospects improved from the rather desperate figure attempting to exploit the uncertain aftermath of rebellion to that of a credible challenger to Richard, heading unified opposition to the English king by the spring of 1485.

In the final weeks of Edward IV's life, Henry personally had no more ability to influence his own destiny than in 1471 or 1475. A change in his status could only come about after a startling political development within England, or in England's foreign relations with France and Brittany. Edward IV's wholly unexpected death threatened both developments, although, initially, harmonious continuity in England seemed more likely than a noble tussle to control King Edward V. The dead king's household servants, his brother Richard, duke of Gloucester, and the Woodville nobles of the queen's blood family, all sought the rapid accession of Edward in May 1483. Brittany knew that he would continue his father's policies, especially as he was under age and would be governed by a protectorate council made up of leading Yorkists.

Richard III's usurpation by 26 June changed the picture once again. By displacing those Yorkists expecting Edward V's accession, Richard effectively created a new ruling elite. It was not a national group, but one focused on his northern power base. This meant a return to political conflict within England as Richard sought to impose himself on the whole country. The usurpation also ended any pretence of Henry Tudor's return to grace. The manner of Richard's coup, with the duke of Buckingham as a close ally, made the unsuspecting Henry his chief rival for the crown.

By becoming king through the military deposition of his nephew, Richard had to combat the anger and betrayal felt by the Yorkist elite. The queen's Woodville family, especially, had invested all of their political energy into securing control of Edward V when he was still Prince of Wales. This would have ensured their command of royal favour once he inherited the crown. While Edward IV was alive and healthy, their dominance of the Prince of Wales was not as threatening as it immediately became when the prince became king. At the close of June 1483, London gossip reported that the princes had disappeared within the Tower. Other Yorkist nobles of the royal blood, such as Edward Plantagenet, earl of Warwick, and John de la Pole, earl of Lincoln, were not threatening to Richard III, and remained part of his royal circle. Henry Tudor therefore represented the sole dynastic threat facing Richard. While Henry remained in Brittany he could be manipulated as part of Breton or French policy; but if his position could be negated, then Richard might contemplate a more stable environment in which to develop his kingship.

Control of Henry, perhaps even his return to England, could be dangled as an incentive to wring concessions from an insecure King Richard.

Louis XI wanted to use Henry as a bargaining tool to exert pressure on England in support of French claims to Brittany. Duke Francis wanted English help for the opposite reason: he might be unable to resist French demands unless England offered troops to defend his border.

Francis was very mindful that Brittany was the last of the semi-independent states (or feudatories) to retain autonomy from the French crown. He knew that after Duke Charles the Bold of Burgundy died in battle in 1477, France had quickly absorbed some of the scattered Burgundian lands. Charles's heir, Mary, had married Maximilian Habsburg, Archduke of Austria, in 1477. When she died in March 1482, the Holy Roman Empire, to which Maximilian was heir, gained nominal control over the Burgundian territories. Louis and Maximilian continued to carve up Burgundian lands with a treaty of 1482. Such aggressive French territorial expansion, and with the collusion of the powerful Habsburgs, made Brittany extremely vulnerable without secure alliances. Only England seemed in a position to help.

Within both France and Brittany there also existed complicated power struggles that elevated Henry's importance. When Louis XI died in August 1483, his heir, Charles VIII, was aged only 13. A regency was set up under the king's elder sister Anne of Beaujeu. The regency immediately conflicted with Louis, duke of Orléans, over governance of the king. Orléans sought international backing to challenge the French regency directly. He identified Henry's position in Brittany as a source of leverage. This policy was effective because a crisis of authority was also underway in Brittany. The lingering illness of Duke Francis meant that his senior officials dominated day-to-day government. Other Breton nobles resisted their influence to the point of open rebellion. Both parties aligned themselves with the rival French factions in an effort to influence politics within the duchy.

The duke of Brittany's only heir was his daughter Anne. Edward IV had been gravely concerned that Anne would be married to the French king and Brittany would lose its independence. The French could then dominate the Channel and be in a stronger position to continue territorial expansion. In February 1482 Edward had promised Brittany 4,000 archers to defend the border. Part of the agreement for this assistance was the surrender of Henry and Jasper Tudor. The situation was unresolved at Edward's death.

King Richard III seized the throne with slightly different priorities. He inherited a naval war against the French, and shipping from the

Low Countries and Brittany suffered in indiscriminate cross-Channel piracy. This led to Breton retaliation and a decline in relations with England. Richard III did not want the distraction of a foreign conflict as he prepared to face domestic resistance to his usurpation. While he was concerned about his Tudor rival, Richard needed to stabilise his relationship with Duke Francis. In July 1483 an embassy sent to discuss maritime matters also probably considered Henry's position. Henry's status had not really changed, despite a probable relaxation of his confinement. Nevertheless, he remained a recurring factor in calculations of the possible threats to Richard III.

## CONSPIRACY AND REBELLION, 1483

Henry was lucky that those political figures already targeted by Richard III as likely opponents were beginning to look to him as the focus of plotting in the summer of 1483. Two separate elements of conspiracy developed. The first was coordinated by John Morton, bishop of Ely, imprisoned at the duke of Buckingham's castle at Brecon. The second was a more complex plot that quickly attracted former household men of Edward IV, Margaret Beaufort and Elizabeth Woodville.

Morton seems to have been a man of exceptional guile and awareness. Thomas More, who was later partly educated in Morton's household, suggested that Morton gradually planted the idea of rebellion in Buckingham's mind by flattering his immense pride in his status. We can be certain that Henry Stafford was acutely conscious of his own royal lineage from Edward III (which was superior to Henry's legitimised Beaufort ancestry). By July 1483 it became clear that opposition to Richard's regime was gaining pace. A rising to free the princes failed in London on 3 July and could have hastened their deaths. With popular rumour rife, it is possible that Buckingham seized the opportunity to forward his own right to the crown. Polydore Vergil suggested that it was he who originated the crucial plan to depose Richard and that he 'unfolded all things to the bishop of Ely'.[2]

Here the duke displayed his subtlety. Buckingham was aware that an outright declaration of his own intentions would isolate him from the momentum being generated on Henry's behalf. By ingratiating himself with the Beaufort and Woodville group of plotters, Buckingham put himself into a position where he could apply his inside knowledge of Richard III's deceptively swift coup to sideline Henry. His own seizure of the crown could then be launched at the vital moment.

Morton quickly realised that Buckingham was willing to gamble everything on deposing Richard III. He was able to use Margaret Beaufort's servants, Reginald Bray and Dr Lewis Cærleon, to communicate information on the state of existing plans. Edward IV's widow, Elizabeth Woodville, must surely have been uncomfortable at the involvement of the abetter in her son's deposition, but she continued to immerse herself in the rebellion from sanctuary in Westminster Abbey. Once she was committed, it was also easier to involve the displaced servants of Edward IV and the household officials loyal to Edward V. Woodville contacts ensured that the conspiracy attracted support in a number of regions across southern England.

Crucial also was the influence of the Stanley family. Sir William Stanley was deeply attached to Edward IV's eldest son, and had headed his household at Ludlow castle. William's elder brother, Thomas, Lord Stanley, was Margaret Beaufort's third husband. Richard's mistrust of his proximity to Henry's mother had brought Stanley near to arrest as Richard prepared his coup. The conspiracy took full advantage of Stanley dominance in the north-west. One of Margaret's servants, Christopher Urswick, was charged to contact Henry with the latest progress of the conspiracy. His most important responsibility was to convey the news that Elizabeth Woodville would welcome the marriage of her daughter Elizabeth to Henry once Richard was defeated.

Several messengers travelled to Henry in the summer of 1483 with news of the acceleration of the conspiracy. The plan was for Henry to procure a military force and sail to Wales to raise rebellion in Jasper Tudor's former estates. He would then join with the massive army that Buckingham was capable of supplying from the Marcher lordships on the Anglo-Welsh border. The duke even took the remarkable step of writing to Henry directly, perhaps on 24 September 1483, providing the intended date of his own rising (18 October), and giving Henry enough information to coordinate his crossing. This short time span hints at extensive earlier communication. Yet as Ralph Griffiths commented, Buckingham 'made no pretence of acknowledging Henry as the next king of England or of welcoming his marriage to Elizabeth of York'.[3] Buckingham's interest went only as far as deposing Richard III.

The startling news that Buckingham was active within the conspiracy convinced Henry to approach Duke Francis with a plea to support an expedition to England. Henry probably disclosed some of the evidence of the plot and extent of the planned risings in England. Most importantly, Duke Francis was no doubt promised English help against France once Henry was king. Francis readily lent his support and allowed messengers to return to England with news of the assistance available to Henry.

The conspiracy seems to have planned a series of risings to confuse and split the king's forces, and to disguise Henry's arrival in the west to coordinate with Buckingham. On 10 October Kentish rebels were near to London. There were at least eight other flashpoints across southern England and the Welsh Marches. Centres of organised rebellion included Brecon (the duke of Buckingham), Maidstone (Sir John Guildford), Exeter (the marquis of Dorset), Newbury (Sir William Berkeley), and Salisbury (Sir Giles Daubeney). It is likely that Henry was declared king and Richard's rule condemned at each of these musters. A later enquiry into the Cornish sector of the rising at Bodmin indicated that the rebels were an unconnected mixture allied in opposition to Richard. This lack of direct commitment to Henry, and the sheer number of areas to be coordinated, made success very difficult.

The key rebel Buckingham also failed to raise his own tenants in the lands so recently acquired from King Richard. Here, the duke suffered by association with the Lancastrian Beauforts and Tudors. His unpopular style of lordship gave many the excuse to fail to muster when called, or to desert outright. He found his own estates under attack from the king's men, who also knocked down bridges over the River Severn and defended others against the rebels. Torrential rain and flooding left the duke with few options and he was captured at the house of a former servant on 30 October. Three days later he was beheaded at Salisbury without the meeting with Richard III that he had demanded. Even then, the rising in Cornwall did not start until 3 November as Richard continued his march to the south-west. Further north, a Stanley army – reputedly 10,000 strong – was ready to set out from Lancashire in mid-October. The quick collapse of the rebellion led to the premature dispersal of this force. By mid-November most southern rebels had either escaped or were captured.

Henry had an opportunity of only three weeks in which to put to sea once he received notice of Buckingham's intentions. Although Duke

Francis freely supported him against Richard III, Henry could hardly dictate the pace of preparations in Brittany. He received a payment to raise
troops and a small personal loan from Francis. Throughout September,
Henry prepared a fleet of about fifteen ships. As many as 5,000 men
were brought together at the port of Paimpol, but Henry was probably
delayed until the first days of November. The same foul weather that had
destroyed Buckingham's hopes also scattered Henry's ships as they fought
the Channel storms. When Henry's own vessel was joined by only one
other off Plymouth, his allies in the south-west had already dispersed.
Henry would not go ashore without more of his force in attendance. When
none appeared he returned towards Brittany. More bad weather dispersed
the Tudor flotilla along the French coastline, and his own landfall was in
Normandy. Henry's friends became scattered, with Morton, Urswick, and
Edward Poynings reaching the Low Countries.

The failure of the rebellion might actually have preserved Henry
Tudor's position. Had Buckingham defeated Richard III in battle, or
if the risings had forced the king to flee the country, it is possible that
Henry's absence would have encouraged Buckingham to play his hand.
In the last months of 1483, fleeing English rebels had no safe haven
other than to seek out Henry and attempt to rebuild their challenge to
Richard III. Henry's followers had been boosted by many senior Yorkist
gentry arriving from England – perhaps a total of almost five hundred
men. But these exiles had fled at the head of Richard's chasing soldiers
with what they could carry. Cut off from estates, communities, and
income it was difficult to gauge how they could once again contribute
materially to Henry's quest for the throne. The loans, cash, and ships provided by Duke Francis had also been squandered. Buckingham's death
might have left Henry as the only dynastic challenger to Richard III,
but he remained impoverished and reliant upon his continental hosts
for support.

After his dismal involvement in the upheavals of October 1483,
Henry had to take a more regal and inspiring lead as he rallied his com-
panions. With experienced figures now in his entourage, such as Thomas,
marquis of Dorset, Sir Edward Woodville, and Sir Giles Daubeney,
Henry took advice from those who had been at the centre of Edward
IV's rule. Intensive discussions at Rennes at Christmas 1483 resulted in
Henry's proclamation that he would marry Dorset's half-sister, Princess
Elizabeth of York, once the crown was won. He also required new oaths

of allegiance to underline the solemnity of their undertaking. Henry effectively became king to his community of exiles – but he was their only hope.

Life became very dangerous for Henry's friends remaining in England. Several messengers were captured and executed. Most others were attainted in their absence. Margaret Beaufort still intended to work tirelessly on behalf of her only son. She supplied the funds to buy Henry's safe passage through French royal territory back to Brittany. Her conspiracy brought her to the point of attainder. Her husband, Lord Stanley, was interrogated by Richard and his council. He convinced the king that he was uninvolved, but was required to keep Margaret under virtual house arrest. Her estates were transferred to Stanley, who continued to disguise his commitment to Henry. Elizabeth Woodville was less resolute than Margaret. By the close of 1483 she perhaps knew, or was led to believe, that her sons Edward V and Richard, duke of York, were dead. She bowed to pressure from King Richard to leave sanctuary after he promised to uphold her position and protect her daughters.

By the spring of 1484 Richard had realised that the promise of military help to Brittany remained the most likely way to get his hands on Henry and the Yorkist traitors. Ambassadors sent to Brittany agreed a ten-month truce in June, and Richard promised to send 1,000 archers to the duchy. The duke was again ill and negotiations were conducted with Pierre Landais, the Breton treasurer. Landais agreed that Henry would be handed over in return for more English support for his own faction. John Morton's secret friends at Richard III's court intercepted news of these negotiations. The network of conspiracy remained healthy as Christopher Urswick was dispatched to Henry with the vital information that he was about to be delivered to Richard. The uncertain situation in Brittany prompted Henry to make tentative approaches for French support. Urswick was redirected to Charles VIII, and he negotiated Henry's passage into France. How this was to be achieved, however, was a matter for Henry and his advisers alone.

The story of Henry's escape from Brittany was recorded by Polydore Vergil who interviewed those involved. Under the pretext of visiting Duke Francis at Rennes, Jasper Tudor and other exiles of noble rank secretly slipped across the border into the French duchy of Anjou. Henry waited for a day or two with his personal servants and, after leaving the town, changed clothes in a nearby wood. Disguised as a servant, he then followed his uncle into France. Henry was only four days away from arrest. Breton troops immediately tried to intercept him and he reportedly reached France only an hour ahead of his pursuers. Duke Francis was certainly ignorant of the agreement with England, but Henry took a great risk in leaving Brittany without his permission. Hundreds of the rank and file of his exiled court still remained in the duchy.

When Francis recovered his health he summoned the leaders of the abandoned Englishmen and offered cash to cover their expenses in joining Henry in France. This was a remarkable gesture of personal support for Henry, even though it robbed Francis of a valuable asset in the diplomatic minefield over Brittany's status. Charles VIII was willing to welcome Henry because custody of the English pretender frustrated the alliance of Landais in Brittany with the duke of Orléans in France. Henry was held under French protection and given financial help to lodge and clothe his companions. Yet in October 1484 he existed purely as a pawn for French policy.

## HENRY TUDOR AND FRANCE

Many historians believe that the help given to Henry Tudor after he reached France was instrumental in the overthrow of Richard III less than a year later. The French feared Richard III so much that they backed Henry with up to 4,000 troops and 40,000 *livres tournois* (then equivalent to about £4,500). For Henry, the difference between his invasions of 1483 and 1485 was determined and comprehensive French support with clear aims in a wider European political context. The French gambled that an unknown and inexperienced Tudor king would have so many problems securing his domestic position that he would be unable or unwilling to help Brittany against French aggression. If Richard III were allowed to continue the stabilisation of his regime then England's historical animosity towards France would almost certainly resurface in time.

Charles VIII's regency government showed how it planned to use Henry's position when he was declared as heir of Henry VI in November 1484. The earl of Oxford joined Henry's group around this time, after being released from imprisonment in Calais when his gaoler, Sir James Blount, declared for Henry. Oxford immediately became his dominant adviser. The sudden French emphasis on Henry's Lancastrian connections might have been due to Oxford's influence. Although some of the Yorkist garrison had defected with him, Oxford's steadfast refusal to acknowledge Edward IV's kingship might have caused some difficulty for the senior Yorkists among Henry's supporters.

In November 1484, Henry seems to have accepted his role as a Lancastrian pretender in return for money from the French king's council. He also began to send letters that declared his outright intent to seize the English throne. Activity at that time could have been linked to an attempted rising in Essex by Sir William Brandon and John Risley. Henry's proclamation of his goal was a step that few previous claimants had taken before entering England. It was dangerously presumptive about the condition of the country, the animosity towards the reigning king, and the appeal of the invader. Henry had not been so confident in October 1483. This does suggest that at the close of 1484 both Henry and Charles VIII were optimistic about the impact French support would have upon the Tudor quest for the English crown. Nevertheless, Henry's public assertion that the crown should be his because of 'rightful claim, due and lineal inheritance' strained credibility. When Henry eventually made his landfall in Wales such specific language was dropped, and he stated that he had invaded to secure the crown 'unto us of right appertaining'.[4]

This Lancastrian emphasis also had the potential to shatter the circle of supporters that had developed around Henry in exile. A distinctly Lancastrian recovery of the English throne would leave very little opportunity for the Yorkist exiles to re-establish themselves with anything like the status they had enjoyed under Edward IV. A possible wholesale reversion to the pattern of landholding and power-broking that existed before 1460 was more alarming still. Richard III was able to appeal to the common, if fractured, Yorkist bonds that before 1483 had united him with many of those now following Henry.

Richard made calculated gestures of reconciliation. Some, like John Morton, were offered but refused pardons. Shortly afterwards he departed for Rome to begin a campaign on Henry's behalf at the papal curia. Others, most notably the marquis of Dorset and his uncle Richard Woodville, were persuaded to return to England by March 1485. To Dorset, Henry's capabilities were questionable, as was the likelihood of Richard III's deposition at his hands. Dorset was only intercepted by Henry's men with French help and he was not fully trusted by Henry again.

French acknowledgement of Henry Tudor's position brought endorsement of his right, title, and claim to the English throne. He appeared in public in Rouen during the final months of his French exile with the precedence that his sudden status as Prince of England afforded. He also received a grant in his favour of 40,000 *livres tournois* (£4,500) to recruit and equip a military expedition. The French publicised their generosity, and the facts and figures of sums of money and numbers of troops were exaggerated by contemporary commentators. This became more explicit after the Tudor victory, when the French were keen to take credit for establishing Henry in England.

Richard was well aware that a promise of support was wholly different from the delivery of that aid when the moment of need arrived. He was certainly confident of defeating Henry, regardless of the extent of his foreign backing. The mere fact that Henry relied upon England's ancient enemy for shelter and assistance allowed Richard to maintain a flow of hostile denouncements. One assertion stated that Henry Tudor would surrender Calais in return for French sponsorship of a Lancastrian recovery. Such claims were intended to galvanise English domestic support against a foreign-backed invasion.

Since the French policy towards Brittany in the early summer of 1485 was also reactive to English intentions towards the duchy, Richard held some initiative over how the French might regard Henry's usefulness if their policy was made to change. Charles VIII's regime was also involved in the ongoing rebellion of Ghent, Bruges, and Ypres against Maximilian's claim to be regent for his son in the Low Countries. War had started in January 1485, but by July the violent conduct of French forces gave Maximilian control of the region. Recent research by Michael K. Jones indicates that Henry received only the first quarter of the 40,000 *livres tournois* promised in April 1485, perhaps because of the pressure on resources for the campaign against the Flanders towns. Jones has also found further evidence that Henry was forced to accumulate the considerable shortfall from personal loans and bargains. This evidence shows that Henry's cause was officially abandoned at the start of July 1485.[5]

The reason for this change was that the expected English expedition to assist Brittany did not materialise. Under the French terms of agreement with Henry, English military intervention should have meant the launching of his counter-invasion to restrict English freedom of movement in the Channel. At that moment, on 24 June 1485, Breton rebels had risen against the malign influence of Pierre Landais and the Breton army had failed to resist them. Breton government collapsed, Landais was captured and executed, and military threat from the English melted away. Without any regime to uphold, Richard III had no need to send his archers. And without this English menace, Henry could serve no purpose for French policy.

Henry believed that nothing further would be forthcoming from Charles VIII and by mid-July was negotiating personal loans in Paris. Henry's few valuable possessions were handed over as security, and he was obliged to leave the two Yorkist lords within his entourage, John Bourchier, Lord Fitzwarin, and the marquis of Dorset, as pledges for a private loan of 30,000 *livres tournois*. The scarcity of Henry's resources on the eve of his embarkation is shown by a later repayment to William Bret, a draper of London. He spent £37 purchasing six complete suits of armour, twelve brigandines (padded jackets sewn with metal plates) and twenty-four sallets (visored helmets) for Henry. If this represents the kitting out of Henry's personal bodyguard, then he was almost completely reliant upon what could be gleaned from his fellow exiles and whatever his loan could purchase for the main body of his army.

What Henry got for his money were certainly French mercenary soldiers. Charles VIII allowed Henry to recruit skilled captains to lead his ships and French infantry units. Henry probably spent his initial funds on bringing together quality troops such as a contingent of Charles VIII's Scots guard and Bretons supportive of the French regency government. The bulk of Henry's forces, however, were reported to have been recruited at the last minute.

Michael K. Jones has argued that in July 1485 Henry was permitted to recruit troops from the camp of the leading French captain, Philippe de Crèvecoeur, then being disbanded. Jones suggests that Henry's loan was sufficient to attract up to a thousand pikemen trained in the latest techniques by Swiss mercenary captains.[6] This body formed the backbone of the invader's army at Bosworth. The original source for this evidence is now lost, but it was published in France in 1897. Livia Visser-Fuchs has countered by stating that this same source suggests that the Normandy war camp was disbanded in 1481, and that the mercenaries hired by Henry were not described accurately.[7] Henry's recruits were *francs archers* or regional militia troops, units of which were composed of longbowmen, crossbowmen, handgunners, and bill or pikemen.

These irregular troops were by no means the most highly skilled soldiers in Europe.

One of these *francs archers* wrote a letter from Leicester on 23 August 1485 on which this current controversy hangs, but the presence of pikemen is questioned. Given that troops had been mustered for the French attack on the Breton border at the end of June 1485, and that some of Crèvecoeur's forces were still then in the Low Countries, parts of northern France were certainly militarised regions at the time when Henry's force was assembling. This made it at least likely that he recruited a cross section of experienced soldiers that might have included contingents of pikemen.

When the invading army left the mouth of the Seine on 1 August 1485, the total number of soldiers at Henry's disposal probably fitted into seven vessels and numbered no more than 2,000, according to Cliff Davies.[8] Only about 400–500 of them were Englishmen. Yet with a large contingent of Scots, Bretons and demobilised French troops still looking for further fighting, Henry commanded an experienced international force that was very much in keeping with the small armies that had recently fought in Europe. It was, however, much smaller than the Breton army embarked on his behalf at the end of October 1483. Henry could not be sure how this amalgamated expedition would fight in the face of Richard's well-prepared army waiting in central England. There was also no prospect of simultaneous domestic rebellion. Henry's best chance of boosting his invasion force was to persuade men to join him once the landfall was made, and to hope that the Stanleys would openly commit to his cause before he was captured or defeated at Richard's hand.

## THE ROAD TO CONFRONTATION

Henry's departure for England was the final gamble of a man with no alternatives. His own life was in danger of stagnating until his usefulness to European rulers could be revived. It was much more likely that he would be sold to Richard III as French policy changed yet again. Henry could be considered to have been as foreign as the majority of soldiers who accompanied him. After fourteen years in Brittany and France it was likely that he only had a pressing reason to use the English language after November 1483. His childhood recollections of Wales must have been minimal; and he seems to have had no personal knowledge of England. Few senior men in his expedition had known him for more than eighteen months. As far as we know Henry had never taken part in or witnessed a battle; his military expertise and capacity to inspire, lead, and dominate his companions had only been tested since 1483, and then never in conflict. Additional to these difficulties was the prospect of confronting an experienced military leader with a committed base of support, who was confident of his ascendant position.

Henry's forces headed for the Pembroke peninsula in west Wales, an area linked to Jasper Tudor's lordship as former earl of Pembroke. They landed in Mill Bay on 7 August. The invasion was very well organised, with roles and responsibilities already worked out, and a clear plan of campaign in place. The change from a political to a military operation was marked by the prominence given to Sir Richard Guildford as master of ordnance. Numerous other relatively lowly Englishmen were also conspicuously rewarded for their campaigning skills after Bosworth. Henry no doubt bore in mind the total failure of his attempted English landing in 1483 and the proximity of Richard's soldiers to any suitable landing point on the English coast. The situation was worse in 1485. The king's northern followers had moved south to manage the lordships and government posts vacated by the rebels who fled overseas. Wales was more isolated and held better prospects of drawing the assistance of friendly gentry. This decision was also almost certainly based on intelligence and careful preparation. Even so, it was a highly dangerous enterprise.

Richard's committed knight Sir James Tyrell commanded the eastern counties of south Wales. Other household men were on the spot as guardians of Pembroke and Tenby castles. Richard had calculated where in his kingdom Henry was likely to have felt most confident of support. Lordships dominated by men active on Richard's behalf blocked many routes from Pembroke towards England. Uncertainty over the allegiance of major local figures like Rhys ap Thomas, meant that Henry had little option but to head north, into still-less-populated regions where residual Lancastrian loyalties might be encouraged. Henry also had to get closer to the north-western English lands of the Stanleys. Only there could the fruits of pre-arranged communication boost the Tudor army into something that could face Richard with confidence.

The exact timescale of the march through Wales is still problematic, but the route taken passed across the Pembroke peninsula to Haverfordwest, over the Preseli hills to Cardigan; then along the coast to Aberystwyth (occupied about 12 August); the following day Machynlleth was reached and Henry turned inland up the valley of the River Dyfi. The difficult journey over upland valleys and plateaux that then followed must have delayed progress. It was probably not until 17 August that Welshpool was passed and Shrewsbury (and England) stood before Henry's army.

Immediately upon landing Henry sent out numerous letters in the royal style and dispatched riders to call upon the assistance that had previously been offered. He appealed directly to the longing within the principality for a native leader to throw off English rule and restore the ancient rights of the Welsh. This sentiment rode on what remained of Jasper Tudor's reputation and had very little connection with the unknown Henry. It had some effect nevertheless, as on 8 and 10 August men at defended centres such as Pembroke and Cardigan declared for the Tudors.

As he marched, Henry must have expected some resistance and skirmishing from Richard's loyalists. The longer he was unchallenged the more his confidence would have grown. He also had time to amend plans made in France and to communicate his intentions to allies waiting in England. By 14 August the Tudor force had marched unopposed beyond Aberystwyth. Although his army was small in the context of the confrontation for the crown to come, several thousand soldiers were more than a match for any of the garrisons based at Cardigan or Aberystwyth, or the retinues raised by Ricardian loyalists in Wales. Henry was also lucky that the troops shadowing his progress were raised by men he had been in touch with from France.

Richard did not receive the news of Henry's arrival in Wales until 11 August. The king immediately set about his own military preparations and was therefore reliant on the initiative of his men in Wales to do their best to delay Henry's progress. That they did not hinder him must have encouraged the invader and could be the reason why powerful figures such as Rhys ap Thomas and Rhys Fawr brought substantial numbers of troops to Henry during the march through the bleak hills west of Welshpool. Henry's progress was naturally cautious. He must have spent much of his day sending scouts and analysing information received. Local guides would have been a source of advice and counsel, but constant vigilance forced Henry onwards with as much urgency as his growing army could manage.

The crucial phase for Henry was the entry into England. On 17 August the expedition was approaching Shrewsbury. Henry desperately needed his most influential friends to declare their support, not least because of the difficulty in keeping his mercenaries paid, supplied, and motivated enough to continue. At Shrewsbury, however, Henry met resistance for the first time. The gates were closed to him – perhaps because of the fear the burgesses had of foreign troops, or of reprisals from King Richard once he learned of their treason in admitting a rebel force. Henry tried reasoning with the townsmen, promising to honour their oaths to Richard. Yet they clearly did not consider him to have much of a chance of deposing Richard, or that he held any authority over them other than the threat of force. The use of violence at that stage would have been disastrous to Henry's prospects of persuading other towns to grant him safe passage and provisions. A stand-off was avoided when messengers from Sir William Stanley arrived and persuaded the mayor to open the gates.

On 20 August, Henry moved forward to Stafford, where he held a long-awaited meeting with Sir William Stanley. Having safely escaped Richard's loyal servants in Wales and by successfully coordinating his march into Shropshire, Henry might have allowed himself a prayer for deliverance. The prospect of Stanley troops swelling the ranks of his army would also have made the inevitable battle with Richard III easier to plan as a tactical engagement. Stanley poems written after 1485 suggest that reassurances were given to Henry at Stafford that the Stanleys were fully committed to him. Lord Stanley could not declare himself openly because Richard had taken Lord Strange, his son, hostage for his father's good behaviour.

We get some indication, now Henry was in the English midlands, that he intended to combine his forces with the Stanleys and head down Watling Street towards London – an arrangement agreed two years earlier but finally almost ready to be put into effect.[9] With as many as 6,000 troops, the Stanley military machine might have doubled Henry's fighting capacity. Lord Stanley was doing his best to deceive Richard by following a parallel course to the invader, but keeping close enough to his route to engage Stanley troops against either the king or Henry. From a strictly personal viewpoint it is likely that Lord Stanley was manoeuvring to be on the winning side rather than to throw his weight publicly behind Henry before there was no possibility of Richard winning the day: an approach consistent with his involvement in most political crises since 1459.

Lord Stanley had been through Lichfield when Henry arrived there on 20 August, and then moved from Tamworth towards Atherstone on Watling Street. This small town could well have been a pre-arranged rendezvous, since Lord Stanley halted here after days of constant marching. There would have been little sense in moving north of this key highway as Henry intended to use it as a fast route to London, or as sure means of retracing his journey in retreat. Stanley probably had reasonable knowledge of the king's intentions, and would have had a first-hand appreciation of Richard's determination to confront Henry. Richard left Nottingham for Leicester on 19 August, certain of finally facing his enemy in the coming days.

On 20 August the two Stanley brothers met at Atherstone. Here they must have discussed how best to deploy their forces, both to depose Richard III but also to preserve the life of Lord Strange. That same day, Henry was about seven miles away, between Lichfield and Tamworth. Here he was joined by various knights who had slipped away from Richard's army. Their knowledge of Richard's manoeuvres should have buoyed Henry, but he seems to have been struck by uncertainty. That evening, Henry managed to become detached from the main body of his troops and was lost in the countryside around Tamworth until dawn on 21 August. We can only imagine how horrified the other commanders were at his absence.

Henry explained himself with news that he had received further information from the Stanleys, and he did finally meet with Lord Stanley and Sir William at Atherstone on 21 August. Discussions about battlefield tactics could not persuade either Stanley to place their troops under the command of the earl of Oxford. They did promise to array in three separate formations, each under separate command, and Lord Stanley offered four of his best knights and their troops to strengthen the Tudor vanguard under Oxford. The last-minute arrival of other deserters from Richard perhaps still did not dispel the uncertainty over how the Stanleys would become involved once the arrows were flying.

## THE BATTLE OF BOSWORTH

The battle that placed Henry Tudor on the throne has always been subject to dispute and conjecture. The poor range of contemporary sources
makes it difficult for modern historians to write with certainty about
what happened on 22 August 1485. This battle is now once again the
centre of debate among late medieval scholars. Recent research and
theories by Michael K. Jones and local historian John D. Austin have
created an alternative battle site in the fields north-east of the town
of Atherstone.[10] This has brought into sharper focus evidence already
proposed by Peter Foss, historian of Market Bosworth, for a location
nearer to Dadlington.[11] Meanwhile the traditional site at Ambion Hill
has received a boost with Leicestershire County Council sponsoring further geophysical analysis and redevelopment of the visitor centre.[12] This
debate evolves the narrative of the battle's topography, logistics, and tactics. It also permits some re-evaluation of the contemporary accounts
that have proved difficult to interpret with the established site alone.
Space does not allow a full discussion of the alternative theories, but this
is a rewarding debate, not least for its demonstration of historians' skill
in analysing evidence.

With the armies of Henry and the Stanleys in the vicinity of Atherstone
we can assume that most of the available large open spaces would have
been occupied by groups of soldiers, possibly 10,000 of them. Tradition
and antiquarian sources suggest that Henry's forces camped on the
Outlands, what is now Merevale Park, to the south-west of the town.
Surviving stained glass figures of the Breton dragonslayer St Armel and
Tudor roses associate Merevale Abbey directly with the Tudor victory.
Later compensation to the abbey for damage to its lands and property by
Henry's army indicates much military activity on its land.

Having gathered his forces in the vicinity of Atherstone and with
command of Watling Street, it is doubtful whether Henry and his captains would have seen sound military sense in marching north-eastwards
to seek out Richard. Henry could not have doubted that a massive royal
army was coming his way: knights like Walter Hungerford and Thomas
Bourchier had fled from it only days previously. After safely completing
his link-up with the Stanley leaders, it was also in Henry's interests to
delay the confrontation. He was increasingly likely to attract deserters
from the king's army the longer the battle was deferred. It would be no

chivalric contest between respected noble adversaries or the rulers of rival nations. Richard wanted to eliminate his Tudor adversary as quickly as possible. Had the king seen an opportunity to attack Henry at any point during the battlefield preliminaries he would surely have taken it.

King Richard had left Leicester on the morning of 21 August. The exact location of his resting place that night is still not known. There is evidence that his scouts were closely watching activity in Atherstone, since Lord Stanley was reported to have raised an alarm on 20 August. Richard's spies should have informed him, therefore, that Henry was camped in the vicinity of Merevale. The continuator of the chronicle of Crowland Abbey, who refers to the 'battle of Merevale', suggests that Richard remained close to the abbey to restrict the invader's options.

The discussion over the site of the battle does not affect the story of how the crown was won and lost. Both camps were active early on 22 August. Henry hoped to confirm the agreements with the Stanleys. Lord Stanley still refused to join him and told Henry to put his own troops in order and to expect help when the time was right. Henry therefore had to organise his army without the Stanley infantry, and perhaps cavalry, that he had relied upon to withstand Richard's superior numbers. The main sources – Vergil, the Crowland Chronicle, and the Stanley poems – suggest that the king's army was nearly twice as large as Tudor's. Once Henry knew that the Stanleys would watch and wait, he had little choice but to move the earl of Oxford and his force into position for the opening exchanges of fire.

The fighting probably began with an artillery volley from both sides, perhaps with time only for one round from the various heavy guns brought to the field. Vergil states that it was at this point that Oxford's troops had to navigate around marshy ground as they struggled towards Richard's vanguard, commanded by John Howard, duke of Norfolk. If the invader's forces had marched from Merevale to a position north of Dadlington that morning, it is possible that boggy ground around Sence Brook at the foot of Ambion Hill was traversed as the army moved northwards with the late morning sun then at its back. Richard ordered his vanguard forward when he saw Oxford's advancing troops wheel around the marsh. With superior numbers of archers facing him, Oxford's manoeuvre could also have aimed to attack the flank of Richard's vanguard and to move his force away from the full effect of deadly flights of arrows arriving from Norfolk's soldiers.

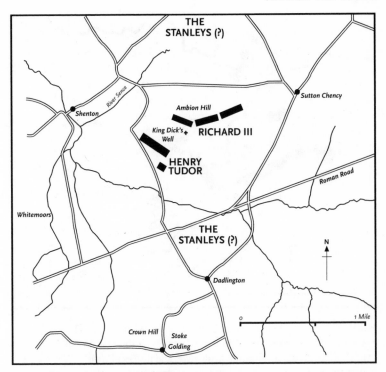

*Map 1* The traditional battle site of Bosworth Field, with Richard III on Ambion Hill and Henry Tudor approaching from the west. This flanking manoeuvre, described by Polydore Vergil, is almost impossible to achieve and the position of the Stanleys unknowable. The name 'King Dick's Well' dates from the late eighteenth century

Henry's commanders perhaps realised that their best chance of victory without the Stanleys was to use a powerful infantry attack to break Richard's vanguard and exploit the resulting confusion. With the uncertain commitment of many of Richard's supporters a knockout blow might have caused panic and battlefield desertions before the king's cavalry could be brought into effect. Many of Henry's French mercenaries were vastly experienced and formed themselves into small companies of about one hundred men, each identified by its own battle standard. In the fierce hand-to-hand hacking and thrusting combat the organisation

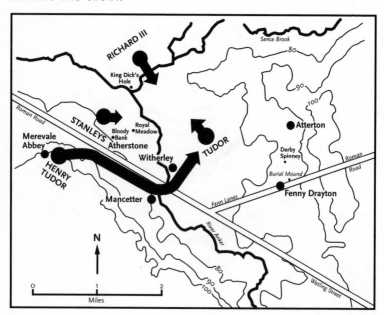

*Map 2* The proposed alternative battle site of Bosworth Field. The map shows
(i) the possible start positions of the rival armies on the morning of 22 August
1485; (ii) Henry Tudor's flanking manoeuvre and final deployment; (iii) the position of the Stanley forces in Atherstone, midway between the two armies; (iv)
the parishes named in Henry VII's compensation grant (Mancetter, Witherley,
Atterton and Fenny Drayton). The clusters of place-name evidence might suggest that the clash of the vanguards took place north of Atherstone, in the
vicinity of Royal Meadow and Bloody Bank, and that Richard's engagement
with Tudor occurred further east, with the fighting spilling into the parishes of
Fenny Drayton and Atterton, and culminating close to Derby Spinney and the
burial mound. (Modern roads have been omitted.)

of Oxford's men began to take effect against the archers and billmen of
Norfolk's contingent. The Stanley poem, 'The Song of Lady Bessy', suggests that where Rhys ap Thomas's men were fighting their ferocious
attack threatened to move them too far ahead of the rest of Oxford's unit.
Orders were given not to move further than ten feet from the standards. As the French, Welsh and Scots momentarily drew back from their
English opponents, confusion held sway in Norfolk's ranks. Oxford

regrouped his troops into a tighter wedge formation, a highly effective Roman infantry technique, and continued to press forward.

While the grinding clash of the vanguards went on, Richard realised the difficulty facing Norfolk. However, we do not know if this division was supported by fresh troops closing ranks behind the duke. The narrative sources agree that at a similar moment in the fighting, the king's attention was drawn to Henry's isolated and exposed position at the rear of his troops. Richard then initiated a charge with his mounted household men and a large cavalry division. A rapid cavalry attack around the confrontation of the two vanguards was most likely to have occurred because Richard saw the chance of killing Henry quickly. Richard's own military experience suggested that the death of an opposing commander soon sapped the spirit of his troops and would rapidly end the killing. A hammer blow to Henry and his small bodyguard could achieve this aim before Oxford's committed infantry could recover ground, and the Stanleys had time enough to decide finally which side to support.

This brings into focus evidence of the crucial role of pikemen among the French mercenaries in Tudor's ranks. The letter from one of these soldiers explains how, upon viewing Richard's charge, Henry dismounted and took refuge in their midst. Michael K. Jones believes these soldiers were pikemen because this unit withstood the impact of Richard's mounted charge. Only staggered ranks of eighteen-foot long spears were likely to have resisted the force of armoured horses and men charging at full tilt. Even compact units of infantry armed with bills would have broken in the face of hundreds of determined riders.

The evidence cited to counter Jones's viewpoint has already been mentioned. Livia Visser-Fuchs goes further in suggesting that the Spanish captain, Jean de Salazar, who was present as a military adviser to Richard, would have known exactly how pike formations would be deployed, having spent the previous decade fighting for the Burgundians against the French. Richard would surely have been advised not to risk a mounted attack against pikes without infantry support. Concentrated fire from handgunners (arquebusiers) or archers could have negated the devastating effect of pikes against horses. Richard made a calculated decision to charge, and it must be assumed that he weighed up the consequent chances of victory and defeat, and in that instant decided to ride out with his most trusted followers.

The Atherstone site allows Richard's full cavalry charge to be more of a tactical military possibility than does Ambion Hill. Yet if Richard's military acumen was demonstrated by his concern to get his army into a position where massed cavalry could be used effectively against Henry's infantry units, it is difficult to believe that he would have been caught out by the tactics of pike units (who must have been very conspicuous), since only a few battlefield options were available to set up an effective defence quickly against cavalry approaching at speed. Perhaps the majority of Henry's pike troops were already thrown into the murderous push-and-shove with Norfolk's men, and Richard knew that he could discount their ability to protect Henry.

It seems unlikely that pikemen alone were present around Tudor in sufficient numbers to withstand the initial shock of Richard's cavalry assault, because we are told that the basis for Richard's decision to attack was that Tudor was spotted in a vulnerable position. A more plausible alternative is that in the few minutes it took for Richard to move across the battlefield, a combination of pikemen and less-specialised infantry from elsewhere in the invading army were able to assemble and hold a defensive formation that desperately resisted Richard until Sir William Stanley's men intervened.

The clash of forces at the moment Richard's riders met Henry's bodyguard was the most chaotic and bloody of the short battle so far. Richard's momentum was broken. His horsemen were scattered in smaller units around Henry's position. Some would have ridden past; others dismounted to fight on foot. The king was in the thickest part of the fighting. With a group of loyal men he began to cut his way towards Henry, still identifiable by his Red Dragon standard. Richard must have realised that his gamble had failed in its initial aim: Tudor had not been swept away.

The initiative was now lost. Richard's riders were effectively trapped between Henry's bodyguard and the deadlocked vanguards. The king's own inactive infantry under the earl of Northumberland were too far away to have any impact upon the personal crisis Richard now faced. Having resisted the shock of Richard's charge, any pikemen surrounding Tudor would now have fought with more effective bills, axes and swords as organised formations descended into a bloody toe-to-toe mêlée. With great determination, Richard now did what Oxford's units had earlier accomplished. He massed his men around the royal standard and drove forward, still with the intention of killing Tudor.

He came very close, since Henry's standard-bearer Sir William Brandon was killed, and the formidable knight Sir John Cheyne knocked out of the way by Richard himself. Richard and Henry must have been only feet apart. Later writers commented that Henry fought with great courage and surpassed what many had expected him to achieve in the press of battle. There might be an element of flattery in this, but it was clear that in resisting Richard's ferocious attack on his own position, Henry stood his ground long enough to convince Sir William Stanley that the time to attack had arrived.

An overwhelming number of Stanley soldiers descended on the vital struggle and rapidly killed Richard's companions. The king himself refused a final chance to escape on horseback and was mercilessly battered to death.

Evidence of Richard's death, probably from the cheering of Stanley's red-coated troops, prompted the duke of Norfolk's forces to break and run. It was now that many of the casualties were likely to have been inflicted. Lord Stanley has been ignominiously credited with engaging his forces against the panic-stricken remnants of Richard's vanguard as they ran for their lives. If this was true then his contribution was barely creditable. Other troops, most notably the northerners forming Richard's rearguard and brought by the earl of Northumberland, simply began to march away from the battlefield. Since they had not engaged against Henry they were allowed to pass unhindered.

In the final spasm of fighting Richard's coronet was knocked from his head. The later Tudor symbol of the crown and thornbush is unusual enough to suggest an element of truth in the story that Lord Stanley discovered the crown in undergrowth and placed it on his stepson's head. This was a symbolic gesture of obedience and was accompanied by acclamation of 'God save King Henry' from the soldiers and nobles around him. Richard's body was stripped and humiliated. He was tied over a horse and taken in Henry's train as it left the battlefield for Leicester.

Henry was likely to have been so exhausted by his personal efforts, the stress of combat, and the slaughter he had witnessed, that the full realisation of his triumph was hard to take in. He had won a victory that very few could have hoped for and seriously believed in. Richard's larger army had stuttered and stalled on the battlefield, with only a fraction of his forces engaging. The king's calculated risk had been a disaster that cost him his life. Even the timing of his charge, had it been delayed or launched earlier, might have had a wholly different effect on the outcome of the fighting. Henry was delivered to his destiny by the slenderest of margins and God's providence. All he had to do now was to keep the crown, something that every king since Henry V had failed to do.

This brief period in Henry Tudor's life was disproportionately important to the way he later developed his ruling style. Henry's pre-1485 relationships with Brittany and France resonated throughout English foreign policy for his entire reign. His own status as a challenger to an established king and puppet of international politics made him particularly aware of how conspiracy might be revived against his own regime. It was also likely that the defections Richard III suffered, and the equivocal behaviour of many nobles at Bosworth, played some part in establishing Henry's attitude to lordship and the means by which nobles had determined the fate of the crown since 1459. Henry resolved never to be in a position to suffer defeat by indifference and disloyalty. The Tudor crown would come to dictate and dominate relationships with ruling elites.

The weight of despair and disappointment of his exile bore heavily on Henry. The memory of his penury and hopelessness contrasted absolutely with the opportunity now before him. With the crown in his possession, Henry's overwhelming aim was to build quickly on the amazing victory and extend his dominance over the country. Because he had been 'a lens through which different parties could focus their energies against Richard III',[13] his backers were an inconsistent amalgamation – anti-Richard, but only pro-Henry by necessity. To keep them constant in allegiance to the Tudor crown, Henry felt that he had to rule through enforcement rather than consensus.

Above all, he wished to pass the crown to his heir. Since he had not yet married, this in itself was a dynastic lottery. Even more disconcerting was his inexperience of the responsibility of authority. With no knowledge of managing even a collection of manors, as most of the gentry in his army had, Henry faced a truly daunting task. The challenges he had to face in keeping his crown would be even greater than those already overcome in achieving it.

# 3

## FORGING THE DYNASTY

### STARTING TO RULE

As Henry VII faced up to the challenges of creating a royal household and establishing his personal authority, it was immediately obvious that the body of loyalists available was inadequate as the agency of national rule. Only in the localities where the royal family dominated could the king be sure that his representatives were wholly reliable, although even the restoration of figures like Jasper Tudor would take time to have an impact. In 1485 Henry had few experienced blood relations. The only way he could rule the entire nation effectively was to turn to the administrative skill, social connections, and political ability of those families that had served Edward IV and Richard III.

By broadening his base of servants to include former opponents, Henry increased his own vulnerability by institutionalising a dependence on men whose loyalty could not be assured. Henry had to work phenomenally hard during his first years, both to create the stable government that would breed confidence in his abilities and to contain the vulnerability of his regime to internal plotting. The support soon shown to Henry's enemies by Margaret, dowager duchess of Burgundy – sister to Edward IV and Richard III – made it essential that Henry devoted his energies towards discovering and destroying internal and external conspiracy to prevent a duplication of his own seizure of the crown. Henry had to deal with all of these dangers immediately and simultaneously. Never were the skills of kingship so precariously learned.

Henry sought to demoralise and nullify the remnants of Richard's army scattering across north Leicestershire. Henry showed a ruthless side by displaying Richard's mutilated body for two days. Such treatment of an anointed king was perhaps vindictive, but it was necessary to quash rumours that Richard had escaped the battlefield.

To stifle potential rallying of support in Richard's name, Henry decided to date his reign from 21 August. This act would have been scorned had he lost at Bosworth, but it now became an effective way of employing the letter of the law. All those who had opposed the Tudor standards could be classed as traitors. Richard's status was reduced to that of duke of Gloucester, 'calling and naming himself by usurpation King Richard III'.[1] Henry then had a free hand in choosing how to confront the many servants of Richard who were not defeated in battle. This decision was made law in the attainder of Richard and his twenty-eight leading supporters in parliament at the end of 1485. It did set a dangerous precedent, since Richard was an anointed king. His soldiers had been honouring their loyal oaths of allegiance. Prosecuting those who followed their king could dissuade others from turning out for Henry should any future challenge to his crown come to be determined in battle.

In a few days, immediate tensions subsided. Henry issued a proclamation protecting the property of returning troops. This and other measures spread the message that sound rule was in place. The dispatch inaccurately detailed the Yorkist casualties at Bosworth. In announcing the deaths of Richard's friends and allies Thomas, earl of Surrey, John, earl of Lincoln, and Francis, Viscount Lovell, possible opposition figureheads were removed. Although news of their survival was soon circulated, this misinformation gave the Tudor crown vital days during which likely opponents would be confused about how to react to Richard's death. Henry eliminated a further possibility when he sent troops to Sheriff Hutton in Yorkshire to capture Edward, earl of Warwick, the inheritor of the male Plantagenet line. Henry was determined to contain opposition before it had a chance to arise.

The new king acted with remarkable leniency after Bosworth. William Catesby, beheaded at Leicester three days later, was the only notable follower of Richard to be executed immediately. The earls of

Surrey and Northumberland were imprisoned. Other survivors, such as Viscount Lovell and Sir Humphrey Stafford, reached sanctuary at Colchester. Another group of north-western Yorkists fled to the hills of Cumberland. Henry was prepared to be magnanimous because he needed the skills these nobles and knights possessed. On 11 October 1485 a general pardon was offered to all but those who had fled. Realistically, however, the acceptance of the pardon was the only guarantee of the loyalty of many ex-Ricardians.

Henry was also constrained by his own inexperience of high office. His instinct was to entrust his kingship to the abilities of men who had shared the hazard of exile, and the uncertainties of the campaign to Bosworth. The Tudor dynasty was entirely embodied in Henry at that time, and unlike his Yorkist predecessors, who took the throne backed by stable personal retinues, Henry's private authority was rooted in the combined skills of the few hundred Englishmen who had fought at his side. At the close of 1485 the Tudor king had little choice but to extend the influence of this war band.

Henry was forced to take a major gamble that the skills of his followers would match the requirements of national governance. Henry therefore identified key requirements and appointed officers in a way that utilised the experience of Yorkist officials without compromising security or ignoring the need to reward his allies. The men who were appointed to his household were drawn from the ranks of pre-Bosworth supporters. This allowed the connections between personal service and regional rule to develop as the king's friends recovered their estates and local connections. Such men were also given the more honourable posts in government. The roles that required specialised skill were left to career civil servants who had worked under the Yorkist kings.

Henry's initial appointments as Lords Chancellor were experienced Yorkists. The service of Thomas Rotherham, archbishop of York and, by 7 October 1485, John Alcock, bishop of Worcester, demonstrated how links to the Yorkist elite were exploited to stabilise Tudor power. By 6 March 1486 Henry was more confident about his control over government. Morton's appointment as chancellor was a key factor in the development of a distinctly Tudor ruling identity. Morton, more than any other man, had engineered the flow of conspiracy in Henry's favour. During his time in Rome after April 1485, he had done his best to promote Henry, and especially to secure dispensation for his marriage to Elizabeth of York, which progressed quickly. Morton's work might also have involved a campaign pointing out Richard III's violent coup and marriage without dispensation. His promotion to the archbishopric of Canterbury later in 1486 was an acknowledgement of his efforts on Tudor's behalf, and he became Henry's partner in government.

Henry did not interfere with the operation of the legal system. All his appointees as justices at common law had served previous kings, including the chief justice of the King's Bench, Sir William Huse, who had been in post since 1481. At the Exchequer, Sir Humphrey Starkey, the chief baron, had been one of Edward IV's sergeants-at-law in 1478. The three barons who served under him were all trained under the Yorkists. Other survivors from the Yorkist period included John Fitzherbert as King's Remembrancer. His notebook of debts owed to the crown shows how royal financial processes continued to work right across the transition from Ricardian to Tudor rule.

More honourable posts, such as the chamberlainships of the Exchequer, were given to Henry's allies William Stanley, Richard Guildford, Richard Edgecombe, and Giles Daubeney. These were perhaps the four knights who had done most for Henry in August 1485, so these grants were rewards with little expectation of real responsibility. Conspicuous also were the men associated with the defections at Calais in October 1484. John, Lord Dinham, and his stepson John Ratcliffe, Lord Fitzwalter, became, respectively, treasurer of England and steward of the king's household.

Where possible, however, Henry's leading supporters were offered rewards that compelled them to become fully involved in establishing Tudor power. The king gave very little away to his key servants without tying personal influence to the prosperity of Henry's own kingship. To prevent his accession from becoming the dictatorship of a narrow elite, former opponents also had to be accommodated. The longer this was delayed, the more likely it was that Henry's weak claim and incomplete victory would invite a backlash. All of these difficulties therefore forced Henry to focus on the keystones of government under his own direct control – the royal household, the royal council, and central departments of state – as the arenas where the nature and direction of Tudor policy and governing style could be organised quickly.

Henry's first priority was to confirm God's judgement by becoming anointed king of England, France and Lord of Ireland. He was crowned at Westminster on 30 October 1485. The absence of a wife meant that changes had to be made to the order of service taken by Richard III. The king's oath was probably also identical to that of his predecessor. The coronation service had changed very little since the fourteenth century, but Henry used the badges and heraldry of his family and ancestors to emphasise that Tudor rule was different to that of the Plantagenets. Those who had been at Henry's side at Bosworth took central roles in the ceremony. This emphasised that while the crown had been won by force, the realm had been delivered from Richard's tyranny and sound rule was restored in a new dynasty.

## THE FIRST TUDOR PARLIAMENT

Parliament met on Monday 7 November 1485. Henry's own status had already been discussed by the judges. His attainder was considered to be void by the very fact that he had become king. Henry's right to the throne was also not addressed by parliament. Close investigation of the subject would quickly have brought up the superior claims of Edward, earl of Warwick, Margaret Beaufort, and even John II of Portugal (who had a superior Lancastrian ancestry to Henry's Beaufort ancestors). Henry could never establish authority if he exposed the weaknesses of his lineage. Since Henry had stated before Bosworth that he was king, and victory in battle had confirmed it, parliament was called to endorse this expression of divine will. If Henry were believed to hold no royal authority then his summons to parliament would have been largely ignored. The lords and representatives of the Commons who responded to Henry's command had already acknowledged his right to rule.

The crucial declaration of the king's title was presented to parliament as a petition of the Commons agreed to by the Lords and king. This implied that Henry was king by invitation of the majority of the population through its representatives. At his death, Richard III was the sole embodiment of his own dynasty. Without an heir or son, his death vacated the succession and left Henry free to define quickly the terms upon which his own kingship would be based. Parliament declared that Henry and the heirs of his body yet to come inherited the sole right to the kingdoms of England and France, the royal dignity and all other things thereunto belonging:

> to the pleasure of almighty God, the wealth, prosperity, and surety of this realm
> of England, to the singular comfort of all the king's subjects of the same, and in
> avoiding of all ambiguities and questions ...[2]

This statement used the authority of parliament to end any speculation about Henry's royal rights and his personal regal qualities. Although none of the points was elaborated upon, this statement stopped formal debate about the Tudor succession. Further discussion was deemed seditious and treasonable.

Henry also needed parliament to clarify Elizabeth of York's position. She was still legally illegitimate following the terms of Richard III's act settling the crown upon himself in January 1484. Henry could not build his dynasty on heirs born to a woman with the stigma of bastardy recorded in the formal records of England's highest court. This was probably the reason why no reference was made to the children of Edward IV when Henry repealed Richard's parliamentary title. Orders that copies of the bill and act be surrendered for destruction, and that the original enrolment should be erased, were also less about negating Richard's title than preventing uncomfortable questions about Elizabeth's status.

Henry's own title invested the future of the regime in the heirs of his own body. It did not specify that he would marry Elizabeth, nor anyone else. This seems ambiguous, especially as his intention to marry her was publicly known. Henry was unlikely to abandon his promise to marry Elizabeth since this was the basis of his Yorkist support at the close of 1483. A reduction in Elizabeth's status would be a humiliation that could threaten Henry's rule before it had even started. Yet it could be suggested that the slowness with which Elizabeth's position was defined allowed Henry time to find out what had truly happened to her brothers, the Princes in the Tower. The investment of a dynastic line in Henry alone suggests an allowance for the possibility that Elizabeth might not be the only surviving heir of the House of York.

If this were so, marriage to Elizabeth would lose its dynastic impact. Of course, Henry would also lose the majority of his support as Edward V's right to be king would revive. Had Henry been certain that Richard had murdered Elizabeth's brothers he would surely have presented the evidence to parliament in November 1485. The creeping uncertainty over Perkin Warbeck's identity would not have tested the allegiance of Henry's elite Yorkist supporters in the 1490s. Instead, Henry offered the vague assertion that Richard had shed infants' blood as part of a catalogue of wrongdoing. The lack of definitive wording in this respect in a parliament where the drafting of other documents was meticulous implies that Henry could not discover the fate of the Princes. It remains unlikely, but possible, that they were still alive at the end of August 1485 only to be killed by Tudor hands. Only their deaths would have made Elizabeth the sole Yorkist heir, and only her marriage to Henry would maintain his Yorkist support.

Henry addressed the Commons in person and offered some evidence of his hereditary title to the crown. This must have focused on his Beaufort bloodline, and not on his connection to the Lancastrian kings, which carried no dynastic weight. The Beauforts had been legitimated in 1397 but barred from succession by Henry IV in 1407. Subsequent kings by their royal authority had the power to remove this impediment, but the necessity had not arisen. The Yorkists would never have undermined their own grip on the succession by allowing a rival Lancastrian claim. In 1485 this strategy of a legitimate Beaufort right could have been something for Henry to fall back on had not the circumstances of his accession allowed a complete acceptance of his title through God's judgement.

Parliament reversed the attainders of the leading Lancastrians defeated in 1471, including Henry VI and his royal family. Also restored were Henry's own mother, her cousin Edmund, duke of Somerset, her half-blood Wells relatives, and Edward Stafford the young duke of Buckingham. Henry's own followers, attainted in 1484, recovered what Richard III had deprived them of. Elizabeth Woodville also received her lands and goods. An act of resumption turned the royal landholding clock back to 1455. This could have been devastating to the Yorkists now loyal to Henry were it not for an enormous list of provisos. The parliamentary restitution of Lancastrian inheritances and political influence did, however, highlight Henry's true familial focus. The marriage to Elizabeth of York seemed little more than a dynastic expedient to gain and retain Yorkist support after 1483.

Henry brushed aside any doubt by marrying Elizabeth, as soon as dispensation was received, on 18 January 1486. The fact that little is known about the ceremony or who attended, despite the importance of the union to Henry, indicates some uncertainty on his part. Elizabeth was not crowned queen until an heir had been born (eight months later) to the royal couple – a sure sign that businesslike security and not romance was his overriding concern.

Henry VII had a golden opportunity to establish stable government on his own terms. Since parliament had offered no resistance to his demands, he had been able to achieve all of the political unravelling and reconstruction he intended. Richard III's closest male heirs, John, earl of Lincoln and Edward, earl of Warwick, had respectively made their peace with Henry or were safely under lock and key. The failure, for whatever reason, of Richard's other leading subjects to fight for him at Bosworth indicated to Henry that he was successor to a king few had been willing to support at the decisive moment.

In 1485 Henry could not afford to give away too much of his weakly held power in an effort to buy support, nor could he be seen as parsimonious or reluctant to rule in the expected manner of his royal predecessors. He boosted the status of his loyal nobles Jasper Tudor (now duke of Bedford), Thomas, earl of Derby, and John, earl of Oxford, by allowing their absorption of many of the offices in the crown gift in Wales, the north-west, and East Anglia, notably in the duchy of Lancaster estates. Their service was cemented with royal annuities to their followers. This encouraged strong leadership and meant that Henry did not have to deploy his own household servants throughout the entire country. Henry now had a period of grace before his rule came under real scrutiny. He used this opportunity to confront the legacy of Richard III directly.

## HENRY IN THE NORTH, 1486

Henry's progress to the north in March 1486 was the first real test of his kingship. The journey into the region that had been dominated by Richard since 1473 would determine the effectiveness of the new royal household. It was also a test of how Henry was accepted in the provinces. He had to gauge carefully which of Richard's servants would cooperate with the Tudor crown, and which would resist. Taking the Tudor regime into the north was a bold move into the heart of opposition territory.

The expedition was primarily a public relations exercise. While he was keenly aware of the narrowness of his victory, Henry wished to demonstrate his own majesty and the support he enjoyed from a unified royal household and nobility. Henry would be judged on his regal qualities and how he performed the symbolic and public aspects of his role, such as celebrating mass, dining in public, and tending to the poor. To most of the population, a monarch might be seen in such a context perhaps only once in a lifetime. The impact Henry made, both as a kingly figure and as a man in tune with the mood of his realm, could determine the allegiance of a region and perhaps the nation as a whole.

The king's journey also had the urgent political purpose of pacifying the region most at risk from rebellion. Many former Ricardians had already accepted the general pardon and were serving on commissions of array issued on 25 September 1485 against the threat of Scottish invasion. This was a first step to their rehabilitation but also a sign that Tudor England was seen as vulnerable as the Scots threatened to take advantage of Henry's weak control in the north. Henry's determination to preserve his security brought a belligerent statement from the royal council. England would go to war with Scotland rather than yield any foot of English land in the crown's possession when Henry became king. Henry's capacity to put this threat into practice was dependent on the resources of nobles rather than his own royal power. The Stanleys policed the behaviour of the commissioners themselves, and their army offered an imposing military threat. The mobilisation of the north under Stanley guidance resulted in a three-year truce with Scotland, agreed in July 1486.

Henry Percy, 4th earl of Northumberland, was the natural candidate to inherit control of the north-east. His indecisive behaviour at Bosworth, however, caused his imprisonment until 6 December 1485. Henry promoted Lord Fitzhugh as an initial political leader. Henry's personal earldom of Richmond made him direct lord of Richard's favourite northern residence at Middleham in north Yorkshire. Fitzhugh was the local head of the network centred on this lordship. This appointment singled out Richmond men as the core of the new power in the north, and built upon a continuity of lordship that pre-dated Richard's own possession of the estate. Henry kept most of Richard's officers in post, and another, Sir Thomas Markenfield, became first Tudor sheriff of Yorkshire. Such a measured response to those clearly aligned with his former enemy prompted others to submit to the new regime.

Northumberland's restoration ended uncertainty and it was he who welcomed the king to Yorkshire near Doncaster on 10 April 1486. By then the earl's retinue included many former Ricardian knights who were pragmatic enough to recognise the shift in northern power. The preservation of their own positions was more important than undirected resistance to the new king. This transfer of loyalty continued to influence others to conciliation. Some knights, such Sir John Conyers, recovered their former posts and were also appointed to King Henry's household. This personal connection to the Tudor king became instrumental in diluting loyalty to Richard III.

As Henry celebrated Easter at Lincoln on 23 March he received accurate news of the escape from sanctuary of Viscount Lovell and Sir Humphrey Stafford. They attempted to coordinate rebellions in Richmondshire and the west Midlands. Jasper, duke of Bedford, was also active against disturbances in the Welsh Marches at this time. Many English nobles not already travelling with the court assembled quickly once Henry summoned them, or followed his instructions to secure their own localities. When Henry dispatched troops to deal with Lovell's rising between Ripon and Middleham he chose from an immense crown retinue. The troops mustered by Henry's nobles presented a surprisingly united front, and the rebels dispersed as they advanced. They were pursued into the Dales with promises of pardon rather than threats of execution: further evidence that Henry's wish for conciliation was no hollow claim. The imposing army and a magnificent Tudor court were used in conjunction with flexible and decisive government to encourage a sense of obligation to the Tudor crown. As more men acknowledged Henry, fewer risked everything by standing against the tide of regional submission to visible Tudor power.

Key to the Tudor relationship with the north was the way that the city of York responded to Richard III's death. The combined approach of threats and promises, conciliation and the menace of overwhelming military force were brought to bear on the city as Henry arrived on 20 April. Key figures, such as the recorder of the city, Miles Metcalfe, had already submitted to Henry, and his lead influenced the city's stance. The king was welcomed with apparent uniform enthusiasm. In the pageantry of their greeting, the city authorities had already decided to pander to Henry's merits, to emphasise his right to the crown, and to proclaim the benefits of the union of Lancaster and York. Real menace existed under this veneer of loyalty, however. An attempt was made on Henry's life that was thwarted only by the personal intervention of the earl of Northumberland. At the same time, men from Middleham tried to persuade Richard's nephew, John, earl of Lincoln, to rebel. Lincoln was still a member of the king's council at that time, but within a year he became the main organiser behind Lambert Simnel's invasion.

Henry's developing authority was also demonstrated by the first widespread use of bonds and recognisances to control behaviour once the rebellion was crushed.[3] This evidence from the start of the reign suggests that bonds were used so extensively later on because they were successful against conspiracy when Henry's control was weakest before 1490. The rebellions of 1486 showed Henry very clearly that many of the servants he had kept in office in 1485 had been lukewarm in their resistance to conspiracy. Members of the leading Richmondshire families of Conyers and Metcalfe, and William Beverley, dean of Middleham, were brought to London and bound under thousands of pounds. There they remained until thoroughly instructed in what was now expected of their service. Only then were they allowed to return north under strict conditions. Senior figures, such as Sir John Conyers, also lost their established posts to outsiders more closely trusted by the king – in his case to Lord Clifford who became bailiff of Richmondshire on 2 May 1486. The policing of other men through these bonds, like Sir Christopher Ward of Givendale near Ripon, required the earl of Northumberland to watch those who had recently joined his household.

The king also required that more of the gentry who guarded his castles and lordships guaranteed the terms of these bonds. For example, Sir John Everingham, steward of Pontefract castle, joined the marshal of the royal household, Sir John Turbeville, as a pledge for the Conyers and Metcalfe bonds mentioned above. Henry was creating a network of shared responsibility, which would make all involved equally tied to the observance of the king's conditions. With bonds to back up his position, Henry re-admitted many of the suspects of 1486 back into local office and onto regional commissions by the end of the year. Henry's clemency became enforced through the conditions attached to bonds. Here Henry attempted to break up the networks that conspirators would target, and to bind their behaviour to loyal crown service. Such bonds ensured that as an increasing number of men became involved in suspended fines, fewer still would be willing to risk their wealth and influence in support of rebellion.

Henry's definite strategy for controlling the allegiance of former opponents seemed to be making his reign more stable at the end of

1486. The birth of a male heir, Arthur, on 19 September was a very welcome first step towards a secure dynasty. The gathering of the nobility at Arthur's christening in Winchester that month, with a prominent role given to his godmother Elizabeth Woodville, suggested that the patchwork identity of Tudor rule was growing harmonious.

## FROM IRISH INVASION TO YORKIST REBELLION, 1487–1489

The dangers of assembling a new regime from the scraps of older loyalties, however, were fully exposed by the rapid eruption of a new conspiracy in favour of Lambert Simnel. This culminated in the only invasion of England by an Irish army and their massacre in a close-fought battle near Newark on 16 June 1487.

Simnel was probably a joiner from Oxford, although his name, identity, and occupation are certainly confused in contemporary records. He was spotted by a disloyal priest and trained to impersonate a Yorkist prince. By the spring of 1487 he was acknowledged as king by the Yorkist lords in Ireland. How such an obscure plot rapidly involved leading Yorkist figures in England, Ireland, and the Low Countries is still difficult to fathom. Simnel's backers did not rake up the mystery of the Princes in the Tower, but threw him into the role of Richard III's nephew, Edward, earl of Warwick. With his rights overridden in parliament, the plotters perhaps hoped to merge sympathy for Warwick's claims with lingering disappointment at Richard III's death. Warwick might have been thought dead, or in danger of vanishing within the Tower like his cousins. The impersonation of a living nobleman is otherwise puzzling.

The plot probably aimed for a sudden deposition of Henry and the quiet dislodging of Simnel for the real Warwick, or even his chief English promoter, John, earl of Lincoln. The backing for such an obvious impostor in 1487 has also discredited the reliability of Perkin Warbeck's later identity as Prince Richard of York, more than might be warranted. Simnel's plot was, however, a major challenge to the unformed skills of the Tudor king, and one that came close to destroying Tudor rule at its outset.

In February 1487 the queen's mother, Elizabeth Woodville, suddenly forfeited her lands and entered Bermondsey Abbey on a relatively meagre royal pension. This change in fortune could have been coincidental with Simnel's appearance, but her son, Thomas, marquis of Dorset, was arrested at the same time. A serious Yorkist conspiracy sent a shiver of uncertainty through the Tudor elite, and provoked the king's suspicion. Other nobles with Yorkist blood also reconsidered their acceptance of the Tudor accession. John, earl of Lincoln, had helped Lovell and the Staffords in 1486, and he collected funds to aid their escape at the end of the year. By the spring of 1487 his treason emerged fully and he joined the conspirators in the Low Countries. His aunt, Margaret of Burgundy, united him with an existing circle of displaced Ricardians. They began to work out ways of grafting their shared connection to Richard III onto the existing English and Irish conspiracy against Henry VII.

To stifle the appeal of the rebellion, Henry paraded the real Warwick in London. This move probably convinced Lincoln to revive his own royal status as Richard III's nearest adult male heir. He had served Richard in Ireland and Yorkshire, the two regions where Yorkist loyalty remained strongest. These old ties were exploited fully in the coming months. Margaret of Burgundy probably encouraged Lincoln's ambitions and made available highly skilled German mercenaries under the expert commander Martin Schwartz. The rebels and their army arrived in Dublin at the start of May 1487. Simnel was crowned and anointed as Edward VI by Irish churchmen and nobles the same month. Many no doubt believed that Warwick had genuinely escaped. Others were certainly hoodwinked by the few who knew Simnel's true identity. The support of the dominant Fitzgerald family, led by Gerald, earl of Kildare, swept away doubt and resistance. Kildare supplied thousands of Gaelic warriors to an invading army that landed in Furness on 4 June 1487.

Henry had begun to prepare an army to invade Ireland. His plans were halted amid fears of a direct rebel attack from the Low Countries. Once he learned of events in Dublin, Henry moved to the midlands to await news. The king used his north-western connections to assess where the invaders might land and who their contacts would be. His spies had already started to deliver intelligence of the plot and he used this to work out a detailed programme for mustering his forces.

The landing place of the rebel army allowed them to link up with Richard III's chief friends in north Lancashire, like Sir Thomas Broughton. He had accepted a pardon in 1486, but abandoned Henry once rebellion gained pace. The invaders also followed a route that brought them close to other sympathetic gentry. By 8 June the rebel army had crossed the Pennines and received a warm welcome in Richard III's heartland of Wensleydale.

The presence of a massive rebel force did much to influence the loyalty of the Yorkists in Henry's own lordship. The rebel advance was deliberately provocative and caused many to switch sides, headed by Thomas Metcalfe, supervisor of the lordship of Middleham. Later fines for other gentry, nearby abbeys, and townships could indicate widespread sympathy for the Yorkist invaders. They could also represent a heavy crown reaction to the slightest evidence of disloyalty. Despite this support among Richard III's ex-servants, 'King Edward VI' did not stir the North Riding into open rebellion. Henry already had a strong grip on the region and many people thought twice about openly declaring their support for his enemies.

Henry's information of the rebels' movements arrived when only a few days old. He sent cavalry northwards to track their route. The earl of Lincoln kept his army moving quickly. York was caught out by their speed, and loyalists like the earl of Northumberland and Lord Clifford were not able to boost the garrison until the rebels were almost at the gates. Lincoln did not wish to confront York but to bypass it. By doing this he maintained his momentum and kept Northumberland's soldiers away from the royal army. The rebels also gave a bloody nose to Lord Clifford south of York around 10 June as they continued southwards. On 12 June troops from Richmondshire under the two Lords Scrope attacked York. Northumberland had just left the city to pursue the main rebel force and was forced to retreat to defend it. Once things were secure, he considered it too late to travel to the king, and took his large army away from York northwards: perhaps to cut off the rebels' retreat; to chase the Scrope forces; or to find a safe spot to await the impending re-run of Bosworth.

The royal army reached Nottingham on 13 June. After some confusion over billeting and rumours spread by spies that the king had fled, Henry prepared to meet a very stern test of his leadership. He made certain this time that the Stanley units were billeted among his own forces. The herald's report for the campaign shows that a very impressive collection of lords and senior gentry had joined the king. On the night of 15 June the Tudor forces secured Newark and awaited their opponents. The rebels camped to the south-west at the village of East Stoke. On 16 June the two armies faced each other from early morning. The rebels were probably 8,000 strong and arranged in a single unit. The

Tudor army was perhaps twice as large. Henry did not have to hazard his life in the thick of the fighting since many of the Tudor commanders at Bosworth repeated their service. The earl of Oxford would bear the brunt of the fighting as commander of the king's vanguard, but Henry wisely ensured that Stanley contingents were merged into its units.

The odds had been reversed from two years earlier when Henry was the unfancied invader. Even though outnumbered, Lincoln's forces sought strength from hopes or promises of inactivity and desertion among the king's troops. Henry was very safely in the rear, but many of his best and most trustworthy soldiers would be committed first. Any early rebel success might have pressurised other sections of the royal army. If this became prolonged there would be a tipping point where the king's men would start to flee or change sides. It became vital that Henry crushed his opponents quickly.

An initial exchange of archery inflicted massive casualties on the Irish forces. Rather than be annihilated, they launched a ferocious mass attack downhill and at full speed. Against Oxford's vanguard of perhaps 6,000 troops, their numbers and momentum were effective. More slogging slaughter ensued as each side hacked into the other in the hope of forcing a breakthrough and retreat. Since Oxford's men did not crumble, and soon regrouped to force the rebels back, Henry must have become aware that only last-minute treason could prevent his victory. By that stage, no one leader could alter the course of the battle decisively. The rebels were pushed back beyond their starting point, with many hundreds hacked down in a bottleneck soon named Red Gutter. As the rout continued, it seems that the German professionals and some Yorkist commanders deliberately fought to the death.

Henry's instructions to capture Lincoln and his captains were ignored and their bodies were discovered. Lovell escaped the slaughter. Scottish records indicate that he reached James III's court, but his importance as a rebel leader ended in 1487, and his ultimate fate is a mystery. Broughton, too, made his way home but did not trouble Henry again. The king had hoped to interrogate them for a fuller picture of the strands of conspiracy. It seems possible that some of his commanders deliberately targeted the opposing leaders to draw a firmer line under the suspicion and recrimination still bubbling after Bosworth.

Simnel was captured, presumably a fair way from the fighting. His placement in the royal household, first as a kitchen spit boy and later a falconer, suggests that he was innocent of the political danger his conspiracy had stirred up. Henry's national security was still fragile. Large parts of his army had not fought in the battle and Oxford's vanguard had been left to struggle for three hours before victory was won. There had already been considerable debate, even among Oxford's East Anglian servants, about whether to march to the king without viewing the proper commissions. Although malicious rumours of Henry's defeat brought Yorkists onto the streets of London, where the king's men and their property were targeted, the precarious state of the north obliged Henry's government to remain in the region for over a month after the battle.

Rather than clamping down on the Yorkists whose allegiance had been cast in doubt, Henry accelerated their integration into his regime after Stoke. This process was capped by the belated coronation of Queen Elizabeth on 25 November 1487. The ceremony took place during the session of Henry's second parliament, which met on 9 November. Since most lords and leading knights were present at Westminster, the timing of Elizabeth's investiture might also be seen as an acknowledgement that Henry's failure to endorse her status had contributed to the rebellion just faced. Crowning Elizabeth formally proclaimed Henry's dynastic reliance on Yorkist blood, but specifically that of Edward IV. The earl of Warwick's rights were publicly extinguished. The danger he posed as a potential focus for conspiracy condemned him to lifelong imprisonment.

Before parliament met Henry blended magnanimity with a careful extension of his control as he unravelled the roots of the 1487 plot. The pattern of bonds seen in 1486 was repeated. His failure to back up the royal pardon the previous year had freed many dangerous rebels to join Simnel. By the summer of 1487, Henry enforced royal clemency with very real financial threats. The two Lords Scrope bought their lives with a bond of £3,000 and were imprisoned in the south. Scrope of Bolton perhaps owed his life to the family influence of Margaret Beaufort. He had previously married into Margaret's step-family, the St Johns, and this connection perhaps diminished royal anger at his treason. Scrope's first cousin Elizabeth was also the countess of Oxford. Appeals to these family ties show that Tudor authority was becoming accepted at the higher echelons of the nobility. Security also bred greater stability. The earl of Surrey reportedly refused a chance to escape from the Tower during the crisis. Such sound judgement gave him the opportunity to rebuild his career and brought his great abilities into Henry's service.

The business of the second parliament was dominated by measures to shore up areas of weakness in Tudor security. Henry received papal support for a clampdown on sanctuary – the main way that rebels were able to escape justice. Lincoln and his English supporters were attainted, but Simnel's Irish backers escaped the formal censure of parliament – an indication, perhaps, that Henry appreciated the delicate balance of English lordship there. Even after overt treason the crown was looking to encourage rather than coerce the Anglo-Irish lords into acceptance of Tudor authority.

In England, too, Henry started to address the ways in which lordship worked, and how political behaviour could be regulated by the intervention of the crown. Control of allegiance through bonds was a part of this process. Another was the greater royal supervision of the ways in which lordship operated. A statute against abducting heiresses and widows had at its root royal control over the transfer of the estates of tenants-in-chief. There is a hint that Lincoln's sudden treason was also mirrored by plotting within the royal household. Another act allowed senior household officers to investigate the involvement of servants below noble rank in conspiracy against the king and his councillors. Problems of lawlessness, riot, and manipulation of justice were addressed by the creation of judicial sub-committees of the council with the misnamed Star Chamber Act.[4]

The problem of the king's stewards potentially mustering royal tenants for rebellion produced an act that dictated how crown officers managed tenants under their control. Other acts concerned arrangements for the garrisons at Berwick and Calais, and a grant of taxation for the defence of the kingdom. Henry was fully aware that his rebels had combined with hostile rulers seeking his downfall. The business of parliament helped to enhance Henry's capacity to resist future challenges. A rigorous defence of his security as early threats were faced and overcome helped to shape the Tudor ruling style that emerged later.

Henry's victory confirmed his tenacity. It also broadcast to European observers that a more stable England could have a useful role in international politics. While Henry was still enjoying the glow of success after Stoke, he was approached at Leicester by French ambassadors with an appeal for English help to annex Brittany. Henry could not ignore his debt of honour to Duke Francis for his dogged preservation of the

Tudor cause before 1484. He would not allow Brittany to be absorbed by France without some form of English intervention.

An English naval force and small land army was offered to Brittany in February 1488. When this proved ineffective, and after more French success in battle, Henry backed down and sought a truce with France. With English interference ended, the French continued to attack the Breton border. In July a French army successfully invaded and won a decisive battle at St Aubin du Cormier. The sickly Duke Francis agreed to the Treaty of Sablé to end the conflict on 20 August 1488. By this treaty Francis agreed not to marry his daughter Anne without French permission. But with his death two weeks later, the Breton nobles set up a regency for Anne, and Henry was again able to promote himself as defender of Breton independence.

This time, Henry did not rush to arms but offered English diplomats to negotiate a solution that involved other countries already hostile to France. Henry's improved security allowed a coalition of himself, Maximilian, Archduke of Austria, and King Ferdinand of Aragon, to formulate a strategy against France that benefited all three rulers. Henry's status as defender of Brittany was also recognised by Duchess Anne's government. At discussions that led to the Anglo-Breton Treaty of Redon, also in February 1489, Henry forced Brittany to agree to pay the wages of 6,000 troops he intended to send in April. This was a serious expedition, with over £1,300 eventually being spent on weapons and supplies over the following year.

A draft agreement with Aragon and Castile at Medina del Campo on the 27 March 1489 was particularly important to the future of Tudor England. The negotiations suggested that Henry VII was considered to have a future as king. The treaty incorporated the first agreement for an Anglo-Spanish marriage. Henry had first proposed an alliance the previous year, based on the marriage of Catherine of Aragon and Prince Arthur. Both were young children, and the possibility of the marriage heralded closer relations until they were old enough to wed. The treaty also included clauses requiring neither state to assist the rebels of the other, and complex arrangements for recovering territory in the event of a war with France.

Just as successful intervention in Brittany seemed to be improving Henry's international reputation, events in northern England once again forced him to rearrange his priorities. Henry's policies in the Ricardian north bit hard as the differences between Tudor assertiveness and Richard

III's good lordship became apparent. Henry increased the tax burden in the region. He not only pressed for collection of the parliamentary tax granted in November 1487. Some ex-servants of Richard, like William Beverley, dean of Middleham, were also made responsible for collecting the cash. Employing these men in a most unpopular job sought to undermine their status where they had previously incited rebellion. By turning such Ricardians into apparent Tudor loyalists, Henry broadcast the message that good behaviour could bring reward once past allegiance was forgotten.

In the north, the strong crown lordship in place since 1487 began to hurt a region struck by economic decline. Delays in collecting the 1487 taxes added to the burden imposed by a further subsidy in 1489. In April that year, a protest gained momentum in Cleveland, perhaps taking advantage of Henry's distractions in Brittany. Led by a yeoman, John Chamber, the protestors marched south towards York. Their aims were simply to plead their case against royal tax demands. The king instructed the earl of Northumberland, who was repairing Scarborough castle, to confront the dangerous and growing band of petitioners. Percy set about his task in the company of more recently recruited servants.

The earl asked for more troops to meet him at Thirsk, so he probably felt ill-prepared to confront an unknown group of several hundred rebels. As the king's lieutenant, Northumberland was expected to face down their challenge. The protestors also sought a meeting with him because he could intercede personally with the king on their behalf. When the confrontation came on 28 April, Northumberland pressed for collection, was deserted by his retainers, and murdered by the rebels – probably the only fatality in the entire uprising. Northumberland's death prompted further unrest near Richmond and in the East Riding. The king feared that an escalation of this popular rising could undo his hard work in securing the loyalty of the north-eastern nobles and gentry. There were also Ricardian undertones to what followed.

A sympathetic alderman of York, Thomas Wrangwash, allowed the rebels to enter the city on 15 May. Sir John Egremont, an illegitimate member of Northumberland's family, stirred up the country and directed the rebels as far south as Doncaster before turning back towards York. Henry immediately mustered another imposing royal force for the north. Thirteen peers brought hundreds of troops, but the backbone was again supplied by Derby and Oxford, with the earl of Surrey proving his

worth after release from the Tower. The rebel army of up to 5,000 protestors looked to be heading into Richmondshire as the king approached:
perhaps further evidence that old loyalties were only dormant. Without
a powerful royal leader to direct resistance on the ground, the allegiance
of the region appeared in danger of haemorrhaging.

The rebels melted away as Surrey led the king's vanguard towards
York. The rising generated very little threat to Tudor rule and Henry
pardoned around 1,500 men. Many others trudged off home and only six
were executed. The mood of conciliation continued as Henry based himself at York. Those caught up in bonds in the aftermath included some of
the king's own officers, like the constable of Sheriff Hutton, who allowed
the protestors to pass unhindered. Other men ensnared as the rising was
investigated were the new Percy retainers who seem likely to have been
those who deserted Northumberland.

Some contemporary sources, including the Great Chronicle of London,
suggested that Northumberland had been killed because of his failure
to support Richard III at Bosworth. Members of his retinue secretly
favoured Richard III's political heirs and acted indirectly against Henry
VII to threaten his hold on power. There is no direct evidence of this,
but the king was forced into a risky strategy to ensure that a lid was kept
on disloyalty in Yorkshire. Henry pressed ahead with tax demands and
extended the enforcement of allegiance.

Northumberland's murder enabled Henry to change the pattern of
regional rule. Men whose status was derived entirely from Tudor service,
not landholding, came to control the administration of the north-east.
In June 1489, Henry made the earl of Surrey his lieutenant in the north.
He was based at Sheriff Hutton castle and revived Richard III's ruling
regional council.

The Yorkshire rising also distracted the king from his military campaign to help Brittany, and without his personal attention English
policy began to lapse. Maximilian had his own domestic problems, and
the ongoing rising of the Flemish towns became so serious that he was
forced into an independent peace with France in July 1489. Henry tried
to remain resolute, even in defiance of the pope's efforts to force a truce.
Yet it was clear that England was still not in a position to act alone
against France, and Henry entered into negotiations.

Although the 1489 protest alarmed Henry, its dynastic undertone
was nothing but a spectre. Overt plotting in favour of Richard III's

legacy was in decline after the battle of Stoke. Yorkist conspirators were no less determined to depose the House of Tudor, but their options and resources became more limited, certainly within England. The focus of rebellion moved from the north, since the region now had too much to lose by maintaining Richard's memory.

Tudor enemies began to broaden their appeal for support to the areas connected with the real earl of Warwick. By the end of 1489 English intervention in Brittany had also aroused French resentment. Charles VIII saw an opportunity to retaliate against Henry VII by drawing English rebels to France. Most active was John Taylor, formerly a servant of Warwick's father. In 1489 Taylor began to discuss financing an invasion in Warwick's name.

In the west midlands, the minority of the duke of Buckingham and the earl of Warwick's imprisonment left a power vacuum. Henry's relatives stepped into the breach. To run local government Henry preferred to use gentry servants of the royal family. The search for security broke up long-standing patterns of local lordship and excluded some knights, like Sir Simon Mountford, who were experienced leaders and who might have created county-wide loyalties to the crown. They were not given the opportunity and drifted into rebellion as a result of this exclusion.

Increased public exposure of the earl of Warwick after Simnel's rebellion soon declined. Nobles like the earl of Derby extended land-holding and promoted their own servants into the west midlands. The royal family ensured that even knights attainted after Bosworth, like Sir William Berkeley, were already becoming rehabilitated. Such bias gave little opportunity to others overlooked or excluded from the favoured elite. This policy was a symptom of Henry's insecurity that could only be addressed by opening the door to the most able and experienced gentry, rather than only those closely connected to more trusted royal relatives and nobles.

The Tudor crown still had a dilemma in retaining and expanding control over lordship and loyalty after 1490, even if it appeared to be resolved within some regions. The leading anti-Tudor conspirators therefore began to revive old Yorkist connections in East Anglia and Calais. The earl of Oxford's return to regional dominance had created some friction as disputes dormant since Edward IV's reign reappeared. Lord Fitzwalter's surprise appointment as steward of the king's household in 1485 brought a closely linked group of Calais Yorkists back to prominence.

Although a Norfolk landholder, Fitzwalter had spent much of his career in Calais after 1471, and he retained strong family ties there. Henry was perhaps relying on an existing experienced network to run England's last continental outpost. In 1485, Fitzwalter probably hoped to exploit the earl of Surrey's attainder. He bullied Surrey's wife and he stepped up his involvement in East Anglian land deals. Surrey's return to favour in 1489 only heralded a future for Fitzwalter of power-sharing under Oxford, and it is from this time that he began to fall under suspicion.

Fitzwalter was not regularly styled with his title of Lord Steward from 1487, and it is probable that Sir Robert Willoughby took over some of his household duties. In July 1489, Fitzwalter lost his regional posts and was bound for his lifelong loyalty. Early in 1490 he was fined for contempt before the council and seems to have permanently fallen out with Henry thereafter. Other bonds suggest that Fitzwalter's circle was already on the fringes of rebellion. His descent into treason by 1493 was the result of his rapid disillusionment with Henry – a process shared by many who were unable to access the narrow network of loyalists representing the crown in the country's regions. This process was accelerated by the careful targeting of sympathisers like Fitzwalter by Henry's committed Yorkist enemies. After 1490, they threatened to turn deeper loyalties against the Tudors.

# 4

## PERKIN WARBECK

### THE ORIGINS AND DANGERS OF WARBECK

English political life in the 1490s was dominated by the 'reappearance' of Edward IV's youngest son Richard of Shrewsbury, duke of York. The historical debate still rages over whether Prince Richard survived imprisonment and death in the Tower in 1483. Henry VII and later Tudor writers did not think so – the king could suggest nothing else. The prince was soon proclaimed as an impostor: a young man from Tournai in Flanders named Perkin Warbeck who was trained to play the part. The sole aim of the plot was to reclaim the loyalty of the Yorkists serving the Tudor crown.

The conspiracy was one of the defining events of Henry's reign. It was an almost catastrophic challenge to the king, not least because it aimed to repeat the very nature of the Tudor accession. The plot's longevity tested Henry's abilities to the limit, and altered England's position in European politics. By 1500 key elements of the ruling structure within England were significantly different from those in place in 1491. Above all, the passion with which Henry strove to ensure Warbeck's failure made him a more robust monarch. He emerged from the crisis absolutely determined to command the loyalty and obedience of the country.

We are no nearer a definitive understanding of who Warbeck was. Ian Arthurson has presented Spanish evidence from 1496 that suggests both the Princes in the Tower died in the summer of 1483 and that their murder was disguised as blood-letting. The crucial information was the record of an interview with Perkin's first mentor, Duarte Brandao, and a meeting with Warbeck's Flemish father who confessed his son's true identity.[1] On the other hand, research by Ann Wroe proposes that the real Perkin Warbeck was still a child in 1491 and living with his family in Tournai. Inconsistencies here mean that we should not take the Tudor view of Warbeck as the truth about his background. Wroe speculates that 'Prince Richard' was an illegitimate son of Edward IV who was brought up by Margaret of Burgundy from 1479. An English boy called Jehan le Sage was treated honourably by Margaret and lived in her household from that date. This association could have provided both the resemblance to Edward IV and the knowledge of the Yorkist court that Warbeck reportedly possessed.[2]

Warbeck emerged as a royal figure at Cork in November 1491. As a crewman on a Breton merchant ship, he modelled his master's fine clothes. Despite his protests, bystanders proclaimed him as a Yorkist prince. This confusion was probably an invention of the existing plot designed to stir up Yorkist sympathies. If he were truly Richard, then this would have been the time to proclaim his survival. Such a low-key return to public life for a legitimate royal figure does not suggest real confidence in his initial appeal.

What is more likely is that this was an attempt to broadcast the seeds of a new conspiracy to provide only fragments of a tale of the miraculous return of one of King Edward's sons. A king uncertain of his fundamental supporters might view any contact with rebels as outright treason, making it more likely that former Yorkists would have nothing left to lose by rebelling. Such a carefully managed conspiracy could cause Henry's deposition without the need for open rebellion and battle.

Until 1491, Warbeck also had an itinerant life around Europe – from Portugal, to Brittany, and Ireland. He had relied on his social abilities to ingratiate himself with new masters and changing situations. He had also proved himself successful at self-promotion, having reached the rank of minor courtier in Portugal. Warbeck therefore possessed the bearing, language, and skills to perform the role conceived by his masters. Of course, all of these refinements would have been uncannily accurate had Warbeck actually been Richard of York.

If Warbeck was Richard we could hardly expect to find evidence of his true character among Tudor official records. No independent contemporary account of his origins survives. Warbeck's 1497 confession, repeated at his execution, was copied into the Great Chronicle of London. His very different account of Prince Richard's escape from the Tower in 1483 surfaced in a letter to the Spanish monarchs a decade later. Forcing a confession from Warbeck emphasised his outrageous deception and was a necessary action to refute a true Yorkist prince's survival.

For Henry, Warbeck simply had to be an impostor. As it was, he had enough trouble stifling the rumour and gossip that poured into England during 1492. He ruthlessly dealt with those of his followers who allowed their allegiance to be swayed by the ambiguity of Warbeck's status. During much of the 1490s, therefore, any differences between Warbeck's real identity and that promoted by his supporters made little difference to the massive impact of his conspiracy. Warbeck's credibility was perceived as genuine by enough influential people to shake the foundations of the Tudor regime. A surviving Yorkist prince was likely to reclaim the loyalty of almost everyone except Henry's immediate Lancastrian family.

That family's grip on the crown was strengthened with the birth of King Henry's second son, Henry, on 28 June 1491. He would be made duke of York at the start of November 1494, in a direct challenge to the claims of Warbeck. Although the arrival of two male heirs was a very welcome event for a fledgling dynasty, the survival of Arthur and Henry (and their sister Margaret, born on 29 November 1489) was entirely in the hands of fortune. Edward IV's reign had shown that even when royal heirs were nearing the age of responsibility, the inheritance of the crown remained dependent upon stable political circumstances and avoidance of disease and accident. Henry's deposition by Warbeck's conspirators would almost certainly have brought the death or disappearance of Arthur and Henry. The very survival of the Tudors as a ruling dynasty depended wholly on King Henry tightening his authority until he could pass the crown to an adult heir.

Although Warbeck's role was probably imposed upon him by his chief mentors, John Taylor and John Atwater, it was unlikely that the conspiracy arose spontaneously in Ireland at the end of 1491. English intervention in Brittany in February 1488 had given Charles VIII of France plenty of time to organise the links in a plot to depose Henry. The widespread support for Simnel in Ireland meant that Henry's agent, Sir Richard Edgecombe, reached only a compromise solution in 1487, since the removal of Fitzgerald power would only have invited deeper unrest. In a letter to Margaret of Burgundy, Taylor explained that he intended to goad the Tudor king into actions that could drive Ireland to rebellion by making it known that Kildare had aided Warbeck.

At the close of 1491 Warbeck was undergoing secret training for his royal role. At the centre of this coaching was Stephen Fryon, a former French secretary to Edward IV who had also served Henry VII before defecting in 1489. The king's intervention in Ireland after Stoke made the lordship far less willing to engage with another Yorkist pretender in 1491. King Henry sent troops under Thomas Garth and boosted the power of the Lancastrian Butler family to prevent the Fitzgeralds from making Warbeck even more welcome. Under this English pressure, the French sent a mission to bring Warbeck to Charles VIII's court.

By March 1492, John Taylor's letters announcing Prince Richard's deliverance had reached James IV of Scotland and Margaret of Burgundy. James longed for the recovery of Berwick and greater international status for his country. Charles VIII was preparing for an English military reaction to his campaign to annex Brittany, and welcomed the possibility of threats to England's northern border.

Henry had already considered what the Scots might do to aid their French allies. He developed a plan to kidnap James IV and his brother the duke of Ross at the Scottish parliament in spring 1491. This soon faded, and Henry turned to disgruntled Scottish nobles such as Archibald Douglas, earl of Angus, to lead military action into Scotland. English border fortresses were strengthened during the year, and Angus might even have established a bridgehead at Tantallon by September 1491. But the military activity soon declined into a truce that was unstable, but solid enough to allow Henry VII to launch his attack on France.

In the early summer of 1492 Warbeck was at the French court and seemed about to repeat Henry Tudor's own seizure of the crown. It was essential that England prevented an expansion of Warbeck's conspiracy, and, above all, that Henry stifled any foreign backing for an invasion in the name of 'Richard IV'. The rapid success of Warbeck's appeal for support almost certainly hardened Henry's existing desire to fight the French at the close of 1491.

# THE INVASION OF FRANCE, 1492

Henry VII's military expedition to France in October 1492 provides some idea of Henry's European ambitions during his first decade of rule. Most modern historians have agreed that his campaign was little more than a military parade from Calais to Boulogne with a brief siege at the end. Henry is accused of pretending to emulate Henry V's military glories when he was really only interested in ending French support for Warbeck, and in securing compensation for England's futile defence of Brittany.

Henry agreed treaties with Maximilian in September 1490 that set out the terms by which both would fight the French. At the same time, Henry ratified the earlier treaty of Medina del Campo with King Ferdinand. This revival of the Anglo-Burgundian alliance suggests that Henry VII had analysed how Henry V had successfully used a similar strategy against France after 1415. Henry's policy was no longer simply to protect Brittany, but a more aggressive strategy to counteract growing French dominance in north-western Europe. In December 1490, the alliance developed further when Maximilian married Duchess Anne by proxy.

Henry's rhetoric during 1491 was particularly warlike. In his speech at the opening of parliament in October, Chancellor Morton spoke on the theme of Jeremiah 8:15 ('we expected peace but no good came, and for a time of health, but behold discord'), firmly blaming the French for sowing disruption around northern Europe. This propaganda war hoped to persuade parliament that England's security depended on stopping French expansion and maintenance of Yorkist conspiracy. Defeat of France in battle on the basis of a Burgundian and Spanish alliance would leave no safe haven for Warbeck.

Henry displayed his intentions by picturing himself as an imperial monarch on the printed statutes and ordinances for the war in 1492. He also ordered horse trappings with the fleur-de-lis emblem of France, and minted a new coin that pictured the arms of France in the centre of a Tudor rose. Presumably Henry intended this coin to be circulated in the French lands he would conquer. The council ordinance of 1492, which set up a regency government of councillors to rule while the king was abroad, also developed directly from that established for the young Henry VI in 1430, at the height of England's most recent successes in France.

Henry gauged his preparations against the situation in Brittany. In 1491 the attentions of the allies wandered. Maximilian was required in Hungary; Ferdinand was on the verge of expelling the Muslims from Granada; and Henry heard first reports of new unrest in Ireland. French offensives threatened to overrun the duchy as its protectors looked elsewhere. When no ruler supported the besieged duchess at Rennes in April 1491, she agreed to become Charles VIII's wife, and committed Brittany's future to France. Charles and Anne were married in December 1491.

Henry had been promised repayment for English expeditions to Brittany. Some historians have seen his willingness to accept a truce with France in October 1492 as motivated by his desire for compensation from whoever would pay. In fact, Henry's reputation for avarice has clouded a true judgement of his campaign in 1492.

In October 1491 Henry negotiated a tax from parliament, the third part of which was to be collected in November 1493 only if the king's army stayed on campaign through the winter of 1492–3. That this was even specified suggests hopes for a swift campaign. But it is also possible that Henry intended to seize and hold a bridgehead at the end of the campaigning season, and then to exploit and develop this foothold in France during 1493. By that date, Henry had withdrawn his army, but might justifiably have left some troops overseas as a pretext for levying extra taxes.

Maximilian, too, hoped to use war against France to recover territory lost to France in 1482. As part of that treaty he had promised his young daughter, Margaret, in marriage to King Charles. In April 1491 Charles's marriage to Anne of Brittany doubly insulted Maximilian. At the end of the year he had the money to fight France, and, when Charles refused to release Margaret from her wardship, Maximilian began to assemble his forces.

Henry's own preparations began in July 1491. During the following year weapons were made, ships were requisitioned from Cornwall to Suffolk, and stores ordered. By the spring of 1492 the king agreed indentures for war service to his leading captains. With Portsmouth rather than Dover or Sandwich as the embarkation point, Henry clearly intended to invade through north-western France – perhaps Normandy or Brittany. It is probable that the campaign was planned for early June 1492, the period when Warbeck was in high favour at the French court. Henry's intentions were probably still flexible. In mid-June 1492 a sea force of up to 1,500 men under Lord Willoughby landed near Cherbourg. The expectant French repulsed it and English attacks were not continued. But this raid might suggest an intended English bridgehead for a recovery of Normandy.

Embarkation of the invasion fleet was delayed by French naval activity in the Channel during the early summer. An effect of French promotion of rebellion in the Low Countries after 1488 was the raiding by French vessels from a fortified naval base at Sluis. This disruption of the trade routes between England and the Continent made his defeat an important step in full-scale military preparations. In August, 900 men under Sir Edward Poynings helped Maximilian's forces to blockade the port and a truce was concluded by 12 October.

Henry and Maximilian had been in frequent diplomatic contact to coordinate operations. They also had attempted to secure allies within Brittany, and this communication allowed Henry's enemies to intercept his messages and alert the French. Strengthening of Brittany's defences probably ended English plans to land in the west. Careful and expensive preparations were quickly undone as the mustering army was relocated from Portsmouth to Canterbury and Sandwich – with Picardy and the Pas de Calais now the English target.

Some negotiations for peace with France then began, as Henry was permitted to do under the 1490 treaties with Maximilian. The Archduke, it seems, was doing the same, as his ambassador was at the French court during June 1492. At the end of August, English negotiators secured an offer from Charles of a payment to cover Henry's expenses for the defence of Brittany. Henry had already rejected a similar offer in 1490. If he had been determined only to receive a pay-off from France then this was the time to have taken it. There were deeper motives behind the campaign than Henry's alleged avarice. In fact these negotiations did not stall the speed of Henry's preparation, and might even have been designed to confuse the French.

The difficulty of mustering and manoeuvring the large English army is indicated by the timescale between Henry's proclamation of invasion, on 2 August, and the disembarkation of his army at Calais on 2 October 1492. It took many weeks to acquire the shipping necessary to transport men, stores and equipment, with over 700 ships eventually involved. Henry even confiscated the Flanders galleys of Venice to move his largest cannon across the Channel. His army totalled around 14,000 men and was the largest English force sent overseas during the fifteenth century. By focusing on Calais, Henry also made it easier to link with Maximilian's forces from the east. Yet despite the coordination of their broad diplomatic aims, a unified military campaign did not become possible, because the military objectives of both leaders were not linked from the outset.

When he landed in Calais, Henry was still hopeful of a united campaign. He would have been aware that whipping up the mood for war was a dangerous strategy if he intended only to sue for peace and payment as soon as he landed. The German princes certainly believed in attacking France, and granted Maximilian the necessary funds. A mercenary contingent of 4,000 infantry and 2,000 cavalry was dispatched to King Henry at Boulogne. They enthusiastically captured Arras on the way, but this delayed them long enough to arrive only when Henry had just agreed his truce with Charles at Étaples. An account of this campaign by its commander, Wilwolt von Schaumburg, was damning in its allegation that the English and French had conspired to humiliate the Germans, and had engineered a siege at Boulogne simply to extort money from their subjects.

Recent research by John Currin points to the 1492 invasion as a serious attempt to revive the dynastic conflict with France.[3] Henry's extensive preparations suggest the first phase in a reconquest of England's lost French territory. The attack on Boulogne could be seen as an attempt to obtain a strategic foothold in a region that gave an established army many options after a difficult winter of consolidation. French improvements to the fortifications of the town made it clear to Henry's military commanders that it would not be captured before winter. The English could not secure the strategic base they needed. It was Henry's captains, therefore, who urged the king into negotiations to salvage some honour from the French as part of a truce. The French were worried that Maximilian might launch an attack of his own to exploit the capture of Arras, and were willing to negotiate with Henry.

The peace at Étaples brought accusations from Maximilian's representatives that Henry had violated their treaties of alliance. It is true that Maximilian did send troops to help Henry and that his main army invaded French territory within a month of Étaples. However, Henry's inability to carry through the campaign he wanted left him with little option but to conclude a truce with France. He did try to safeguard

Maximilian's interest as part of the negotiations, but Henry's relative inexperience of dealing with the vacillating Maximilian only created deeper enmity between the two rulers. Of course, Henry could have withdrawn his army through Calais and resumed the campaign the following year, but the French would have been in a far stronger position to resist now English military intentions were known. Henry's subjects, too, would not have financed a lengthy war that again raised the spectre of military humiliation at the hands of the French.

## WARBECK AND THE TUDOR ELITE

The failure of the 1492 campaign can only have increased uncertainty in Henry's capacity as a leader among those whose heads were already turned by the news of a surviving Yorkist prince. Henry's negotiations with Charles VIII at Étaples secured agreement from France to stop harbouring Yorkist rebels, paid for Henry's expenses in Brittany, and agreed an annual pension of about £5,000 to be paid at Calais. France had not persisted with Warbeck because the focus of her foreign policy was shifting. Charles intended to press his right to the kingdom of Naples. The security of France's northern maritime frontier with England was vital to avoid English intervention when the Italian campaign was launched. Observance of the clauses of Étaples was essential if France was to remain secure. This necessity also ended any prospect of a French-backed Yorkist conspiracy against Tudor England.

The hostility felt by England's ally Maximilian at being left out of the peace talks now opened up new possibilities for Warbeck's promoters. It took little time to match Maximilian's pique with Margaret of Burgundy's 'ungovernable envy' towards the Tudors. A change of regime in England would invalidate Charles VIII's treaty with Henry. A Yorkist king restored at the hands of Burgundy would be obliged to stay involved in Maximilian's war with France. Rumours circulated that Charles was even willing to hand Warbeck over to Henry to prevent him becoming a tool of Burgundy. John Taylor and his group of about a hundred supporters quickly bribed their way into Flanders, arriving at Margaret's household on 12 December 1492.

John Taylor stoked the fires of popular rebellion within England by exploiting the disillusionment of military failure against France. He emphasised the miraculous nature of the appearance of a prince long assumed to be dead, and blended in prophecies and popular tales of the king who will return from overseas to reclaim his throne and unite the kingdom. Ties of service to Edward IV's sons were also the chief cause of the 1483 rebellion against Richard III. So there was latent attachment to the Yorkist princes that infused those Yorkists inherited by Henry VII.

Taylor pitched the story of Richard's escape, wandering, and reappearance at exactly the correct level to ensure that Maximilian and Margaret not only believed the truth of the tale but also were willing to assist in a Yorkist recovery. Margaret would look for no elaborate policy to tie to her support for Warbeck: her anti-Tudor venom was enough to maintain this new conspiracy solely on its own merit. The amazement and discussion this revelation generated were quickly passed to England by the merchant community. The emergence of a rival, whose legitimacy could not be confirmed or denied by the Tudor crown in 1492, revived the entire question of Henry's right to the throne. The conspirators had found fertile ground. Francis Bacon described the news as coming 'blazing and thundering' across the channel as all ranks of people were stirred to reconsider their allegiance to Henry.[4]

News of how Prince Richard had been welcomed in Flanders targeted Henry's control at the key centres of his power – within the royal household, in the north-west, and at Calais. Later indictments suggest that as early as 12 January 1493, ex-Yorkist household officers were discussing where their loyalty really lay. With little direct inducement, leading figures associated with Edward V, Prince Richard, and Calais-based East Anglians, agreed to support Warbeck with troops and money. By the second week of March, Lord Fitzwalter, Sir Robert Clifford, Sir Humphrey Savage, Sir William Stanley, and others, were actively preparing to assist in a Yorkist coup. Henry was in serious danger if the treachery of his household chiefs Stanley and Fitzwalter became more explicit, or if he failed to react to suspicions over their loyalty.

The king's immediate practical response was to reassess the situation in Ireland. A military expedition departed there in March 1493. By mid-April a show of force resolved the struggle for influence between the Fitzgerald earls of Kildare and Desmond. The king pardoned both. The recall of Kildare to England, where he remained for several months, was enough to keep the lid on Irish rebelliousness during a summer of uncertainty. Henry had to be equally wary of possibilities in Calais.

The connections there of Fitzwalter and Clifford gave them access to the politically aware permanent garrison. Any long-term subversion of crown control in this melting pot of rumour and suspicion could threaten Henry directly and stifle English shipping and trade.

The degree of overt support for a Yorkist claimant at the core of the Tudor regime, based solely on rumours of his survival, is very difficult to judge over five hundred years later. Much of the key evidence of house-hold treason was drawn out by spies and *agents provocateurs*. It was a sign of Tudor vulnerability, fear of invasion, and domestic rebellion, that Henry ruthlessly rooted out suspects on the slight evidence of treasonable conversation.

On the other hand, Henry did not make up the devastating nature of the threat. The arrival of Warbeck in Flanders created the biggest invasion scare since June 1487. From April 1493 Henry placed himself at Kenilworth with a standing force. Commissions of array and special judicial investigations issued in April and May 1493 show the king's real concern. A focus on Shropshire, the Welsh borderlands and East Anglia suggests a link between traitors and trouble in the localities where they were influential.

The appointments also indicate the beginning of a separation of trust between men who had been in exile with Henry and those who had served Richard III after 1483. Henry's view of events remained murky and the aims of Warbeck's backers seemed to be working. Several royal commissioners, such as Sir Simon Mountford in Warwickshire, later joined Warbeck. Other people were wrongly accused of treason. The clampdown also forced some rebels from cover. At the end of May 1493, Sir Humphrey Savage encouraged Londoners to swear loyalty to Richard IV (he soon fled to sanctuary at Westminster Abbey), and Sir Robert Clifford slipped out of England to Margaret's court on 14 June.

Throughout the summer naval patrols kept watch on the East Anglian coast, and the king's household men in Kent rounded up targets for Warbeck's messengers. The expected invasion did not mate-rialise. Margaret could not raise the funds to supply mercenaries, and Maximilian, who was preparing to take full responsibility as Holy Roman Emperor, faced problems in his eastern lands. As soon as he was able, Henry had sent agents into Flanders to uncover what was known of Warbeck's origins. By June 1493, Henry was confident he had found the truth about his adversary. In a letter to Sir Gilbert Talbot at that time,

Henry linked the plots of Warbeck and Simnel, and laid the blame for both inventions with Margaret of Burgundy.

At the start of July 1493 Henry sent ambassadors to the Netherlands to set out the outrageous pretence perpetrated by Margaret in trying to set a commoner on the English throne. The chief negotiator, William Warham, made the mistake of insulting the dowager duchess too force-fully. Warham secured agreements that there would be no official aid for Warbeck, but Margaret remained free to act as she wished in her own lands. She became even more determined to cause Henry's down-fall. Such was Henry's urgency to destroy Warbeck that he did not build on the encouraging official response of the Netherlands, but prepared an economic blockade to force a complete abandonment of Warbeck.

Maximilian became Holy Roman Emperor in August 1493. Prince Richard's kinship to Margaret of Burgundy now allowed both patron and pretender to enjoy the unrestricted support of one of Europe's most ambitious rulers. This escalation forced Henry to place Warbeck at the centre of all his policies. Henry's trade embargo began on 18 September 1493. By May 1494 Archduke Philip responded with a ban on the import of wool from England. It deprived England of key markets for three years. Both England and the Netherlands suffered economically while the future of the Tudor dynasty hung in the balance. The block-ade resulted in a number of riots within London, especially against the opportunistic Hanse merchants,[5] as workers were laid off. The Calais staple was made the only point of access to the continent for merchants based within England.

The conflict between England and Burgundy escalated through propaganda during the autumn and winter of 1493–4. Margaret and Maximilian strained to detach the Spanish monarchs from Henry. The kings of Scotland and Denmark found it in their interests to endorse Prince Richard's survival, and 'Richard' himself was happy to supply the details of his escape in 1483. Warbeck's welcome as a true Plantagenet prince was proclaimed to the whole of Europe when he accompanied Maximilian to his father's funeral in Vienna in December 1493. The time they spent together convinced the emperor that Richard was gen-uine and worthy of help to recover his birthright.

## BREAKING WARBECK'S ENGLISH SUPPORT

The plausibility of Richard of York's reappearance generated real confusion of allegiance as 1493 turned to 1494. The king's use of spies escalated dramatically, but the volume of rumour and evidence coming into the council often disguised hard facts that Henry needed to act upon. It was reported that men were afraid to meet and discuss events for fear that misplaced words would lead to imprisonment or worse. Henry was perhaps conscious that a premature savage attack on the leading suspects might provoke broader unrest. He therefore needed firm proof before acting, but the insidious nature of the conspiracy made it difficult to distinguish loyal from malicious information.

Henry certainly knew the status and type of recruit Warbeck's backers were targeting. He asked his chamber officials to keep specific lists of bonds and fines in order to master the interconnecting information that had to be sifted. He secreted spies into the households of suspects and even interviewed the chaplains and confessors of his knights and nobles. Henry brought the kinsmen and servants of known suspects before the royal council. Their knowledge was extracted before they were bound under large sums for their loyalty. This was part of the process of gathering proof. Henry knew that many elite men were acting in favour of Warbeck through servants and third parties, so Henry exploited existing service ties to ensnare retinue leaders.

In the first weeks of 1494, for example, bonds from Cheshiremen indicate that Sir William Stanley's servants were being monitored long before his arrest. These measures represented bail for those who had provided information to the king and council. In 1495, acceptance of heavy bonds saved many men from indictments of misprision (concealment) of the treason that their friends and relatives were suspected of. The imprisonment in the Tower of Stanley's illegitimate son Thomas in 1494 was perhaps stronger proof that his disloyalty was discovered. Without real evidence against him, however, Stanley kept his nerve. He and other household conspirators remained around the court into the final weeks of 1494.

By early summer 1495, the French warned Henry that Maximilian was massing ships and supplies to send Prince Richard and a large army over to England. Charles wanted England to remain neutral while he fought for Naples. Warbeck's possible invasion would guarantee that

Tudor troops remained on alert around England's coast during the summer months. Henry's response to the French was full of bravado and downplayed the danger from Warbeck. Henry was probably aware that Maximilian had his own problems to contend with, and having failed to finance an invasion in 1493 he was less likely to do so in 1494, as the French attacked Italy.

The ceremonies surrounding the creation of Prince Henry as duke of York on All Hallows Day 1494 tried to present a united court honouring the only true living duke of York. The spectacular jousting and feasting even allowed the king to gather in one place the conspirators he had known about for over eighteen months. Henry must have demonstrated his skill as a dissembler during these celebrations. On the one hand, he entertained lavishly; on the other he scrutinised the behaviour of those men intent on his deposition, all without any outward change in his demeanour.

Through this crucial and stressful time Henry remained one step ahead of the plotters. Sir William Stanley was present at a council meeting on 11 November 1494, but the conspiracy was not discussed. Publicly, the king seemed calm. Behind the scenes, his officials began to arrest conspirators. Throughout November and December Henry also supervised a secret scheme to get Sir Robert Clifford out of Flanders. Clifford's familiarity with Henry's daily routine and his contacts acquired in royal service had placed him at the centre of Warbeck's advisers. We can't be sure if he realised that Warbeck was the impostor Henry claimed, or whether his intimacy with Warbeck's plans suggested that he was incapable of bringing off an English coup. Either way, Clifford made it known that he wished to return to the king's grace. In exchange for immunity he was willing to provide the letters and seals that identified the network of elite traitors in England.

Clifford was pardoned just before Christmas 1494. After a dangerous escape he was in London by 12 January. Henry had already moved his household and council to the Tower. He stage-managed Stanley's appearance before the council and ensured the chamberlain was condemned by the evidence supplied by his turncoat confederate Clifford. Clifford informed the king that on 14 March 1493 Stanley had promised to assist Warbeck with all of his resources once he had received messages for mobilisation from Margaret. Clifford's information spurred the king's allies and loyal household servants into rapid action. On 20

January Lord Fitzwalter was examined, and five days later Henry's men had completed the round-up of enough plotters to conduct a special trial at London's Guildhall.

Sir William Stanley was tried and convicted as a traitor on 7 February. He had saved Henry's neck at Bosworth but was reported to have considered his rewards too few for his transfer to Tudor service. The involvement of Stanley retainers with Warbeck suggests a genuine willingness to aid Prince Richard, rather than the vague assertion that if Warbeck truly was the Yorkist prince then he would not be opposed by Sir William. Stanley's castle at Holt in the Welsh Marches was found to contain the astounding sum of £10,000 in cash, sufficient to keep an invading army in the field for many weeks. On 16 February, Stanley, the most powerful knight in England, was spared the horrific end of hanging, disembowelment and butchering, and was beheaded on Tower Hill.

The apparently disparate group of plotters were, just as John Taylor and Warbeck had hoped, very firmly linked to the surviving senior figures of the House of York. The household of Cecily Neville, mother of Edward IV and Richard III, bred several members of the conspiracy. A core group of rebels had Hertfordshire connections to Cecily's castle at Berkhampstead. The key connection between others who had broken their oaths since the end of the 1480s was direct royal service to Edward IV and his sons. Many, like William Stanley, had been body servants to King Edward and had made real sacrifices on his behalf from 1469–1471. The Warwickshire group centred on Sir Simon Mountford had fought for Richard III and were part of the network that John Taylor had wished to provoke in 1489. Strong links to the Woodville family of Henry's queen also emerged. Another strand focused on deeper foundations formed by the real Prince Richard's childhood marriage in 1478 to Anne Mowbray, daughter of the duke of Norfolk. Warbeck's backers believed that the fundamental adherence to the Yorkist crown that had brought power and influence to these families would provide a range of support sufficient to smash the ties that maintained Henry's kingship.

Henry's need for information was demonstrated by the sparing of those whose life offered him a further advantage in the political war against Warbeck. Whereas Stanley was killed because his landed power threatened to open up the north-west, Fitzwalter's influence was based on office and connection in Calais. His life was spared and he was imprisoned in the town. His steward, Thomas Cressener, was reprieved with his head upon the block. A wider Calais group became ensnared in bonds. These men were required to keep their eyes and ears open to the flow of information passing through England's continental frontier. Henry's mercy and attempt to mine the cells of conspiracy that remained overseas had mixed results, as several men resurfaced in later incarnations of Warbeck's plot.

## THE INTERNATIONAL PLOT THICKENS

The breaking of the English conspiracy in 1495 was a massive blow to Warbeck, but it was only ever one part of his overall strategy. The plot's powerful backers ensured that the attempt to dethrone Henry VII continued. While the rebellion in England was picked apart, Warbeck was negotiating loans in the Netherlands to finance an expedition. Prince Richard increased the stakes when he made Maximilian the heir to his realm of England if he should die in the attempt to recover it. The perennial Habsburg difficulty of ruling the scattered lands of the Holy Roman Empire might have given him the option of nominating another Yorkist king in England should Warbeck fail at the final hurdle.

Messages were sent to surviving rebel networks in England. Henry perhaps heard of the plans since northern English defences were placed on alert in March 1495. In Ireland, the earl of Desmond's rebellion continued and threatened to draw in the other Fitzgerald leaders. Kildare's arrest and removal to England in February 1495 was shocking, and took away internal Irish controls. Desmond was soon in alliance with Scotland, and he received support from Warbeck and Margaret for a full-scale rebellion in the spring of 1495. What seemed most dangerous to Henry were the closer ties of Scotland, the Low Countries, and rebels in the chaotic Irish lordship that heightened the danger faced in 1487.

At this point Margaret of Burgundy appealed to Pope Alexander VI to withdraw earlier papal endorsement of Henry's royal rights. The nature of this petition confirmed the preparation of a substantial invasion force intended to force Henry into battle. One of Burgundy's best soldiers, Roderick de Lalaing, was given command as Warbeck's ships were launched at the end of June 1495. The shortest route to likely sympathisers in England was to East Anglia. However, strong winds scattered Warbeck's fleet and he appeared with a much-reduced force off Deal in Kent on 3 July 1495.

Henry awaited events in the Severn valley. Defence of the east had been left to Archbishop Morton and the earl of Oxford. Beacons and fast-riding messengers within the Cinque Ports[6] brought troops to the coast by the time the first invaders reached Deal beach. Morton's men tricked them into believing that the area had declared for Prince Richard. As others were enticed out of their boats, Henry's forces attacked with showers of arrows before cutting down over half the landing party of 300 raiders. The survivors were abandoned and soon rounded up. Warbeck regrouped his ships and headed for Ireland. Secure in the knowledge that the feared invasion had been defeated by the power of the weather and a quick skirmish, Henry remained on the move. He deliberately targeted the region dominated by the Stanleys and visited the earl of Derby near Liverpool at the end of the month.[7]

The setbacks of 1495 placed Warbeck's plot once again in the larger frame of international diplomacy. Warbeck drew England and the Low Countries into the more massive ambitions of Europe's great powers. In 1493 Charles had been able to safeguard his borders through treaties with Ferdinand and Maximilian. However, French military success was so rapid after September 1494 that Ferdinand engineered the League of Venice in March 1495 as a counterweight. Milan, and the central Papal States welcomed Spanish intervention. Maximilian already had his own reasons to fear French expansion and was a willing signatory to this Holy League.

Around Europe, England's neutral position interested all parties involved in the League, and, of course, the French whom it opposed. There was pressure from Ferdinand to steer England and Scotland towards peace so that Henry could be brought into the war against France. Maximilian was still actively interested in making Warbeck king of England. He continued to argue that a Yorkist puppet would be a better guarantee of English hostility towards France. Ferdinand was wary of forcing Henry into seeking stronger links with Charles VIII to balance the support for Warbeck in the Netherlands. Charles's best hope of a free hand in Italy was to prevent a Yorkist takeover of England.

During 1494 and 1495, Henry grasped the key position England held as the rest of Europe fretted about French intentions in Italy. Maximilian had to balance his fears of an aggressive France with his belief that he could manipulate a Yorkist king of England. He had neither the finances nor serious political desire to chance the deposition of Henry when France threatened his lands on many fronts. Although he was more

likely to have been distracted by the implications of Charles VIII's clash
with the League's forces at Fornovo in July 1495, Maximilian was also
led to believe that the people of England would rise against their Tudor
oppressor at the first appearance of their rightful king.

Meanwhile in Ireland, Warbeck tried to make the most of a land on
the brink of political disaster. The earl of Desmond's rising was turning
into full-scale war. By the end of June 1495, Desmond was besieging
Waterford and Sir Edward Poynings and his allies appealed urgently
to the king for help. Henry, who was still in north-western England,
could do little to raise a substantial force quickly. Desmond was greatly
encouraged by the arrival of the 'Duke of York' with eleven ships, on 23
July. Warbeck sailed right up into the town and tried to land his Flemish
troops on the flooded ditches that had become makeshift defences. The
citizens bombarded the ships, and those invaders taken prisoner were
ruthlessly beheaded. Fighting continued for eleven days before Poynings
arrived with a loyalist force. Warbeck and Desmond were forced into
retreat by 3 August. Warmly chased around Ireland during the summer,
Warbeck renewed contact with Scotland and resurfaced at James IV's
court in November.

King James was aged 22 and desperate for military glory. He wanted
Scotland to be taken more seriously as part of the emerging European
balance of power. He used Scotland's ancient alliance with France to bargain with Ferdinand and Maximilian at the first meeting of the League
at Worms. Aid to Warbeck and a revival of the Anglo-Scottish war were
threatened in order to restrict England's ability to help the League.
Ferdinand pushed Scotland further into confrontation when James intercepted ambassadors' mail and learned that Spain had no intention of
taking Scotland's aspirations seriously. The Scottish council decided to
admit Warbeck to their country to hear his plea for help to recover the
English throne.

For Warbeck and Taylor this was almost a fresh start. A retelling of
Prince Richard's escape and wandering life received a mixed reaction
from Scottish lords. Many saw that a Yorkist prince could be useful to
Scottish policy. Others were suspicious that Maximilian and Margaret
wanted Scotland to do what they had been unable to accomplish
– invade England and force a Yorkist coup. The king was convinced
enough to offer Warbeck a substantial pension and a marriage to a royal
cousin, Lady Katherine Gordon. Despite his generosity, it is still unclear

whether James genuinely believed in Prince Richard's survival, or used the plot to further his own ambitions.

Elsewhere, Warbeck's failure increased the pressure on Maximilian to admit Henry to the League. By the close of 1495 plans for the marriage of Maximilian's son Philip and Ferdinand's daughter Joanna boosted the coherence of the League against France. The proposal also threatened to give Spain stronger influence in the Netherlands. Henry, too, realised that he could juggle Maximilian's stretched resources against Spanish willingness to help resolve the problems posed by Warbeck if it allowed England to join the League. Henry banked on Ferdinand's ability to influence Maximilian and began to negotiate directly with Philip for a resumption of trade with the Netherlands. Margaret and Maximilian's pro-Warbeck intentions were thwarted by the reluctance of the Low Countries to continue to endure economic blockade. By the end of February 1496 a treaty – the *Intercursus Magnus* – restored trading links and established an alliance between England and the Netherlands.

Henry also sent ambassadors to Maximilian to discover just how his support for Warbeck would continue under pressure from the other members of the League. Maximilian twisted and turned, but refused to abandon Warbeck. Henry flirted with France, knowing that Warbeck was just as likely to return to French protection if England declared war as part of the League. Charles VIII tried to persuade the Scots to hand Warbeck over to French protection. This would be a further guarantee of English neutrality, since French backing for Warbeck would heighten the internal discord Henry had worked so hard to contain. English pressure on France was also more likely to reactivate the ancient Franco-Scots alliance, moving Warbeck from one enemy to another.

Diplomacy circled inconclusively. Henry joined the Holy League on 18 July 1496, but as a neutral. England would not fight the French or supply money for anyone else to do so. Spanish pressure on Scotland continued. James sought a Spanish marriage for himself and was willing to drop Warbeck if it allied Scotland and Spain. Ferdinand's delaying tactics backfired when the Scots discovered that he did not have enough daughters to make the match a reality. Warbeck promised Berwick and a payment of £50,000 if James would aid a Yorkist rebellion. James could not resist the opportunity to thrust Scotland into the diplomatic spotlight. Even a renewed proposal that he marry Margaret Tudor came too late to avert the military build up on both sides of the border during 1496.

Preparations for war with Scotland prompted an apprehensive Henry to renew measures against English traitors. Household conspiracy created an atmosphere of distrust that distanced Henry from senior families such as the Stanleys. His intelligence network also assessed the loyalty of Yorkist nobles planted into the heart of the regime. We know from later evidence that George, Lord Abergavenny, and Edmund, earl of Suffolk, were thinking hard about where their loyalty lay. In August 1496 the marquis of Dorset was again heavily bound for his allegiance. Defections occurred in Cumberland; Warbeck's agents were active in Northumberland. Henry received intelligence that Carlisle might be vulnerable to treason. He was also concerned that the Scots might stir Ireland to rebellion once more through the earl of Desmond and his allies, who had refused pardons in 1495.

During 1496, after Warbeck had been driven from Ireland, Henry tried to get the Yorkist Anglo-Irish lords to negotiate once more. To everyone's surprise, Henry's careful offer to Desmond of limited power in southern Ireland brought his submission. Desmond's surrender also encouraged hope of stability in Ulster – the most disrupted region and vulnerable to Scottish intervention. Henry maintained the momentum. The real power in Ireland, Gerald, earl of Kildare, had been at court under a cloud since the spring of 1495. Henry used the opportunity to make him Lord Deputy once again and to force through a settlement between rival nobles. Kildare was honoured by becoming part of Henry's small royal family with his marriage to Elizabeth St John. Once he returned to Ireland at the start of September 1496, Kildare began to act like the king's true kinsman. He distributed Henry's pardon and ensured that Ireland was closed to Warbeck and as a second front for Scottish forces.

Henry's negotiating efforts continued in the north. It soon became clear, however, that the abandonment of Warbeck by James IV was never likely. James also resisted further French embassies that offered cash to take Warbeck to France if it meant an end to the war between England and Scotland. James, perhaps blinded by the prospect of recovering Berwick, continued with his war preparations.

## NORTHERN WAR AND WESTERN RISING, 1497

As 1496 progressed, greater stability in Ireland and improving relations with Philip the Fair left Scotland as Prince Richard's only hope for a significant military challenge to Henry, who had successfully kept the strands of the conspiracy apart through vigilance and careful diplomacy. His efforts ensured that Warbeck was forced into reliance on Scotland in a war that James IV had no chance of winning. The tax offered to Henry in November 1496 to finance the war was itself over twenty times James IV's yearly income.

Nevertheless, in mid-September 1496 a fully equipped Scottish army accompanied by foreign observers crossed into English territory. Warbeck remained in high favour with James, and his English traitors continued to agitate for uprisings in coordination with the Scottish attack. Although he had reigned for over a decade, Henry was still wary of indifference or treason on the battlefield. The king instead made the northern counties responsible for their own protection since they would suffer first. After he had destroyed a few isolated towers, and briefly bombarded Heton castle, James retreated back into Scotland by 25 September in the face of a northern army approaching from Newcastle under Richard Neville, Lord Latimer.

This raid demonstrated that Warbeck's backers still had the potential to persuade other powers to fit conspirators' aims into their own anti-Tudor or anti-English policies. The far north of England, however, had remained indifferent as 'Richard IV' entered his realm. James IV, too, was underwhelmed by the reality of Warbeck's appeal south of the border. Having committed himself to action by breaking the truce, James had little choice but to continue the war. Fortunately for the conspirators, Henry was still unsure how a well-directed attack would unsettle his intimate supporters and catch the enthusiasm of the common people. In his favour was the fact that Warbeck was in danger of repeating the mistakes of 1487. The north was unlikely to rise against the king when the alternative monarch arrived at the head of a largely foreign army. James IV's claim that he had crossed the border simply to restore the rights of his cousin of York cut little ice in a region constantly watchful after 200 years of war with Scotland.

Henry decided that ancient border hostility could be used to prop up his rule and, perhaps, detach Warbeck from Scotland. Henry gathered his councillors early in October 1496 to work out a war strategy. James had deliberately broken the seven-year Anglo-Scottish truce agreed in April 1494. Henry decided upon invasion after studying records of previous attacks on the Scots. The border garrisons were boosted by hundreds of troops, and massive sums were sent to Durham and Newcastle to supply a larger army. Henry then called a Great Council to meet at Westminster at the end of the month.[8] It promised a loan against taxes of £120,000 for the preparation of a land and naval invasion of Scotland. By November 1496 the cash from the loan was needed urgently to fill the gaps left in Henry's finances by the rapid purchase of weapons and supplies. Berwick and the East March bore the brunt of the build up, and ships were brought from the south and Calais to carry supplies and troops into the region. Henry left the earl of Surrey in command, confident that his past loyalty to the House of York would not resurface as betrayal.

The dragnet tightened on Yorkist plotters as more bonds and restrictions sought to paralyse Warbeck's network. Henry seemed confident that the back doors to England were closed to them. At the end of November Lord Fitzwalter was beheaded at Calais. With Warbeck in Scotland, he had probably outlived his usefulness as bait for other conspirators. The earl of Kildare remained loyal in Ireland despite the opportunity that Anglo-Scottish war provided to stretch crown control in the lordship.[9] For the first time Ireland would not contribute to Warbeck's cause against the Tudors.

After preliminary raiding by both the Scots and English during January and February 1497, Henry began to place the border region under martial law, with Carlisle becoming a closed town. The vanguard of the royal army was dominated by the retinues of the king's household men and not the major noble forces seen on earlier campaigns. Recently purged, and commanded by the new chamberlain Lord Daubeney, the campaign would be a test of how well Henry had reconstructed the core of Tudor power.

Henry soon learned that Warbeck and his captains were with King James in the borderlands during the first week of June. His pension was still paid by the Scots, and James allowed him to maintain contact with Irish rebels and Margaret of Burgundy. Henry was right to see the defeat of Scotland and the ejection of Warbeck as the key to England's position in Europe and security at home. As Daubeney finalised the assembly of the 7,000-strong vanguard at Newcastle, and Lord Willoughby's fleet waited off Sandwich with most of the bulky equipment, unrest in the far south-west of England halted the Scottish war in its tracks in the last week of May 1497.

Pressure to raise funds for the war brought the first spark of protest in Cornwall. Cornish people perhaps felt that they had contributed disproportionately as captains like Lord Willoughby had already recruited troops and miners in the county. In the Lizard peninsula, allegations of corruption prompted a blacksmith named Michael Joseph to organise discontented protestors. By the end of May, a major uprising was underway as a growing band of rebels left Cornwall for Exeter. They bullied their way into the city and rapidly spread their protest into Somerset. Taunton rose in open rebellion and soon parts of Wiltshire had joined. As support developed, so too did the aims of the rebel leaders. James Tuchet, Lord Audley, became the only noble leader of the rising as it passed through Somerset. He had been assigned a role in Henry's northern army, so his surprise treason was suggestive of real problems of allegiance for the king.

Audley's involvement in anti-Tudor rebellion falls into the pattern of Yorkists who initially worked with Richard III but then fell out of favour. Henry, too, was suspicious of such men, and the restoration of his southern exiles after 1485 closed the door to lords like Audley who had done little to deserve a share of the patronage offered to men who had endured hardship with Henry. In fact, Audley could have been pushed into rebellion because some of his father's lands had gone to John Cheyne, one of the king's most loyal knights. Other West Country gentry, excluded from the favoured circle of royal beneficiaries, followed his lead. Warbeck's proclamations in 1496 highlighted what he saw as Tudor reliance on a clique of base-born men who deliberately excluded rightful noble councillors.

In 1497 Audley, Joseph, and the other leaders became bolder as they progressed unopposed. By blending the appeal of a Yorkist Richard IV with regional anger at Henry's tax demands, the rebel army had become a formidable force when it camped near Wells at the start of June. Audley decided that speed was his best means of catching Henry unprepared. The rebel army by-passed Exeter and divided into two columns. One led by Joseph marched towards Guildford, while Audley set off for Oxfordshire. He perhaps hoped to cross the Thames to approach London from the north. It is also possible that he had received encouragement from the earl of Suffolk, who was visiting his Thames valley estates with another Yorkist peer, Lord Abergavenny. Suffolk was ordered to move his forces to defend the Thames bridge at Staines. When both lords discussed their next move, Suffolk was all for carrying out his orders. Abergavenny was less sure. In case he should be associated with Abergavenny's hesitation, Suffolk hid his shoes so that he could not immediately ride. Doubtless many other lords faced similar decisions when faced with the choice of defending Henry or moving to oppose him in battle.

One noble had a particularly difficult decision to make. The king's chamberlain Daubeney, commanding the royal vanguard further down-river, had turned back from Newcastle and was shadowing Joseph's force. A brief skirmish near Guildford was all the resistance he offered as the rebels continued towards London. By 13 June he was at Hounslow Heath but did nothing further to stop the westerners moving south of London to Blackheath. Daubeney was a Somerset landholder. He faced neighbours within the rebel army. His prominent service with the king meant that he would be one of the main orchestrators of their destruction when battle came.

Henry was not pleased that Daubeney's caution brought the decisive battle almost to the gates of London. On the other hand Daubeney's position made him the focus of rebel appeals when it became obvious that Henry's nobles had not deserted him. The rebel captains would be handed over on the promise of a general pardon. Henry refused this because the stated aims of the rebels now went far beyond tax protests. Audley and Joseph wished to destroy the Tudor royal family. The coming battle was about dynastic survival. By 16 June the king's army had joined Daubeney's vanguard in Lambeth. His massive force of perhaps 25,000 troops marched away from London to confront a rebel army that was at least 10,000 fewer in number.

London was well defended and secure for the Tudors, unless of course the king was defeated, captured or killed. Queen Elizabeth and the royal children moved to the Tower. The royal army manoeuvred into positions during the night of 16 June to surprise the rebels who had dug in around Deptford village. The vanguard of the westerners threatened the royal manor of Greenwich and the road to Kent. They remained spread out, however, with the main force still arrayed up the hill on the heath itself. There seems to have been some skirmishing early in the morning of 17 June along the river at Deptford Strand, and this attack caught Audley's forces unawares.

Daubeney fought with reckless courage at the front of the vanguard. In this vulnerable position he managed to get himself both wounded and captured. The fact that he was not killed but rescued or released shows that some rebels perhaps still hoped for his intercession. Even without the vanguard leader, the battle moved swiftly. The rebel army was unable to reinforce the contingent at the bridge, and the king's forces fought their way onto the top of the heath. Without artillery or significant cavalry, the rebel force was little match for the earl of Oxford's main charge that broke the opposing ranks and led to a bloody rout. Unlike at the battle of Stoke, there was no heroic last rebel stand and Audley, Joseph, and the other leaders were captured alive.

Henry knighted London's officials and rewarded the important contribution of the East Anglian gentry with knighthoods and promotions. The rebel captains replaced the royal family as prisoners in the Tower and were executed on 27 June. Audley was mocked with a suit of ripped paper armour and beheaded on Tower Hill. Their heads were boiled, tarred, and spiked on London Bridge, while various sections of their bodies were nailed to London's gates or carted to south-western towns. This grisly end for the leaders was not inflicted upon the rank and file and no more executions followed. Henry attempted to conciliate the Cornish rebels through lenience, but it was a mark of their alienation that many simply returned home and threw themselves once again into rebellion.

## WARBECK'S FINAL FLOURISH AND FAILURE

The victory at Blackheath did not resolve the situation Henry had faced at the start of the summer of 1497: a military challenge from the Scots and the prospect of a linked invasion or rebellion in Richard IV's name. The abortive war had cost as much as £90,000.[10] The Blackheath campaign still had to be paid for. England was in no position to finance a lengthy northern war. It was in Henry's interests to use his northern army to scare James IV quickly into peace on England's terms.

James had done very little to advantage himself from the English king's discomfort during May and June. In the week before Blackheath, the Scots offered some half-hearted raiding but missed an opportunity to attack when the English were fully distracted. Lord Willoughby had continued north with his large naval squadron during June, and he arrived off Aberdeen by 10 July. This force applied pressure to negotiations, since it was now Scotland's turn to face a possible war on two fronts.

Discussions continued across the border, with the Spanish still keen to broker a truce. Henry instructed his chief negotiator, Bishop Richard Fox of Durham, not to seek peace without an agreement to get Warbeck out of Scotland. Protection of Warbeck was now hampering the international recognition that James craved and he encouraged Warbeck to sail to Spanish protection. Warbeck left, probably with that intention, on 4 July. Within weeks he had latched on to new unrest in Ireland.

Scottish policy supported Warbeck right up to his departure, so it is likely that James still wished to extract concessions from England. Scotland again mustered for war. Henry responded by arraying another northern force under Thomas, earl of Surrey. The Scottish build up on the border was impressive, particularly in gunpowder weapons. With Norham castle their first target – only six miles from Berwick – this was a more serious campaign than the raids since September 1496. Even without Warbeck, James was determined to be taken seriously as a chivalrous military leader.

Norham, with Bishop Fox and his team inside, was besieged for ten days from 1 August. The ancient keep withstood everything fired by the Scots. Surrey's force was expected to try to raise the siege, but on 16 August he set out towards Edinburgh. Lord Willoughby had moved his fleet into the Firth of Forth and was landing marines by 15 August. A combined attack on Edinburgh looked likely. The English commanders coordinated well and Surrey demonstrated his intentions by bombarding Ayton castle as he marched into Scotland. James managed to move part of his army to catch up with Surrey at Ayton.

A pitched battle looked imminent, but was very risky for James. The English had superior numbers and a strategy that was crippling Scottish communications. In desperation, James challenged Surrey to single combat, gambling that he would either recover Berwick or become Surrey's prisoner. Surrey declined to fight a king when he was merely his own master's lieutenant. He preferred to risk the decisive battle. On 19 August, James began to withdraw his forces. He did not know that after two weeks marching around in the rain the English troops were in no condition to fight. Surrey decided, against Henry's instructions, to arrange a truce. Henry seemed to have detached Warbeck from the Scots and brought King James to a more realistic view of his own abilities and Scotland's diplomatic position. On 5 September 1497, and with the Spanish as interested arbitrators, a seven-year truce was agreed at Ayton.

Warbeck almost inevitably ended up in Ireland. He was probably invited there by Sir James Ormond – Henry's long-time ally who was by then embittered at the Fitzgerald ascendancy. He was the king's rebel by the end of May 1497. By 26 July Warbeck was in Cork, having failed to find any remnant of support elsewhere. Ormond's rising was snuffed out when he was killed by a kinsman. Warbeck was now pursued by Fitzgerald men and narrowly escaped to sea. They had already learned that he hoped to take Irish Yorkists into Cornwall to make the most of the anger still felt there against Henry. By August 1497 there were very few Irish Yorkists left who could add anything substantial to Warbeck's enterprise. It was therefore as an isolated figure that he arrived near Land's End with three ships on 7 September 1497.

This was the first time that Warbeck had appeared in England. Henry knew he was coming and had laid his plans. Since Blackheath had already been fought by the time Warbeck left Scotland, he had missed his chance to exploit the most dangerous rebellious fervour of the westerners. Nevertheless, survivors of Blackheath were confident that the region would rise again as 'King Richard' appeared among them. That trust soon seemed well-founded.

By the time Warbeck arrived at Bodmin on 12 September, about 3,000 rebels had joined him. Henry had entrusted Edward Courtenay, earl of Devonshire, to prepare the defence of the major towns. Devonshire was forced to withdraw into Exeter as some of the county levies deserted to Warbeck. The king expected Warbeck to head to Exeter. Devonshire was given time, money, and equipment to prepare a solid defence. Lord Willoughby's Scottish force was quickly diverted to Portsmouth to await any southern rebel breakout from the west. The king also dispatched Lord Daubeney to muster Somerset and neighbouring counties. He was to tackle Warbeck head-on to prevent any advance from Devon. The king also headed another reserve force in Oxfordshire. Henry already had enough troops to break Warbeck on the walls of Exeter.

The king had devised a comprehensive strategy to draw the rebels into annihilation. For a fourth time during 1497 English soldiers were marching to fight within their own country. Had all these challenges arrived simultaneously then Henry would have been hard pressed to keep the crown. The scattering of the threat diluted the impact of each event and enabled a coordinated royal response. By demonstrating that he was willing to pay almost any price to rid Tudor England of internal rebellion, Henry was broadcasting the growing strength of his kingship.

Exeter defied the rebel army of about 8,000 men from 17 September. Hundreds of rebels were killed trying to break the gates of the city. Twenty-four hours of vicious fighting caused Warbeck to retire to Taunton to lick his wounds. By that stage, the king's three armies had him encircled. The earl was prepared to follow Warbeck once he had regrouped Exeter's defenders. Daubeney was only a day's march away from Taunton by 20 September. In danger of being cut off and ensnared, few of the remaining rebels were willing to die for 'King Richard'. John Taylor must also have realised the end was near, for on the night of 20 September he, Warbeck, and about sixty followers left their army to Henry's mercy. It soon broke up as the king began his advance into the south-west.

Warbeck's retreat was blocked. His ships were attacked at Penzance and he became separated from Taylor as his small group of fugitives scattered. Warbeck dashed across country to the New Forest. By 22 September, in disguise and with only three companions, he sought sanctuary at Bealieu Abbey on the Solent. The abbot soon realised just who his guest was, and word was sent to the king. Within days, Daubeney's cavalry and soldiers from nearby Southampton arrived and forced Warbeck's surrender. His life would be spared, but Henry wanted the full facts of his life and conspiracy.

Warbeck met the king and several former Yorkist lords at Taunton on 5 October 1497. One of Henry's heralds reported Warbeck's full confession of his impersonation of Prince Richard. The text was hastily broadcast and had reached London within the week, where it was circulated. We shall never know if Henry himself still held any doubts about the identity of his most persistent adversary. It was essential that any trace of evidence that Warbeck was indeed Richard was erased. Henry publicised that Warbeck wrote to his mother in Flanders – a document that reveals a great deal about his confusion, fear, and relief as he escaped the role put upon him for almost six years. Warbeck remained with the king as Henry moved onto Exeter to begin the process of re-establishing control in a region in revolt since May.

The royal household remained there for just under a month. Many rebels were rounded up as the judicial process separated captains and real traitors from deluded and enthusiastic hangers-on. Henry then returned to London with Warbeck. Queen Elizabeth and Prince Henry had joined the king at Westminster from the safety of East Anglia by 21 November. Warbeck was paraded and quizzed so that the citizens could see the man who had been at the root of England's troubles for most of the decade. Like Lambert Simnel, Warbeck was treated leniently. He posed no personal threat and could expect a life in royal service.

He was allowed little contact with his wife, Katherine Gordon, who had landed with him at the start of September; Henry was certainly in no mood to release Warbeck to exile or rural seclusion. When, at the end of November, Maximilian sent high-ranking ambassadors to discuss trade matters and secretly to buy Warbeck's return to the Netherlands, they left empty handed. The king saw Warbeck as a victim of his more determined managers. Cutting Warbeck off from his sponsors preserved his life and ended the threat of 'Richard IV'. What it did not do was resolve the lingering belief that another prince with better royal blood than Henry Tudor – Edward Plantagenet, earl of Warwick – had been deprived of his birthright since 1485.

## THE END OF WARBECK AND WARWICK

Warbeck seems to have settled down to a steady life with the court. He accompanied the royal family on their progresses throughout the first half of 1498. At this time, Henry entered into negotiations with the new French king Louis XII to renew the Étaples agreement. Much stronger terms were agreed relating to the harbouring of rebels. Henry was tightening the net around those Yorkists still at large. The king's confidence was probably growing, but at that time Warbeck inexplicably turned his back on Henry's sympathy.

He escaped from his locked chambers in Westminster palace on 9 June 1498. Henry panicked. He initiated a frantic search throughout London and sent instructions as far away as Lincolnshire. Warbeck's re-emergence threatened to whip up uncertainty once more. Numerous Yorkist small-fry still were at large and doing their best to combine in conspiracy. Several prime movers of rebellion, such as John Taylor and

John Atwater, remained outside Henry's grasp. Above all, the earl of Warwick had become the only focal point for Yorkist sympathies.

Warbeck was soon picked up in the grounds of Sheen priory. The prior managed to secure a pardon for his life, but Warbeck had condemned himself to lifelong imprisonment. On the way to the Tower he was humiliated in the stocks on Cheapside. It was suggested that King Henry himself had created the opportunity for Warbeck's escape as a test of his contrition and faithfulness. The king could also have renewed plans to gather suspected rebels to Warwick's cause, and used Warbeck to draw them from cover at an early stage. Although Warbeck's keepers within Westminster were charged with creating keys to free him, a broader plot to spring Warwick from the Tower did exist.

In midsummer 1498 this was little more than tavern talk between pardoned rebels and Warwick's servants. Henry drew Warbeck's pathetic condition into sharper relief when he was taken on the royal progress to East Anglia in July. Henry arranged an interview with ambassadors from Philip the Fair who were forced to hear a repeat of Warbeck's confession. Warbeck asserted that 'Richard IV' was a cunning invention of Margaret of Burgundy created solely to persuade Europe's rulers into aiding Henry VII's deposition. As part of discussions over the cloth trade between England and the Netherlands, Henry pushed for a formal renunciation of support for Yorkist rebels on Margaret's estates in Flanders. Under pressure for some gesture, that would ensure she kept her personal lands, by early September Margaret amazingly wrote to Henry to ask forgiveness for her role in sponsoring his enemies.

With the myth of Prince Richard's survival now dead and buried, Henry launched commissioners into the western counties to broadcast his discovery of the imposture and to extract the familiar penalties of fines and bonds. The king's long investigation into the extent of western disloyalty revealed a deep level of hostility towards his kingship. The punishments meted suggested that opposition was as entrenched in Somerset as it was in Cornwall. Such extensive discontent had bubbled under the surface of regional political life for a long time. The clampdown Henry initiated was certainly an indication of harsher policies yet to come.

At the end of 1498 Henry perhaps allowed himself to feel more secure than at any time since 1490, but this apparent stability had come at high personal cost. Pedro de Ayala wrote to Ferdinand and Isabella at that time to inform them that the Tudor crown was at last undisputed and that Henry's government was secure. Nevertheless, Henry appeared old for his age, despite being only 41, yet young for the difficult and careworn life he had led.[11]

The birth of Prince Edmund in February 1499 provided renewed hope for the Tudor dynasty's longevity. At the time Edmund was born, however, the spectre of Yorkist royal rivals appeared once again. In January 1499 a Cambridge scholar, Ralph Wilford, proclaimed himself to be the earl of Warwick after a dream that he would be king if he announced as much. He was executed more for launching his rising in East Anglia than for the empty threat he posed. Ambassadors reported the shock this incident caused to the king – he aged visibly in a matter of weeks. Such strain moved Henry to resolve Warwick's position as the final weak point in his security. Despite much more serious risings earlier in the reign, Warwick had survived in the security of the Tower since the age of ten. Other factors now combined to cause Henry to execute the tragic young earl in 1499.

After Prince Edmund's birth, Henry was thinking about his own future. In March 1499 he consulted an astrologer. Henry did not learn the time of his own death, but discovered that he was in danger while enough committed Yorkists were free to cause him trouble. Henry was a superstitious man in an age where astrologers held influence over all degrees of people. This type of vague prediction, which was little more than a reading of unresolved threats, could have had a hand in guiding royal policy. It is also likely that during the negotiations for the marriage of Arthur and Catherine, the Spanish applied pressure to close off the obvious routes of conspiracy within England. They wished their princess to rule a safe and stable nation without any fear that she would have to rush to sanctuary or dash overseas to escape rebellion.

The plot that unfolded in the summer of 1499 aimed to take advantage of the summer progress of the royal family. Warwick's servant, Thomas Astwode, learned of the royal itinerary. He planned to use contacts in the Tower to secure the earl of Warwick's escape when the king was on the Isle of Wight. The plotters drew together many survivors from the 1493 household plot, with Warwick as their figurehead. The germ of the king's awareness to a new plot may have been planted by more sinister developments.

At the end of June 1499, Edmund, earl of Suffolk, departed to Flanders without permission. The immediate reason for this was fear of repercussions of killing a man in a London street fight. There was also a possibility that this nephew of Richard III was associated with the new Yorkist conspiracy. He was frequenting the part of the city where Warwick's men were hatching their plot. Suffolk was soon persuaded to return, but not before Henry had displayed his unease by threatening trading sanctions with Archduke Philip to ensure de la Pole had no safe haven. As a result, surviving Yorkist networks were monitored more closely.

The focus for Henry was obviously Warwick and Warbeck. They were locked in adjacent rooms within the Tower. But the Tower was not simply a closed prison. It was a royal palace, treasury, and armoury. Prisoners held there had to make provision for their own upkeep. This arrangement allowed servants to come and go with supplies and news. The Yorkists took advantage of this apparent laxity, as the king knew they would.

Later indictments set out the bones of the plot. Warbeck was accused of urging Warwick and his servants to help to seize and burn the Tower. In the confusion they were to ransack the king's treasury, dash to the riverside, and ship Warwick abroad. The official version made Warbeck the instigator of the plot, but Warwick was willing to join him in rebellion. This crucial connection sealed their fate.

It is entirely possible that the king deliberately manipulated Warbeck to trip Warwick into treason. Warbeck had appeared confused and close to collapse when the Spanish ambassador had seen him in prison. The lieutenant of the Tower, Sir Simon Digby, had been an effective rebel-hunter previously, and was capable of using Warbeck's broken state to ensure that Warwick became tied to the plot. By 4 August, Digby knew the details of the imminent attempt to rescue Warwick through the defection of some of his garrison. The king was informed but allowed the plot to unravel. Under careful observation, the connivance of the two chief prisoners was proved to Henry's satisfaction.

In early September 1499, Henry's agreements with the French brought about the delivery of the chief rebel John Taylor. Taylor's capture gave access to the inner workings of all the conspiracies since 1489. Although we have no evidence of the information he delivered, the fact that his life was spared suggests that Taylor and the king reached an agreement. He certainly had intimate knowledge of Warbeck's true identity. As Warbeck himself had been interviewed, so Taylor, who spent the rest of the reign in the Tower, could supply the proof to foreign ambassadors and English nobles that Warbeck was a counterfeit prince. All the doors of conspiracy had closed but one.

The earl of Warwick would always attract the interest of the half-hidden fanatics still hoping for Henry's deposition. The king was again advised by his astrologers, and perhaps more forcefully by the Spanish, that Warwick was a danger to the crown while he lived. Imprisonment had proved no barrier to his involvement in conspiracy and his death seemed the only solution that would finally free Henry from Yorkist agitators. When the members of a very full royal council meeting heard the evidence on 12 November 1499, they agreed with the Spanish.

Warbeck, John Taylor, and John Atwater, mayor of Cork, were tried on 16 November and sentenced to traitors' deaths. At the moment of his execution, Warbeck confessed to the crowd that he was indeed an impostor (at least Tudor accounts tell us that he did). Warbeck was hanged at Tyburn on 23 November. Warwick appeared at Westminster before the peers of England on 19 November and confessed his treason. A week later his head was cut off. As he had done with William Stanley, the king paid for Warwick's burial. By 29 November a third trial began of the other conspirators. Some of those indicted did not stand trial at all, while others escaped the punishment they might have deserved. This has only fuelled the speculation that the king had constructed most of the plot.

Warbeck's execution ended one of the most protracted and dangerous conspiracies faced by an English monarch. Although Edmund de la Pole was to adopt the Yorkist challenge in 1501, the danger of mass appeal to broad Yorkist sympathies had been overcome by Henry's tenacity and the trust he placed in nobles like Oxford and Surrey. Henry's former Yorkist household knights were by then Tudor men through and through.

Things were not so clear earlier in the decade. Henry's regime was maintained only by a transfer of allegiance. Prince Richard's reappearance was intended to demonstrate to Edward IV's old servants that they had acted in ignorance when they propelled Henry Tudor to power. A true Yorkist prince, waiting overseas for the chance to recover his throne, made their support for Tudor morally wrong and indefensible in terms of their prior oaths to Edward IV. Warbeck used this context to make all prominent families question where their loyalty lay. This act created hundreds of personal dilemmas across the Tudor state in the 1490s.

Warbeck, as Prince Richard, could be manipulated and paraded by Maximilian and Margaret of Burgundy, but Henry's propaganda had ensured that enough doubts remained over his identity to stop wholesale defections from 1493 to 1495. Claim and counter-claim created a fog of uncertainty that helped Henry to keep the links of his authority in place against very determined opponents. For a coup to work within England, Warbeck's appeal had to reach an audience beyond those who had been intimately involved with the Yorkist elite. Many families might have owed the crucial rise in their status to service under the House of York. But by 1495, after two generations of wearing civil conflict, most land-holders were willing enough to acknowledge the authority of the crown, regardless of who sat on the throne.

The static reaction of the majority of northern gentry, who refused several good chances to rebel before 1490, showed that overwhelming evidence and powerful motives were needed if the groups targeted by plotters were to be pushed into treason. Those on the cusp of rebellion shared the king's urgent search for the hard facts of Warbeck's identity. Without it, the risk to livelihood and inheritance was too great. The only inherent Lancastrian or Yorkist loyalty was found among those who shared the royal blood of either dynasty. Even among the Yorkists ele-vated into the Tudor hierarchy, the conspirators' options were restricted when persuading would-be rebels to mobilise troops, money, and them-selves. Treason against Henry VII required direct action.

Richard of York's status as an underage prince, without a concen-trated group of lands or a powerful personal following, restricted his appeal beyond the superficial level of curiosity about his survival. Had Edward, earl of Warwick, fled the country in 1485, anti-Tudor con-spiracy might have developed very differently. His service networks were sufficiently deep-rooted in the west midlands to become a basis for national support. The range of supporters Warbeck had drawn out between 1487 and 1495 indicated that the initial level of commitment to his cause was too dispersed to be the basis for a revolution. The shift in rebel focus to the Tudor royal household did not work either because Henry was able quickly to draw on the loyal Lancastrian and Beaufort servants that balanced the former Yorkists at the amalgamated core of Tudor power. Warbeck's conspiracy was an audacious and potent chal-lenge to Henry. In defeating it, he became a far stronger ruler. From the uncertainties and insecurities of the 1490s emerged an experienced and ruthless monarch, and one obsessively focused on preserving his hard-won security.

# 5

# THE RIGOURS OF KINGSHIP

## PERSONAL LOSSES AND A CRISIS OF AUTHORITY, 1499–1504

The 1490s had seen a transformation in England's position in Europe. To crush Warbeck Henry had been willing to squeeze England's traditional export markets in the Low Countries and to purge his close circle of men who were not absolutely loyal. Through such impressively ruthless kingship, Henry proved to observers that England was no longer stricken by the leaderless government and unstable institutions that had invited civil conflict since the 1450s. It was for this reason that monarchs like Ferdinand, and eventually Maximilian, came to accept that England once again had a role in European state politics.

The execution of Warbeck and Warwick also left Henry's grip on internal power at its strongest. Henry had never before enjoyed a time free from rebellion or conspiracy. The year 1499 should have been the start of a period of stability for Tudor kingship. Instead it turned out to be but a brief interlude in the story of dynastic setback and personal tragedy that plagued Henry's personal rule. It was during the period 1499 to 1504 that opportunity slipped from Henry's grasp. His regime developed a narrow and restrictive focus on the containment of threats and the control of individuals – policies that almost led to a return to civil conflict in his final years.

Warbeck's capture took away any leverage the Scots had against Henry. The truce of Ayton of September 1497 still held firm. In the early summer of 1499, peace negotiations took place along the border. A treaty was agreed at Stirling on 12 July 1499 – the first full agreement between England and Scotland since 1328. This was a major achievement for both monarchs.

During the same period Henry sealed England's alliance with the Spanish kingdoms in a treaty of 10 July 1499. The political understanding that created this agreement was formed a decade earlier at Medina del Campo. In 1499, the earlier proposed marriage between Arthur and Catherine of Aragon finally took shape. Catherine would come to England at the age of 12. The treaty set out the dowry demanded (200,000 crowns agreed to be worth 4s 2d each), and the jointure land she could expect as princess and when she became queen. Free of the Yorkist menace, the Tudor crown would be a far more stable ally in Spain's struggles with France. Henry's greater confidence in his stability meant that he could adopt a tougher negotiating position. Trading agreements were guaranteed, as were undertakings not to aid the rebels of the other state. Ferdinand was wary that Henry's good relations with France might also make him more concerned to use England's newfound security to strengthen diplomatic relations in northern Europe. Indeed, Henry was already thinking of using the marriage of Prince Henry to smooth his previously troubled relationship with England's main trading market in the Low Countries.

Henry's growing band of children meant that cadet branches of the royal family seemed inevitable. England's new prominence, however, meant that the Tudor offspring were likely to strengthen Henry's links through marriage to other ruling houses, rather than within the English nobility, as his royal predecessors had done. With the duchies of York and Somerset held by the king's immediate family, there was little scope for would-be rebels to begin to undermine Tudor power by raking up the York–Lancaster struggle.

Henry was familiar enough with the unexpected ways in which his destiny had moved. He could do nothing to ensure that fortune would provide him with a comfortable old age, but with the birth of his third son he was able to begin to plan the longer-term future of his dynasty (a luxury his successor never enjoyed). In naming this son Edmund, after the English royal martyr who, in 870, had died rather than surrender his East Anglian kingdom to Viking invaders, Henry invoked a spirit of resistance found among England's past rulers that he had tried to emulate.

Arthur's name conjured associations with the valiant and unifying king of legend. Henry, duke of York, took his father's name and, aged 10, in Easter 1501 was already actively involved as Marshal of England (with Lord Willoughby as a mentor) in the sessions of the court of the Verge of the Household.[1] The king was broadcasting the kind of dynastic roles and characteristics he hoped his sons would develop as he prepared for the transition of power. Having secured the Spanish match and taken most of the steps to marry his daughter Margaret to James of Scotland, Henry's kingship had moved beyond resistance to conspiracy towards more constructive dynastic building through diplomacy and marriage.

The new century started well enough. Henry travelled to Calais to meet with Archduke Philip in May 1500. The agreements reached when negotiating the earl of Suffolk's return promised a full restoration of the beneficial trading links between England and the Low Countries. Soon after, however, the new confidence of the regime began to shatter. It was in youth and not maturity that the first shock was felt. Prince Edmund, the 16-month-old duke of Somerset, died on 19 June 1500. Despite his infancy, Edmund's death was a blow to the king's vision of balanced Tudor power. The formal account of his funeral suggests a ceremonial for a prince of greater age and status. Infant mortality was a risk all late medieval parents endured, but for a newly arrived dynasty it must have been gravely alarming.

Prince Henry was then aged only 8 and far from the beefy, athletic youth who acceded as Henry VIII in April 1509. It was in Arthur's status as proxy-husband to Catherine of Aragon, therefore, that all Henry's hopes of immediately stabilising his regime rested.[2] With this loss came a sense of renewed vulnerability. New instructions were issued for the negotiation of a marriage between Margaret Tudor and James IV during the summer of 1500. Henry also gave commissioners new powers to settle Marcher disputes with their Scottish counterparts in July of that year, lest unrest at another dynastic setback threatened to open the north to rebellion once again.

Other shocking but not unexpected news came soon after. Henry's oldest ally Cardinal John Morton died on 12 October 1500. Morton was undoubtedly the architect of Tudor's successful capture of the throne.

He had engineered the 1483 conspiracy and had gone to Rome in January 1485 to secure papal backing for Henry's marriage. As chancellor he headed the king's legal clampdown on abuses of lordship and saw through a number of ecclesiastical developments that also enhanced Henry's authority, especially reform of sanctuary and benefit of clergy.

Morton's grasp of the new direction in which Henry was taking the English polity was encapsulated in his promotion of Henry Medwall's play *Fulgens and Lucrece*. Medwall was Morton's chaplain and wrote this 'interlude' to be performed before courtiers in 1497. In struggles between a nobleman and a commoner for the attention of an heiress, it is the hard-working commoner, rather than the shallow and arrogant noble, who wins her affection. *Fulgens and Lucrece* satirised the decline of aristocratic servants around the king in favour of the new men who succeeded through their good service.

Morton's replacement as keeper of the great seal, Henry Deane, enjoyed far less political prominence that his wily predecessor. Deane cut his political teeth in Ireland with Poynings in 1494 and 1495 and was a close friend of Bray, who was chief executor of his will. Deane had the misfortune to die in the same week as Queen Elizabeth in February 1503. Despite being a monk, he was experienced in politics and the law, but he was Henry's second choice as chancellor. Morton's intended replacement, Thomas Langton, had died before his translation from Winchester. Nevertheless, Deane would have brought confidence and a steady hand at the centre of government. He also helped his chaplain Thomas Wolsey to move into royal service.

Deane's death only added to the uncertainly Henry must have felt as the experienced allies, attuned to the pulse of the regime, began to depart. William Warham was a natural choice as Deane's replacement. He had been Morton's deputy as master of the rolls from 1494 and was an eloquent English ambassador during the 1490s. He seems to have had little impact within chancery, and many of the key interests Morton had held were redistributed.

It is probable that Sir Reginald Bray acquired many of the political responsibilities Morton had held. The western rebels of 1497 had condemned both men as the chief agents of the king's financial repression. They also seem to have been among Henry's closest advisers in decisions of policy, as stated by various ambassadors. Bray's death in August 1503 robbed Henry of an intimate adviser and a man of vast experience.

Whether this was deep enough to be real friendship is questionable, but men like Bray and Morton had shared Henry's hardships in the early 1480s and had grown wealthy and influential in pursuit of his policies.

Henry's implicit reliance upon those who had shared his exile left him dangerously exposed when members of this elite began to die. This inflexibility weakened the basis of Tudor authority. Henry's choice of replacements sought to recreate the ties of fidelity that had propelled him to the crown. Much of Morton and Bray's closeness to the king was transferred to servants who were entirely dependent upon their personal relationship with Henry. But this was not a connection based in the trying times of 1483 to 1485. It was a purely professional relationship created to streamline policy, and one that made Henry's new men more accountable and easier to supervise.

We find the first real evidence for Henry's failing health from the summer of 1501. That July he complained of failing eyesight when writing to his mother. If the erosion of his health became incapacitating with greater frequency thereafter, we might see the return of the politically astute Surrey to a central role as Lord Treasurer in 1501 as an attempt to compensate for Morton's death. Surrey, Fox, Lovell, and Warham came to represent an established and traditional body of royal councillors that counterbalanced the more aggressive work of Richard Empson, Robert Southwell and, eventually, Edmund Dudley. There was clearly a tension in the way that Henry's immediate advisers cooperated around the king after 1500. Henry's own diminishing ability could also have complicated an increasingly difficult power-sharing arrangement. This became very apparent when Surrey and Fox delayed the announcement of Henry's death for 36 hours in April 1509 to arrange the arrest of Empson and Dudley.

After a decade in the north, Surrey was also an expert in maintaining Henry's authority. His recall could have been linked to a sudden resurgence in Yorkist plotting. By August 1501 Edmund de la Pole, earl of Suffolk, escaped over the Channel with his brother Richard to the court of Maximilian. Uncertainty once again flowed the other way. Henry took steps to isolate and restrain de la Pole's followers in England, but he could not know how Maximilian's policy would develop with another Yorkist pretender desperate for his help.

Suffolk's treason cast a shadow over the departure of Catherine of Aragon for England at the end of September 1501. She and her entourage arrived at Plymouth on 2 October and were met by a party of Henry's household knights. Her journey to London took several weeks, allowing many people in the southern counties to catch a glimpse of their future queen. Catherine was almost 16 years of age and about 6 months older than Arthur. Although they were young by today's standards they were at the prime late medieval age in which to herald a brilliant new phase of recognition for the Tudor dynasty.

Henry was determined to put on a show that matched the political opportunity then in his hands through this marriage into the most dynamic monarchy in Europe. The king planned a grand formal entry into the city. Delays in Catherine's departure from Laredo had given Bishop Fox a great deal of time in which to devise and supervise the creation of a spectacular ceremony that tells us much about how the Tudor dynasty viewed itself at the beginning of the sixteenth century.

Catherine entered London over London Bridge from the south on 9 November. She was welcomed with speeches from actors representing St Catherine and St Ursula (in Geoffrey of Monmouth's version of her life, a virgin martyr sent to marry a usurping king). In the city itself, Gracechurch Street was blocked by a wooden castle decorated with the unifying Tudor rose emblem. Figures representing virtue, noblesse, and policy – the three anchors of just and chivalric kingship – gave welcoming speeches from the castle that praised the princess but also spelled out what her role would be within the Tudor ruling elite. Prince Arthur awaited his bride at the centre of an amazing array of mechanical models of the heavens and devices of the zodiac. Another pageant placed God himself in a giant red rose, a direct representation of Henry's belief that his dynasty was maintained by heavenly favour.

The lavish spectacle continued with feasting and jousts for the preening young noblemen of the court to impress the king and the Spanish representatives. Henry was concerned that English hospitality sent the appropriate messages to Ferdinand and Isabella. He personally wrote to praise the welcome Catherine had received from all the people of London. Arthur did the same at the end of November, expressing his happiness at the marriage.

Arthur and Catherine immediately travelled to Ludlow to begin their lives as Prince and Princess of Wales. The king had already started to create a powerful ruling structure for Arthur's regional rule in Wales.[3] With his heir's future now clearly established, by October 1501 Henry was also ready to use the marriage of his daughter Margaret to cement England's relationship with Scotland. The fine detail of Margaret's dower, the itinerary of her journey into Scotland, were worked out by the end of December 1501. Negotiations resulted in three new treaties, all agreed on 24 January 1502: the treaty of marriage, a treaty of perpetual peace, and a treaty for preservation of order on the marches.

With two dynastic marriages underlining Tudor England's resilient status, Henry was free to turn his attention once again to the crushing of dissent and conspiracy connected with the earl of Suffolk's treason. By the spring of 1502 the earl of Oxford and Sir Robert Harcourt had placed Suffolk's most prominent servants and tenants under heavy bonds. Other Yorkist figures were rounded up. The arrest of Sir James Tyrell, William de la Pole, and Lord William Courtenay indicated the seriousness of the potential threat posed by Suffolk at Maximilian's court. Henry seems to have used double agents to completely undermine Suffolk's threat before it had a chance to develop. Sir Robert Curzon, captain of Hammes castle in Calais, was alleged to have encouraged Suffolk's second flight from England. He remained with Suffolk long enough to expose the conspirators' plans to the king.

As with Sir Robert Clifford in 1493, Curzon perhaps initially let his Yorkist background lead him into conspiracy. He might have been alarmed by Henry's ruthless execution of Warwick. Any thoughts of rebellion he had soon evaporated as the hopelessness of Suffolk's position quickly became apparent. Curzon was excommunicated and condemned as a traitor along with Suffolk in 1504, and his sureties did forfeit their pledges for his loyalty. This would have been ruthless action indeed had Curzon been an *agent provocateur* from the start. Curzon was received by the king after Suffolk was imprisoned in 1506, and he received a large annuity from Henry. This is the strongest evidence that Curzon was Henry's man on the inside of this last Yorkist rebellion of the reign.

Henry seemed to have mastered the web of conspiracy. But the provision for the future of his dynasty that Henry had worked so hard to create was torn apart when Prince Arthur died at Ludlow castle on 2 April 1502, probably from a severe chest infection or tuberculosis. King Henry and Queen Elizabeth were shaken to the marrow by Arthur's death. One of the very few real insights into the king's personal feelings comes from the report of his reaction to the news of his son's death. The king's confessor was charged with waking Henry and giving him the shattering news.

Henry sent for Elizabeth and together they shared their pain with words of comfort. The queen tried to remind Henry that he was an only child and had been preserved by God through all his troubles. The responsibility for consoling the king was too much for his wife and when she retired to her own chamber she broke down uncontrollably. Henry then came to her 'of true gentle and faithful love' and they both retired into privacy to remember Arthur and to give thanks for his life.[4]

Arthur's death threatened to destroy Henry's carefully balanced relationship with Spain. The fundamental reasons for the alliance still applied. As a way to maintain the amity between the two countries, and to get further concessions from England, Ferdinand sought ways for Prince Henry to marry his brother's widow. The success of the policy depended on whether Catherine was still a virgin. Prince Arthur's teenage bragging during their four months together suggested that she was not. The Spanish monarchs initially believed so and asked for a return of the payments towards her dowry and marriage portion. By July 1502, French armies were once again on the offensive in Italy. Queen Isabella was prepared to accept that Catherine's marriage had not been consummated if it meant England could join the war against France either in the north or in Italy. Ferdinand used the carrot of a possible English recovery of Normandy, but Henry was reluctant to commit England with his dynasty once again in a precarious state. The marriage agreement was quickly settled and the draft of a treaty was drawn up by September 1502, but ratification was delayed for a year by the death of Pope Alexander VI in August 1503. Papal dispensation was needed because Catherine and Henry had become related within the accepted degrees by her marriage to Arthur.

Henry and Elizabeth had to pick up the pieces of their dynasty. The king's immediate political reaction was repressive. Arthur's death came in the first months of the de la Pole challenge to the Tudors. Suppression of conspiracy apparently forced the execution of Sir James Tyrell and two other crown officers in May 1502. Henry also made it known that Tyrell had confessed to the murder of the Princes in the Tower. This declaration prevented a tried and tested route to externally sponsored rebellion from reopening. No evidence has ever been found of the substance of Tyrell's confession. Tyrell was killed and William de la Pole and William Courtenay thrown in prison because their Yorkist credentials and previous treasonable associations coincided with the death of Henry's heir.

Henry brought all of his experience and consolidated power to bear on the crushing of any new signs of rebellion linked to former Yorkist loyalties.

Henry pressed ahead with the peace process towards Scotland. The treaty regulating Marcher government was an important indicator of Henry's concerns at that time. It allowed up to twenty days for the arrest of murderers and robbers in the marches, even if they were more than one hundred miles within the opposing country. James agreed not to attack the castle and town of Berwick, and Henry was bound not to use the standing garrison there to wage war on the Scots. After a last-minute delay over the presence of the word 'France' in the English king's titles – an indication that the Franco-Scots 'auld alliance' was still maintained – the treaties were ratified and exchanged on 17 December 1502. English preparations for Margaret's journey and marriage were made throughout the winter of 1502–03.

The losses of the royal children Edmund and Arthur put further pressure on Queen Elizabeth. She was again pregnant by May 1502. She had tried to comfort her husband in 1502 with the hope of future children. But at the age of 36 Elizabeth was not a young woman. She was probably already weakened by six pregnancies and the residual anaemia that many medieval women endured through a combination of an iron-deficient diet and repeated childbirth. Elizabeth's death on her birthday, 11 February 1503, a week after the birth of her seventh child – the short-lived Princess Catherine – was to be the hardest personal blow Henry would endure.

Henry had sought frantically to ensure a successful birth. On 20 January 1503 a groom of the chamber rode to bring the queen's surgeon, Master Robert, to Richmond. Another expert physician was brought from Plymouth on 10 February. Henry was disconsolate at Elizabeth's death, and remained alone with his grief for some time. He paid for masses at various shrines; Walsingham burned over 56 pounds of wax during prayers for the queen. In the weeks after Elizabeth's death, Henry himself suffered a severe illness. He was unable to eat or drink for six days following contraction of a throat infection, or quinsy. He was close to death. The coincidence of this incapacitation with the sudden vulnerability of his crown suggests that this unhappy and trying time had a direct physical effect on Henry's abilities. It was over a month before he began to resume some of his former activities. The royal crossbow maker was paid for cleaning all the bows on 19 March 1503, and Henry rewarded his kennel master at Stratford by the end of the month, following a successful hunt.

After almost eighteen years of what seems to have been stable and affectionate living, the end of Elizabeth's companionship was a tragedy for Henry. Having been almost alone and friendless until the age of 28, he then grew into a relationship that offered real support and strength to the recurring uncertainties of keeping his crown. Although only a fragment of Queen Elizabeth's personality comes through the royal records, she was the companion with which Henry Tudor sought to create a dynasty. The impact of her death brought about a deep change in Henry.

By the end of June 1503, Henry escorted his daughter to Margaret Beaufort's palace at Collyweston in Lincolnshire in preparation for her final journey to Scotland. This was a very strenuous time for Henry and his mother, but her support was surely key to the triumph of policy over emotion. In marrying his daughter to James of Scotland, Henry knew that the future of the Tudor dynasty was then invested in the survival and development of 12-year-old Prince Henry, who was cosseted thereafter. Any further dynastic mishaps would have resulted in the throne of England devolving to Margaret and her heirs as kings of Scotland. This took exactly a century to come about. But Henry's belief in the dynastic value of the marriage, which occurred in Edinburgh on 8 August 1503, was indicative of the good personal relations that Henry and James had worked very hard to establish after 1497.

Princess Margaret's wedding coincided with the death of Henry's oldest surviving friend Sir Reginald Bray. The marriage and the deaths of Arthur, Queen Elizabeth, and Bray in the 16 months from April 1502 left Henry isolated, dispirited, and vulnerable. The dynasty could not be revitalised without the king's remarriage. The search for a new wife advanced slowly, and as it did so, Henry focused his energies on security, international recognition, and protection of his surviving children. As he had done in response to the crisis of 1493–5, Henry became more private and disconnected. In the final years of his life, Henry's personal status was once more tied to the stability of the nation and the survival of his dynasty, but he no longer was the dynamic driving force behind the nuances of policy.

## ILLNESS, DECLINE AND DEATH, 1504–09

Although Henry's major personal rivals were dismissed, dead, or imprisoned by 1504, his dynasty remained as precarious as it had been in 1485. His surviving children were his heir, Prince Henry, and the 8-year-old Princess Mary, but without a wife there was no chance of expanding his legitimate family. Chronicle descriptions of English events in Henry's final years are comparatively devoid of detail. Instead, the Great Chronicle of London and Polydore Vergil's *Historia* contain retrospective assessments of the changes wrought in Henry's reign before 1509, and a catalogue of oppressions and grievances that suggest the appearance of a new basis for Henry's kingship.

The period of Henry's increasingly friendless widowhood saw the ascendancy of bureaucrats and lawyers as agents of crown policy. Many historians have identified a change towards more rapacious, unreasonable, and oppressive measures that were fuelled by Henry's increasingly dominant greed and autocracy. He oversaw a pre-emptive political and financial clampdown on the abilities of England's most powerful subjects to destabilise his throne. His own ill health and the spectre of dynastic failure made Henry's final years an unpleasant exercise in the retention of power.

The effect of the way Henry was forced to replace the core members of the royal affinity was seen in a report of a conversation at Calais in September 1504. The rule of Calais had always been a very sensitive issue for the crown, and posts there were reserved for trusted loyalists. In 1504, Sampson Norton, Hugh Conway and Richard Nanfan doubted the loyalty of their boss, the lieutenant of Calais, Lord Daubeney. The officers discussed other gossip that the senior men of the regime believed the king was ill and likely to die. None apparently spoke of Prince Henry as the next ruler. Rumours even suggested that many of Henry's closest servants like Daubeney, Guildford, and Poynings had already made provision for their own secure future should a Yorkist restoration take place. By 1504 the level of suspicion in the Calais pale had grown. Conway, the treasurer of Calais, reported that the king was once again being bombarded with malicious gossip and rumour of treason, as he had been at the end of 1493.

Wavering crown control in Calais reflected the uncertainty of the king's control but also marked the way Daubeney had ruled the town.

He was probably already under suspicion of embezzlement and by December 1506 was forced to pay to the king 2,000 crowns from the French pension agreed at Étaples. That even Daubeney may have been making financial preparations for his own security at Henry's expense suggests a renewed crisis of confidence in Tudor staying power.

Against this background of a growing lack of commitment to the Tudor crown, it might simply have been coincidence that Edmund Dudley entered Henry's service in September 1504. The effects of Dudley's efforts on behalf of the crown are highlighted elsewhere.[5] The appointment of a specific enforcer of royal policy was perhaps a response to Henry's growing incapacity. There can be little doubt that Henry was generally unwell after the family deaths of 1502–03 and suffered more frequent bouts of illness. This disability was severe enough to reduce the mobility of the court. As their severity increased, hunting trips to Henry's favourite southern estates all but ended in the final three years of the reign.

These events, and the possible fear that his enemies would again exploit the vulnerability of the regime, could well have been enough to transform an already suspicious ruler into a calculating despot. The key questions are, did Henry disengage his previous vigorous control over policy to allow his bureaucrats to assume direct control of the system of governance? Can we then blame them for the most repressive period of Henry's rule?

Henry had already constructed ruling agencies centred upon council-based specialists.[6] The only alternative to any reduced royal input after 1504 was their increased responsibility to maintain the momentum of the king's overall aims in government. There was no possibility that the Tudor regime would revert to the noble-dominated crown admin-istration seen in the mid-fifteenth century. Only the king could have initiated the policies enforcing royal prerogative rights, and made them work flexibly in response to the surprises of real life. Dudley could not fully have manipulated the sale of offices, decided the king's favour in the law, or managed the delicate relationship with London's govern-ment, without the support and advice of Henry. We can also see an active king behind the containment of Stanley power and the removal of Sir Richard Guildford's influence in Kent in 1506. Henry might have delegated business to his council officials, but he still pulled the strings of government – even monitoring Dudley's performance. Henry forced him to take a pardon in 1508 for entering family lands without the proper fine. The king also exchanged lists of bonds with Dudley and worked closely with him to manage, cancel, and renew bonds against a range of people. Henry's continuing workload was demonstrated by his handling of foreign affairs after 1504.

Evidence from Dudley's own hand also perhaps refutes the idea that Henry was not in personal direction of this policy during the period of his alleged decline. As he awaited execution in the Tower of London in 1509 on charges of constructive treason, Dudley recorded the instances where he felt individuals had suffered oppressive treatment, and been forced to submit to unreasonable fees, in their dealings with Henry.[7] Although Dudley had pressed relentlessly for payment of these sums, and found many ways to make himself wealthy as part of the process, crucially his petition strongly suggests that he was working under the king's personal direction.

As he faced execution Dudley perhaps had little reason to be anything other than honest in the assessment of his role in Henry's government. Henry VIII had already made it clear that his father's reputation was not to be sullied by public allegations of rapacity or tyranny. So attempts to blame Henry VII for the implementation of his own unpleasant policies were not likely to find much sympathy in Henry VIII. Dudley remained the king's man. Like other specialised servants before him, Dudley was perhaps 'a small scale and rather grubby' Henry VII,[8] elevated to compensate for Henry's own inability to maintain an omnipotent grip on the finely balanced policies of financial threat and control. Nevertheless, he continued to work at the king's right hand.

The strongest narrative to emerge from Henry's later years is his reaction to European events as England's position was threatened again. The alliances of the European powers were changing quickly around 1504. France and Spain had already partitioned Naples in 1500, but by 1503 Louis XII of France was nearing agreements with Maximilian that threatened to unbalance existing alliances against France. Even more important for the European balance of power, and the future of Henry's alliance with Spain, was the death of Isabella of Castile in November 1504. Isabella had wanted her husband to rule as a guardian for her daughter and heiress, Joanna. Joanna was married to Maximilian's son, Archduke Philip, and Philip pressed his claims to rule Castile in right of his wife. The consequences of the struggle for control over Castile spilled over into cautious rivalry between Henry and Ferdinand as widowers searching for a stabilising second marriage.

Henry's public alliance with Ferdinand led him to look first to another marriage into the Spanish royal family. In June 1505 his ambassadors interviewed Ferdinand's niece, Joanna, queen of Naples. Henry's list of instructions for his representatives makes fascinating reading and reveals evidence of his attraction to large-breasted as well as solvent women (who did not suffer from bad breath or facial hair).[9] Henry's servants went on to a meeting with King Ferdinand in July in an attempt to gain information on how Ferdinand and the Habsburgs might resolve Archduke Philip's claim to Castile. Henry was still calculating the most advantageous policy for England's welfare.

Ferdinand obviously wanted to keep control of the other half of his joint Spanish monarchy. To cement his ties to France, and to acknowledge his rule in the kingdom of Naples (to be occupied for three years by a truce of March 1504), Ferdinand agreed a treaty with Louis XII at Blois in October 1505. Henry also knew that Ferdinand intended to marry the French king's niece, Germaine de Foix, as a way of gaining support to keep the Habsburgs out of Spain. The wedding occurred in March 1506. The alliance at Blois did much to reverse the way foreign policy had developed during the previous decade. As with Henry, Ferdinand felt that maintaining his security at home was more important than consistency in foreign policy, although to his credit Henry was remarkably reliable in a period when rulers shifted their loyalties to suit changing priorities.

Henry also tested the water in other areas for his own remarriage. As the European powers rebalanced, he was also negotiating with Maximilian over support for the earl of Suffolk, and Archduke Philip's intentions towards Castile. Maximilian's daughter Margaret, widowed duchess of Savoy, was a possible bride in March 1505. By the summer Henry had also received a proposal from Louis XII that a marriage to another royal niece, Margaret, daughter of the duke of Angoulême, might induce positive French action over the earl of Suffolk.

Perhaps because of Henry's continuing concern over Suffolk's continental support, he was most interested in a marriage to Margaret of Savoy. Henry's fears over Maximilian's previous support for Warbeck prompted Henry to bribe his way into Habsburg favour. After October 1502, when Suffolk became resident in his lands, Henry began to lend considerable sums to Maximilian. With Philip's interest in Spain a primary concern for the already overstretched Maximilian in 1505, Henry increased his magnanimity with some extraordinarily generous payments, such as £108,000 in April 1506. This financial power demonstrated to other rulers that massive personal resources backed Henry's rule. The time when external sponsorship of rebels could threaten his position was passed. Maximilian perhaps realised this and did little to assist the earl of Suffolk, but fortune took a further turn in Henry's favour in January 1506.

That month, Archduke Philip and Joanna were blown by storms into Weymouth on a journey from Zeeland to Spain. Henry took full advantage of such good luck. Through hastily arranged but copious hospitality, in just over a month the two rulers agreed a secret treaty at Windsor that acknowledged Philip as king of Castile and offered further English financial and military help to his kingdoms. Henry's earlier loans probably made Philip more amenable to England's negotiating position.

By 9 February 1506 Henry was allied to Philip, and agreed a beneficial trade treaty that ended a third trade embargo between England and the Netherlands. The Netherlanders called it the *Intercursus Malus* because it so favoured the English. These agreements between the rulers also secured formal arrangements of dowry for a marriage with Margaret of Savoy. Most importantly, Henry secured Philip's agreement to surrender Edmund de la Pole, which occurred at Calais on 16 March. Henry looked to have secured for England a leading role in the counterbalance between France, the Empire, and Spain. Maximilian even took up the theme and soon started negotiations for the marriage of his grandson, Charles, to Henry's remaining daughter, Mary.

With Archduke Philip's death on 25 September 1506 diplomacy rapidly reversed again. Ferdinand secured control of his daughter Joanna, who was alleged to have been showing signs of mental instability, perhaps brought on by Philip's death. Her father in fact held her in virtual imprisonment, and tales of her breakdown were possibly designed to deter Henry. He certainly considered her as a possible wife (unlikely had she been truly mad), and he had spent three months in her company at the start of 1506. Margaret of Savoy also turned down the prospect of an English marriage at this time, making Henry's interest in Joanna more understandable.

Margaret of Savoy assumed control of Philip's lands in the Low Countries on behalf of her nephew, the new Archduke, Charles. Both Maximilian and Henry became wary of French attempts to take advantage of the situation. At the end of 1507 a formal treaty between England and the Netherlands attempted to maintain the agreements worked out in 1506. The firm betrothal of Princess Mary with Charles capped this agreement and led to great celebration within London. Henry thus ended his reign as he had begun it: in alliance with Maximilian against French threats and to isolate France's recent ally Ferdinand of Aragon.

Further delays from Ferdinand ensured that Henry's proposed marriage to Joanna of Castile never progressed beyond the exchange of encouraging letters. When the old adversaries from 1494 – Maximilian, the Archduke (now Charles), the king of France, the pope (Julius II), and Ferdinand – met at Cambrai at the start of December 1508, it was to form an alliance to carve up the republic of Venice. The adversarial nature of diplomacy had turned relationships on their head, and it was England that was again omitted from the gathering. Henry might have felt snubbed by this, but it is clear that England was in a far stronger position than in 1494. The range of alliances, marriage proposals, and agreements that Henry was able to negotiate and conclude during his final six years all suggest that he was accepted as a ruler worthy of consultation and involvement at the high table of European politics.

Henry's conduct of foreign affairs, and his misreading of the intentions of the League of Cambrai at the end of 1508, does suggest that illness was taking a toll on his faculties. We already know that his changing health was noticed as early as the late 1490s. By 1500, Henry suffered from a recurring disease that caused a gradual decline thereafter. Any physical illness was also likely to undermine Henry's resistance to the mental stresses he had endured during his life. To a king obsessively and personally involved in the everyday aspects of his government this was a heavy setback.

Polydore Vergil provides a brief but graphic physical description of the king, probably around 1506. Henry's face was thin, as was his body, but he was well built and seemed strong. His blue eyes continued to sparkle, and he became animated and expressive when speaking (Ayala also comments on this). His teeth were decayed and many were missing, and his hair was thinning and grey. Despite signs of ageing, physical decline, and illness, Henry's memory and brilliant mental strength were apparent at the time of Vergil's description.

Henry's ailments were often referred to as quinsy, a tissic, or consumption that became particularly bad in spring. Quinsy was usually a generalisation for an inflammation of the throat, or tonsils. Henry clearly had severe bouts of this condition. In March 1503 he could not eat or drink for several days because of an ailment of his throat. This condition would only become fatal after infection brought on secondary complications. It seems likely that real debilitation developed in conjunction with a respiratory disease. A tissic was a general cough, but most historians agree that this cough and Henry's wasted, sunken appearance towards the end of his life suggests pulmonary tuberculosis.

Surviving portraiture of Henry does show a quick physical decline from Micheil von Sittow's portrait of 1505 (National Portrait Gallery), to the grey-haired, drawn and emaciated figure in the second of two portraits at the Society of Antiquaries, London (Scharf XXIV). Both of these might be near contemporary images, and reflect the king's physical changes in his final years. There was perhaps an element of flattery in Sittow's representation, especially as it was commissioned as part of the marriage negotiations with Margaret of Savoy in 1505. Nor should we rely on either as an accurate image of the king's real appearance. However, both pictures clearly resemble the likenesses of Henry's death mask, Torrigiano's terracotta bust, and Henry's tomb effigy. Henry's uneven and sunken eyes, his hollow cheeks, and thin lips correspond to the physical descriptions of his later years.

Henry was losing weight and may have suffered a loss of appetite associated with the symptoms of tuberculosis. He was certainly less active. In February 1508 Henry was too ill at Richmond to travel to Westminster for the anniversary service for the death of Queen Elizabeth – something he observed with deep reverence after 1503. In January 1509 Henry became gravely ill at his manor house of Hanworth, just over the river from Richmond. News of his illness spread and the royal chamber paid for masses and prayers around the country to secure his recovery. By Easter 1509 he was unable to attend church, despite setting out from Richmond palace. The final draft of his will was drawn up on 6 April, and by 10 April his death was expected any day.

Henry began preparation for his will and memorial over a decade before his death. While this may indicate that he was aware of his physical decline, Henry had a clear programme in mind for his physical and spiritual legacies that were independent of any thoughts of mortality. Most medieval people revised and renewed the planning about their death, and Henry was no different. Henry originally hoped to be buried in the Lady Chapel at St George's, Windsor, and started work on a tomb in 1501. This intention celebrated the royal association with his uncle Henry VI. Henry VI's cult was attracting great popular attention at the close of the 1490s, and Henry VII tried to capture this movement by linking his own memorial to that of the saintly king and legitimate Lancastrian rule.

In 1498 the abbeys of Chertsey and Westminster disputed Henry VI's intention to be buried at Windsor. Westminster obtained a favourable judgement in the royal council and Henry transferred his memorial plans to St Stephen's Abbey. His memorial would be the magnificent chapel built to replace the Lady Chapel. Building work started in January 1503. In 1505, Henry hired the Italian sculptor Guido Mazzoni, who had worked on the tomb of Charles VIII of France. The design for Henry's tomb intended to install a life-size bronze figure of Henry above the recumbent figures of the king and queen on the tomb itself. This double representation of the deceased king was abandoned by the time Henry's final will was drawn up, but the reference to Tudor's military accession was not. In fact, the martial image of the king became even more symbolically dynastic. Henry's final will ordered that a gilded wooden statute of him was to be placed on the shrine of Edward the Confessor. The form of this figure could have been intended to resemble the silver image of Henry V nearby. In the hands of the armoured king was to be the crown Henry had won at Bosworth. The statute was to be positioned so that this imagery was clearly visible to all.

By placing his own shrine next to that of St Edward and in proximity to Henry V, the Tudor king was planting his own family among the honoured royal elite of England's past. Henry also ensured that Tudor heraldry and badges were displayed across the chapel, in the glazing, sculptures and ironwork. Even the priests charged to say masses for the king's soul in the perpetual chantry chapel would wear copes embroidered with his emblems and arms. Visitors and pilgrims could not fail to be reminded that the new Tudor dynasty had created this magnificent memorial.

Henry's new dynasty had used every public opportunity to broadcast the magnificence and authority of his regime. As Sydney Anglo has pointed out,[10] Henry's red rose, red dragon, Beaufort portcullis, and greyhound devices appeared on documents, treaties, seals, coins, glass and stonework alike. His wealth and power was made obvious from such indulgent building projects as the chapel at Westminster. The repeated proclamation of such symbolism did not assume any sophisticated level of interpretation. For Henry, understanding among his subjects of the precise meaning of Tudor and royal heraldry was probably not as important as the claim to dynastic legitimacy that it represented.

The text of his will and the plans for his tomb and chapel offer examples of the strength of Henry's piety and the typically rigorous planning that went into preparations for his death. This evidence offers some insight into Henry's true personality, but even here precedent and formulaic documents sometimes disguise rather than clarify Henry's personal intentions. Immediately obvious is Henry's private devotion to the Virgin Mary. Henry considered that Mary,

> in this mortal life has ever been my most singular trust and confidence, to whom in all my necessities I have made my continual refuge, and by whom I have hitherto in all my adversities ever had my special comfort and relief. [11]

Henry genuinely believed that the Virgin had helped to secure and preserve his crown and had guided him during his most troubled years of conspiracy.

Henry acknowledged God and the Virign's role when he presented his standards to St Paul's upon his first entry into London in September 1485. He offered prayers of thanks to Mary in Newark immediately after Stoke in 1487. The Virgin remained his solace in times of stress, and again after the victory at Blackheath. A powerful religious dimension therefore motivated all aspects of Henry's personal rule, but was particularly important in the hazard of conflict.

Among the saints Henry most often prayed to was St Vincent, the patron saint of Vannes in Brittany. It was in this town that his quest for the crown began to gather momentum in the early 1480s. Over twenty years later Henry sent expensive gifts to the cathedral at Vannes, and Vincent duly appeared among the imagery of Henry's tomb and chapel at Westminster. The Breton saint Armel also had a strong following in the area of southern Brittany where Henry was exiled. Two images of Armel are found in the memorial chapel, although he was not mentioned in Henry's will. Armel was credited with delivering Tudor's expedition from disaster during the storms of October 1483, and with preserving Henry to his landfall in August 1485. This saint is also represented on stained glass previously at Merevale Abbey, suggesting that Henry and others who had a hand in Tudor's victory considered his intercession to have been vital on 22 August 1485.

A figure of Armel on Chancellor Morton's tomb at Canterbury cathedral, and his appearance in the books of hours of early Tudor insiders, further indicates that Henry's companions from 1483 also shared an interest in the cult.. This powerful private association with Henry Tudor's emergence explains why Armel's popularity disappeared completely in England after 1485. The popularity of Breton saints during the reign might also be a symptom of how other French ideas and practices accompanied Henry in his journey across the Channel.

Henry VI, Edward V, and Richard III had all suffered less than regal treatment at their deaths. Henry left precise and elaborate instructions for his own magnificent funeral. They ensured that the first king of the new dynasty had a powerfully symbolic internment. After lying at Richmond for two weeks while masses were chanted for his soul, Henry's corpse was placed on a chariot beneath his effigy. Lords accompanying the body carried banners of Henry's patron saints, while knights held images of his lands, titles, and royal ancestors. Seven hundred torchbearers accompanied the procession, which contained over 1,400 mourners. This was the burial of a king of noble descent: far from the pretender denounced by Richard III in December 1484 as of 'no manner, interest, right or colour' to the name and title of royal estate.[12]

By the time Henry's corpse reached St Paul's, all the lords, bishops, councillors and ambassadors were in attendance. When the cortège moved to Westminster, yet more standards and banners surrounded the effigy on a magnificent wax hearse. Heralds conducted a very solemn ceremony at which Henry's armour, helm, shield and sword, his battle standards, and even his warhorse, were displayed. At his magnificent tomb, Henry's officers broke their batons in the vault and proclaimed Henry VIII as the new king. Such pomp and tradition emphasised that the Tudors sat comfortably in the royal descent.

In his will Henry acknowledged that wrongs had been done to many individuals, but that these were necessary measures to ensure the succession. It is clear that those rewarded in Henry's will were those who had remained loyal throughout all of the difficulties faced before 1509. They had shared Henry's purpose and were closely allied to what the king hoped to achieve and the measures that were acceptable to bring those aims about. The will shows that Henry's fundamental personal motivations were to ensure spiritual absolution, the preservation of perpetual memory, and the grounding of dynastic prosperity.

# 6

## TUDOR GOVERNMENT AT WORK

### THE IDEOLOGY OF TUDOR ROYAL POWER

The favour shown to Henry by the God of Battles in August 1485 placed the king in a very straightforward and powerful hierarchy that all late medieval people would have recognised. Richard III had made this explicit in the grant creating John, Lord Howard, as duke of Norfolk in June 1483. In the text of the grant, Richard comments that:

> the ray of His light and glory in many and diverse ways shines upon all his crea-
> tures and marks out those who share in His goodness. And whereas we, who
> under his providential design rule and govern His people, endeavour by His grace
> to conform our acts to His will ... and consider it fit by natural and prudent reason
> to walk in His ways and ... to mark His footsteps ... [1]

Henry IV had struggled to find similar heavenly backing for his deposition of Richard II in September 1399. He emphasised to parliament his blood descent from Henry III. Since God had given him the right, he was claiming the crown with the help of his powerful kin and friends. Richard II had proved to be an unworthy ruler. Misgovernment and degradation of the law were the main reasons Henry presented to parliament, but divine favour was a strong basis for his actions.

Almost a century later, with Richard III dead at Bosworth, Henry did not have to justify his personal status so forcefully. But he did emphasise his belief in the sanctity of kingship. Henry invoked the pope's help to support his defence of the throne. Papal threats of excommunication and the removal of sanctuary for traitors guaranteed punishment in the afterlife for crimes against God's anointed ruler. Henry's determination to depose Richard III developed from the belief that in shedding infants' blood he had debased the monarchy and made himself unfit to rule (although Henry never made explicit reference to Richard's responsibility for the deaths of the Princes in the Tower).

God's intervention at Bosworth gave Henry's reign a powerful foundation that had a strong impact on political society – even perhaps restraining the actions of some men who might otherwise have tried to depose him. This connection to divine providence also enhanced Henry's own piety, since to have real evidence of God's preference for one's own cause was the highest endorsement any Christian prince could hope for. The invocation of divine providence and the familiarity of the imagery of Fortune and her wheel in contemporary life enforced the view that there was a hierarchy and order stemming from Heaven in which all figures had an ordained place.

This divine scheme for earthly representation of God's power was reflected in the theoretical structures used to explain how rulers ruled. When investigating late medieval English political and constitutional ideas, modern historians usually take their starting point from Sir John Fortescue's work. The king was but one part of an organic body politic and his function was to 'protect the law, the subjects, and their bodies and goods and has power to this end issuing from the people'.[2] Kings were not dictators and should be bound to the law as much as subjects. Although late medieval law was applied in the name of the monarch, new laws could only be created by parliament, where the members of the Lords and Commons were believed to represent truly the entire nation.

The crown was the chief part of the body politic, but it was only one aspect of the ruling entity. Other parts such as the royal council and parliament were essential for good rule within the realm. A king's role was theoretically well defined when ruling as an embodiment of the nation's power. Henry VII, however, was burdened with particular, if not exceptional, personal circumstances. These factors perhaps obliged him to rule at the edge of the law by pressing his private rights to preserve his public position. Frequently, Henry's role as wearer of the crown required him to work in a conflicting way with the other agencies that made the state work. In doing so he created new ways in which the king interacted and dominated the other centres of crown government.

To medieval theorists, the monarch represented the power of royal authority through the visible magnificence of his court, his clothes, jewels and gold. In an age of conspicuous display, outsiders viewed power of a kingdom and the authority of a king by his most obvious regal qualities. Monarchs absorbed and performed the expected traditions of English kingship. This reassured those involved in governing that the king was part of the same process and not above it. The body politic functioned because the instruments of ruling – the law courts, parliament, chancery, exchequer, and the royal council – operated as independent but interacting units below the level of the king.

Successful kings did not have to control personally the parts of the state that made governance work. Monarchs were meant to be the glorious outward-facing representation of solid and effective rule that was left in the hands of people trained in the techniques of ruling – judges, sheriffs, councillors, customs officers: civil servants supposedly indifferent to party politics. This would then strip away the factionalism that had created rival kings in the mid-fifteenth century, and which had rapidly stifled the agencies that could have ensured effective government.

Part of the reason for the violence and discord within the aristocracy at the end of the 1450s was the distance of the king from his full responsibilities as ruler. Instead of advising Henry VI to become more fully involved in the routine of his political role, texts such as the anonymous *Somnium Vigilantis* found a new way to compel loyalty to a king who remained disinterested in governing. The powerful figures reliant upon a continuation of Lancastrian kingship looked to this prototype of the ideas of divine right that upheld Charles I's regality in the 1630s. The sanctity, power, and authority of the regal facets of kingship became an overriding justification for loyalty to the king in all aspects of his relationship with the body politic. The king deserved allegiance because he was king, regardless of his fitness to rule. Henry VI was not the monarch on whom to make such an appeal. Even then, it took periods of royal mental breakdown before the most powerful lords were provoked into open struggle for the crown.

The slide towards civil war during the 1450s appeared so slow because the English royal government had for centuries been both regal and political. Unlike in absolutist states such as France, the concept of sharing the functions of power along the lines identified by Fortescue had existed as part of English political culture for generations. Edward IV was particularly effective in blending magnificence with a dynamic personal commitment to his role as king.

By 1485, after Yorkist experiments with finance and council government, practical elements of Fortescue's theories of governance did exist within the English polity. The very real problem Henry had to resolve was between the consensual rule that was the best guarantee of good royal lordship and stability in the kingdom and the selfish preservation of his own authority against enemies that sought his destruction no matter how well he might come to rule. Political pressure throughout the reign made the two things increasingly incompatible. Dynastic security soon overrode the promotion of balanced and indifferent rule.

The personal power of the king and the ways he exercised royal lordship influenced how the bureaucracy of government worked effectively. Although the monarch was the most important part of the governing process, he could support or undermine the representativeness of his rule by changing the level at which he interfered in the operation of normal government – the availability of local justice, dominance of parliament, the partiality of the royal council.

By leaving the running of these institutions and processes to the bureaucrats who were suitably skilled, the state would avoid corrupting national rule with the incompatible personal interests of powerful and aggressive men under the king. This might be the defence of their common aristocratic outlook against the demands of lesser subjects. It could also be the protection of the more private concerns of their own local authority through the unlawful promotion of their retainers or manipulation of the law directly. Of course, the reality of late fifteenth-century power relied very heavily upon the authority, cooperation, and involvement of aristocratic influence.

The magnates, peers and lords had a deep vested interest in keeping the polity running smoothly. They owned the bulk of the land, they interacted with local hierarchies, networks and individuals, and they enforced the application of the law. When their rule broke down, the effects were obvious; but it did not collapse frequently. The disorderly effects of local power struggles were usually contained by the application of noble power and effective projection of the crown's authority. Fortescue's work condemned the late medieval council as an institution full of powerful men who only served to secure their own private interests, or those of the elite landowning class they were all part of, through protection of their tenants, servants, and retainers. The interests of the king, and the concerns of the broadest political community, were pushed aside as the elites used their governing authority to secure their own objectives. Such a view implies that all nobles were overmighty, or wished to become so.

Most nobles were happy to support a strong king who satisfied their personal ambitions and those of the ruling elite as a whole. It was only when royal control at the centre weakened that its extension into the regions became unregulated and vulnerable to abuse by competitive lords, suddenly freed from the restraints imposed on them by their roles as crown representatives. The Wars of the Roses had proved that kings themselves had been unable to remain above factional politics. This had led to a failure in the king's role as leader of a political community that defined and managed the interests of the entire realm. It was the effectiveness of the king's position within the polity that was crucial to how the dynamics of late medieval governance worked.

John Watts has developed some intriguing ideas about how Fortescue's theories might have influenced the way Henry VII constructed his regime.[3] Apparent changes in patterns of rule under Henry might not necessarily have been something he consciously engineered. Rather, they may have developed from the continuity in office of the bureaucrats and experts that had kept the government machine running smoothly. Henry's reappointment of the Yorkist-trained judiciary, for example, gave their expert opinions greater weight and emphasised the impartiality of their legal expertise. It made their custody of the law appear as part of representative government that stood above faction.

Henry's unique circumstances perhaps also have played a part in how he approached his duties as king. Henry's adolescent political isolation prevented his absorption into the accepted codes of aristocratic rule. He had not gone through the training and stages of responsibility that nobles needed to develop the skills for political life. This detachment from the abilities shared by his peers and gentry gave Henry's ruling style a particular character that was different from the way the crown had done things before.

It acquired a physical dimension when, by the early 1490s, the privy chamber within the household began to control the personal space the king occupied. The extra layer of royal service was staffed by lower-ranking grooms and yeomen. They became influential because of their closeness to the king, but Henry allowed them to shine most brightly only at court. The buffer created by the privy chamber limited the access to the king of the aristocratic body servants so prominent in the Yorkist household described in Edward IV's *Black Book*.[4] This did not diminish the projected power of the early Tudor household and court. It merged the magnificence of the king's role more fully with that of the aristocrats that attended court. At the same time their responsibility to serve the king in person diminished.

The great figures of the kingdom had previously surrounded the monarch and projected his power into the counties where they held their land and dominated local society. This made late medieval rule a highly cooperative exercise. From the mid-1490s, the principal role of the lords and leading knights became part of the pageantry of court life. They remained close to the crown as an institution when they sat in the royal council or on local commissions. Some were undoubtedly the king's friends and social companions. But Henry began to select those men that shared royal rule at the centre of things primarily for their ability, flexibility, and loyalty.

Rank and prestige no longer ensured a natural right to be close to the king or to share his responsibilities within the body politic. New nobles such as Daubeney and Willoughby were very much at the centre of this trend. It did, however, bring problems associated with the perceived right of lesser councillors like Empson and Dudley to wield the king's authority.

A reduction in the level of aristocratic service in the household was matched by a rise in the influence of professional servants in other areas of the regime. Henry began to take over the governing agency best suited to enforce his personal ruling priorities: the royal council. The infrequency of the king's decision to summon parliament and Great Councils brought greater focus onto the royal council as the mainstay of interactive Tudor rule. Henry's council met regularly and involved the full range of mighty nobles and wealthy prelates – the natural councillors of any king. But they had little training for the enforcement of the detached and legalistic role within the body politic Henry chose to develop for himself.

He became directly involved in the council and shaped its members and the way they worked solely to benefit Tudor security rather than magnanimous and indifferent rule. Henry's council became less of an advisory body and more of an executive agency of the head of government. This meant that bureaucrats and administrators became vitally important to Tudor power because they were not normally distracted by the concerns of estates, retainers, and spheres of influence. When they became wealthy, they acquired wealth for its own sake and not for the political influence that land had previously brought. Their authority rested solely on the power of their role as councillors.

By forcing the aristocracy to share more of the regal role of kingship, was Henry emphasising that his political supremacy was shared only with his executive councillors? Did he wish to free the crown from the direct influence of the aristocracy? Ambassadors reported that Henry was subject to his council in 1498, but by 1507 had few confidential advisers except his mother. He continued to develop the outward brilliance of the Tudor court, its visual propaganda and display, but was not widely loved because he was not a great man, in the sense of the larger-than-life regal figure that his father-in-law Edward IV had been.

Henry's personal attention to the minute detail of kingship underlined a ruling style based on legal trickery, the squeezing of royal rights, and enforcement of the letter of the law. This required masterful expertise. Only focused professionals could offer this level of skill. While Henry sought to acquire these administrative abilities himself, it was the lawyers and judges who came to dominate the heart of the regime. Henry's most effective agencies became the committees of the royal council charged with specific roles in the law. The king could bypass established structures altogether, as Henry was to do through the use of bonds. This was council with very little apparent counsel.

Fortescue's advice was that the executive council should be separated from the ruling function required from the major nobles – that of looking after regional rule on behalf of the centre. Councillors should work only with the king and each other to protect and enforce lawful rule. If impartial power at the centre of the regime became too indistinct from the private interests of those who carried the king's laws and policy into the counties, then royal authority would be compromised. At first glance Henry seems to have been following Fortescue's advice: the effective governing committees of the council did become separated from the broader advisory body. Yet Fortescue's council was always envisaged as a restraint on the king's dominance of government. Because it was in theory the chief agency that managed the king's political role in the body politic, it also controlled the way in which royal power was blended with that of the other ruling agents. By making the council and its professional executives the enforcers of political decisions and policy, Henry was removing the natural checks and balances on his potentially tyrannical power.

Henry began to ignore the formal advice usually offered when he interacted with the other representative parts of the realm in parliament or the full advisory council. This was a dangerous path, which risked confrontation and had direct political effects. The king had been forced to back down when he had pressed for a feudal tax in 1504. He responded by calling no more parliaments, although his previous one had met as long ago as 1497. Henry effectively ended the most visible interaction of the king with the wider realm through its representatives. This closed the door on one form of consensual rule and allowed Henry and his council-based agencies to dominate the ruling process.

After 1504, royal interaction with, and control over, political communities became dependent on technicalities and legal procedures such as obligations and recognisances. During this period the king's status as a widower, his withdrawal from the more public side of his role, and his physical decline meant that he had to delegate significant parts of his regal role to other ministers and representatives. This move could only dilute the royal aspect of governance while extending the power of the political agencies of the crown, and therefore of the crown itself. It was probably from this shift in the balance of Tudor rule that a repressive regime emerged after 1504.

Bonds are the most interesting example of how the narrow council of professionals wielded the king's power in a way that seemed to target the landholders and aristocrats increasingly exiled from the administrative engine room of the regime. The controlling nature of bonds was also used as ideological glue to enforce the loyalty that Henry's policies were testing to the limit. A new doctrine of service stood alongside Tudor restructuring of existing institutions to transform the mentality of the ruling elites. In the conditions attached to the thousands of bonds issued during the reign, Henry demonstrated his authority (through acceptance of his right to demand payments), defined acceptable behaviour, and enforced an obligation of loyalty upon the powerful figures of the nation. This was moral regulation to control conduct and enforce conditions of service.

The activities that many councillors undertook on behalf of Henry provide clear indications of how Henry tried to elevate both the crown's power and the status of his intimate allies. Long before Dudley joined Henry's service, the sections of 'remembrances' in the chamber books contain a huge range of evidence that suggests how the king's councillors supplied a constant stream of beneficial information and gossip to the king. Primarily it boosted his revenue, but it also ground out the message that the Tudor crown was the dominant ruling power in the kingdom. A snapshot of memoranda from October 1502 suggests the practical value of the type of loyalty and service the king instilled in his councillors.

Reginald Bray notified the council of all the offers he had received on behalf of the king: from Lord Willoughby's son requesting his father's offices as overseer of the Cornish tin mines, to Lord Dudley using him as an intermediary to secure three wards in Staffordshire. Bray used his own position as a channel for information to offer the enormous sum of £600 for choice fees in the king's gift. Sir John Mordaunt, presented evidence of a massive riot involving 2,000 of the earl of Shrewsbury's followers. He and the bishop of Carlisle notified the king of various northern wardships, and of treasure trove in Yorkshire.

The buying and selling of office was well demonstrated, with insiders able to bid for vacancies for their own friends and servants. The king's secretary Thomas Routhal offered £40 and a letter of introduction for John Berst to become one of the chamberlains of the Exchequer. Various councillors were assigned to work out the fines and incidents arising from the earl of Suffolk's lands, and the debts due to his co-conspirators Sir James Tyrell and Sir John Wyndham. The embezzlement of a few collectors of clerical taxes in Lincoln and Exeter dioceses brought commissions to all bishoprics to investigate the same offences. Someone presented sufficient information to begin process against Lord Stourton for treason. John Durrant, one of the treasurer's deputies at Calais, presented a scheme for saving the king 500 marks per year from the wages due for the Calais garrison.

This range of information continued month after month. It offers compelling evidence of how Henry and his councillors were in tune and how the cumulative effect of the council's role was established. The range of interference for which Dudley was more famous existed for many years before he became Henry's servant. The period of his service was marked by a higher price on the king's favour, and this, rather than the novelty of demands for payments, could be what sparked real resentment at the king's methods.

Financial vigilance, oppression, and virtual extortion must have done little to endear to the crown those men and women on the receiving end of these policies. The very extensive employment of bonds, and the predatory nature of the council in its relationship with the elites, suggests that Henry intended to dominate the institutional power of the crown and not simply the personal power associated with the king. Any pressure on the nobility during the reign grew from this desire to prevent aristocrats from rising out of the class of near-royal kinsmen to challenge for the crown as Henry himself, Henry IV, Richard, duke of York, Edward IV, and Richard III had been able to do. Henry imposed royal authority upon them by watchfulness and knowledge of how their relationships with the crown worked.

There was also a point during the reign when the use of bonds ceased to be a reaction to the circumstances surrounding incidents of disloyalty and became the core of a crown policy of control. Some evidence points to the response to Warbeck in the mid-1490s as the crucial time period. The origins of the privy chamber at the end of the 1480s might point to an earlier origin. There is also an interesting linguistic change in the text of many bonds at the beginning of 1500.

Before that date bonds concerning allegiance specifically mentioned that reason and set out the sums involved and the conditions to be applied. During 1500 clauses appear that state more vaguely that the main signatory to the bond acknowledged himself to be bound to the king under a certain sum. There was also a move away from networks of sureties and a greater emphasis on individual responsibility. We might look to the executions of Warwick and Warbeck in November 1499 as key to this change. Free from Yorkist figureheads, Henry could become more proactive in refining ways to contain the loyalty of his leading subjects. This suggests that the tempo of the Tudor regime changed in 1500 and that a more vigilant and restrictive policy was put into effect. We see some of this oppressiveness in the evidence from 1502 noted above, but it was much more apparent from Dudley's workload after September 1504.

The control exercised by the council seemed inappropriately heavy handed when gauged against any aristocratic threat to the Tudor dynasty arising before 1509. We cannot know if emerging noble challenges were crushed at birth by the bludgeoning effect of Henry's financial threats.

Warbeck's revival of deep Yorkist loyalties did cause a great deal of questioning of the Tudor right to the throne. The likes of Stanley and Fitzwalter were perhaps sacrificed to demonstrate that Henry's regime would be ruthless in the face of wavering allegiance. But many threats were simply paper brinkmanship. Henry threatened the estates and wealth of those forced into bonds but acted to enforce his claims only if men and women were foolish enough to continue the behaviour that had made them suspects in the first place. Loyalty on the king's terms posed no danger to estates, although it might cost a hefty fee for his prerogative assent to inheritance.

In 1498 the Spanish ambassador Pedro de Ayala reported that Henry was unable to escape the dominance of some of his councillors, although he had tried to do so. Towards the end of the reign it was apparent to others that the power of many councillors was running without restraint. Some of the harshest policies credited to Henry personally might have been the product of councillors appropriating his political power. Yet the case of Thomas Sunyff, and no doubt many others not yet studied in great depth, shows that Henry was fully aware of what Empson and Dudley were doing in his name after 1504.[5] Whatever the true extent of Henry's complicity in Tudor oppression, his regime had departed from the type of personal monarchy displayed by Henry V or Edward IV. Henry's contact with his leading subjects was made via his elite agents in the council and it was conducted through political control of the law.

By doing this Henry was, in a way, undermining his personal power as king and reinvesting it in the machinery of crown government through the council. The institutional power of the crown became stronger and Henry ensured that no challengers threatened his capacity to wield that power. A shift in the way monarchy worked was a result of these changes. The physical and ideological distance Henry put between himself and the traditional ruling tasks of the king meant that his chief governing role became the management of the councillors ruling in his name. Henry stayed closely involved in the daily tasks of ruling despite developing a framework that allowed him to withdraw physically and administratively from the process of ruling.

Many of Henry's policies did not survive beyond 1509, but their effect on how England was ruled did. The success of Henry's shake-up of the relationship of the crown with its leading subjects may have set back the acceptance of change for many years. Henry VIII's early years, with a vibrant youthful court and the pursuit of military glory in France and Scotland, were certainly more like those of Edward IV's reign than the more sombre final years of Henry VII's. It was only in the 1530s that a new generation of officials was prepared to implement revolutionary policies on a grand scale. Henry VIII was able to become an indulgent and distracted monarch, disconnected from the administrative brilliance of ministers like Thomas Wolsey and Thomas Cromwell, because Henry VII had developed ruling structures that did not require the monarch to exercise his personal good lordship and constant intervention. Whether Henry VII's monarchy was new monarchy is still debated. Yet something deeply important to the long-term development of England's ruling structures occurred during Henry VII's reign that transformed the 'merry but unstable England ruled by Edward IV to the tame, sullen and tense land inherited by Henry VIII'.[6]

## FINANCE AND TAXATION

### The financial root of security

Henry VII still has a powerful reputation as a cash-loving king. Many of his policies did have finance as their basis. At the heart of late medieval English financial policy was the belief that solvent monarchs lessened the impact of royal power on their subjects. Kings in command of their resources were less likely to cause the friction in the search for income that had dogged monarchs like Richard II and Henry VI. Where financial planning and the machinery of gathering royal wealth went wrong, the rest of the crown's ruling structures would be undermined. Because Henry's dynasty was vulnerable for all but a few years, financial security and the capacity to control wealth became the broad foundation for early Tudor policy. Henry did not follow this line because he necessarily needed the money of his aristocrats. He worked hard to guarantee his personal income from the crown lands and other usual sources. Rather, intimidation of their personal resources gave the king overwhelming leverage in the struggle for political dominance.

To project Tudor power required predictable and measured wealth generated on the king's terms. As his reign progressed, Henry's financial strategies avoided less controllable influences such as the Commons in parliament. He set out to improve the mainstays of royal income from the crown lands, the customs and trade. Henry also evolved a flexible approach to less formal resources like loans, feudal payments (or incidents), and improved financial administration.

Henry asked parliament for only one grant of taxation between 1497 and 1509. In fact Henry only asked for ten direct taxes during his 24-year reign, with seven of those before 1497. Parliament was not called during Henry's final five years, suggesting that royal finances were becoming self-sufficient. Fundamentally, Henry's command of wealth dominated the resources that could be brought to challenge his dynasty. He knew that financial power gave him the capacity to ruin his enemies, and control of the nation's assets gave him a greater chance of passing the crown to his heir.

## The crown lands

When he became king, Henry Tudor inherited the estates of his royal predecessors. Henry's first parliament made him the legal heir of his father Edmund, earl of Richmond, and of King Henry VI. Henry also acquired the private estates of the Yorkist kings – Edward IV's earldom of March and Richard III's personal lands in the north. Many noble estates were in crown hands because of minority (the duke of Buckingham) and forfeiture (the earl of Surrey). From the start of his reign Henry made a decision to hold onto this enormous group of lands. The immediate royal family were given limited grants from this pool of forfeitures, but many such lands returned to Henry's control during the course of the reign. Elsewhere, the allegiance of other loyal families, like the Stanleys, was bought by select generous gifts. Outside this group very few others received outright rewards of land, a policy that continued up to 1504 when fifty-one attainders added to the range of Tudor crown estates. Henry received a range of lands unsurpassed in the late medieval period.

Henry had to master the basics of governing before he could reshape things to operate they way he wanted. In 1485, the Exchequer recovered its status as the place where normal revenues from the counties, fee farm rents of towns and the profits of justice were paid. Officers accounted for their revenues at the upper Exchequer and not in the chamber. Henry began to rearrange the administration of his income once he received his first grants of taxation in 1487. The chamber handled these payments in a revival of a similar Yorkist system.

The chamber receipt books show that its income from land rose from about £3,000 in 1489 to £40,000 in 1505. His gross receipts through the chamber increased from about £17,000 to £105,000 over the same period.[7] Diversion of these sums to the chamber gave Henry a more direct influence over his cash flow and the men he appointed to manage it. This evidence might not present the full picture of Henry's wealth or Tudor cash flow. The chamber was operated by a small staff, headed by a treasurer and accountable only to Henry himself. The Exchequer system, based on draft accounts, tallies, and a complex auditing paper trail, seemed rather cumbersome in comparison.

Henry separated the administration of some blocks of noble land in his hands from the revenues of the existing crown lands in a particular county. This improved efficiency but it also allowed the king to discover just what could be raised through direct royal control. The Salisbury, Despenser, and Beauchamp estates of the Neville family (many belonging to the earl of Warwick) were kept separate in the chamber accounts of receipts.

Forfeitures were handled in the same way, so that Henry had a clear idea of their feudal value should any restoration to heirs be negotiated. When Simon Wiseman managed the duke of Suffolk's estates in 1491 and 1492 (during the minority of his heir, Edmund), his assessment of their value was a key factor in downgrading Edmund's rank to that of an earl. This process allowed fines and bonds to be set at levels where they were most politically disabling. Hugh ap Rhys was responsible for Lord Scrope of Upsall's lands during his imprisonment after 1487. Rhys must have had a role in assessing Scrope's fine at a crippling 12,000 marks, paid in December 1489.

Henry's allies realised the profits could be made from managing the estates in crown hands, and the king allowed them to seek these grants as an alternative to direct gifts of land. Sir Thomas Lovell accounted for the lands of Lord Roos; John Hayes looked after the earl of Northumberland's lands in Devon. The king was aware that a well-placed steward, like John Saville at Pontefract, could benefit the crown if a grant boosted his local standing.

The range of lands in the king's hands at any one time was therefore piecemeal: a mixture of Henry's own possessions, lands due to be restored when heirs reached 21, and estates forfeited after treason that might not be recovered. Royal landholding was also fluid. Lands with a more temporary royal status were vital political tools in the management of the local influence of Henry's servants. Restrictions on the giving of royal land forced the aristocracy to recognise that under his kingship, stewardships, leases, and temporary possession were the only viable ways for individuals to build up their local connections and authority. This begins to explain why he did not attempt a reform of royal landholding towards a single system of accounting based on crown lands in each county.

Early in the reign, the main strategy behind the management of crown lands was to reward courtiers and improve the local status of the king's men. When Henry's dynasty again became vulnerable after 1503, crown land was managed on a very different basis. Some tenancies were offered on the basis of who would pay the highest rent. The more lucrative grants were gained after bribes for the king's favour. In 1504 Miles Gerard was able to find 200 marks to be receiver of the duchy of Lancaster, while Robert Marshall had to offer £20 for a post in East Anglia. Further down the service scale, there was competition to be the king's tenant as Henry sold the farm of lands belonging to royal wards. James Barkley paid £78 for the yearly rent of the lands of William Vale in Gloucestershire. Some wards' possessions were leased as a block, but large estates such as the 5th earl of Northumberland's were partitioned to maximise the profitability of individual manors.

Men who were eager to manage royal manors and parks subjected themselves to the close scrutiny of senior officials and the agencies established to police their conduct – the Council Learned, and the Court of General Surveyors. The fact that they were willing to take this responsibility suggests that there was still ample opportunity to carve themselves some advantage.

Henry applied the techniques of land management in the duchy of Lancaster lordships to the organisation of all crown land. From the duchy came the innovative administrators Reginald Bray and Richard Empson. They were joined by other skilled officers: Robert Southwell as surveyor of crown lands; Edward Belknap as guardian of Henry's prerogative rights; John Heron as financial mastermind in the chamber. These were professionally trained men who began a coordinated step-change in the organisation of the departments, committees, and small teams that, together, made Henry's regime so effective. As the inner circle of

Henry's most able servants these new men took over many of the roles filled by nobles in previous reigns.

## Prerogative rights

Professional men, skilled in the application of the law, also spearheaded the king's interest in exploiting the full range of ancient rights due to the crown. Although Henry was keenly aware of the weakness of his claim to the throne through descent – seen in the sometimes-gaudy display of Tudor imagery and heraldry – he certainly did not underestimate the hereditary rights he acquired when he became king. Most important was the investigation of lapsed royal prerogative rights that targeted the resources of his powerful subjects. In the king's eyes they were legitimate royal rights, but many subjects felt them to be unjustly demanded, or that they paid more than their fathers had done. The new agencies set up to enforce Henry's legal system led landholders to fear the solid legal basis whereby Henry could enforce his feudal rights.

It is possible from the mid-1490s to see the emergence of Henry VII's intention to focus on his prerogative rights as a means of asserting his authority and of filling his coffers. Edmund Dudley was an expert on *quo warranto* (the holding of private rights from the crown). In 1495 both Robert Constable and Thomas Frowyk read on the king's prerogative at Lincoln's Inn. These two top law students probably chose this topic to appeal to the legal direction in which the king and his judges were then moving. Constable died before his judicial career took off, but Frowyk was a king's sergeant (equivalent of a modern QC) by 1501. He became chief justice of Common Pleas in 1502. Dudley and Frowyk served together on the royal council and its specialised legal offshoots after 1504. They brought a wealth of expertise to the king's armoury as he hunted for crown rights at the very edge of the law.

Near the start of his reign Henry issued grants to loyal followers in reward. By 1508 he demanded fees beyond the usual costs for processing and enrolling grants paid into the hanaper (the office responsible for collecting these fees). In that year, Sir Sampson Norton and his wife were asked to pay £20 to renew a grant. This payment ensured that the lands were not given to anyone else, but Norton must have monitored what was going on and petitioned widely to be certain that no one had dangled a higher bribe before the king.

Profits from the sale of wardships and marriages rose rapidly after 1494 as Reginald Bray took over responsibility for arranging guardians for under-age tenants-in-chief. Bray himself paid only £20 for the royal ward Richard Buckingham in March 1491. The value of young Buckingham's estate might have been small, but Chamber income from wards rose from about £350 that year to just over £1,500 in 1494 as Henry realised the profitability of bargaining wardships and marriages. In 1501 the post of master of wards was created for Sir John Hussey. His attempt to offer wardships for bribes led to a scandal in 1502, which the king quickly stifled through a series of rolling bonds scheduled for the next decade. Hussey's private enterprise was very much frowned upon, although Henry was doing nothing less. Hussey held onto his office with the threat of immediate sacking hanging over him. He worked tirelessly and improved annual profits from wardships to over £6,000 by 1507.

Marriages were even more lucrative. Under Dudley's scrutiny, the price of securing the marriage of a royal ward went through the roof. In 1507 Nicholas Vaux and Thomas Parr paid over 9,000 marks for the marriage of the two daughters of Thomas Green. Henry also interfered in the remarriage of widows of his tenants-in-chief. In 1504 Edward Jernyngham was told he would have to find £200 if he wanted permission to marry Dame Margaret Mortimer. When in 1506 John Carr was planning to marry Anne Conyers he was made to agree to provide whatever sum Henry demanded for the licence within 40 days.

Henry made his influence felt in other areas where he could exercise his royal rights. The marquis of Dorset's widow had to pay £200 to allow the marriage of her daughter to take place as the marquis had requested in his will – perhaps a symptom of Henry's long and vindictive memory towards those who had disappointed him. The livery fine demanded from the new earl of Arundel when he entered his lands in April 1488 was 200 marks. When the second earl of Derby took up the reins of power in the summer of 1504 he agreed to obligations of 2,000 marks to cover the entry fine. By 1508 the price of special livery could be as high as 1,000 marks, as Sir Robert Curzon paid for livery of a ward. There were political dimensions to grants such as this that were possibly unrelated to the value of the estates.

What is important here is the vast difference between 1490 and 1504 in the range of royal feudal and prerogative transactions for which hefty payments were required. The king's financial health benefited from the expert scrutiny of Henry's legal councillors in areas where royal rights could be exploited fully. Crown officers pored over records and documents to wring out cash owed to the king. In 1507 a debt of Lord Fitzwalter was uncovered twelve years after his execution. Henry even lent Dudley a 'great boke called Jura Regalia'[8] – perhaps a running record of royal rights and precedents. The combined effect of this pressure crushed any doubts that Henry would dominate the feudal relationship with tenants-in-chief. The policy extended the growing gap between the royal family and the next social level among the aristocracy. We cannot know if Henry's exploitation of his prerogative rights increased tenfold, but it is certain that the entire financial focus of the regime moved towards underdeveloped sources of cash during the 1490s.

The heirs of tenants-in-chief found that a tightening of royal prerogative powers gradually led to yet more land becoming preserved solely for the crown. Henry became more like a landlord than the chief part of a political community sharing an elite and specific outlook. From being the first among equals, as even Richard III and Edward IV had been, Henry's actions set him above the political and social communities from which medieval kings had previously emerged. Henry's active enforcement of his rights in the areas of vacancies to title, wardships, marriages, and with a policing agency in the council learned in the law, was a great departure from accepted crown behaviour.

Pressure for a feudal aid in 1504 indicated how confident Henry was of enforcing his rights and incidents. This focus in the latter half of the reign on patrimonial taxes (payments arising through inheritance), rather than the more traditional parliamentary taxes for specific sums, was particularly innovative and, no doubt, loathed. And although the king was rebuffed a number of times, the surviving records of his benevolences and forced loans are powerful evidence of Henry's desire to master the residual feudal power of the great nobles and gentry. Henry used the law to justify these impositions, and many of the requests were legally grounded and adapted by later monarchs.

## Customs and taxation

Most fifteenth-century kings could expect parliament to grant to them the customs duties on wool and the 'tonnage and poundage' or import and export tax, on commodities like wine, cloth, grain and minerals such as alum. Unlike previous kings, Henry received both grants immediately in 1485 – possibly an indication that the Commons wished to stabilise crown finances after the uncertainty of the previous three years. Once formally granted the customs duties, Henry's income from this source depended absolutely on the health of England's trading relationships. The king could influence the ease with which goods flowed in and out of the country, but the trading wealth of the nation was at the mercy of economic forces across Europe.

Henry's revenue from customs became tied to early Tudor foreign policy. Henry was willing to sacrifice customs income when political security demanded closure of trading links, as with the Netherlands in 1496. He threatened a further trade embargo with Archduke Philip in 1499, and for a third time in 1505–06 to challenge continental support for English rebels. Annual customs income may have averaged just over £40,000 by the end of the reign – a few thousand more than the usual income from a parliamentary tax of a fifteenth and tenth.

Taxes were normally granted to the crown with the agreement of the nation in parliament. The usual justification was national warfare or the expense of an unexpected campaign to suppress rebellion. The burden of Henry's direct taxation was not as frequent or financially onerous as that of many of his predecessors. His clashes with the representatives of his subjects came over the methods used to assess who would pay and how they would pay. His move towards feudally based assessments that were not agreed by the Commons implies that Henry hoped to use the precedents and records of his tax grants as tools to enforce his rights in related areas like lordship and landholding. Although experimentation brought resistance and open rebellion in 1487 and 1497, it did boost the income to the crown beyond the equivalent of the most traditional assessments. The pressure to fund the Scottish war of 1497 generated up to £120,000, but this was an exceptional demand. Henry eventually abandoned attempts to find a new approach to taxation by consent.

Henry's first tax grant, in 1487, was popularly demanded of resident foreigners. Four his other nine grants were the most usual late medieval taxes: 'fifteenths and tenths', granted in the parliaments of 1487, 1490, 1491, and 1497. This tax had been standardised for 150 years and was based on a fixed value of land and goods within parishes and townships. In country areas the rate was a fifteenth of the value of the goods assessed; in towns, one tenth. Since this tax reproduced contributions made before the Black Death, it was out of tune with the fifteenth-century wealth and economy of England.

Both the king and the country expected about £30,000 from each fifteenth and tenth. Henry and his council knew he was likely to be given this type of award by parliament if reasonable need was demonstrated. In the aftermath of conflict within England, Henry did indeed opt for more conventional taxes. But parliament was aware that most of Henry's military costs were generated while fighting English rebels in civil war in 1487, 1489, and 1497. The expense in meeting these challenges were largely beyond Henry's control. Parliament knew exactly what it was committing the country to when it offered a fifteenth and tenth, and preferred the stable and traditional means of acceding to the king's requests.

Henry was more innovative in his requests for taxation in anticipation of planned military campaigns, and it was here that parliamentary resistance appeared. In 1489 Henry needed around £100,000 to send 10,000 archers to Brittany for a year. He wanted this sum to be raised by an income tax. Parliament was reluctant because the yield was open-ended and based on an estimation of wealth. The Commons also recognised the danger of creating precedents through the formal documents, and requested that none were returned to the Exchequer. Parliament was to hold details of the sums raised locally. The Commons also pushed through a compromise whereby the clergy would pay one-quarter of the sum. The relative novelty of an income tax, last tried by Edward IV in 1472, led to evasion and reluctance. It also prompted the rising that caused Northumberland's death and incurred the vast expense of a campaign in the north. Only about £27,000 was collected. The 1490 parliament made up some of the shortfall by granting another fifteenth and tenth, but the experiment was a failure that the king did not try to repeat.

Instead, the Tudor crown again followed the Yorkist lead during the financial preparations for an invasion of France. In July 1491 Henry appointed commissioners to assess relative wealth of leading subjects in each county so that they could offer a contribution to the Tudor war chest. In return they received royal goodwill or benevolence. Demesne land (that used directly by a lord) was not taxable in the fifteenth and tenth, nor was wealth held in anything other than land or movable goods. Some prominent subjects had therefore failed to make appropriate contributions to earlier taxes. Imminent war with an ancient enemy allowed Henry to ask for emergency financial help. Unfortunately, the benevolence of Edward IV's reign was deeply resented, not least because there was no fighting in 1475. Richard III went so far as to outlaw similar forced gifts. Henry was therefore on dangerous ground in pressing for a type of loan that had been condemned within living memory.

The Tudor method of assessment also adapted the dilemma Edward IV had put to his contributors in 1474. If a potential donor appeared to be wealthy, he could probably afford to pay; if he seemed to have a frugal existence then he was perhaps hoarding or investing his cash, so could contribute generously. This trap has become known as 'Morton's Fork', and it is often cited as typical of Henry's deviousness. Even though its origins were Yorkist, it does indicate a belief that information was the key to Tudor power.

The benevolence arrived on top of existing requests for loans. It took parliamentary authority to secure the eventual collection of about £50,000, but this sum trickled in over five years. The immediate cost of the expedition to France had to be met from existing reserves. Administrative confusion and the evasion and resentment aroused by its novelty meant that this approach was not repeated. War with Scotland in 1496 brought promise of a loan to be offset against future parliamentary taxes, not as an outright gift. Although it was intended that the loan would be repaid when parliament granted the king his tax (and almost £50,000 was repaid by the end of 1498), the formal record of the relative wealth of over 2,700 contributors created the kind of precedent that made the late medieval elite uneasy.

The extent of preparations for the 1496 Scottish expedition resulted in intensive pressure for funds. The Great Council agreed to a grant of £120,000, which parliament was asked to endorse. The first half of the subsidy aimed for a specific total, and collection could be focused locally on those best able to pay. The administration of this tax functioned much better as commissioners appeared committed to their task. It was an important step in the development of workable subsidies to replace the outdated fifteenth and tenth. The second half of the subsidy was not needed as the Scottish war was postponed after the eruption of the Western Rising. Henry considered that a national tax for a national war of conquest was appropriate. The south westerners did not want to pay for a northern war. Regional differences remained strong and the king heeded the warning. Henry even paid for the Blackheath campaign from the £15,000 in fines imposed on the rebels. This sum probably allowed the Scottish campaign to continue in 1497.

Henry waited a further eight years before requesting another tax from parliament. In the intervening period other forms of royal income were refined and exploited. The king's final tax request must be seen in the light of these developments. In 1504 Henry asked for a feudal aid for the knighting of his son Prince Arthur (knighted in 1489 and dead for two years), and for the marriage of Princess Margaret to James IV of Scotland, which took place in 1503.

The crown's ancient feudal rights allowed Henry to demand these taxes, but by this stage of the reign there were reasons other than finance behind the king's decision. A feudal aid was a further extension of the calculations of wealth associated with earlier benevolences, and one that the Commons was not prepared to allow. The knights of the shire and burgesses argued that so many tenures were ancient, unrecorded, and uncertain that they might not stand up to crown scrutiny. After a difficult debate, the Commons offered a subsidy of £40,000. The extent of opposition worried the king and he did not challenge parliament's decision. He sensibly allowed them a deduction and accepted a subsidy of £30,000. The Exchequer handled collection, but payment was passed to the chamber and £25,311 had been received by John Heron by the end of July 1506.

This rebuttal was not the end of Henry's focus on feudal tenures. Edmund Dudley was speaker in this parliament, and entered the king's service soon after. Parliament denied Henry the opportunity to compile a definitive record of land tenures and service requirements, but Dudley was given the role of searching them out and charging for renewals and extensions anyway. It was the lords and leading gentry, as tenants-in-chief, who ended up paying twice for denying Henry his aid: once as contributors to the 1504 subsidy, and again as holders of the lands and liberties dissected during the last five years of the reign.

Henry's determination to acquire his entitlements led to the persistent pursuit of outstanding sums. In 1488 the council began to demand bonds from officials who had failed to deliver their revenues. In some cases this search continued for many years. The 1495 parliament authorised the recovery of undelivered contributions to the 1491 benevolence. The council also investigated delays connected to other taxes. In the summer of 1495 collectors in Shropshire faced imprisonment and personal bonds of £1,000 unless they settled the amounts due. A Cambridge officer had to explain to Bray why his sums towards the 1491 benevolence were still unrecorded in the royal chamber. This type of awareness of what was due to the crown and by whom could only be effectively followed up through accurate documentation and study of records.

In March 1496, William Spencer was discovered to have 'greatly misbehaved himself' in the Lincolnshire collection of the clerical subsidy granted in 1491. The king fined him 300 marks and demanded repayment of the missing cash. For his own 'profitte and lucre' William had caused the king to lose legitimate income. It was also perhaps a small step for Henry from ruthless collection of income due to a vigorous pursuit of new ways to fill the royal coffers. Pressure on the political security of the regime would turn the screw of financial dominance ever tighter, making the acquisition of profit and lucre the cornerstone of royal policy during Henry's final decade.

## Financial management and government innovation

When Henry took the throne, crown finances were managed through the established procedures of the Exchequer. It was originally the court through which people owing money to the crown were called to account. At its twelfth-century origins, most of the chief officers of the royal household sat to take payments from sheriffs and bailiffs of the king's counties and other liberties – half-year income paid at Easter, and the balance made good at Michaelmas, when paperwork was drawn up.

By the fifteenth century, the Exchequer was based at Westminster palace and was divided into two parts. The Upper Exchequer was a court that managed royal revenue and the officials who collected it. The Lower Exchequer handled the receipt and issue of money. It was closely linked to the Treasury, where currency was stored in strongboxes. The Exchequer had developed specialist officers as the accounting and auditing processes expanded rapidly during the fourteenth century. Business became more complex as accounts of income other than that of the sheriff – the 'foreign accounts' – began to be paid there and not within the royal household.

The Yorkist kings experimented with a more flexible system of financial management, based on the king's chamber within the household. Without surviving records it has been difficult for historians to analyse exactly what occurred. From early in Henry's reign, however, we do have evidence that money was paid out of the Exchequer to the treasurer of the chamber, but without audited accounts at the Exchequer for its expenditure. This indicated that new methods of financial management were in place, probably in direct continuation of Yorkist practice.

The role of the king's chamber in handling Henry's income is at the root of any investigation of his financial policy. The records of money coming into the chamber have survived from 1487, while the books of payments showing what the chamber spent exist from 1495 (with later copies of a book from 1491).[9] The chamber was managing cash from all kinds of sources by 1488. Bray paid in over £650 in pennies in December that year and the king's solicitor Thomas Lucas deposited £114 from the profits of justice in February 1488. The 1489 subsidy of £100,000 was paid directly to the chamber, and the chasing of officials was conducted by chamber officials and the council. Records show that forfeited bonds were also directed straight into the chamber at that time. The full range of payments and activities more familiar at the close of the reign were already in operation by the end of the 1480s.

Historians have thought that the treasurer of the chamber presided over a court treasury that managed the king's income from lucrative but unpredictable sources, such as prerogative rights. It was believed that the books famously signed on every page by Henry were thought to have been the only records of the treasurer's financial dealings with him. What was presumed to be a development that emerged forty years later, to cope with the income from monastic land, was actually in place around 1500. The survival of the accounts of John Heron's clerks, John Daunce and Robert Fowler, between October 1501 and September 1505, shows that the treasurers employed a team of clerks to handle the vast sums passing through chamber control. These records reveal the mechanics of Henry's financial system for the first time.[10]

This evidence might suggest an administrative innovation or the revival of a Yorkist precedent. Yet no similar documents have been identified from the Yorkist period. Nevertheless, it is very difficult to pinpoint when any changes occurred. Copies of lost records suggest that the later chamber system was functioning by 1491. The service function of the chamber had changed by 1492. Certainly, the statute creating a court to investigate conspiracy in the household (1487), and the threat to Henry's personal safety posed by the disloyalty of Lord Fitzwalter at the end of the 1480s, both point to changes within the household during the first years of Tudor rule.

There is also evidence of a much stronger interconnection between officials across the crown's financial institutions. In 1504 Daunce was one of the four tellers of the Exchequer, as well as Heron's clerk. Tellers received revenues at the Lower Exchequer and raised the tallies that discharged officers depositing cash.[11] Daunce considered many sums that he dealt with as a teller, such as those raised by the 1504 subsidy, to be payments directly to the king's chamber. It seems likely that these officials managed a great deal of business that was not recorded on the chamber books. Their accounts show large sums delivered to the king's cash treasuries, and also the transfer of coin to the mint in connection with coinage reform in 1504. Money also flowed other ways to meet Privy Purse or more substantial expenses, such as the wages of household servants or repairs to castles.

By comparing the working and accounts with the signed chamber books we get a new view of Henry's wealth. In April 1505, Heron's books record the massive payments to Archduke Philip and Maximilian, but nowhere do the chamber receipt books indicate a similar level of income to the king in the first place. For example, in October 1505 only £22,729 appears to have remained in the chamber after all payments had been removed. Yet between the end of 1495 and the close of the reign Henry probably spent in excess of £500,000. He was able to do this despite the gap between the record of apparent income and what was paid out, because the chamber books were not the only record of the financial transactions made.

Many funds were moved without ever becoming recorded in the treasurer's books. The French pension of about £5,000 was, from 1492, accounted and stored at Calais and was never recorded at Westminster. Edmund Dudley's cash receipts from obligations were passed directly to Heron's assistants. Other junior officers handled large amounts of cash. The groom of the stool managed the coffers of the privy chamber. He was important not only for his intimate service with the king but because the personal chamber staff took control of the monarch's private spending cash from at least the early 1490s.

The Exchequer was often used to replenish the supplies of cash that existed under the control of the chamber. The collection of subsidies was usually so slow that expenses could be met from the cash stored at the Tower or in Heron's offices at Westminster. The immediate costs of defeating the Cornish rebellion of 1497 were met in this way, with almost £8,000 paid from royal coffers before the proceeds of the subsidy were diverted through the Exchequer of receipt. The sum was repaid by the fines imposed on the rebels in 1498 and 1499.

Does this indicate that Henry passed responsibility for his finances to servants within his household and council? Stores of cash kept in the nearby office of the chamber or at more secure sites, but not in the royal rooms, imply that the king perhaps did not have the direct hands-on management of his finances that previous scholars of Tudor finance have suggested. This would be consistent with the autonomy given to council groups in defending Henry's legal rights. Rather than suggesting a disinterested king, this evidence indicates a monarch who had already mastered the way that he wanted the agencies of his government to operate.

## PARLIAMENT

Parliament today is the place where laws are made and unmade. While this was also the case in 1485, parliament's primary function was as the highest court under the king. The superior legal status attached to parliament was shown by the regular presence of the king in person at the start of parliamentary sessions. Few monarchs ever sat in the King's Bench, and it was rare for them consistently to act in person even in the royal council. But parliament, which embodied the representation of the entire nation, required a more visible royal contribution.

Henry recognised the importance of his personal role in parliament, especially at the start of the reign. He spoke to the Commons to explain his right to the crown in November 1485. He received in person the parliamentary oath against retaining, rioting, and maintenance at the end of that first parliament.[12] The ruler was also required to give personal assent to the acts that parliament agreed upon. Parliament was an extension of the role of the royal council. Most of the lords in parliament had attended council or Great Councils during the reign. Many of the prominent knights of the shire and burgesses had also advised the king in the council on specific issues, so were familiar with Henry's relationship with the nation's great men and how issues were resolved.

From the king's point of view, parliaments were not called to pass legislation. Their main functions were to give authorisation to royal requests for extra income in the form of taxation, and to bring the highest form of the law to bear upon the king's traitors through acts of attainder. This type of act removed the civil rights of the traitor, their estates and possessions became forfeited to the crown, and their bloodline became corrupted so that all titles and claims were extinguished. Attainted persons usually suffered a traitor's death – although Henry rehabilitated several attainted opponents, such as Thomas, earl of Surrey, and John, Lord Zouche.

Parliament was called only upon the instructions of the monarch. Secular and spiritual lords were summoned by royal writ. In the same way that lords became admitted as councillors by the king's request, so a royal invitation was necessary to attend parliament. Landholding did not confer an automatic right to sit. Other lords, like Lord Stourton in 1504, were given licence to be absent, or were asked to send a proxy representative. Because Henry inherited a body of lords after a civil war, those that were prominent within his regime (and hence in parliament) were his allies and friends. Attendance was almost always lower than the potential pool of lords. Henry could draw on two archbishops, nineteen bishops and twenty-eight abbots and priors. In his first parliament thirteen senior clergy and seventeen abbots actually attended.

The king assembled his parliamentary lords in the parliament chamber in Westminster palace. The chancellor, who normally opened a new parliament with an instructive or topical speech, oversaw the discussions of the lords and the crown, even if the king were present. The representatives of the Commons met separately, usually in the chapter house or refectory of nearby Westminster Abbey. Each county sent two knights to represent its interests – a total of seventy-four knights of the shire. To be eligible, these men did not have to be knighted but had to possess land worth £40 per year. They were elected by the freeholders of their county, who were men possessing land worth 40s per year. Boroughs, towns, and ports sent a further 224 MPs. For many of Henry's parliaments no formal returns of the Commons survive, and evidence of who sat for which constituency has to be gathered from scattered sources.

Members of the Commons observed the debates of the king and his lords spiritual and temporal, but only their formal representative, the speaker, was authorised to present to the king the business upon which the Commons agreed. Even this range of responsibility was at the king's invitation. Nevertheless, the speaker's post became vitally important to regimes victorious in civil war. Kings made a point of giving their chief allies this duty. Sir Thomas Lovell was speaker in Henry's first parliament in 1485, Edmund Dudley in his last of 1504. In between other allies like Sir Richard Guildford and Sir Richard Empson had served as speaker. Through closely allied directors of the Commons, kings hoped to gain more control over what the Commons debated and how its decisions were made. By manipulating what they proposed, kings were less likely to have to reject bills that an antagonistic or unruly Commons put forward. Nevertheless, the king and the Lords gave careful consideration to bills originating in the lower house.

Within the Commons there was also a division in status between the numerous burgesses, who appeared for towns, and the superior knights of the shire, who sat for all counties except Wales, Chester, or Durham. Since the king's household knights and councillors were also likely to be the most influential county gentry, there was a regular circulation of loyalists through parliament. Many counties must have welcomed the election of a royal councillor or household man as their MP since it gave them greater chance that their concerns would be lobbied successfully.

A 150-year-old dispute between the dean and canons of Windsor and the poor knights of St George's chapel was settled in favour of the dean and canons in the 1485 parliament, but only through the extensive lobbying of Henry's friends. The canons petitioned and bribed tirelessly, even paying Oliver King, Henry's secretary, to put in a good word. Dean Morgan was clerk of the parliament, Speaker Thomas Lovell was paid by the college, and one of the king's sergeants at law probably spoke in favour of the bill. Such labour lay behind many of the private acts passed in Henry's parliaments.

Although the Commons was reactive to the discussion in the Lords, the king also had many avenues by which to ensure that royal priorities were met throughout the whole parliamentary process. The direct influence of leading royal servants and the denial of initiative to the Commons allowed strong kings to direct parliament's business. Henry overcame grumbling in 1485 to pass the attainder of Richard III and his followers on exactly the terms he required. The king could manipulate acts already passed with the creation of provisos that negated the terms of legislation against named individuals who had petitioned for exemption. These measures were most common in acts of resumption that recalled crown grants since a certain date. Henry and his closest advisers sifted 421 provisos to his 1485 Act of Resumption. After the brief civil war of 1485 this was undoubtedly a highly charged political process. Similarly, those selected to be triers of petitions at the start of each session made decisions on what went forward to be discussed and what was disallowed. Parliament's status as the most senior court made it an appropriate place for individuals to secure private rights by definitive act rather than the king's seal alone. In these ways parliament was part of the king's arsenal of patronage and was recognised as such in the way lobbying and petitioning worked ceaselessly throughout parliamentary sessions.

Actual procedure was established and guarded by the clerks of parliament, whose medieval manual, the *Modus Tenendi Parliamentum*, was entered into the first Lords' Journal in 1510. The surviving fragments of private commentary on Henry's parliaments suggest that he did little to change its operation. The king and council monitored the conduct of elections and were aware of major attempts to influence who sat in parliament. Riots at borough elections resulted in appearances before the council and bonds for good behaviour. It was rather the measures he sought to push through that provoked comment and sometimes resentment. Occasionally, we have evidence of debate and resistance to Henry's wishes. The diary of a burgess sitting for Colchester in 1485 suggested that the bill of attainder aroused a great deal of opposition, since it questioned the right of men to support their anointed sovereign against his opponents. These concerns prompted the treason, or *de facto*, act of 1495. Henry rethought his tax demands in 1504 under pressure from the commons.

Henry clearly needed parliament. He used its authority to endorse his capture of the crown. He called it during times of political and military crisis to enhance his response to those crises. In 1504 parliament was recalled to reconnect the king to his community in the widest and most formal sense. Parliament was essential for the public demonstration of Henry's kingship. The discussion in other sections of this book of statutes passed by Henry's parliaments indicates his overwhelming concern with law enforcement, rather than crime creation or new ways to generate income. Henry's legislation programme in the 1495 parliament, addressing riot, perjury, juries, and the performance of sheriffs, demonstrated his good lordship and concern for sound rule in the face of Warbeck's external threat and internal English conspiracy. The 1495 treason act can be seen in this same light.[13]

On the whole, because the king, lords and leading gentry worked closely through the council, Henry's parliaments gave him little trouble. Royal policies were criticised and crown demands over taxation negotiated in parliament, but this was a constructive interaction. Henry did not dominate or threaten the Commons into submission. The king listened closely to the combined requests of the Commons and the petitions presented by individuals. Important assessments of the economic and commercial priorities of the nation emerged through legislation like the Navigation Acts to protect English shipping, or revision of weights and measures in 1491. Parliament was also used to safeguard the money supply, the quality of the coins in circulation, and the jurisdiction and strength of the courts. Henry was mindful to heed the requests of the Commons. Their major concerns over order and trade were aligned with Henry's broad aims and surfaced in many of the acts passed.

Henry was pragmatic about calling parliaments when he needed to do so. Because parliaments became infrequent after 1495 it is likely that substitutes to the legislative process were found in petitions to the council and council decrees and proclamations. But this was not the same thing as the two-way exchange of information between the rulers and the representatives of the ruled that parliament had come to embody. A decline in the discussion and debate that the Commons had enjoyed regularly during the first decade of Tudor rule helped to enforce the view that Henry became a withdrawn king, ruling through a narrow council elite. By 1504, in the final gathering of the reign, parliament even devolved to the king directly its own major role in reversing acts of attainder. By then, the refinement of bonds and financial pressure could create the same effects as attainder and forfeiture. Henry was using the institutional power he had created for the crown to absorb more of the executive functions that had been previously wielded by other parts of the ruling elite. Parliament retained a very important role under Henry VII. The scarcity of its meetings after 1497 suggests that this was becoming specific and specialised among the ruling institutions of the crown.

## JUSTICE AND THE CENTRAL COURTS

### Henry VII and the law

Those living at the close of the fifteenth century would have been keenly aware that crown control over the law and how justice was applied were among the chief factors by which monarchs were judged. The law regulated the lives of the entire population and shaped individual relationships from the manor upwards. It was a mysterious presence in the fabric of national life that set the boundaries for daily existence to most subjects. To others who were entangled in its processes, it perhaps provided as powerful an impact as the Church. Even at the level of national events, evidence from chronicle sources, private letters, and bills and indictments in the courts, indicates that the operation of justice was a fundamental concern of all communities.

The Wars of the Roses had developed partly from inconsistent royal assurance that the law was impartial; from insufficient respect for the rule of law by the aristocrats who were meant to uphold it; and from domination of the law for private means. For the law to work well, co-operation between all its agencies – king, council, judges, JPs, officials, jurors – had to be seen to work primarily in the interests of the nation.

The organisation and operation of the late medieval legal system created an intricate series of dependencies that could be accessed at various levels. Losses of many records and the inaccessibility of others have made it very difficult for modern historians to analyse how the system worked. Assessments of the effectiveness of the king's influence over the operation of the law are now hard to judge. During Henry's reign, however, we can detect many new approaches that have left distinct evidence of how a determined monarch could influence the established legal system.

The king was the focal point of the law. Justice was done in his name and he controlled the appointment of officers, commissioners, and judges who made the system work. In established medieval thinking the law was given to the realm for the security and benefit of all subjects, and of the king himself. From the early thirteenth century in England, Magna Carta had given the component parts of the body politic rights that the monarch was bound to uphold as the chief part of the same commonwealth. The king and the legal power of the crown were part of the judicial system. This brought the king down from a level where he appeared to be above

*Plate 1* A bond under £400 from November 1502, requiring John ap Elys of Ruabon in the Marches of Wales, and his 'part-takers', to behave themselves towards the king's officers in the lordship of Bromfield and Yale. They were to appear when summoned to Holt castle and were ordered to Westminster to answer before the council at Easter following. This type of bond is typical of those instruments that used financial threats to enforce behaviour on the king's terms (see pp. 127 and 216). TNA: PRO, C 54/376, m. 40.

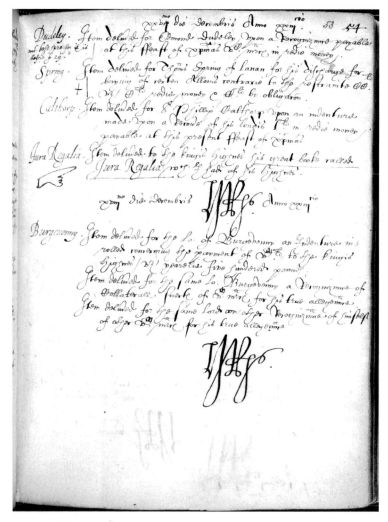

*Plate 2* A seventeenth-century copy of Edmund Dudley's notebook, complete with reproductions of Henry VII's sign manual. This page contains reference to Henry's receipt of the book 'Jura Regalia' from Dudley in December 1507 (see p. 137). It also notes Lord Abergavenny's payments towards his massive retaining fine (see p. 179). This document is one of the most important sources for Henry's reign. British Library, Lansdowne MS 127, fol. 53.

*Plate 3* Arthur, Prince of Wales, c.1500. Arthur is aged about fifteen in this fine portrait, completed before his marriage to Catherine of Aragon in November 1501. Arthur's death in April 1502 almost destroyed King Henry's plans for the stable development of the Tudor dynasty (see p. 106). This picture is now held at Hever Castle in Kent.

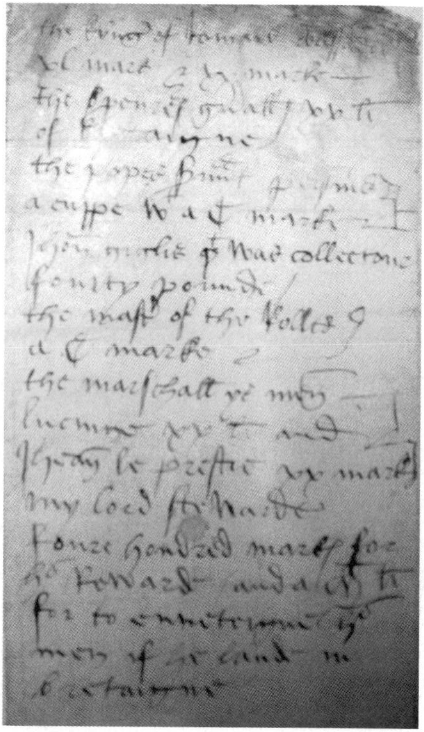

*Plate 4* This fragment, from 1488–89, is written in the king's own hand and records cash sums and gifts he required to be allocated to various people. Included are 20 marks to Maximilian's ambassadors, a gilt cup to the pope's servant, and a provision of £1,000 to the Lord Steward (Lord Willoughby) should his army land in Brittany (see pp. 60, 64, and 255). This document indicates Henry's close interest and control over how the crown's money was spent, even early in his reign. TNA: PRO, E 101/691/25.

*Plate 5* Explicit Tudor imagery on the new gold sovereign, introduced in 1489 (see pp. 69 and 250). The obverse shows Henry enthroned in state robes with the orb and sceptre. He is backed by a canopy of fleur de lis and wears a closed crown. The reverse of the coin depicts the arms of England inside a Tudor rose. The deliberate merging of established royal heraldry with Henry's Tudor and Beaufort family devices sought to proclaim the regal status of the new dynasty. British Museum, CM E.4841.

*Plate 6* Henry VII's sign manual on this first surviving page of his last will (with minor changes from one drawn up in 1507). Although damaged, the will is over 13,000 words long and is the most comprehensive of any medieval monarch. It records in great detail Henry's instructions for his tomb imagery, the completion of his chapel at Westminster Abbey, the masses he required, and alms to be distributed after his death, his funeral arrangements, the completion of churches he had endowed, specific bequests, and the appointment of his executors (see pp. 115–16). TNA: PRO, E 23/3.

*Plate* 7 An illustration of Henry VII's deathbed scene, on the night of 21 April 1509, from Sir Thomas Wriothesley's heraldic collection relating to funerals of prominent people, produced in the middle of Henry VIII's reign. The chief officers of Henry's household and other nobles are identified by their heraldic shields. British Library, Additional MS 45131, fol. 54.

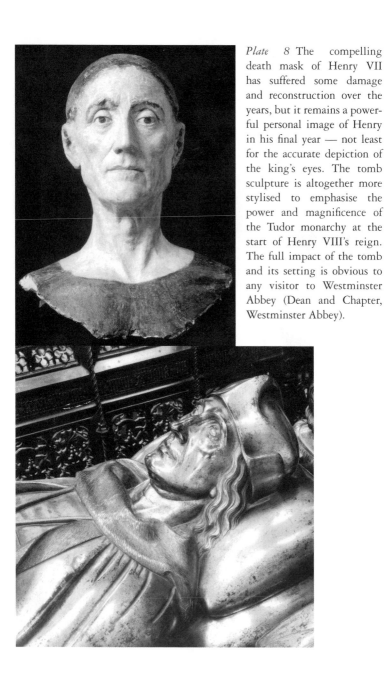

*Plate* 8 The compelling death mask of Henry VII has suffered some damage and reconstruction over the years, but it remains a powerful personal image of Henry in his final year — not least for the accurate depiction of the king's eyes. The tomb sculpture is altogether more stylised to emphasise the power and magnificence of the Tudor monarchy at the start of Henry VIII's reign. The full impact of the tomb and its setting is obvious to any visitor to Westminster Abbey (Dean and Chapter, Westminster Abbey).

the law, to one where his own power was defined by his relationship with it. The king's role was also to provide an idea of just law.

Royal justice not only wielded the punishing power of crown authority but also blended ideas of mercy and persuasion. This was where the king's relationship with justice could inspire or undermine confidence in the law. Henry VI's frail grasp of his judicial responsibilities and the manipulation of the law under his rule had cast England and Wales into civil war in the 1450s. An inconsistent monarch could sow decay throughout a system that was the most important pillar of crown authority. Henry VII's most critical task, and the one that could effectively secure his own kingship, was to revive confidence in the law. Historians now agree that Henry's reign did witness a novel attitude to the legal system. Whether this made him a great and fair legislator, or a ruler determined to manipulate legal structures purely for dynastic security, is still the subject of debate.

Traditionally, specialist legal knowledge had been reserved for the judges and lawyers, who were experts but not necessarily the king's friends. They operated the central common law courts of King's Bench and Common Pleas strictly on the centuries-old legal process that grew from the issue of writs. These documents initiated established but limited methods of starting a case – called forms of action. An existing legal framework enforced rigorously was some guarantee of solid belief in the law. Yet the procedures of the central courts and the related local action to get defendants to appear at the dock to answer indictments – known as mesne process – were cumbersome, complicated, and riddled with opportunities for delay. Henry had a disconnection from the structure and impact of English law because he had never been involved in its practice. As the giver of law to the country after 22 August 1485, he was in a unique position to shape what that law was.

It was likely that the Tudor adaptation of existing procedures was intended from the outset to benefit both the nation and the strength of Henry's grip on the crown. The political pressure placed on the Tudors by rebellion and family disaster meant that for the major part of his reign the application of justice became only a component of the early Tudor necessities of survival and security. This was where Henry's application of a legalistic and dynastically obsessed form of kingship began to undermine his temporary possession of the monarch's ancient role as the leader of a commonwealth of carefully balanced influences.

Henry was content to let his common law judges continue to direct things in King's Bench and Common Pleas, and in their mobile jurisdiction as assize and gaol delivery justices. The general isolation of the Yorkist judges from the political events of 1483–5 virtually guaranteed their reappointment after Bosworth. They managed the law, but Henry was immediately concerned to examine how its organisation could be improved against his own ruling priorities, and how its enforcement could be better ensured.

The consecutive chief justices of King's Bench, Sir William Huse and Sir John Fyneaux, and Sir Thomas Bryan in Common Pleas before 1500, were enthusiastic allies in this process since judges grew wealthy on fees as cases were processed. Their priority was to maintain the business of their jurisdictions by preventing a draining of cases to the equity courts because common law procedure was inflexible. A major part of Henry's investigation of common law deficiencies, therefore, concerned the speeding up of procedures and a clarification of practices. Henry realised that common law writs were not being handled properly by sheriffs and their Westminster agents. The processes concerned with outlawry and the arrest of murderers needed particular attention.

Political upheaval during the 1483 to 1485 period probably hindered the performance of gentry officers serving as sheriffs. It might also have highlighted the inflexibility of a formulaic range of writs available from chancery to people bringing their cases to court. More general forms of writs were introduced from the 1490s that encompassed a wider range of offences. They could be adapted by lawyers to fit each case as it arose. These forms were known as actions on the case. A new armoury of legal tricks and fictions was soon created that made the law more flexible but also required greater royal and judicial control.

Fictitious Bills of Middlesex permitted defendants to be brought into court from anywhere in the country on the fabricated grounds that they had committed a trespass within that county. They were then found lurking elsewhere. Westminster was in Middlesex and the King's Bench had a standing jurisdiction that allowed it to hear cases arising there. Once the defendant was in court, the real cause would emerge and the case would be in a position to proceed by bill much more quickly than under the previous writ system.

Through the various legal agencies at his command, Henry also demonstrated that the law stemmed from him alone. Evidence exists of manipulation of the legal process by the crown that tarnishes Henry's increasingly outdated reputation as a promoter of impartial justice. The number of cases where the king intervened is relatively small when compared to the volume of business passing through the courts, but it suggests that the law was increasingly used as a vehicle for the crown to pressurise its subjects.

The process of the common law could be stopped or Henry's pardon assured for payment of the appropriate fines. Yet the demand for payment for the king's legal favour is not something found at the start of the reign. The *recorda* files of the King's Bench contain numerous privy seal warrants returned from Chief Justice Huse or the king's attorney in the court, Henry Harman. The warrants show that Henry halted cases where prosecutions of individuals had been shown to be in error. He wrote to the court to stop process against Worcestershire men indicted of treason after Sir Humphrey Stafford's rebellion in 1486. Henry was made aware of their innocence and halted proceedings without further explanation. He discovered that a riot in Staffordshire allegedly involving 700 men on behalf of the Delves family was a twisting of the facts. In February 1488 Henry decided that some Kentish indictments for illegal retaining, outstanding since 1474, had been brought through malicious information.

This was the area where, towards the end of the reign, lingering indictments might be quashed for a fee rather than the king's will in the interests of good justice. Although the chamber books of payments survive from July 1487, fees for favour in the law are not immediately obvious – although they might be disguised in sums received from the king's solicitor and attorney.[14]

Royal intervention in the law was therefore a highly personal decision by the king or his intimate councillors. Solutions brought about in this way frequently required an appearance before the council or the king himself. Henry's decision-making still backed up this policy and he was responsible for the boundaries in which his legal officers worked. The evidence from after 1500 suggests a far harsher outlook towards royal mercy and favour at the law. This change tipped the balance of early Tudor judicial policy towards repression and tyranny.

After deliberating, Henry might allow some suitors to proceed at common law, as he did for the bishop of Exeter in 1507. The king intercepted and cancelled indictments like those for murder facing the

Staffordshire knight Sir John Montgomery and a Lincolnshire priest, John Cultard, in 1505. James Molyneaux compounded with the king for rioting by his tenants in Lancashire in 1509, and a council settlement of their offence then followed. Henry could deny petitions for equitable judgement and demand that cases should be heard at common law; Thomas Newton's claim to the patronage of the church of Alderton in Suffolk was directed in this way in 1506. In some cases, Henry ensured that legal process favoured the man who offered the greatest bribe, although there could have been additional factors that allowed him to trim the power of great men through his decisions.

Where the law had run its course, Henry also intervened in a very wide range of offences to sell royal clemency. He pardoned murderers from the gentry class, like Sir John Ferrers and two members of the Egerton family of Cheshire in 1506. The king reversed the outlawries of several knights, including Sir Thomas Parre, as well as lesser men and clerics. Henry's pardon was extended to wool stealers; those whose misprision and seditious words had come to the council's attention; murderers, thieves, rapists, and illegal hunters.

Henry's need to extend his base of support meant that the application of his laws became very pliable. He forgave many offenders who had something to offer the crown (cash, lands, information, or political contacts), or whose rehabilitation benefited the public face of royal authority. Others who stepped too far beyond the limits of the king's generosity, or who showed themselves to be security risks, were removed as awesome examples of royal power. Previous kings had intervened in the normal course of legal process, but Henry was unique in tying his legal favour so extensively to financial payments and to bonds. He might have seen the extra material benefits of selling his pardon, but this was not done haphazardly. This hard and soft flexibility demonstrated Henry's ownership of the law and his absolute determination to wield it where necessary to strengthen his dynasty.

The economic basis to much of Henry's intervention in the law on a case-by-case basis stands in contrast to his determination to flush out similar abuses by royal servants running the law in the counties. While it might not show a resolute belief that justice should be left entirely to its expert practitioners, we see a monarch eager to wield his personal control of the law in the political arena. It also perhaps demonstrates a ruler anxious to set himself above the law when it came to his own security. Very few previous monarchs had tried such a forceful move because the established balance of rights and liberties that existed between the crown and its subjects was so delicately poised.

Henry was playing a dangerous game by advertising that his laws could be bypassed and royal favour gained for the right price. Loyalty and support might come from the grateful beneficiary of royal intervention, but resentment could follow if the cost of the king's favour was too high. Those priced out of the bidding war, or unable to make the contacts to get the king's ear in the first place, could be equally frustrated at being denied an impartial hearing of their case. There was a very real possibility of them turning to other powerful figures for alternative and perhaps illegal remedies that challenged royal authority in different ways.

Legal pressure could generate political hostility, as occurred when Henry tried to manipulate the position of Edmund, earl of Suffolk, at the end of the 1490s. Such a progression might be seen as a direct consequence of a royal attitude to the law that was inconsistent, partial, and saleable. Henry maintained a stranglehold on the dispensation of remedies through the recruitment and promotion of expert lawyers to his service. It might suggest a structure that was itself highly organised and thorough but which pushed to the very edge of their allegiance some subjects who had the most frequent need to use the law. Henry's death released them from a legal system that by 1509 was appropriated for the security of the Tudor dynasty.

## The royal council and the law

Although Bacon has strongly influenced Henry's reputation as a great legislator, many early Tudor statues did not create new crimes. Henry was clearly concerned at the conduct of his law officers and refined the ways that existing laws were enforced. Fourteen of his statutes tightened up legal procedures, but only a handful of JPs were prosecuted for malpractice. It was in the royal council that Henry scrutinised the performance of his servants most effectively. The council possessed its own commanding legal jurisdiction as the extension of the king's personal lawgiving capacity. The senior judges and aristocratic JPs and commissioners formed a major body of royal councillors. They worked closely with Henry to refine crown dominance of the legal system.

From the council stemmed the equity courts staffed by royal councillors and supported by specialist officers. Chief of these, and established since the fourteenth century, was the Lord Chancellor's Court of Chancery. Henry's chancellors, John Morton and William Warham, had a strong personal identification with their king. This association gave their court a powerful alignment with royal will. The chancery equity court handled many thousands of petitions that flooded into the king.

Procedure was clear, straightforward, and quick when compared to the common law. Bills, answers and proceedings were in English; writs of subpoena under the king's private seal compelled appearance on pain of a fine; examinations were made under oath; depositions were taken from witnesses, often by commissioners in the locality; preprepared questions called interrogatories could be put to witnesses by each side; fines and recognisances were used to enforce decisions and compel behaviour, often to abide by judgements or the arbitration of councillors.

By Henry's reign, the separate equity jurisdiction of chancery from the council was still relatively recently established. The council had always possessed the legal flexibility to deal with sensitive political cases or those where the king's personal input was necessary. As a king intent on defending his weak grip of the crown, the legal authority that already existed within the council gave Henry a potent tool by which to control the enforcement of his laws. The Tudor council heard cases between individuals by petition; acted on information from private subjects; investigated riot, retaining, and customs offences; and managed the operation of the local legal system through supervision of juries, inquests, and the proper progress of cases.

Although the council used chancery procedure, Henry's challenge to the powerful legal influence of his foremost subjects required even more of a flexible approach. Where procedures at assizes, quarter sessions, or in the Westminster courts broke down because of disruptive external influences, the council took over the prosecution or punishment of offenders. It was then that fines, damages or recognisances were imposed as punishment, reprimand, or guarantee of future behaviour.

The use of bonds to enforce behaviour and allegiance from the beginning of the reign also created a stronger connection between common law process and the council's legal interests. Chancery writs were required to instruct sheriffs to act on forfeited recognisances. Many instances of failure to abide by conditions attached to bonds first came to the attention of the crown's legal servants at local level and were followed up through common law process. The king and council were then alerted to misbehaviour and potential disturbance and intervened as necessary.

At the close of 1486 Sir Robert Green had been bound to appear in the council in February following, probably as the result of a riot and the murder of another knight's servant in Westminster earlier that year. In the meantime he was to behave himself and cause no disturbance within Northamptonshire. On 10 November, the constable of Towcester, William Cooper, reported to the council that he had arrested one of Green's servants on suspicion of murder. Green appeared with armed followers, broke open the gaol to free his man, and almost beat the constable to death. The council then asked the sheriff to force the immediate appearance of Green and his sureties in chancery to explain why the first bond should not be forfeited.

Green did appear by his attorney, denied everything, and opted for a jury trial of the allegations made. He escaped serious punishment and was again in trouble during the 1490s for failing to control his followers in London. The forfeiture of the bond enforceable through the council and chancery was dependent upon the outcome of trial at common law. This type of case linked the council, chancery, and criminal justice at Westminster. It also shows the importance of smooth connections between central justice and local law enforcement.

The 1487 Star Chamber Act suggested the probable breakdown of contacts between central direction of the law and regional enforcement of it. The Act identified areas where legal challenges to abuses of lordship were neglected. It implied that the king and his officers were almost powerless to curtail maintenance, the giving of livery, embracery, corruption by sheriffs in packing juries and falsifying the return of writs, riot, and unlawful assembly.[15]

The worst offenders were those lords who were meant to uphold the law, but whose non-cooperation blocked royal investigations. As a result, murder, robbery and general insecurity spread throughout the realm. The Act allowed a committee to be formed by the chancellor, the treasurer, and the keeper of the privy seal. They were to call upon a bishop, a noble councillor, and the two chief justices, to act by writ or privy seal against offenders who would be punished as if they had been convicted in a court of common law.

The Act also incorporated seemingly unrelated clauses about other legal activities. JPs were empowered to inquire after avoidance of their verdicts. They could take recognisances for keeping the peace and to call those bound over to the next sessions. Any defaults were to be certified into the central courts. The Act also tightened procedure over the investigation of murder. 'Great boldness' was given to murderers because coroners, constables, and officers did not know procedures. Towns were to be fined if murderers escaped capture, and they were to pay the coroner's fee for investigating the death. He was to forfeit hundreds if he failed in his duty.

We do have evidence of a great deal of theory and planning behind the judicial policies that emerged from the council. Henry experimented imaginatively in the way the council coped with the expanding volume of business attracted by its broadening interests. Small bodies of councillors took on responsibilities that exerted crown demands upon the legal system at various points. These council committees worked in areas where the law lacked clarity, where the king's rights were neglected, or where there was an urgent threat to order and security.

During Henry's reign there was an enormous increase in the number of suits that were presented to the main council at Westminster, and to a smaller group of councillors attending the king as he moved between residences. In the latter area, Henry acted upon Richard III's appointment of masters of poor men's petitions to develop another council committee led by his almoner, the dean of the royal chapel, and other clerical councillors. In reality this court heard business in a similar way to chancery from plaintiffs who were rarely stricken by poverty. But it did travel widely – hearing cases when the king was in Calais in 1500 – and its connection to a royal charitable role provided another means by which the crown could encroach upon ecclesiastical jurisdictions. This committee would develop into the Court of Requests under Wolsey in the 1520s.

The council and chancery courts indicated an active government that seemed willing to offer legal avenues that were supplementary or even alternative to the common law. The year 1487 also saw the council take over the policing of the royal household, as a body of councillors was empowered to investigate conspiracy among the king's personal servants. A similar tribunal challenged dishonest juries between 1495 and 1504, although this has left little record. From about 1499 a group of about eleven expert legal councillors formed the council learned in the law. This committee provided specific legal advice to the king and the main council, but also managed crown prosecutions chiefly in the area of feudal landholding. Other bodies such as the general surveyors of the crown lands protected Henry's income from the royal demesne estates and managed disputes between the king's tenants. These latter bodies gave Henry's council more of the appearance of an oversized noble council – chiefly concerned with land management, the defence of rights, and the proper administration of revenue – than did previous royal councils.

This equitable jurisdiction was also broadcast geographically as Henry revived or developed special councils of the Marches of Wales, of the north, of the king's mother in the east midlands, of the chancellor duchy of Lancaster in Westminster, and of the warden of the Cinque Ports in Dover. The chancery courts of the palatinate of Lancaster and Durham applied the king's delegated authority uniformly through his appointed officials. The popularity of this procedure led to more and more appeals to the crown.

These areas where equity jurisdictions were established or renewed frequently coincided with localities where nobles held large tracts of land or were crown stewards. Equity's emphasis on a decision reached through evidence, argument, and conscience encouraged the demonstration of the skills that successful good lords already employed. Chief of these were arbitration and interaction with the grievances of suitors – often their own tenants or servants. Intervention to settle disagreements before they escalated into conflicts was an important part of the preservation of a lord's influence.

The threat of legal proceedings and the issue of writs often became sufficient to force a compromise agreement out of court. The king's aristocratic allies were encouraged to take this example to their own councils and legal jurisdictions. Their role as commissioners to take depositions in council cases, or as agents acting for the king with full legal powers, helped to project Henry's authority into the regions. The extension of equity did require an enhancement of the means of enforcement, and here again King Henry's preference for financial pressure through bonds went some way towards ensuring that suits were genuine and that default on judgement or arbitration could become very damaging.

## The Church, the crown, and the law

In England, Church and civil pleas had been separated for centuries. Although chancery writs could enforce appearance before bishops' courts, there was a comprehensive ecclesiastical legal structure to try moral offences such as the sins of blasphemy and adultery, and suits like the validity of wills or marriages. The pope, and not King Henry, was at the top of the Church's legal structure in England and Wales. Churchmen had the right to appeal outside the kingdom to Rome, and this had often been a concern for English kings. Additionally, in the late medieval period the Church was a landowner and secular lord second only to the crown. Where vulnerable English rulers struggled to establish control, the influence of the Church within the temporal arena could be a distraction.

A system of law based on the rules and decrees of popes since the 1100s (the canons of Church law) ran alongside the common law within Henry's kingdom. The functioning of these two structures overlapped as the king's law dominated regulation of the Church's landholding, while the Church's punishment of mortal sins interfered constantly with the lives of all subjects. For both systems to work well cooperation between the king and the clergy had to be worked at. One such compromise was achieved over the benefit of clergy.[16]

Henry's quest for political control obliged him to challenge the superior interest of Rome over the English Church. Undermining ecclesiastical courts on many fronts was an important part of this process. Henry effectively reduced the right of the Church to offer sanctuary to criminals. The fifteenth-century growth of equity and conciliar justice had already diverted suitors from the Church courts. Chancery, in particular, robbed bishops' probate courts of their control over disputes about wills and inheritances. The King's Bench responded to this legal tug of war by allowing actions on breach of promise, an area previously controlled by Church courts.

The statutes of Provisors and *praemunire* had been introduced by Edward III in 1351 and 1353 respectively to stop Rome interfering in Church appointments that were the king's to give, and to prevent English clergy using the pope's courts in Rome to bypass common law jurisdiction in England. To elevate his own kingship, Henry began to treat the authority of the Church courts as a foreign influence. He used *praemu-*

*nire* to widen the gap at the points where ecclesiastical and common law overlapped. He encouraged the King's Bench as a court of appeal to allow cases that sought to overturn judgements in Church courts. Various other rights of ecclesiastical courts were challenged during the reign, such as that to award costs in 1497. The dilution of ecclesiastical legal jurisdictions had an important role in containing the impact of the Church on Henry's personal kingship.

## JUSTICE AND LOCAL LORDSHIP

### Community, lordship and the law

All late medieval kings dominated a system of lordship that worked through personal leadership. Henry's accession created opportunities to change the existing structures of national lordship. His disconnection from the way England was ruled meant that the trust associated with royal and noble lordship had to be earned on both sides of the balance. Henry created few new nobles and was reluctant to promote or reward his servants excessively. Rebellion and attainder after 1485 diminished the pool of leading peers. Henry also kept the personal estates of the crown in his own hands. With little royal family to endow, it was more beneficial for him to make the royal lands work harder for the crown rather than to give them away as rewards. Where land was granted, it was primarily as stewardships or leases. Local appointments were therefore more easily tailored to fit with Henry's priorities for a particular county or network.

He deliberately split up forfeited estates, such as those of the rebel Sir Humphrey Stafford after 1486, to prevent the build up of blocks of concentrated power – even among his own followers. The enhancement of regional councils in the north or Welsh Marches disrupted the traditional means of noble lordship in those areas. It also had a major impact on how adherence to the law was enforced. It has been seen by some historians as Henry's ill-judged attempt to tinker with the existing system in a way that indicates his lack of understanding of the king's role within it.[17]

This policy sharply defined the network of king's supporters in the regions and created a clear role for royal stewards and officers – most notably in defending the king's laws. In many cases this conflicted with traditional arrangements for effecting local rule through noble and gentry retinues. Conflicts between the Lancashire Stanley family and Sir Thomas Butler, or the earl of Northumberland and Sir John Hotham in east Yorkshire, emerged for this reason as the king's servants were promoted against noble power.

A king was at the top of a service structure that connected him to all levels of society below. One of the monarch's most important roles was to know and manage the qualities and skills of his leading servants. Kings staffed their household with trusted followers, but they also had a wider responsibility to tenants-in-chief – the hundreds of wealthy and influential people who held land directly from the crown. This group were the aristocratic elite, who might know the king as a man rather than a power, or come into personal contact with him in the royal household or at court. There were also less-defined ideas of royal leadership for the broad politically aware landholding classes as a whole.

Even further removed, the majority of subjects whose focus did not extend far beyond parish or town life shared a different view of the crown's power. What bound all of these levels of society together were the concepts and practice of justice and lordship. And while these ideas were crafted into real policy at the centre of government, they were put into effect within the overlapping units of local society – villages, manors, parishes, boroughs, cities, hundreds, counties and regions. It was here that Henry's authority and abilities as king were felt keenly, and also where his leadership can be judged accurately.

The connection between the law and society was managed at the local level by the members of these regional and local political communities. By regulating their local legal roles, the Tudor crown found new ways to encroach upon the political and social freedoms of the landholding elites who had, to some extent, been responsible for the descent into lawlessness during the mid-fifteenth century. Order and respect for the law were only maintained by a careful balance of strong royal leadership at the centre and the delegated freedoms to lords locally. When King Henry swore at his coronation to uphold equal and merciful justice to all subjects he could only hope to get close to achieving this by having a group of conscientious representatives to make his laws work universally.

Each broad level of the population was responsible for different aspects of the judicial system away from the centre of royal power. Henry's courtiers and friends were also the main agents of the law in the counties. Westminster judges would visit a county twice a year to hold the Lent and summer assizes or to empty the county gaol by commission. But it was the nobility and gentry within local communities who promoted the king's laws on a day-to-day basis. The status of peers and knights as leading landowners required them to serve as JPs, sheriffs, escheators and special commissioners.

Their personal knowledge of the law stemmed chiefly from the pressing need to defend the titles to their estates from predators. These concerns and the complex nature of late medieval land law provided many landholding gentlemen with enough legal experience for them to be classed as skilled amateur lawyers. By the close of the fifteenth century a growing number had also been educated at the legal universities – the Inns of Court. Their legal roles were backed up by books of relevant statutes and a clerk of the peace to advise on legal technicalities and procedures. County leaders also oversaw the courts connected to the manors they owned or leased. These manorial and urban borough courts controlled local landholding and tenancy, trading and markets, and small-scale violence, trespass and debt cases where values fell under a 40s (£2) limit.

The legal abilities of educated aristocrats developed through the commercial availability of printed books. Henry's legal system was perhaps the first to benefit extensively from a boom in the printing of legal textbooks. Greater literacy meant that more trained lawyers could practise away from Westminster and still stay connected to legal developments and ideas. Many thrived in the larger regional and county towns where assizes and quarter sessions were held. Their training ensured a stronger connection between legal practice and legal management from Westminster. More immediate access to accurate legal opinion ensured that suitors found outlets for their grievances at the specialist council courts of equity that expanded quickly under Henry's leadership.

At the points where individuals became involved in the regulated practices of lordship and the law, they were obliged to participate. Lesser members of local communities formed the juries that provided the verdicts in various courts, commissions, and inquests. At the level of manor courts they were the jurors who protected copyhold tenancies and common land against outside interference. It was also not unknown for communities to use the law to preserve their own rights if challenged by aggressive or unreasonable lordship.

A duplication of the royal judicial role also occurred at lower social levels. Abstract social concepts such as power, virtue, chivalry, hospitality, and honour appeared in the contemporary literature that informed the attitudes and experiences of the landed elites. These were shared ideals that influenced the king as much as his foremost servants. The interdependence of all levels up and down the lordship structure meant that the king's lead was followed. Subjects not only reacted to royal proclamations, laws, and decrees, and tried to adapt the way they did things to fulfil the king's wishes, they also followed royal fashions, tastes, and trends in the hope of catching royal favour and progressing their own careers. All kings therefore found their own lordship mirrored in that of their inferiors. The way the king crafted his policies in regulating local law and lordship suggests much about how the Tudor crown wished to govern.

## Lordship and the abuse of power

The manipulation of the law was the negative side of the reliance on nobles and gentry to promote impartial royal justice. Perversion of justice occurred constantly throughout the fifteenth century because the power of lords was based upon possession of land – whether by title or by stewardship. The aristocratic struggle to gain and retain land bred the violence and disorder that kept the courts busy. It also drew socially competitive late medieval men and women into a greater struggle to develop estates and inheritances as a way to guarantee advancement. The build-up of hereditary estates maintained the traditional local influence of lords across generations of royal service and private land dealing. This accumulation of concentrated landholding in a parish, county, or region encouraged a stable network of service, since political dominance absorbed the gentry connections that formed the relevant local community. Lords preserved their power through the creation of affinities and networks. They used their followers to defend their rights and influence. In return, lords supported their servants' concerns, problems, and quarrels.

The crown had always allowed this to happen since kings needed nobles and their gentry servants to manage local affairs and to ensure that royal power was represented. At the start of Henry's reign, however, royal office holding in itself was not a sufficient mark of status to match the more potent power of large groups of retainers commanded by the major families. During the course of the reign this situation was gradually reversed. Because noble power underpinned so much of royal power, Henry could not deprive the peers of their traditional means of lordship. If anything, the small Tudor royal family magnified the responsibility placed upon the dukes, earls and lords to manage the regions for the crown. Only they had the land-based connections that matched, on a regional or county level, the king's national influence. Strong nobles gave the crown stronger resources on which to draw. All Henry was concerned to do was to ensure that this was done in compliance with his laws and with his wishes foremost. But royal efforts to bring this about required the king to tread carefully.

The 'bastard feudal' system of lordship based on service in return for payment and protection was entrenched and accepted. Under powerful royal leadership it worked. It was unwise for a monarch to intervene within this finely balanced system without very clear objectives and certain means of forcing through change. Henry VI's abject lack of leadership during the 1450s had allowed noble jostling for influence over freely available royal patronage to escalate into lawless violence. Edward IV had worked hard to restore royal leadership and a stable system of lordship. His solution was to develop regional power blocs dominated by major noble affinities. Edward's royal authority was delegated to Warwick in the north, Clarence in the midlands, Herbert in Wales, and Lord Stafford of Southwick in the south-west. This was medieval personal leadership at its finest. Edward dominated his leading nobles and restored stability to English kingship. His approach ensured that his system survived the removal of all four from the picture by the 1470s. However, the inherent weakness of a lordship structure managed chiefly by the king in person was that the death or incapacity of the ruler would cause the system to collapse. Within three months of his death, his heir Edward V was deposed and Richard of Gloucester again split the political nation. When Henry VII presented himself as a unifier he realised that the rift among the political classes would only be repaired if the king could get his idea of productive lordship and impartial justice to work in the counties of the realm.

## Making the law work

In practice, the day-to-day nature of offices like JP, sheriff and escheator was not attractive to those men expected to fulfil these roles. They wanted the freedom to appoint deputies and agents to do the menial work attached to particular posts. Nevertheless, the responsibility was theirs. By 1485 the powers of JPs and sheriffs were extensive and perhaps even onerous. The real possibility of being out of pocket prompted some men, such as Sir John Rainsforth of Essex in 1506, to pay fines or promise lands, rather than serve. Henry had to find a balance between enforcing what was required from these roles and ensuring that they remained prestigious and interesting to the landholders who normally occupied them.

There seems to have been no intention by the early Tudor crown to place county law in the hands of lower-ranking administrators. Henry realised that the only way local law enforcement and local lordship could be transformed was for lords and gentry to participate fully in the process. Although directed from Westminster, Henry's main measures in this area were designed to make the local agents of the crown improve their own conduct and efficiency as lords and legal agents. The 1488 Justice of the Peace Act stated bluntly that there were enough laws but that JPs were failing to enforce them. It is clear from the payments made to those JPs who actually heard the sessions that most of the mundane legal work was left to more expert lawyers. Being part of the quorum was a mark of status within the county, but Henry was not prepared to elevate the influence of individual gentry by appointing them to the commission without demanding something in return.[18] The king's requirements also tied his agents into an extensive system of control.

What Henry offered to aristocratic JPs (and what really interested them) were expanded legal responsibilities that were effective all year round. Chief of these improvements was the right granted in 1495 to determine certain offences summarily without a jury and on the evidence of informers. In the year Perkin Warbeck's conspiracy was particularly threatening, this legislation boosted the powers of the landholding class and the king's reliance on their diligence. Other laws passed in the same parliament to speed the local legal process included acts to allow rioters to be prosecuted *in absentia* if they avoided repeated summonses to sessions. JPs also acquired greater control over the composition of juries when they were able to reject members suspected of bias towards defendants.

In reality, the practical restrictions that Henry extended in parallel to new statutes meant that these measures were most favourable to members of the royal household and other loyalists acting locally. Boosting

JPs' legal powers without careful management invited abuses of lordship among county elites. Justices were tempted to dishonesty. Richard III's parliament passed a statute to allow JPs to bail suspected felons who could find sureties for their good behaviour. This law had been abused and, according to the Taking of Bail by Justices Act of 1487, many murderers and felons were allowed to escape the law. The Act allowed JPs to bail prisoners, but it fell to sheriffs to note those in custody and to ensure their appearance in court.

JPs were also in a position to favour themselves, their friends, and the networks they were part of. There were numerous examples of senior JPs using their positions to promote their own servants and continue their disputes. Lords Maltravers and De la Warr were summoned before the council from Sussex in July 1486 for rioting. Lord Grey of Codnor and Sir Henry Willoughby were bound to keep the peace towards each other under pain of £500 in May 1488. Lord Grey of Ruthin, Sir Nicholas Vaux and Sir Thomas Green were ordered to disarm their servants within London in November 1498, lest the violence of their dispute escalate.

A spectacular example of JPs resisting royal attempts to reform their behaviour is provided by Sir Thomas Cornwall and Sir Richard Croft, who were both JPs in Herefordshire from the start of the reign. Their quarrel had grown under Edward IV but they used Henry's initial preoccupation with the Ricardian north to set about each other with renewed enthusiasm. In 1486 Cornwall used his retainers to break open the gaol of the abbot of Leominster and released two of his men arrested by Croft, who was also treasurer of Henry's household. Cornwall claimed that he was simply using his powers as a JP to release them since they were bailed to appear at the next quarter sessions. Other charges of riot and attempted murder only emphasised that these two knights acted to defend the status of their lordship, despite the strict requirements of their office as JP. Henry seems to have been more concerned with the disruptive competition to retain men illegally within Leominster. Despite several appearances before the council, recognisances, outlawries and cases in the King's Bench, this conflict rumbled on into the mid-1490s in defiance of crown efforts to end it.

Henry managed appointments to commissions of the peace as a reward for good lordship and behaviour. Lords favoured by the crown were more likely to have their trusted influence extended by promotion of their servants to county office or as JPs, as was the case with the earl of Surrey in his native East Anglia after 1501. The king could also dismiss and reappoint JPs as their conduct required. In 1507, Sir John Cottesmore of Oxfordshire was obliged to agree to the king's solution to his offence of misprision at a price of £400, but he worked his way back onto the bench by 1509. The constant undercurrent of rebellion meant that the king and his council were quick to dismiss suspects and rebels from these influential posts. In this way Henry and his Lords Chancellor created new JPs who were more fully acquainted with the king's expectations from their period of service.

Jack Lander has shown that Henry remodelled the composition of the peace commissions during the 1490s.[19] This was apparently done more for reasons of poor performance and corruption than from a fear of heightened political insecurity. Early in the decade, Henry began to appoint his more trusted knights and relatives to the bench in counties where they held no lands or major influence. This was a symbolic rather than practical change, since men already with multiple roles inside the regime could not spend the year riding to sessions across the country. But it sent a clear message of supervision, if not outright interference, from the centre.

At every level of the county judicial system, Henry's regime monitored the practitioners of the law. The 1488 Justice of the Peace Act made this explicit.[20] At each quarter session JPs were to proclaim that they had failed to prevent local disorder and violence. The king's subjects were invited to report negligence to, and seek remedy from, individual JPs, gaol delivery or assize judges, or ultimately the king and his council. The intention of such intervention was to make a county's legal officers self-improving. It worked not only against JPs. In 1499 John Vavasour, a justice in the palatinate of Lancaster, was reported to the council for taking bribes. Various sheriffs and escheators found that their conduct was harshly assessed by Edmund Dudley at the end of the 1504–05 Exchequer year (although this could have been Dudley's zeal to impress his new employer).

Stronger royal monitoring of conduct under the law simultaneously made lords aware of royal scrutiny of their leadership in other spheres of county life, such as retaining and land transactions. Some individuals also seem to have been made to serve as part of their rehabilitation after offending the crown. As part of a pardon in August 1506, Piers Stanley was obliged to serve as sheriff of Merionethshire during the king's pleasure. Where lordships allowed men to appoint officials, Henry sometimes intervened to ensure that his conditions were met. Sir John Warburton had the right to appoint the undersheriff of Cheshire but had to pay the king £40 for confirmation of it in 1505. The suitability of his choice of officer also required the king's agreement.

The status of almost all substantial landholders at some stage brought them to the bench, to sit on special commissions, or to hold local office. Defence of that landed status by legal and illegal means often cut right through any period service to the crown within a county. Common law prosecutions for 'force and arms' offences to seize and retain real and movable property suggest that the responsibility to represent royal authority apparently made very little difference to how the personal concerns of the ruling elites dominated their behaviour. This was the main problem for all medieval kings, but one which Henry VII was determined to overcome.

Without enforcement, respect for the law would be eroded. Riot, conspiracy, insurrection and rebellion stemmed from such a disregard for the foundations of royal power. The selfish and inconsistent approach to the law shown by knights like Croft and Cornwall makes it easier to understand why the king tried to control excessive displays of lawlessness by bypassing cumbersome legal channels that often relied upon the cooperation of such wayward gentry in their official capacities. Henry's ability to manipulate appointments and to enforce adherence to the law through men's purses was expanded by the flexibility of the council and chancery procedures he developed.

## Early Tudor sheriffs

Henry VII cannot take credit for extending the powers of JPs in a novel way. The social composition of his commissions of the peace was similar to previous monarchs. As he did in the central courts and across the Tudor regime as a whole, Henry continued to rely on the collective experience of men who had worked hard for Edward IV and Richard III. Over half of those from Richard's final commissions of the peace were appointed by Henry in 1485. Even a major piece of legislation against local legal corruption such as the 1495 Sheriff's County Court Act sought to remedy obvious deficiencies by reinforcing existing practice. This statute condemned the 'subtlety and untrue demeanour' of sheriffs and under-sheriffs who had allowed juries to make false verdicts, and permitted rioters and those guilty of illegal retaining to escape the law.

Until the start of Edward IV's reign the sheriff managed the regular justice within a county at his own county court. Edward transferred this role to the JPs and agreed to legislation that extended their supervision of other county administrators like escheators. With so much responsibility falling upon sheriffs' shoulders the annual appointment in many counties did not guarantee a continuation of the kind of legal competence the crown demanded. The Yorkist kings had made JPs the main practitioners of the law in the counties of England. The sheriff became more like the head legal administrator of the county who was required to ensure that all aspects of the business of governing the county were observed.

Although the earlier dominance of the sheriff within county society had declined by the late fifteenth century, these officers remained the linchpin of early Tudor county justice. The sheriff put the law into practice through the delivery of writs intended for other people, and the observance of those directed to him. He acted on instructions from the civil and criminal sides of the law to arrest suspects, imprison them until trial, detain goods, cause appearance at court, and begin the process of outlawry. Sheriffs also managed the selection and performance of juries and executed judgements and verdicts.

The men who served as sheriff were drawn from the ranks of the senior gentry of their county. They were lords in their own right. For example, the sheriffs of Northumberland and Durham arranged the muster of 500 soldiers for the relief of Berwick from Scottish threat In January 1488. Sheriffs came from the class that could handle political responsibility and absorb the cost of office. Because they were not paid directly, but were expected to draw expenses from the regular income of the counties they managed, sheriffs faced considerable costs during their year in office. Numerous warrants to the Exchequer in Henry's first years repaid sums spent by sheriffs in attempting to perform their duties. As the face of the law they were wide open to influence from the lordship structure in which they operated. Just like JPs, many abused their power within their existing associations and networks.

Temptation to fraudulent or dishonest behaviour could result in bribery, selection of weighted juries, misdirection of writs, or the deliberate failure to arrest suspects. Opportunities for embezzlement and subornment were also presented by sheriffs' responsibilities for seizing felons' goods, collecting the regular income of county administration such as fee farm rents and legal fines, and organising elections of MPs. Where these were isolated offences, they were easily confronted by the crown. However, the civil wars of the mid-fifteenth century had drawn out the worst aspects of lordship as leaders sought to dominate localities and intimidate or exclude the servants of rivals. The alignment of aristocrats in the struggles for the crown between 1455 and 1485 perhaps heightened the politically sensitive aspects of the sheriffs' role in a way that was not apparent during earlier, more peaceful, times.

Sir Edward Stanley's appointment for life as sheriff of the county palatine of Lancaster in 1485, for example, invited complete Stanley command of the legal and lordship systems in the north-west region. Sir Edward's biased dominance of legal process – packing juries and retaining officers – was alleged by Stanley opponents in 1502. Sir Edward was indicted and fined for illegal retaining in 1502 and 1506, and was guilty of keeping profits from the estates of convicted felons. His activities were by no means unique during Henry's reign. The hereditary shrievalty of Westmorland belonged to Lord Clifford, but his control of the post was closely watched. In June 1507 he bought a pardon for 4,000 marks for fixing a *quo warranto* inquest into his right to the office, for influencing the coroner of the county, and for forfeiting earlier related obligations.

Where failings were uncovered, Henry demanded fines for the discharge of offenders. It is likely that informers and opponents of those in post provided the evidence that generated royal investigation of particular officials. Since JPs and sheriffs were from exactly the same county elite it is debatable whether there was any real censure of their behaviour when their friends and colleagues would circulate through the same posts in future. The shared outlook of all senior officers in a county made it difficult for Henry to disrupt existing patterns of lordship and affinity.

This was why he relied excessively on some whom he trusted, like the prominent pre-Bosworth household knights, and attempted to use outsiders to break up deeply entrenched dominance of others.[21] Henry turned to unorthodox means of thrusting crown influence into the heart of local networks. This was done through a shake up of who received crown appointments and what was expected of them, the demand for bonds after almost every transaction with the crown, and an almost obsessive scrutiny by the council of performance in post and observance of statutes by those representing the king locally. Even then, all but the most treasonous rebels were allowed an opportunity to pay a suitable price to ensure rehabilitation.

Supervision of JPs and sheriffs fell to the royal council. Evidence survives for around eight cases before the committee against corrupt juries under the 1487 Star Chamber Act, and perhaps a further five under a 1495 statute against jurors who took bribes. Despite this small body of evidence, there is little indication that the common law courts shared in the clampdown on these offences. King Henry's close personal supervision of council business ensured that he could intervene readily to control local officials whose work and conduct were bound by statute, proclamation, and direct royal censure. This approach allowed Henry to bypass the more rigid common law punishments and to impose bonds or to extract stringent conditions for his pardon or leniency. An approach to abuses of lordship and the law that was more supple and subtle than that laid down in statutes was a very powerful tool.

# 7

## LORDSHIP, THE CROWN, AND THE REGIONS

### NOBLE POWER AND THE RULE OF THE COUNTIES

A thorough study of Henry's approach to regional aristocratic power would make a lengthy book in its own right. This section can only offer a limited snapshot. Henry used different techniques to achieve the degree of control he sought in the networks addressed below. In Lancashire, once the loyalty of the established power-brokers was called into question, he promoted a takeover of regional offices by local gentry recruited to the royal household. This displaced the entrenched influence of the Stanley family and its servants, and allowed a redefinition of their regional role. In Kent he exploited to breaking point the talents of the leading royal servant, Sir Richard Guildford. The king ruthlessly cast Guildford aside and accepted the natural progression of Lord Abergavenny, his noble supplanter, albeit with a complex and rigorous system of financial penalties to ensure loyalty. In Suffolk, Henry maintained the authority of one of his trusted noble allies because he was entirely sure that the earl of Oxford would uphold Tudor influence. Henry allowed Oxford to develop his network to eclipse other nobles in the region. Yet the king was pragmatic enough to make provision for how things would change after Oxford's death. He allowed the recovery of Thomas Howard, earl of Surrey, and ensured that Oxford and Surrey worked cooperatively after 1501.

*Allies and enemies I: Henry VII, Sir Richard Guildford
and problems of influence in the royal dominance of Kent,
1485–1506*

Sir Richard Guildford's rewards after Bosworth involved him at the centre of Tudor rule, yet his career was dogged by a sequence of financial setbacks that prevented him from realising the possibilities his service and personal bond with Henry should have brought. Guildford was a vital cog in all aspects of Henry VII's government machine, yet the demands of household office and regional leadership eventually combined to such a degree that his effectiveness collapsed in both areas.

The Guildford family had made some connection to Margaret Beaufort's household in the mid-1470s, when Richard Guildford and Reginald Bray coordinated loans and marriage arrangements. This was probably Guildford's way into the pro-Tudor conspiracy after 1483. Margaret Beaufort's influence over her inexperienced son during the first months of the reign ensured that a known quantity like Guildford received suitable reward for previous service.

Kent was a county traditionally dominated by the influence of members of the royal household. Before Bosworth, Henry's band of exiles had been boosted by the defection of many Kentish knights who had been prominent under Edward IV. Along with Guildford, his own father Sir John, Sir Edward Poynings, Sir John Fogge, and several others had all been rebels in 1483.

Guildford's role in organising Henry's Bosworth campaign placed him at the head of supporters of the Tudor crown. Responsibility for running Kentish administration and justice fell immediately upon him and those others associated with Henry's victory. They were appointed to the first Tudor commission of the peace within Kent, and by 1488 were established as royal servants and councillors. This was the stable base on which Henry sought to secure his national authority during his early years.

The strong royal connection in Kent only highlighted the weakness of Henry's authority in other regions. He exploited such links by demanding extra effort from the likes of Guildford and Poynings. In Guildford's case, the pressure to perform multiple roles began to draw out what might have been existing financial difficulties, since in February 1486 he faced arrest for £160 owed to a London alderman. The machinery of the

Tudor crown may also have stuttered during its early months in control, as Guildford had to petition for payment of his wages as master of ordnance – a vitally important role as Henry's opponents began to gather.

As a courtier, the king relied on him to buy gifts, such as a gold collar for a Flemish ambassador in 1486, yet he inexplicably lost a lucrative honorary post as one of the chamberlains of the Exchequer in May 1487. King Henry was alarmed enough to examine the matter personally. Despite background money problems, the range of Guildford's responsibilities and skills quickly expanded. He attended the royal council regularly, was a personal servant of the king, and organised the jousts at the coronation of Queen Elizabeth in October 1487. Between Michaelmas 1489 and Easter 1490, he organised military supplies for the English expedition to Brittany – including the construction of Henry's most powerful ship, the *Regent*.

Guildford moved closer to the king after Perkin Warbeck's appearance, when he became controller of the royal household by August 1495. His role as master of horse was even more indicative of his personal relationship with Henry. This was one of the most sensitive appointments within the royal household, since the master accompanied the king when travelling and hunting – times when much of the regime's vital counsel, advice, and decision-making was worked out informally. Guildford's strong personal connection to Henry VII's Beaufort relatives Sir David Owen, chief carver, and Sir Charles Somerset, captain of the guard, also indicated that he remained acceptable to Henry's mother. Other members of the elite recognised Guildford's position. He became one of the key intermediaries between the court, country, and the king. In 1501, for example, he passed bribes for royal favour to Henry, and took money to obtain wardships for other lords. His appointment as knight of the garter in 1500 placed him in the inner circle of Tudor servants.

With key roles at Westminster, Guildford's prominence in Kent and Sussex was also extended. In October 1487 he was granted the manor and lordship of Higham, but was obliged to build defensive towers there and at Camber at his own cost. The king clearly trusted Sir Richard's regional influence to secure the Kentish coastline. His presence was enhanced by control over the port of Winchelsea. Guildford's command of the political resources of the region led to the arrest of rebels in 1493, and he was instructed by the king to thank the Commons of Kent for resisting Warbeck's landing at Deal in July 1495. By 1497, Guildford's political connection was credited with controlling the traditionally volatile Kentish yeomen, who did not join the rebels at Blackheath.

It was a lack of major landholding that seems to have concerned Guildford, since his efforts to acquire it became increasingly desperate. In the parliament of October 1495, he secured an act that allowed him to sell Kentish land on the open market. Two years later he commenced a series of agreements with three local monasteries that eventually led to the acquisition of 5,000 acres of marshland on the Kent–Sussex coast. This was not the type of gift to provide easy income in the short term, yet this seems to have been Guildford's chosen way of acquiring a major estate. Although men like Guildford had a great personal investment in Henry's success, without land they faced a potential drought of royal patronage under his natural successor, and even fewer opportunities should the Tudors be deposed. Guildford was well supplied with income from office, but he sought land rather than more fragile political success for his wealth and income. In his case, the king's determination to retain royal lands in his own hands did cause problems for his loyal followers, who might have expected a greater share of the Tudor windfall.

By 1503, his growing debts were transferred to the management of the abbot of Battle. Other problems with payments for wardships, and for the costs of repairing the royal ships, forced Guildford to fall back on the help of friends like Reginald Bray. Even the king showed personal favour to Sir Richard by reducing the costs of mortgages and leases.

Guildford's financial failings did not have a major impact on his status because for much of the reign he functioned with the assurance and authority that Henry required. Guildford's wider circle of Kentish gentry held similar levels of responsibility. The Kentish network, based upon service in the royal household, also deterred any noble challenge to the gentry-led hierarchy within the county itself. The two resident nobles within the county had a distinctly Yorkist background. John Broke, Lord Cobham, and George Neville, second Lord Abergavenny, were related to Richard III's friend John Howard, duke of Norfolk. This connection brought them little favour under Henry VII, and Kent had little difficulty with powerful noble retinues. This was to change with the accession George, third Lord Abergavenny, in 1492.

Kent remained a difficult county to govern on behalf of the crown. Ten commissions of the peace and three commissions of oyer and terminer were issued in Kent between 1497 and 1503.[1] Evidence suggests that Lord Abergavenny and his retinue were at the root of many disturbances during that period. His household servants were frequent defendants before the courts and Henry's council. Many controlling bonds also involved Neville's retainers after 1499. A royal proclamation of 10 March 1502 addressed the problems of retaining in Kent, with Guildford and Abergavenny singled out. Abergavenny was indicted for retaining offences in Trinity term 1503, and forfeited a related bond the following November. In fact, the declining situation in Kent might have prompted the review of the retaining laws that resulted in the new statute of 1504.

Abergavenny was able to become more assertive precisely because the grip of royal control in Kent weakened. The political resources of the king's household officers such as Guildford and Poynings became thinly spread as Henry's reliance upon his pre-Bosworth supporters increased after Prince Arthur and then the queen died in close succession. Guildford's money problems affected his ability to carry out his political responsibilities. Abergavenny's aggression accelerated his decline at precisely the period in which Henry needed the range of skills and personal qualities that had previously made Guildford such an effective royal servant. The re-emergence of Tudor dynastic insecurity after 1503 made Abergavenny's actions even more threatening than they might previously have been, especially as he seemed to be recruiting servants with previous Yorkist connections, such as Edward Ferrers. The later discovery of his rebellious intentions in 1497 only heightened the king's suspicions further.[2]

The extent of Lord Abergavenny's transformation is found in a 1507 indictment in King's Bench for illegal retaining. Between June 1504 and December 1506, Abergavenny actively recruited followers directly from the previously dominant royal network in Kent. He retained twenty-five gentlemen, including members of the prominent Gainsford, Culpepper, and Appleton families, and hundreds of yeomen and artisans. The growing retinue was based upon Abergavenny's seat at Birling near Maidstone, but also impinged on areas where Guildford had influence, such as his lordship of Cranbrook. It is noticeable that there was no challenge to the local influence of Henry's other Kentish servants such as Sir Edward Poynings near Folkestone, or Sir John Fogge at Ashford.

The rise in Abergavenny's attractiveness as a lord was most marked by the recruitment of Edward Culpepper and George Norton, who were members of families previously associated with the Guildfords. Another retainer, Alexander Culpepper, was sheriff of Kent in 1503, while Lewis Clifford had married Sir Richard Guildford's sister Benetta. By 1504 there was a real change in Abergavenny's attractiveness as a leader. Many of the sons, grandsons and close kinsmen of the rebels of 1483 were then established within Abergavenny's retinue.

This shift in local power directly challenged the system of service established in Kent since 1485. It also became a personal feud. At Easter 1503 Abergavenny's household servants attacked the manor court at Aylesford near Maidstone, where Sir Richard's son George was steward. Guildford servants then assaulted Maidstone men at a market at Sir Richard's manor of Tenterden. In May 1506 George Guildford was pardoned for illegally influencing the jury against Abergavenny's servants in a resulting lawsuit.

Henry also stoked the animosity on both sides. From 1496 Guildford had controlled Southfrith Park, but in December 1500 Abergavenny was made keeper of this major hunting area. He then used servants from Southfrith in the riot at Aylesford. This grant was also a token of Abergavenny's progress in the king's favour after 1503. Just one week after Queen Elizabeth's death, Abergavenny was made master forester of Ashdown, a major duchy of Lancaster estate in Kent. He offered three northern manors for the endowment of Henry VII's chapel at Westminster in July 1504, and continued his good favour by sending gifts to the king, such as a hind at Christmas 1505.

Guildford's decline became obvious to everyone in July 1505, when he was arrested for not returning accounts as master of ordnance between March 1486 and November 1494. Guildford's lands were already in possession of John Nailor, who occupied them the previous month under a separate action for debt. Abergavenny perhaps timed the manipulation of this situation for maximum effect, since John Nailor was his kinsman by marriage. Guildford was imprisoned in London's Fleet prison for five months before he appeared in the Exchequer. Around the same time, his government colleagues, such as the master of the rolls Christopher Bainbridge, attempted to secure money Guildford owed to them. Even after Sir Richard's death, his sons entered into repayment agreements with senior figures like William Warham, archbishop of Canterbury.

In his will of April 1506, Guildford's debts had swamped the value of his estate. All he owned went towards satisfying his creditors. This evidently took many years, since Guildford's second wife, Joan Vaux, seems never to have received an annuity of 50 marks left by her husband, and Henry VIII felt sufficiently charitable to pay her £20 yearly by 1514. Sir Richard's private debts remained a long-term problem, and the settlement of his estate was still the subject of a chancery suit in 1536.

Guildford had handled vast sums as master of ordnance, yet if he were embezzling he gained little material benefit, since he struggled to pay for wardships and land deals. Guildford certainly accomplished much for his royal master, and it is Henry's reliance on his skills that probably delayed a reckoning over the financial formalities of his posts. By 1505, Abergavenny's lordship in Kent was becoming more aggressive in direct relationship to Guildford's declining leadership. The dangers of continued crown reliance upon the Guildford connection were outweighed by the necessity of controlling Abergavenny's potentially dangerous lordship.

Against a background of renewed Yorkist threat, Henry could afford no weak links in his chain of command. Abergavenny possessed the solid service network and charismatic leadership that was attracting clients in Kent. The timing of his prosecution, and his precisely calculated fine of £70,650 for retaining 471 men over a period of two and a half years, allowed the king absolute control over how Neville's lordship would operate, if at all. This fine was reduced to a more manageable £5,000, payable over ten years, and Abergavenny found sureties to guarantee his allegiance. He was also excluded from Kent, Surrey or Sussex without licence. This compromise preserved Neville's status on the king's own terms. Once he was financially at the mercy of the crown, Henry was in a position to encourage Neville's loyalty in a more productive way. All his debts to the crown were cancelled by a full pardon at Henry VIII's accession.

Henry was ruthless but realistic. The minor gentry of Kent had already moved towards Abergavenny's service. The crown could not intervene directly without heightening the problem. Although Guildford's political usefulness had gone, Henry evidently felt a deep personal obligation to him as one of his most consistent loyalists. Once Guildford's legal and financial position was decided, the king instructed the Exchequer to cease any action against him in December 1505. He remained within the royal household, but by spring 1506 he had taken the drastic decision to travel on pilgrimage to the Holy Land. On 4 April 1506 he secured a royal pardon and made his will at Rye three days later. He died shortly after reaching Jerusalem later that summer.

Henry intervened decisively to preserve and control Abergavenny's status, whereas, despite some supportive gestures, he allowed Sir Richard Guildford's decline to continue and eventually sanctioned the legal action that undermined him completely. After 1503 loyalty to the Tudors was more important than previous allegiance to Beaufort, Lancaster or York. Henry was forging a new dynasty and Abergavenny had demonstrated himself to be more controllable, and therefore more effective, than Guildford. Although Neville's loyalty was closely enforced, his leadership contrasted with Guildford's ruined finances and waning authority by 1505. Despite Beaufort ties, and his long history of service to Henry, Guildford was effectively retired because the king did not believe in his competence. This shows the harsh nature of Henry VII's regime in the continual struggle for dynastic security.

## Allies and enemies II: Henry VII, the Stanley family and how the north-west was won for the crown

Stanley dominance of the north-west presented Henry VII with a complex problem. In 1485 Henry was duke of Lancaster and earl of Chester, and royal manors formed the core of lordship in the region. During the fifteenth century, the increasingly powerful Stanleys had collected many crown stewardships for themselves and their servants. This fact, and a relentless accumulation of private estates, made the family the major political force between Cheshire and Westmorland. Henry owed his crown to the action of the Stanley forces at Bosworth, but their support was hardly deep-rooted. Despite their history of ruthless calculation and self-interest, Henry was prepared to trust the Stanleys because Thomas, Lord Stanley (earl of Derby from October 1485), was married to his mother, and he was one of the few experienced nobles to have survived service to both Edward IV and Richard III.

Although the family as a whole was well rewarded as they backed the Tudor crown between 1485 and 1490, the consolidation of their powerful regional status probably conflicted with Henry's cautious approach to the English nobility. Stanley influence in the north-west emphasised Henry's reliance on a narrow elite over which the new crown had little direct control. In consolidating his victory, Henry by necessity entrenched the influence of his few trusted aristocratic supporters, and he made it harder for the crown to wrest authority from their control when it was in a stronger position.

Stanley rewards after Bosworth were sweeping when compared to those of other important Tudor servants. The cooperation of the family with Richard III made this all the more remarkable, and suggests that King Henry was wary of how the family would accommodate Tudor rule without flattering awards of lands and offices. As well as becoming earl of Derby, Thomas Stanley was chief steward of the duchy lands in the north by May 1486. In February 1489 the north-western estates of Yorkists attainted since 1485 were granted to the earl. Sir William became the king's chamberlain before November 1485 and he was confirmed in other appointments. He and his servants were exempt from the act of resumption of 1485. The earl's heir, Lord Strange, received lands that were more scattered, but some were in the north-west. His youngest son, Sir Edward, became sheriff of the palatinate of Lancaster for life from October 1485, and held important stewardships and estates in north Lancashire.

The family consolidated the interlocking network of their affinities through marriage to regional gentry, mutual enfeoffment of land,[3] and arbitration of disputes. Many of their associates were also granted royal annuities, and received subordinate posts in local government. Legal disputes also indicated that the earl preserved his position through maintenance, embracery and illegal retaining. His careful navigation through the turmoil of the Wars of the Roses, and the refinement of personal power that this unchallenged status allowed, left the Stanley family as the one great regional force within England by 1490.

Henry's personal debt to, and close relationship with, Thomas, earl of Derby, overcame any concern at Stanley loyalty during the first decade of Tudor rule. During this period the Stanleys were the military backbone of the new regime, supplying impressive retinues to all Tudor armies and expeditions before 1492. Once Sir William Stanley dabbled with treason, however, their importance at the heart of the Tudor regime and in the north-west meant that any wavering of Stanley loyalty weakened the power of the Tudor crown directly. Henry was most concerned that while the Stanleys acted in a cooperative way when dominating the north-west, individually their reliability was potentially suspect. Whereas Lord Stanley had been a political chameleon since the 1450s, his brother Sir William had been identified with the Yorkists since 1459. When Perkin Warbeck declared himself to be one of Edward IV's sons, Henry could not be sure that Sir William's curiosity would not drag the rest of the inconsistent Stanley group into rebellion. Stanley's treason removed Henry's trust in the long-term commitment to Tudor rule of the other Stanleys.

The reappraisal of Stanley power initiated by Sir William Stanley's execution prompted a rare royal visit to Lancashire and Cheshire in the summer of 1495. This focus of the king and royal household specifically upon Stanley lordship must have been a very stressful time for Derby as he no doubt calculated how best to overcome the disgrace of his brother's treason. A later tradition suggested that during the visit Henry VII was conducted by his host to the top of Lathom House to view the grounds. Derby's jester then pointed to the drop and prompted 'Tom remember Will' – inciting the earl to push the king over in revenge for his treatment of Sir William (presumably out of the king's hearing). Although anecdotal, this story emphasises that the Stanleys had previously been seen as a united group within Lancashire.

Once cracks appeared in Stanley dominance, others began to push for their own independent rights. The first flashpoint came over the building of a new bridge to replace the ferry at Warrington, over which the king would enter Lancashire in 1495. A contemporary poem, The *Ballad of Bewsey*, suggests that Derby and his nephew, Sir Thomas Butler of Bewsey (who was lord of Warrington), clashed over how the royal party would be received. Derby surely wanted to show his regional dominance in the best light at that time. He had already aggressively tried to recruit Warrington families into his retinue and had clashed with Butler's servants over access rights to the bridge. Butler's resistance upset the earl's plans and Henry very shrewdly identified this local confrontation as a key opportunity by which to intervene to confront Stanley control of the region. Sir William's defection gave the king a pressing motive to restrain Stanley power, but events in Warrington provided a means to bring it about.

During the lifetime of the first earl of Derby the squeeze on Stanley power was applied slowly. Henry bound the Stanleys more tightly to the terms of their posts as regional office holders. He demanded the collection of lapsed duties within Stanley lordships, including arrears of customary rents in Congleton in 1488, and the revival of an obsolete forest tax throughout Lancashire in 1502. Sir Edward Stanley's performance as sheriff of Lancashire was scrutinised, and he was given little scope for personal gain when granted authority to mine for lead in Bowland forest in July 1504. The inability of the Stanleys to prevent the implementation of these unpopular measures tarnished their dominance.

Without Sir William Stanley's ready access to the king (and his control over others wishing to attend Henry at court), the Stanleys lost ground in the struggle for the ear of an increasingly suspicious monarch. This became manifest locally as growing boldness on the part of other powerful north-western families such as the Savages. There was some trouble between servants of both families once William Stanley was identified as a traitor, and they backed rival parties in the protracted Pilkington–Ainsworth inheritance dispute over Mellor in north-western Derbyshire. At Westminster, too, the rapid rise of Thomas Savage from dean of the king's chapel to president of the council, and eventually archbishop of York, eclipsed any remaining Stanley influence within the household. It was during this period also that the core of a royal affinity, based on service in the royal household, began to be formed within Lancashire. This development, and Margaret Beaufort's permanent separation from her husband in 1499, suggests that Henry gradually loosened the ties that connected the Stanleys to the core of Tudor power during the later 1490s.

The Stanley–Butler dispute remained a focus for regional unrest. The Stanleys challenged Sir Thomas Butler's title in a number of manors and sought to bring his tenants into their service. In 1499, Henry Garnett, a tenant of Warrington, withheld rent and sought Stanley arbitration over an unpaid annuity from the manor. Butler complained that Garnett had moved directly into Stanley service. Henry Risley also joined the Stanley retinue and lost little time in leading attacks on Butler's rent collectors. Even in 1505, Sir Henry Halsall, steward of Derby's household, disputed Butler's right to receive homage for lands in Halsall. Butler was forced to protest to the royal council. Henry established Butler as the core of a group of north-western gentry marginalised from Stanley power. This group, which included Sir John Booth, Sir Richard Bold and Henry Farringdon, rapidly saw service in the royal household where they were moulded into a unified group of north-western servants.

This crown connection gave them greater confidence to confront abuses of Stanley power. At a Whitsun market in Warrington in May 1499, servants of James Stanley and Lord Strange bullied a yeoman of the crown, James Cokeson, into retracting a royal proclamation and replacing it with one from Derby that suggested that Butler was answerable to the Stanleys for his authority. Butler's servants publicly protested that the king's business was being disrupted, and the Stanley servants soon backed down. The range of crown measures to contain Stanley power was achieving results by 1502. In this year Butler won a case against Derby in the royal council over land in Great Marton.

Violence escalated after the deaths of George, Lord Strange, in 1503 and the earl himself in July 1504. Servants of the king's knight Sir John Booth and James Stanley, warden of Manchester College, clashed in a series of riots, attempted murders, and violent assaults around Manchester during 1504. This activity was a symptom of the further fragmentation of Stanley authority, the absence of experienced leadership, and perhaps Stanley vulnerability to the growing crown presence in the north-west. The Stanley affinity had been built around the personality and lordship of Thomas, Lord Stanley, after 1459. His long career provided a stable period in which to groom Lord Strange to succeed. The deaths of Strange and Derby left the inheritance with Sir Thomas Stanley III, who had lived quietly at Beethom in Westmorland. His inexperience of high politics gave Henry VII a further opportunity to accelerate the disruption of Stanley power more subtly.

Family deaths by 1504 heralded the disintegration of the relationship of the new earl of Derby and his uncle Sir Edward Stanley. The details of this family dispute are unclear, but even in 1521 the second earl remembered the great unkindness that his uncle had done him. The king responded by courting Sir Edward's service. He remained in office as sheriff when many other Stanley servants were replaced after the earldom changed hands in 1504. A pardon for illegal retaining in March 1506 cost him only a bond for £200, compared with James Stanley's fine of £145,000 for the same offence four months later. Sir Edward also escaped the clampdown on Stanley followers after James Stanley's prosecution.

The 2nd earl was isolated and inexperienced, but the king needed him to master his role. For this reason he suffered only enough financial pressure to remind him of the king's power. Henry immediately forced the new earl to acknowledge debts of £1,865 owed by his grandfather, with repayment by obligations. The crown demanded other payments for livery of his lands and to loans from the king. The freedom of the Stanleys to exercise their lordship became immediately tied to the king's management of their debt. Between 1504 and 1506 Derby was encouraged to consolidate command over his grandfather's affinity. The king's aim may have been to allow the establishment of personal ties, but then to manipulate the earl's financial freedom to perform his expected role as a regional lord. The Stanley affinity was still essential to stability in the north-west, but it was to be wholly dependent on royal goodwill for its influence.

James Stanley's retaining offence escalated the scale of Henry's existing attitude to Stanley power. The chief Stanleys and their retainers were burdened with extensive bonds that substantially increased their debt. In what was a remarkable promotion, given his violent disruption of the peace in Lancashire, James Stanley became bishop of Ely on 18 July 1506. The timing of his prosecution and swift removal from Lancashire suggests that Henry wanted him out of the way – if not to isolate Derby and his affinity, then perhaps to diffuse growing tensions between the king's men and Stanley servants.

Following this development, crown activity was swift. On 10 July 1506, Derby was bound under separate obligations totalling over £3,000, and he agreed to deliver to the king parcels of land. In August, Derby was obliged to buy a 'pardon' from the king for 6,000 marks, half of which was to be found by sureties. By November, he again entered an individual obligation for 4,500 marks. The king also monitored Derby's private financial dealings, recording in 1506 that a loan of £800 to the first earl remained unpaid. It is significant that bonds involving Sir James Stanley himself did not begin to appear until November. Even then, Henry targeted the links between the Stanleys, their leading servants, and often junior or newly recruited clients.

Of thirteen obligations in 1506, nine involved Derby or James Stanley with servants such as the previously mentioned Henry Risley, and senior retainers like Sir Henry Keighley. To emphasise that Derby's regional position then depended on appeasing the king's management of debts and obligations, Henry bound the earl by indenture in a further fifteen recognisances of £400 each at the close of 1506. These debts continued to be manipulated and it was not until 1545 that land exchanges with the crown finally cleared a debt that was over forty years old.

Royal financial pressure ran in parallel to a squeeze on Stanley control of duchy patronage. In June 1505, the king's north-western knights, including Butler, Booth, Bold and Farringdon, dominated the first commission of the peace after the death of the 1st earl of Derby. The Stanleys also lost their grip on crown office. In June 1505, Butler became master forester of the forests around Liverpool, steward of the town itself, and governor of the king's tenants there. This gave Butler great authority in the Stanley stronghold of West Derby hundred.[4]

Sir John Booth became receiver of the duchy in Lancashire in December 1504. The Stanleys had held this post since 1461. The following March, Butler's friend and ally Sir Richard Bold received the stewardship of the hundred of West Derby and the lordship of West Derby itself. The stewardship of other duchy hundreds, manors, and tenants, such as Blackburn and Clitheroe, went to Butler and the other royal household men. Most of these offices had been held by the chief steward of the duchy in Lancashire, who had been the earl of Derby until 1504. The removal of this vast array of patronage from Stanley control further compounded the difficulties faced by the new earl of Derby as he established his authority.

Towards the end of Henry VII's reign the Stanleys were no longer dominant in the north-west as they once were, and the household network established after 1504 checked their remaining influence. The controlled way that Henry pressed the royal rights to Stanley debt suggests that the solvency of the family remained essential to a balanced representation of the king's authority in the region.

### Allies and enemies III: the crown, the earl of Oxford and the containment of the de la Pole influence in East Anglia, 1485–1506

The exercise of lordship in East Anglia provided Henry VII with some of his most difficult challenges. The region was a fertile ground for conspiracy and contained the main lands of two of the foremost Yorkist families – the de la Poles and Howards. It was also the homeland of Henry's most loyal noble ally John de Vere, 13th earl of Oxford. In trying to manage this region and its range of powerful figures, Henry was forced to juggle his immediate security and the long-term planning for the future of his dynasty.

Under the Yorkist kings, the de la Pole family were part of a small East Anglian elite. The unspectacular leadership of John, duke of Suffolk, prevented them from becoming regionally dominant, and offered an opportunity for the rapidly rising Howard family to take the lead in local politics and become influential national figures under Richard III. The duke of Suffolk's eldest son, John, earl of Lincoln, became Richard III's nearest adult heir after 1484, but it was the Howards who invested most in the Yorkist kings, and consequently suffered the greatest disaster at Bosworth. The restored earl of Oxford quickly absorbed their authority in Henry's early years.

Oxford had to accommodate existing networks. The task of imposing himself was made easier initially by the appointment of John, Lord Fitzwalter, as head of the service side of the Tudor royal household. Oxford's strategy of forgiveness and containment worked well. His defence of the countess of Surrey's interests while her husband was in prison was commended. He also courted other junior nobles like Lord Willoughby of Eresby, who appeared to be willing to work with the new regime.

Up to 1498, Edmund de la Pole also ingratiated himself well with Henry. Edmund was under age until 1493, and therefore escaped any involvement in the treason of his elder brother the earl of Lincoln in 1487. Since Edmund's father also declined a role in Tudor national politics, the family did not suffer such a setback as they might have expected after Lincoln's attainder. Edmund seems to have been close to his first cousin Queen Elizabeth. He is mentioned many times at the ceremonials held in the early years of the reign: such as Elizabeth's coronation, Garter chapter meetings, and Christmas festivities. At court he associated with Henry Bourchier, earl of Essex, Lord William Courtenay, and other young nobles of Yorkist blood, who were in much the same social position. That these nobles, related to Henry's queen through marriage, were fairly prominent at court when still minors suggests an attempt by Henry to create genuine loyalty to the Tudor crown among a generation of young peers.

In November 1492, during the invasion of France, Suffolk cooperated closely with the earls of Essex and Oxford at the siege of Boulogne. He took part in jousting and court entertainments, and welcomed the king to his Oxfordshire manor in September 1495. Along with the earl of Essex, de la Pole commanded royal forces at Blackheath on 17 June 1497. At a more local level, Suffolk appeared on various legal commissions after 1494, and he was part of the East Anglian bench of JPs until February 1501. For the first decade of Henry's reign and more, therefore, the young Yorkist nobles avoided the connection with treason that seduced many former gentry servants of Edward IV and his sons.

For Edmund de la Pole, this promising start went disastrously off course during the late 1490s. His discontent with Henry VII probably originated in the treatment of his family after Lincoln's attainder in 1487. John, duke of Suffolk, had settled many manors on Lincoln, but his son's forfeiture robbed the family of considerable income. Although Edmund secured some of this inheritance, the crown retained other manors unjustly when he inherited the duchy as a minor in 1491. Consequently, when Edmund came of age as duke of Suffolk in 1493, he did not possess sufficient income to maintain the status of a duke. As a compromise, in February 1493, he accepted the title of earl of Suffolk in exchange for certain of his brother's manors. The accompanying financial conditions demanded £5,000 in yearly payments of £200 – almost a lifelong burden for the young earl.

For a noble who had spent much of his minority in the public glare of the court, his resentment at the loss of his senior rank perhaps hurt deeply. Suffolk seems to have possessed a personality to make much of an apparently minor affront, and this may also have contributed to disillusionment with the king. More importantly, this demotion must have had some impact on the financial difficulties that were a major cause of Suffolk's ultimate defection. After his attainder in 1503, the annual income from Suffolk's estates for 1503–04 totalled around £876. The yearly payments demanded for the recovery of Lincoln's manors perhaps represented a quarter of his revenue.

The king thereafter took a closer interest in Suffolk. From 1498 onwards, he experienced an increase in legal pressure, both locally and at Westminster. Suffolk had done nothing to incur Henry's suspicion, and his service at Blackheath was creditable. The king viewed things differently. He might have wondered if Suffolk was content to serve the king only through loyalty to Queen Elizabeth. Suffolk's lineage, landholding, and connections made him a potential ally of Warbeck and therefore a similar threat to the Tudor crown as Sir William Stanley had been. Henry no doubt felt justified in testing his loyalty.

In 1498 and 1499, Suffolk was summoned to appear in King's Bench over certain unnamed articles on the king's behalf. He repeatedly failed to appear and suffered seizure of Yorkshire lands as a result. More amazingly, in Michaelmas 1498 he was indicted for the murder of one Thomas Crue in the parish of All Hallows beside the Tower of London. Also involved in the same incident were his upper-class drinking friends

Lord William Courtenay, Thomas Neville, and William Brandon. Henry ordered that the case be stopped. To force an obligation upon the earl, he expected Suffolk to plead for pardon. Rather than suffer this humiliation, Suffolk immediately left England for French territory via Calais without the king's permission.

Suffolk perhaps feared that he was being forced into a corner by a hardening crown attitude towards him. In January 1499, East Anglia was once more strongly linked to dynastic plotting as Ralph Wilford's plot was crushed by the earl of Oxford. When Suffolk again fled overseas in August 1499 – just as the Tower conspiracy to spring the earl of Warwick emerged – Henry did not have to think too hard to connect Suffolk to events. At the end of September, Sir Richard Guildford and Richard Hatton were dispatched to Brussels to treat with Philip the Fair for Suffolk's return. They threatened a trade embargo to secure cooperation. Suffolk was personally assured that only by accepting Henry VII's mercy would he be able to return to England and recover something of his former status. His personal relationship with Henry was now coloured by the clear suggestion of treason.

In Michaelmas term 1499, probably immediately upon his return, Suffolk was obliged to re-grant lands until £1,000 had been paid to the king. At the same time, the earl of Oxford agreed to monitor Margaret, countess of Suffolk. Soon Suffolk's servants Thomas Wyndham and John Wiseman were fined for not appearing before the king and council in connection with his time in Flanders.

Suffolk's absence abroad, and the king's growing suspicion of his allegiance, brought his local influence under threat. In May 1500 he had lost a lawsuit over possession of land in Norfolk. In another case in 1501, Suffolk claimed that a yeoman, William Ryvet, was his bondman. This again was brought to the attention of the king. Suffolk was defeated and paid substantial damages of £100 to Ryvet.

Having offended Henry once and submitting to the king's financial mercy, Suffolk found it increasingly unbearable to remain in England. As Francis Bacon stated, Henry VII had put a 'cloud upon him' after his first flight to Flanders,[5] and in August 1501 he again fled the country, this time with his brother, Richard, to the court of Maximilian. Suffolk's credibility as a dynastic rival to Henry VII was to develop almost entirely overseas.

Suffolk's attempts to rouse his tenants to rebellion were completely extinguished by the earl of Oxford in the autumn of 1501. On 10 October a commission was directed to Oxford and Lord Willoughby, 'to take security for the allegiance of rebels ... followers of Edmund de la Pole, late earl of Suffolk' in the East Anglian counties.[6] Sixty-one individuals appeared before Oxford at Castle Headingham between 10 October and 11 December, and entered recognisances swearing their allegiance either to the crown in person or by acting as sureties to enforce the loyalty of others.

The largest group were yeomen tenants of de la Pole's west Suffolk estates, but there was a strong Norfolk presence also. Men from his possessions around Ewelme in the Thames valley appeared before a separate commission. Twenty-four men of gentry rank appeared in bonds of up to £200. There was one knight – Sir William Waldegrave of Bures, and fifteen esquires, including Thomas Wyndham and John Wiseman.

None of those brought before Oxford were attainted with Suffolk in 1504. Any rising on his behalf was nipped in the bud by Oxford's intervention. The key to the successful containment of Suffolk was intelligence of his intentions and movements. This information was passed to Henry by a network of spies and agents – active both abroad and throughout England. After Suffolk's first flight in 1499, Oxford had mobilised retainers such as Sir John Paston to acquire information on Suffolk's supporters. In the summer of 1503, the king authorised Sir Richard Guildford to send one of his servants to infiltrate Suffolk's circle of exiles and his likely supporters in England. Sir William Waldegrave might have performed a similar function within Suffolk's English affinity. He was knighted at the marriage of Prince Arthur and was eventually an executor of Oxford's will.

Another factor in de la Pole's discomfort was Henry's rapid restoration of Howard fortunes after 1500. Suffolk's desertion of England in 1499 made it clear that the de la Poles had lost all chance of regional leadership. The earl of Surrey probably returned to Suffolk in January 1501 when he became Lord Treasurer of England. Surrey's effective and loyal service in the north had proved his worth for a more prominent national role, and he had maintained ties of family and landholding in the region. The Howard network was growing steadily after 1500, and it was Surrey, not Oxford, who attracted the service of many of the de la Pole followers bound in 1501. The implication here is that King Henry sanctioned Surrey's recovery at Oxford's expense. Howard was only a few years younger than Oxford, but he did have an heir, while Oxford had none. By bolstering the Howard affinity, Henry was looking at a longer-term solution to lordship in the East Anglian region.

There was a degree of understanding and cooperation between the earls of Surrey and Oxford in the aftermath of de la Pole's treason. Servants of both lords served on commissions with local crown servants like Henry's attorney James Hobart. Many who had been involved with the earl of Suffolk in 1501 appeared on the commissions of the peace for the first time after Surrey returned from the north. Surrey's success in accepting men with previous de la Pole connections gave the king confidence that the East Anglian region was run securely. Oxford and the king continued to monitor the Yorkist undercurrent in Suffolk for as long as Edmund de la Pole remained overseas. In May 1504, for example, Oxford oversaw more bonds for the sons of men like Thomas Wyndham, who had followed Suffolk abroad in 1499 or 1501.

Henry VII probably misjudged Suffolk. In an effort to crush Yorkist sympathies during the mid-1490s, he probably achieved the opposite effect of awakening Suffolk's sense of injustice and dynastic status. Despite his royal blood, Suffolk had shown every sign of following the example of the earls of Essex and Surrey in combining a fruitful career at court with loyal service in the provinces. His closeness to Queen Elizabeth could have continued to consolidate Tudor power, and he certainly had the potential to achieve the successful recovery managed by the Howards before 1513. His failure to generate any rebellion in England or military support on the Continent suggests that he had become little more than a token figure in international politics. It also indicates the development of Henry VII's information network, which pre-empted much of Suffolk's manoeuvring.

Even after the chance arrival of Archduke Philip in England in January 1506 allowed Henry to negotiate Suffolk's return, the earl's life was spared. This might have been on the insistence of Philip, but it could also be that Suffolk was more use to Henry alive than dead. Richard de la Pole adopted the Yorkist claim and remained at large overseas. Suffolk remained in the Tower, to be executed in 1513 when his brother took up arms against England. His rebellion was never allowed to develop within England, but it was the last major conspiracy to challenge Henry VII. The manner in which Suffolk's potential threat was negated suggests that Henry's protracted efforts to master the ways that conspiracy could challenge his crown were fully in place by 1502. Had it not been for the collapse of his dynastic hopes with family deaths by April 1503, it is likely that Henry would have enjoyed a period of stable rule in his final years – and perhaps without the repressive retention of power that functioned so effectively in his last six years.

## Conclusion

Exploitation of noble inexperience was not confined to the north-west. In Yorkshire, for example, Henry used the 5th earl of Northumberland's minority after 1489 to bring about 'the intrusion of the royal power into the web of alliance and dependence which bound the northern gentry to the great houses'.[7] Percy retainers, such as Sir Robert Plumpton, Sir Marmaduke Constable, and other northern gentry families, were recruited into direct royal service from the Percy affinity. They became regional office holders in parallel with Sir Thomas Butler and his associates in Lancashire. By 1506, with the new earl of Northumberland trying to assert himself in east Yorkshire, the king's body servants, such as Sir John Hotham, used their connections to the royal council to by-pass noble control of justice in the regions. Northumberland also suffered systematic debt creation and manipulation at the hands of the king's officials. He was fined £10,000 for the ravishment of Elizabeth Hastings, a royal ward. This was commuted to a payment of £5,000 in yearly instalments of 1,000 marks. Northumberland also was obliged to place land in the hands of feoffees to the king's use as guarantee of payment. This intrusion was similar to that directed against assertive or potentially aggressive nobles elsewhere, such as Lord Abergavenny in Kent and the 2nd earl of Derby in Lancashire.

Henry VII needed strong noble power to ensure that local government remained stable. The extensive connections of the great families developed through generations of land consolidation, and gentry networking presented a deeply entrenched structure of county government that the Tudor crown had no intention of deconstructing or threatening. Henry VII was concerned to achieve crown control over the noble–gentry connections that made local society work well but also caused most disruption when social links were abused. Security through dominance seems to have been Henry's pressing concern. This was most noticeable in some areas where Henry deliberately inserted outsiders into local networks.[8] He seems to have treated each set of circumstances subtly and with a clear assessment of the personalities and issues involved. There was no uniform attack on the nobles through bonds. Rather, these tools were used to steer the aristocracy into a new way of thinking about their own power and its relationship to changing crown authority.

# 8

## ROYAL POWER AND PERSONNEL

### COUNCIL AND COUNCILLORS

The royal council was the engine room of late medieval government. Infrequent parliaments and Great Councils meant that there was no other formal gathering of the great men of the realm where events and policy were discussed. The court and household had vital functions for the public face of Tudor power as centres of magnificent display or social refinement. They were also informal theatres for circulating gossip and information. The council, however, was the crown's private agency where the hard business of ruling was worked out. The king also frequently presided over council business in person. The association of the council and councillors with his direct presence made the royal council the most important ruling body of Henry VII's reign.

Councillors traditionally advised the crown at the king's invitation. There was also a professional administrative team, headed by the chancellor and treasurer, which had overseen the implementation of the king's decisions. The polarising nature of royal politics during much of the fifteenth century had the effect of merging the advisory and business functions of the council to create an agency that not only devised policy but also put the king's wishes into effect. Members of the council became identified by their personal and political allegiance to the 'parties' contesting the throne. Fewer men served the crown as a ruling institution during the civil war, and the council became more like a modern government cabinet. By 1485 the council was the main initiator and manager of the king's business. Its composition therefore reflected the priorities and alliances that Henry formed to make his policy effective.

The council was Henry's creation. Any condemnation of the king's advisers was an attack on Henry himself. A strong king would not be led by bad advice or influenced by deficient advisers. Only those with some ability, loyalty, or personal connection to the king were asked to become councillors. This was no place for men who were not trusted, or who did not have anything to contribute to the development of the regime. This does not mean that Henry was surrounded by 'yes' men who simply followed his lead and offered no resistance to his views. Henry required his councillors to give their opinions freely and they in turn expected their ideas and information to be heard. In this way the council was a balanced forum.

In August 1485 Henry Tudor's small group of banished supporters had little else to discuss but their own collective expedition to recover power in England. The victory at Bosworth and the imposition of this narrow group upon the country meant that Henry's backers immediately became the heart of a functioning royal council. As the king's only sure allies with a vested interest in his survival, they also took the lion's share of responsibility as major office holders, in the royal household, and in the rule of counties where they enjoyed landholding or legal influence. Necessity meant that this same group of knights monopolised the exercise of the king's direct power early in Henry's reign. Their involvement certainly helped to cement Tudor authority. It also enabled a limited range of common ruling aims to become established at the centre of Tudor power.

These men were attuned to the way Henry viewed things, making the king naturally reliant on their familiarity with his cause. The duplication of a core of Tudorists at the centre of the council and at the centre of the regime made the council adaptable to the new roles that Henry and his chief ministers devised for it. This was perhaps part of the reason why the early Tudor council was able to become so universal in its interests and experimental in its activities.

The gentry rebels of 1483 maintained a closeness to Henry that was only ended by death. In the three years before Bosworth, Henry's council resembled that of a rapidly progressing noble landholder: a retinue leader surrounded by knights, esquires and gentlemen but with few other peers present until a rise in status made his lordship more attractive. Once king, Henry developed the role of his royal advisory body as if it was an extension of his magnate council-in-exile. Officers like Sir Reginald Bray and Sir Richard Empson, who looked after Henry's private duchy of Lancaster estates, became key figures in council administration. The familiar duchy functions of managing land and deciding the disputes of royal tenants were adopted within the king's council proper. This trend enabled an expansion of the council's legal interests in common law and equity, and further developed its administrative responsibilities. The rise of early Tudor judicial and managing committees separated out more and more specialist functions and led to a core of executives and common lawyers based permanently at Westminster.

Henry had to graft his personal connection onto the larger group of peers and prelates that had survived Bosworth. They expected their natural position as great men to be reflected in their selection as Tudor royal councillors. Henry re-employed thirty-five men who had served Edward IV. He was less willing immediately to open up Tudor rule to others who had profited under Richard III or had hedged their bets about Henry's chances. The blending of councillors' skills and interests was a delicate exercise if the king was to get the best from his chief subjects. During Henry's reign a total of 227 men have been identified as councillors. The loss of many records may make this a conservative estimate and it is clear that some men were recorded only once while others were regular attendees because of their specialist skills.

Peers were the most senior secular figures of the realm. They were considered the natural councillors of the king. Late medieval English kings were the first among equals from this group who possessed similar interests and common concerns about the condition of the country. Henry's exclusion from noble society between 1471 and 1485 made him a special case and he reshaped the royal council on the basis of personal loyalty and security rather than status. Surviving records indicate that about two-thirds of early Tudor peers attended at least one session of the council: a total of forty-three lords.

The practical value of their input to the workload varied greatly, since Henry's lawyers and administrators completed most of the procedural work. The conciliar role of nobles who were not also officers of state was already declining. Henry's reign accelerated the role of professional administrators in royal government, and by 1601 Elizabeth I's Privy

Council contained only five peers. The military power of Henry's nobles kept him safe from rebellion and their presence around the throne boosted the magnificence of his court. The council, court, and household were therefore institutions where the king's aristocratic companions expected to be present. There is no evidence that Henry's council neglected or otherwise overlooked the ranks of the peerage when it came to counselling the crown. As with other councillors, a demonstration of loyalty and sound political experience were the most important requirements.

The most essential body of Henry's chosen councillors were his courtiers – the leading knights and esquires of the regime who served in the royal household and whose wives attended the queen. Many had served Henry before his accession to the throne; others caught his eye at court or in the household. Most courtiers had important local roles as crown stewards or JPs, making their attendance on the council infrequent. Since he created few new peers other than Lord Willoughby and Lord Daubeney, this class of royal followers was static in terms of potential social progression. This made the accumulation of land, wealth, and office a major motivating factor for aggressive courtiers on the council, and council business often discussed their offences.

Clerics and churchmen were a growing presence on the royal council as the fifteenth century progressed, becoming the largest group on the council under Henry. Archbishops and bishops were regular attendees, with several clerics holding the most important offices of crown government. Lesser bishops, clerical officers of the chapel royal, priors of religious orders such as the knights of St John, deans, archdeacons and abbots all attended, but only those with alternative governmental office carried real weight on the council.

Most churchmen on the council were trained in canon or civil law. Henry also made use of legal professionals educated in English common law at the Inns of Court. Important attendees included all chief justices of the law courts, some lesser judges, the chief baron of the Exchequer, and the king's own solicitor and attorney general. The chief justices were among the most important voices on the council since they addressed the legality of particular royal actions and advised on the common law aspects of the judicial business under discussion. As the reign progressed and the dominance of the council spread throughout the legal system, the king's solicitor and attorney general became more powerful. The creation of small judicial committees of councillors also diverted control of the council's role in the law away from the crown's traditional legal experts. When the council defended the king's personal legal interests as a manorial lord, such councillors were essential in preparing the king's position at law.

Administrators and officials provided the most vital role within the council. Many such as Lord Chancellor and Lord Privy Seal were clerics or peers. Henry demanded professional skill in key areas of his government rather than the disjointed attention of his aristocratic friends who had fingers in many other pies. Henry rapidly developed the post of royal secretary in response to the vigorous demands he placed on the professional abilities of his councillors. This was already an important post that brought great personal intimacy with the king's way of ruling. Richard III's secretary John Kendal was one of only twenty-nine men attained by Henry in 1485. Only Oliver King and Thomas Routhal held this post under Henry and this built up their experience and responsibility at the king's right hand.

The secretary managed the king's signet office and the signet seal provided a flexible administrative response to the great variety of crown business. This office was the key link between the king and his other ruling agencies. Routhal is conspicuous in the records of the council – both as a man of expertise whose opinion was valued and as a recorder of business. He personally engrossed numerous recognisances in the chancery records. He also monitored those under bonds and was involved in the management of forfeitures and repayments. As with other councillors the king's secretary was a target for the patronage of others who hoped to attract the king's favour. Both King and Routhal paid rewards to servants bringing gifts or information to the king and his council.

From within these groups, a core of about eight or nine regulars would undertake the main business as the inner council. Under Henry the working council included his Lords Chancellor, keepers of the privy seal, presidents of the council (Thomas Savage, bishop of London, Richard Fitzjames, bishop of Chichester, and Edmund Dudley esquire), as well as the most trusted king's knights like Bray, Guildford, Empson, Lovell, Risley, and Daubeney. They filled major office at home and abroad, and had a fluid council role – sitting as advisers to the king, equity judges, or auditors of accounts on consecutive days' business.

Regular councillors who were also courtiers were in an ideal position to act as intermediaries between the king and those circling outside the inner group of royal favourites. Bray, Daubeney, Guildford and others received pensions and fees from earls, lords and wealthy widows who needed direct routes to the king's ear. Royal councillors manipulated the information and gossip of the court both to the king and his courtiers, and improved their own positions in the process.[1] Men who could offer the king information that extended his control would be used extensively. They also profited personally. Election to the Order of the Garter was a common reward among elite councillors. They were the men relied upon to conduct diplomatic missions, or to organise royal jousts and celebrations.

In the fifteenth century the council met usually at the palace of Westminster, in the Star Chamber, or in the chamber of the duchy of Lancaster, but the functions of the council could be exercised wherever the king was. A mobile council accompanied him on journeys and handled petitions and managed business, but council could effectively be taken wherever the king asked for it, especially on informal occasions – out hunting with a few nobles or ambassadors, journeying between residences, gaming with royal friends, dressing with personal servants in private chambers, or during meals. In fact, relatively low-ranking servants such as the groom of the stool – who looked after the king on the toilet – became powerful figures during the reigns of Henry VII and Henry VIII because they were particularly intimate with, and trusted by, the king.

Advice was offered at the king's invitation and was sometimes required from specific specialists. This could be as diverse as London goldsmiths advising on the coinage, or prominent local figures invited to comment on regional petitions, riots, or events in cities and boroughs. During Henry's reign a static inner council continued to act independently of the king. The administrative processing of petitions, grants, warrants, and licences frequently continued almost every day under the chancellor, president of the council, without the king's direct involvement. The participation in council business of officials from the administrative departments of chancery, the privy seal office, or Henry's personal secretariat ensured that warrants and bills were issued quickly once a course of action was decided upon.

Surviving records do show that Henry's council discussed anything and everything that passed within the responsibility of medieval government. There was no distinction between administrative and judicial matters. The business of any day could vary between foreign affairs, riots, title to land, wardships and marriages, trade and customs regulation, judicial malpractice, piracy, money supply and forgery, criminal trials, and petitions from the destitute. The selection of councillors to provide this advice to the crown was fundamental to the strength of any monarch's rule. Councillors not only debated policy but also kept the king updated on events in the counties where their major landholding was based. They remained the eyes and ears of the king. Henry restructured the functions of the council to ensure that his natural aristocratic councillors (in their capacity as powerful local lords) were monitored by a smaller team of specialist officials accountable to the king directly. Henry reconfigured the medieval council and set in motion the changes that allowed Wolsey and Cromwell to further refine the council's role in Henry VIII's reign.

## COURT AND HOUSEHOLD

The court and household were the agencies through which Tudor power was most effectively displayed and projected. In the rooms of the royal palaces, governed by rigorous social etiquette, Henry, his leading subjects, and servants interacted on a personal level. Foreign observers, ambassadors, visitors, English petitioners, regional nobles and gentry, their sons, wives and servants all revolved around the king and his royal family in the public and private spaces they occupied. It was here that major governing decisions were made as the king gathered information informally and distilled it into the policies directed through the council.

To varying degrees, courtiers and servants also spent private time with the king when he was hunting, gaming, or enjoying court entertainments, feast days, and tournaments. These periods were effective opportunities for both king and subjects to communicate in less formal but highly effective ways. As the reign progressed, Henry's body servants used this contact with the monarch to develop their own influence, while the king realised that his direct links with lower-ranking servants could provide innovative ways of applying his policies and enforcing his will.

The pageantry and opulence of the early Tudor court and household structures were also manipulated via the court as essential parts of Henry's rule. Infrequent spectacular events such as royal marriages and funerals, and the king's journeys to the county towns and great houses of his chief supporters, allowed the wider population to glimpse the king and to form their own assessment of his fitness to rule. The court and household formed the visible powerhouse of the regime, as royal servants were moulded and the Tudor way of ruling was broadcast beyond Westminster. When men were in the household they were also courtiers: the space in which the two functions operated was the same. This was the arena where gossip and reputation were formed and traded, although precious little of it has survived.

Henry's court, household and council were closely connected in that they all served the king's various needs directly. The court was where the major nobles came to circulate around the king and where their sons and kinsmen were positioned to give personal attendance upon Henry in preparation for a career in royal service. The aristocracy knew that the best way to secure favour was to be close to the king. He knew that the best way to assess his servants, their capabilities and loyalties, was to have them around the household and court. They were the only places for meaningful interaction with the crown at a personal level. A strong personal relationship with Henry was more likely to enforce allegiance in the expectation of a share in the successes of the regime.

Royal requirements varied between the formality of the role and the service that the king required at a particular time. Court, household and council could each be personal and private, or public and conspicuous. The staff or members of the three institutions were also interchangeable. They were bound to the king by the service he expected, but Henry was surprisingly flexible in the roles demanded from servants of very different status. This has led to a blurring of the boundaries, especially between court and household, which is not helped by the loss of key documents.

At the very beginning of the reign there was a distinct hierarchy of service around the king. This cut through the entire regime and was even defined by the parliamentary acts that established Henry's rights. A statute in the first parliament pardoned Henry's followers who had committed murder or trespass against supporters of Richard III. This marked Henry's warband from August 1485 as a separate and especially favoured group. Henry's accession inevitably established a culture of favouritism that was compounded by the difficulties of his early rule. The narrowness of Henry's initial base of support became the basis for the court politics that is visible in the surviving sources.

The political nation would have been aware that Henry's most favoured and trusted group were his Lancastrian relatives who had been restored in the first Tudor parliament. Even lower-ranking relatives benefited from Henry's wish to have them close about him. His half-uncle, Sir David Owen, was made chief carver for life in September 1485 with the generous annuity of £50. The servants of this royal Beaufort–Tudor–Stanley network, like Reginald Bray and Christopher Urswick, took precedence over the Yorkist rebels of 1483 whose primary loyalty was to Queen Elizabeth. The intentions of those who had prospered under Richard III's rule were harder to assess. Men like Sir Richard Croft and Sir William Stanley, royal officers since the 1460s, were conspicuous for their former Yorkist loyalty. Their specific commitment to Henry had to be both nurtured and enforced. Easier to identify and more obviously controllable were Henry's opponents from Bosworth. Their sudden change from powerful royal agents to enemies of the crown made Richard III's followers likely either to continue to rebel until captured and executed or to do their utmost to ingratiate themselves with Henry.

Henry tried to merge these groups and their distinct interests as he sought to contain the Yorkist and Lancastrian rancour of the previous thirty years. Despite the efforts of commentators like Vergil and Bacon to play down political faction within Henry's regime, clashes of personality and influence did take place. In 1503 Sir Robert Plumpton was advised carefully to select those courtiers he wished to arbitrate in a legal dispute with Sir Richard Empson. Plumpton was told to avoid Bray, Mordaunt, and others belonging to Bray. These men dominated the administration of the duchy of Lancaster, which Plumpton's Yorkshire lands bordered. Those who might favour his cause were men who had joined Tudor after 1483: Fox, Guildford, Lovell and Richard Weston. More sinister manoeuvring was suggested by the plea that Plumpton should 'keep your friends secret to yourself for fear that you lose them'.[2] Many around the court would feel it unwise to support Plumpton if it meant opposing Bray and his friends.

Political and personal rivalries among courtiers could also have developed from the work they undertook. It is probable that administrators Bray, Empson, and Dudley performed a function entirely different from servants who were intimate with the king for purely cultural, social, and private service reasons. From the mid-1490s the young Yorkist lords Thomas, Lord Harrington (the marquis of Dorset's son), William Lord Courtenay (heir to the earldom of Devonshire), Henry, earl of Essex, and even Edmund, earl of Suffolk, formed a vibrant social group that caught the king's attention through jousting, dances, and other entertainments. They added to the youthful splendour of the court and encouraged the king to believe that he was not only moulding a noble military elite but also converting the Yorkist loyalty of their fathers into a distinctly Tudor generation of future aristocratic leaders. Other younger sons of the peerage and heirs of leading gentry followed a similar path into almost permanent attendance around the king in his household and court.

The older generation of administrator-courtiers could not serve the king in this way, and while Henry presumably sought to be even-handed with his rewards, resentment might have arisen between some groups as interaction with Henry reflected the complexity of the task facing a new dynasty. The court and household were training grounds as well as proving grounds for royal service. Some men were summoned to regulate their future behaviour or to appreciate the power of the regime at close quarters.[3] Others were invited to share proximity to the king because their service was mutually beneficial to Tudor rule. The king needed the loyal service of his councillors just as much as they wished to attract a greater share of royal goodwill. The only effective way that both aspects of this service relationship could be judged was through the personal contact that the court and household allowed.

Under the Yorkist kings the size of royal household had grown dramatically. A larger household meant that fewer servants became intimate with a particular king or his regime, resulting in greater continuity of officials between reigns. However, Henry's destruction of Richard's household resulted initially in a complete change of personnel among those serving the king. Henry's royal affinity was expanded through the ranks of the household and his personal servants soon dominated local government in the most unstable regions.

The first Tudor appointments addressed the king's personal safety from the lowest levels upwards. A secure but low-ranking network of military servants was developed quickly. Almost all the named yeomen of the crown, for example, had fought for the king at Bosworth. They guarded the king at night with weapons ready, and acted as royal messengers and agents. The building of a body of loyal officers who were also the king's personal soldiers was vital to the functioning of the new regime. Many yeomen of the crown were already in post at the close of 1485 without formal appointment.

Henry's awareness of his own insecurity created a new household rank of yeomen of the guard that established a corps of experienced soldiers around the king. Vergil stated that about two hundred men were retained as yeomen of the guard in 1485. At least four sergeants-at-arms were in post by the beginning of October to manage them. Seventeen yeomen of the guard received additional grants of office within a month of Bosworth. Grants such as that to John Byde, made bailiff of Bridgewater and constable of Totnes, brought immediate responsibility to carry Tudor authority into the country. This was also a literal requirement. Richard Wilson, one of the sergeants-at-arms, was paid 24s for riding with letters to Cecily Neville, duchess of York, in Michaelmas 1485. The body of yeomen performed this function ceaselessly. The extension of the royal role given to yeomen and grooms was made explicit with the Yeomen and Grooms Act of 1488. After this statute, the lowest-ranked members of the household received their fees only when serving the king. They might have expected a share of the cash gifts at Christmas and New Year, or have amassed the small sums Henry gave in reward for specific service, but to supplement their staple income these crown servants had to seek additional posts.

Henry's gentry body servants must have been performing the senior household duties from his period of exile. Richard Guildford, John Asteley and Robert Willoughby were the first knights to be recorded as body servants on the patent roll. Along with esquires for the king's body, Richard Pole, David Philip, and Thomas Lovell, they were certain to have been among Henry's most trusted personal attendants during 1485. Henry still had to strike a careful balance between securing his own person and diverting the energies of his gentry loyalists into regions where they had to recover their power. This could explain why Sir Gilbert Talbot and Sir John Savage junior, two of Henry's commanders at Bosworth, did not enter the royal household until July 1486 and February 1488 respectively. Similarly, the exiles Sir Richard Edgecombe and Sir Robert Willoughby were initially given appointments that underlined the restoration of their local influence in south-west England, rather than about the king.

Henry had to take certain risks to create a balance between expanding his base of service and maintaining his security. Henry boldly used the household and court to police the former Yorkists and Ricardians whose service he inherited. The fluctuating loyalty of these men during the 1486 to 1489 period was confronted and contained through contact with the king, his courtiers and household officers. The household was the only body where such prominent suspects could be supervised directly by the king, but this restraint was balanced by the prestige of direct royal service. Henry took on a personal role in this rehabilitation. He interviewed many of the pardoned Yorkshire rebels after the battle of Stoke. He was at Pontefract on 26 and 27 August 1487 when bonds for allegiance were taken from prisoners. Former loyalists of Richard III, such as Sir John Everingham and Sir Thomas Wortley, were absorbed into the royal household at that time.

The necessity that infused the establishment of the Tudor royal household was demonstrated by the 1487 Act that established a household court to investigate conspiracy among royal servants. The presence of many former Ricardians as the king's body servants, and the defection of some and lukewarm loyalty of others during the risings of 1486 and 1487, was an obvious danger if left unchecked. The Act brought tighter control of household servants as part of a package of precautions to counter the dangers of admitting former enemies into the Tudor service.

King Henry's policy of accommodation and rehabilitation through the household became an alarming risk to his security as Warbeck's English conspiracy gained momentum during the 1490s. David Starkey has proposed that 1495 was the date when an ordinance created a new household department of the Privy Chamber.[4] It has already been suggested that Henry's suspicion of disloyalty within the household brought these changes about at the start of the 1490s. This new household division acquired responsibility for Henry's intimate personal service from the existing above-stairs ceremonial branch, the *domus magnificencie* (under the chamberlain) and the below-stairs service and supply department, the *domus providencie* (headed by the steward). The privy chamber was organised under the groom of the stool, Hugh Denys, and was staffed by less than a dozen low-ranked grooms and gentlemen. This structure stood in contrast to that dominated by knights and esquires of the body who had previously offered personal service within the king's private chambers.

A paring down of his household structure reflected the creation of the yeomanry of the guard when Henry's position was similarly precarious in 1485. Both developments surrounded Henry with socially inferior figures who were completely dependent upon household office, and the crumbs of local power they could glean, for their influence and prestige. The changes in place by 1495 attempted to divorce intimacy about the king from the national influence that the king's body servants had previously enjoyed. Henry judged that it was the service structure around him, rather than the aristocratic servants themselves, that had provided the greatest opportunity for treason to stalk the corridors of the royal palaces.

By selecting personal servants who were not, initially, significant local landholders, Henry severed the direct link between potential household treason and related local unrest. The new chamberlain and steward were Lords Daubeney and Willoughby – two trusted royal friends and also the regime's principal military organisers. Their appointments enhanced the protective cordon around the royal family. Related promotions were Sir Richard Guildford as controller of the household, and Sir Edward Poynings as governor of Calais. By 1495 Henry had remoulded the structure of his power more firmly around his own dependent supporters.

Henry again chose to rely on a narrow group of servants at a time when he was just beginning to build upon the accommodation reached after overcoming the legacy of Richard III before 1490. The paths to royal favour became narrower and a more restrictive defence of the king's interests grew steadily for the rest of the reign. The strength of Henry's restructured household was demonstrated by the number of early Tudor officers who went on to serve Henry VIII in the same capacity.

The court and household held a powerful social function for the Tudor crown. The drinking, feasting, and regional rivalry reported in descriptions of visits of the entire court to York in 1486 or to East Anglia in 1487 suggest that Henry used such occasions to get the measure of his main supporters. It was essential for the king to work out the qualities of those nobles and senior knights who were not familiar to him before Bosworth. Social gatherings, the interactions they required, and the opportunities for observing and recording the small signs of personality and character were a highly valuable exercise for the king (if completely unfathomable, 500 years later).

Household men and courtiers were more likely to be trusted to hold local office, both for security reasons and as reward for service. It was they and their servants who managed crown lands and forfeited estates. This varied from Sir Thomas Lovell, who secured custody of Lord Roos's lands for £233 each half year, to Edward Blount who delivered £5 for Lord Morley's Shropshire lands in July 1490. This patronage also cascaded down to the courtiers and household men who were free, with the king's approval, to manage their own responsibilities. In February 1492, Bray and Hugh Oldham became receivers-general of the earl of Warwick's lands. Local responsibility was then distributed to Bray's friends, like John Hayes, who became receiver of the Warwick lands in the southwest. This transfer of authority on the king's terms was nothing new. It does, however, suggest that Henry's way of doing things became dominant within the household, across the social scale, and throughout the country, as courtiers came to control local administration.

Henry's responsibilities to his servants in court and household were extensive. From 20s for the rent of Crotchet the armourer's house, to 16s for the clothes of the boy who cared for the king's greyhounds, Henry was a caring and often paternal figure to those few hundred servants who were constantly around the royal palaces. The royal court also included households of Queen Elizabeth and the royal children. By the end of 1502 Princess Mary's household was costing her father £83 per month. The 11-year-old Prince Henry already had his own troupe of actors, who were rewarded with 20s for their performance at Christmas 1502.

Being close to the king also required personal sacrifices that could threaten the private resources of courtiers and household men. Lord Dinham paid 40 marks to a Spanish herald in September 1490, and Guildford provided bows, food, and wine for Scottish ambassadors when they hunted with Henry at Eltham in 1485. Other officers entertained the king's guests around the court until a personal audience with Henry could be arranged. Although these functions were part of the office and roles these men occupied, courtiers and household men had to have sufficient wealth and social skill to make such outlays function at the highest social level on behalf of the king.

While the king could create a magnificent arena for the powerful display of Tudor kingship, there also had to be a benefit and purpose for courtiers in attending upon the royal person. Much of the evidence of the functioning of the court comes from royal records, and this has created an impression of courtly life from the king's point of view. It is unlikely that the survival of more private letters and papers would do much to change the overtly royal focus, but it might explain a little more about why Henry VII's leading subjects wished to come to court, what they hoped to achieve for themselves, and how the king balanced their needs and his.

There is plenty of evidence that they did make every effort to be seen around the king. At Christmas 1491, for example, the earl of Derby spent almost £10 on 48 yards of medley cloth[5] to make spectacular livery gowns for his servants. Heralds' reports of state ceremonials and royal progresses frequently recorded in great detail the quality of the garments and trappings of those who accompanied the king. Private correspondence, such as the evidence of the Paston Letters, suggests that observers were impressed enough by the physical appearance and quality of the cloth of Henry's courtiers to note it in some detail. In 1506, when Philip, Archduke of Austria, was entertained at Windsor with lavish but hastily prepared ceremonies, William Maketyrr told William Paston of the diamonds and rubies in Lord Henry Stafford's hat, the way that the marquis of Dorset pinned a large white feather to his horse's crupper, and how the earl of Kent wore a magnificent coat of cloth of gold and velvet. Henry VII's court and household were vital windows on the regime. Whatever changes he made elsewhere, Henry ensured that visitors and observers to his court witnessed an increasingly magnificent theatre of Tudor royal power.

# 9

# THE PRESERVATION
# OF POWER

## ANTI-RETAINING MEASURES

Retaining was the practice by a lord of recruitment of followers and the protection of their interests in return for exclusive service. This service was often proclaimed by the wearing of livery (identifiable coloured clothes or 'uniform') and the receipt of badges and tokens, and could be recorded and sealed as an indenture or with a verbal oath. When employed within the law it encouraged good lordship and transmitted royal authority into the counties.

Previous kings had struggled to find a definition of retaining that allowed for legitimate service – within the household, as estate managers, or as legal counsel – that was appropriate to a lord's rank and dignity, but which also challenged abuses. Without the enforcement of carefully drafted legislation, the safeguarding of mutual interest through retaining could soon descend into intimidation of opponents and manipulation of the law and local officials. There were certainly many attempts to create laws to clamp down on unlawful practices. Too often, however, loopholes such as the right to lawful service remained, and enforcement proved difficult because of the crown's reliance on aristocratic military might in times of crisis.

Lords bypassed the law by expanding legitimate roles within their service. Household positions were multiplied and title to land that carried tenure by knight's fees was sought out. Most importantly, no English king could keep a fully prepared royal army on standby to tackle emergencies as they arose. The armies that fought for Henry at Bosworth, Stoke, Boulogne and Blackheath were essentially private forces raised from the estates of the most powerful men in the country. The accounts of wages for these campaigns show that even provincial knights could put several hundred soldiers into the field. Henry himself could not have held onto this throne without the private military power of the earls of Oxford, Derby, Shrewsbury, or the duke of Bedford. This vital dependency made unworkable much of the late medieval legislation to curb retaining: restrictions on lawful aristocratic retaining limited the effectiveness of royal power.

Henry could not tackle the independence of noble affinities directly. As was the case with most of his policies, he sought to enforce compliance to the crown's wishes rather than to punish powerful landholders and debilitate their resources directly. He could not threaten to strip the aristocracy of its rights to retain servants. The key was an effective means of control on the king's conditions. Most historians and some contemporaries were sceptical of Henry's seriousness when, during the parliament of November 1485, he obliged the household men, lords, and Commons to swear to uphold royal authority. A central part of this oath was an agreement not to retain by indenture, token, or livery. It also incorporated clauses not to aid or bail known felons, engage in maintenance, embracery, rioting or hindering of the king's writs. Henry followed the form of similar oaths in 1433 and at the start of Edward IV's reign. It was also indicative of a distinct crown policy to take the initiative over the deficiencies of lordship and compliance with the law that Henry had recognised at his accession. A council committee was established in 1487 to tackle most of the offences noted in the earlier parliamentary oath.

Statutes from the start of the fifteenth century had tried to restrict the right to retain only to those great men with whom the king would associate as his natural partners in government. A mutual aristocratic outlook would, it was hoped, ensure that retinues and affinities were created and employed within the law. None of the legislation, including the most recent act of 1468 in force at Henry's accession, had curbed the potential danger from private armies. The cycle of civil war had fuelled the need for aristocratic military power.

Four acts were passed by Henry's parliaments against the practice of illegal retaining, which did little more than rearrange the problem.

Royal policy was steered towards limiting retaining to the household servants and officials stipulated in the 1468 Act, but also to tenants of lands held directly from the king and tenants of crown constableships, stewardships, and bailiffships.

An Act in the 1495 parliament made explicit the link between royal office holding and the military duty owed to the king. Holders of offices, fees or annuities in England and Wales who failed to muster with the king in time of war (reasonable excuses and licences allowed) were to forfeit their grants. By January 1504 this was refined to state that those men in possession of royal honours, castles, and lordships were more bound than holders of annuities and fees to give their attendance for the defence of the king and realm against internal rebels and external enemies.[1]

Dominic Luckett has shown how during the 1490s Henry's reliance upon the retaining power of crown stewards and constables replaced that previously held by aristocratic servants in the royal household.[2] Household knights and esquires kept a magnificent role as part of the court, but military power was passed to the guardians of crown lands and castles. The same men could function in both groups, but the connection was no longer automatic. Henry could command stewards to dispense his red rose livery to muster crown tenants. Officers who did not perform acceptably were removed. The 1504 retaining Act clarified this process through a system of licences.

By allowing his local servants to retain on his behalf, Henry created a virtual standing army. The roots of this are seen in the wages lists for the retinues sent to France in 1492. Lords and knights brought men from their scattered estates, but some who held few personal lands drew their troops from the royal manors they supervised. As the reign progressed, this trend became more pronounced. By 1497, Sir John Cheyne was paid over £500 for the crown tenants he brought to Blackheath. Other loyal knights, like Thomas Lovell, had a retinue of over 1,300 men drawn from offices such as constable of Nottingham castle and steward of Sherwood Forest.

Continuation of the local power these men came to enjoy obliged them to invest their own efforts more completely in the survival of the Tudor regime. Henry denied men like Cheyne, Guildford, and Lovell extensive gifts of land. By offering temporary control of the crown's tenants during his pleasure, Henry ensured that this royal connection grew into a powerful peacetime affinity as well as a potent force for war. Through this licensing system the king could reputedly call on 50,000 men from the royal lands, and gather them together far more quickly than noble retinues or county levies could be mustered. By avoiding war, this retinue of local captains became a commanding agency, enforcing Henry's domination of local networks.

Henry's reluctance to make new grants of crown lands also meant that he avoided new concentrations of aristocratic landholding in particular regions (although there remained many blocs of ancient noble landholding). Even where he was sure of the loyalty of the recipients, the build-up of private interests through land was limited to the royal family. Others had to be content with stewardship of royal estates. By extending the requirement to petition for royal grants, Henry's patronage policy also favoured those who had a good working relationship with the crown and the private trust of the king. Over time, Henry could be more confident that the most powerful retinues were also likely to become the ones headed by his closest followers.

The absence of evidence of common law prosecutions for illegal retaining was undoubtedly linked to Henry's reluctance to clamp down on a practice that he needed to maintain. There were plenty of indictments, but few offenders received serious punishment in King's Bench, assizes, or quarter sessions. The 1504 Act extended the powers of JPs to use quarter sessions' juries to investigate local abuses of retaining. JPs were required to send cases into King's Bench. Prosecutions could continue under common law procedure, or in the Star Chamber, or at the king's discretion. This new Act attempted to create a more flexible approach, and formalised a role that the council had performed for much of the reign.

The conciliar enforcement of retaining offences seems to have extended considerably, as such abuses of lordship could be closely linked to lapses in allegiance. Fines were managed by obligations while behaviour was defined by explicit conditions in recognisances. Thus on 6 December 1488 John Egerton of Chester was bound under £300 without time limit not to be a retainer of any lord. In September 1491 the rumbling conflict between the Cornwall and Croft retinues in Herefordshire brought recognisances of £500 for Cornwall and Sir Ralph Hakulet that neither would retain nor accept into their service any man from the town of Leominster. Elite knights such as Cornwall and his ally Sir Richard

Corbet were just the class of men Henry relied upon to enforce retaining legislation in the localities. If their violent servants were the root cause of many offences, the crown had a real struggle to stop this type of abuse.

Henry and his council therefore approached illegal retaining through its effects – rioting, embracery and more sinister problems of allegiance. Henry did not need to prosecute offenders at common law or through the legal jurisdiction of the council if other methods could be made more successful as means of restraint. Even where common law indictments were spectacularly pressed home, as with Lord Abergavenny in 1506, the final stage of such cases could be stopped before judgement and taken out of court on the king's instruction.

No evidence has been found for Bacon's report that the earl of Oxford incurred Henry's anger for the size of his retinue during a royal visit. Oxford reportedly compounded with the king to avoid prosecution. It is a plausible story of Henry's reaction, but unlikely to be true. Henry needed these powerful and trustworthy retinues actively to defend the crown's interests, with the immediate lord's concerns secondary. Records of King's Bench show numerous cases that were halted and passed to the king and council for completion. Historians who have written on Henry's retaining policies have identified the development of compounding for offences. One writer has concluded that 'we are dealing with some form of conciliar procedure whose detailed records have not survived and do not therefore appear as Star Chamber cases'.[3] Many cases that targeted illegal retaining focused on the way retinues were used and the behaviour of those involved in incidents, rather than the fact that many of the servants involved might have been recruited illegally. If retinue leaders thought twice about employing their followers in local rioting and intimidation, the destabilising effect of affinities would diminish and the recruitment of servants who were not part of the lord's domestic service would become less necessary.

Loyalty and allegiance became the root of Henry's approach to retaining, as they probably had been for all other late medieval kings. The two most spectacular retaining fines of the reign were Lord Abergavenny's, already mentioned, and that of James Stanley, warden of Manchester College. Stanley's indictment at Lancaster Assizes in 1506 resulted in a massive fine of £145,610 following the calculations set out in the 1468 and 1504 Acts of £5 per month for those retaining and 40s per day for

214 THE PRESERVATION OF POWER

those unlawfully retained. In neither case did retaining offences end the careers of the men involved. Stanley was made bishop of Ely in 1506, while Abergavenny remained politically active.

The crown also sent a very clear message that recognisances would become forfeit if retinue leaders continued to disregard the conditions attached. In 1504 Sir John Booth and James Stanley forfeited bonds of £500 for actively encouraging the vicious rivalries of their servants in a struggle for influence around Manchester. Booth was a knight for the king's body and Stanley a regular councillor at that time. Since Booth became regional receiver of the duchy of Lancaster in December 1504, he risked loss of office if violence continued, although it evidently had not prevented his initial appointment. The following month Henry wrote to his esquire, Henry Farringdon, to cause royal tenants in Lancashire to swear not to be retained privately, and to wear the king's red rose badge.

Royal measures to tackle such conflicts seldom mentioned illegally retained servants. It was quite possible, given the status of those involved, that brutal quarrels could have been conducted by legitimate retainers. To contain other instances of rioting and illegal assembly where retaining was mentioned, bonds were used against retinue leaders to address the behaviour of their followers rather than the specific issue over which their retinue had been put. An example is Leo Percy's indictment for expelling Robert Sheffield from a Lincolnshire manor in 1490 by force of a private army of 200 of his own tenants. The inflexibility of the common law response to retaining and riot was demonstrated by a major riot in Derbyshire between followers of Sir Henry Willoughby and Viscount Lisle and those of Henry, Lord Grey of Codnor. Most of those involved were not actually from Derbyshire, making it difficult for the sheriff to serve the required writs to bring those indicted from elsewhere in the midlands before a Derbyshire jury. A Special commission forced a number of Willoughby and Lisle men to enter into bonds that were managed by the council.

By 1504 the early Tudor peerage and gentry were painfully aware that Henry sought to dominate feudal relationships with his tenants in chief. The king could not then create and try to enforce legislation that attacked the feudal rights lords enjoyed over their own tenants without risking resistance. Henry's fundamental reliance on privately raised troops meant that the problems of retaining remained as prevalent at the end of the reign as they had been at its beginning. Henry had tried to restrict the practice and had expanded the ways that unlawful retaining was detected and reported. The use of the king's secretary to licence leaders to retain servants after submission of a list of names to the council was an innovation. Henry also developed the clauses in the 1468 Act that offered rewards to informers, the further punishment given to those denying their offences if found guilty, and the voiding of indentures and agreements upon judgement. The interest Henry took in the effects of illegal retaining makes it likely that all of the legal tools at the king's disposal would have been employed to tackle the abuses that weak controls on retaining could encourage.

## BONDS AND RECOGNISANCES

The one outstanding aspect of Henry's reign that all early Tudor historians have agreed upon is his use of bonds, recognisances, obligations and suspended fines as instruments to manipulate the behaviour of his subjects. Bonds have come to define Henry's way of ruling, but the survival of most evidence of their employment after 1500 has led to a focus on Henry's desire to control relationships with his most powerful and wealthy subjects in areas such as inheritances, wardship and marriage, the purchase of pardons, and the sale of royal favour. Scholarly emphasis on this aspect of Henry's reign has disguised a broader and more long-lived role for bonds. It has allowed historians to present Henry in the way that has become familiar – suspicious, manipulative, and paranoid of the independent power of his subjects.

One major paradox about Henry's use of bonds is that they did not seem to become widespread until the major political threats to his crown had been overcome. These measures became instruments of enforcing, rather than of achieving Tudor control. As we have already seen, however, Henry was no freer of potential dynastic problems after 1497 than he had been before.

Bonds were an established crown method of peacekeeping and enforcement of good behaviour long before Henry won the crown. Chancery documents show many instances where recognisances were used politically by previous kings. In 1413, for example, Henry V demanded a recognisance of £10,000 for the good behaviour of the earls of March and Arundel. Henry, earl of Northumberland, found his allegiance monitored by a bond of £5,000 upon his restoration by Edward IV in 1470. Other legal studies have shown how bonds helped to keep the peace under the Yorkist kings.[4] Bonds enforced harmony in serious gentry disputes such as the Stanley–Harrington quarrel in north Lancashire in 1470, and Richard III employed recognisances to support grants of pardon to former rebels in 1484. A pedigree for politically motivated bonds existed throughout the fifteenth century.

Familiar sources indicate that after 1500 Henry elevated bonds to become the linchpin of his entire ruling system. These sources are the books of payment and receipt of the treasurers of Henry's chamber, the close rolls of chancery, Edmund Dudley's notebook,[5] and from Dudley's 'petition'.[6] Of these, the only published sources are the *Calendar of Close Rolls* and Dudley's petition. The chance survival of these records also favours the latter half of the reign. The *Calendar of Close Rolls* in particular shows this discrepancy clearly.

Before 1500 about twenty-five bonds per regnal year were enrolled. Many were routine agreements in chancery between private individuals to honour arbitration in disputes, or to ensure payment of commercial debts. Henry also intervened to bind one or both parties to the crown when resolving equity cases. The political and manipulative aspect of these instruments is apparent only in isolated examples, such as bonds agreed by the earls of Westmorland and Northumberland, and Sir William Zouche, before 1487 that required allegiance and good behaviour as a condition of pardon.

Where modern historians have addressed Henry's use of bonds, their work has focused on his employment of bonds only against the nobility.[7] Contemporary evidence also supports this viewpoint, and suggests an increase in bonds after 1500. A royal decree in December 1499 made it an offence for chancery officials to fail to enrol recognisances connected to cases of treason or misprision. This could point to laxity beforehand, which might account for a lack of evidence from the first half of the reign. Dudley's explanation of Henry's policy in his petition, and Vergil's similar comments, have also linked bonds to the period after 1500:

> the pleasure and mind of the king was much set to have many persons in his danger at his pleasure ... wherefore divers and many persons were bound to his grace or to others to his use in great sums of money, some by recognisance, and some by obligation without any condition, but as a simple and absolute bond payable at a certain day, for his grace would have them so made.[8]

An explanation for the apparent discrepancy between the numbers of bonds at the beginning and end of the reign, and the related absence of politically motivated material before 1500, is found in Edmund Dudley's service with the king after September 1504. Dudley was principally employed to enforce collection of the payments that were due to Henry from his semi-feudal relationship with his prominent subjects.[9] It is here that we find the arbitrary and ruthless enforcement of royal rights through bonds that has done so much to colour Henry's reputation.

For those who wanted to carve out a career in the king's service, or even maintain the status that they already enjoyed, Dudley ensured that royal goodwill had a price. Thus in November 1507 Robert Rede had to pay 500 marks to be chief justice of the Court of Common Pleas, and Andrew Windsor had to find £200 to be sure of his own office as keeper of the Great Wardrobe. It is difficult to ignore Henry's avaricious reputation in payments like George Dalason's offer of 40 marks in 1508 to be one of the auditors of the Exchequer – a post that was already occupied. The king's leading councillors and servants did not escape this range of fees. Sir John Risley paid 500 marks for a general pardon, and in 1507 he also agreed to pass his manor of Tottenham to the crown after his death. This evidence for the king's favour suggests that the financial pressure exerted was applied universally – to those serving the king as well as those under a personal or legal obligation to him – and not just towards the nobles Henry wished to control through their purses.

There also seems to be very little explicit provocation or political motivation behind many of these entries, as Dudley himself confessed in his petition. The main reason for setting a price on office holding or the securing of existing rights was not necessarily to generate money for the crown. It created a financial obligation that would remain on record to be manipulated as Henry required. This was why the fees that the crown demanded were fairly high, but almost all the entries in Dudley's notebook record the payment of a fractional sum in cash and the remainder by obligations. When set against the likely revenue from occupying a post over a long period of time, or securing lucrative lands or temporalities, many of the sums were perhaps the reasonable cost of seizing opportunities that were in the king's gift. Despite what may be seen as excessive charges, there was no shortage of applicants willing to pay the financial price of entry into Henry's service.

Because the granting of office or privileges was effectively a gift of regional influence, there was a broad motivation to attach suspended financial penalties to contracts representing Henry beyond Westminster. Many of Dudley's bonds did just this – either directly through office that enforced the law, or indirectly with the holding of land and the influence that went with it. Since Dudley's role was so specific after 1504 it was always likely that he continued and extended a proven royal policy. Evidence for this has never been found, and historians have looked to some change in Henry's personality by 1503, rather than a combination of circumstances and the progression of royal policy, to explain the hardened attitude towards his subjects that the policy of rule by recognisance represented.

Some historians have dismissed as irrelevant the differences between bonds, obligations, and recognisances, since all involved promises under financial penalties. But the distinctions are important in order to understand how Henry used them. The bond was effectively an agreement between an individual and the crown, and an obligation or recognisance was used to enforce it. The difference between the two forms is precise. An obligation, although enforceable at law, was not necessarily created by a court. It was effectively a private contract, which included a condition and expressed a penalty in the event of default. It might also have established a right or liability by force of the agreement, often incorporated into the condition.

A recognisance was a more specific tool, in that it was created as part of legal process. Agreements to perform certain conditions were usually included, but these were often directly linked to the legal issue from which the recognisance emerged. Many conditions required appearance before the council or chancery at some future date, and demanded payments to defer larger fines; they might have required the maintenance of the peace against another person or against the king's subjects more generally; and they could also restrict movement from a specific place.

A recognisance also frequently required the main person bound to bring pledges to ensure performance of the conditions. These sureties had to be acceptable to the crown, and it was often a requirement that deceased or incapable sureties were replaced within a specified period. Neglect of the conditions ensured that all sums became forfeit to the crown.

A crucial factor is that Dudley dealt almost exclusively in obligations. The obligations he processed were demanded mainly from individuals, without sureties, and often with payments spread over an agreed period of time. Recognisances, on the other hand, did involve sureties to guarantee that the behavioural conditions were met. Dudley's specific role utilised obligations because the king was making outright grants of crown interest, benefits, or rights to individuals or corporate bodies in return for a fee. Part of this bargain could have been met by a cash payment, but most of it was agreed by obligations, usually because the sum demanded by the crown was beyond the means of immediate payment for those involved.

King Henry was not offering anything in return when issuing recognisances because they were not part of any transaction. Recognisances are more usually associated with the manipulation of behaviour, and therefore have a stronger relationship with politics, loyalty, and security. More specifically, they were more likely to be used once an individual had violated the king's laws or wavered in his allegiance. This also ties recognisances more closely to the law enforcement activities of the royal council.

No historian has yet satisfactorily linked the bonds familiar from the close rolls and chamber books with the evidence from Dudley's notebook. It does seem likely that many of the obligations recorded without conditions in the close rolls can be related to the work of Dudley, Bray, and Empson on the king's behalf. Some evidence linking bonds to the endemic conspiracy Henry faced before 1500 has recently come to light in the form of almost 600 memoranda of bonds agreed during appearances in chancery, before local commissioners, or even directly before the king on progress. The material shows categorically that bonds were employed at the start of the reign and in the context of the politics of loyalty to the king.[10]

This material highlights the key role of local crown agents acting on Henry's behalf as bonds were prepared. Some commissioners, like Guy Fairfax, justice of the King's Bench, and the earl of Oxford, were given regal powers to deal with rebels under writs of *dedimus potestatem* early in the reign. Other men were commissioned to identify and recruit sureties acceptable to the crown. This required deep knowledge of local networks and a clear understanding of why bonds were required. In July 1500 commissioners were appointed to extract obligations from Ralph and Christopher Dacre in Cumberland that they would produce four sureties with lands valued at 20 marks per annum to ensure that the Dacre brothers appeared at subsequent sessions of the peace until a local dispute was resolved. In 1504, John Scott, a commissioner in Buckinghamshire, confirmed to chancery that he had identified five individuals of sufficient status to be bound to uphold the lifelong allegiance of Richard Neville. Scott must have known those individuals who were willing to risk much on Neville's good behaviour.

There was an established procedure for ensuring appearance before crown commissioners. In November 1502 a group of sureties were required to appear before the king's officers at Holt castle within seven days of a proclamation made at the market cross in Wrexham. The onus was on all loyal subjects to pass on the requirement, and this must have closely followed the system of royal proclamations issued by yeomen of the crown acting as king's messengers.

Local knowledge also ensured that the council was aware of the deaths of those acting as sureties. This was part of a development after about 1495 when bonds with numerous sureties often contained clauses requiring acceptable alternatives to be named within a certain period of time after the death of any of the original group. A notable case involved the rebel Humphrey Savage. The original bond dated from 1499, but six years later his brother Thomas, archbishop of York, replaced the deceased prior of St Bartholomew's hospital in London. The crown evidently was quickly aware of the demise of sureties. There was certainly some process whereby Henry monitored the status of sureties, the effectiveness of bonds, and the longevity of the individuals involved.

The new evidence emphasises the links between the king, council and chancery, and the crucial role of the chancellor's department in managing writs and instructions on behalf of the king's council. The enrolment of memoranda of appearances might have been a chancery copy of recognisances related to key council business. An item from November 1487, concerning land in Elwell in the Welsh Marches, is explicitly linked to a case already in discussion before the king and council. Other memoranda of recognisances originating from council business were signed by Thomas Routhal, its secretary.

Royal councillors also had a direct role in managing how these bonds were applied. In July 1503 followers of Sir George Herbert were suggested as his sureties. Richard Fox and Lord Daubeney assessed their suitability to be bound under £500. The vetting process also involved consultation with his opponents. They were invited to confirm the acceptability of any further sureties, should some of those already listed refuse to act. Ultimately, the king and council had the final say on the suitability of sureties. In November 1507, despite having found twenty-seven peers and knights willing to act on his behalf, Lord Abergavenny was still given only until 9 February following to find substitutes for those 'thought insufficient' by the king and council.

Crown attempts to resolve the quarrel between the earl of Northumberland and archbishop of York in December 1504 make the link of council and chancery very clear. Since the charges of both men alleged riots and 'other enormities', they appeared before councillors in the Star Chamber and were placed under recognisances of £2,000 to keep the peace. The text of the recognisances was copied into the council minute, which also contains the statement that the recognisances were 'made and entered of record in the king's chancery more plainly doth appear'. The bonds were, however, taken in person before the chancellor in Westminster Hall, since the entry book also records that both lords were told 'not to use to come to Westminster Hall with so much company as they used'.

Equally as important as the dramatic increase in bonds issued during 1494 is the related rise in payments towards forfeitures. Most of the bonds issued during the first five years of the reign were for lifelong allegiance, with no requirement to pay unless conditions were broken. The rise in cash payments might be indicative of greater ruthlessness by the king as he tackled a sea change in the threat from internal conspiracy.

Where Dudley's activities indicate persistent pressure on the feudal connection of tenants-in-chief to the crown, the material that records appearances in chancery suggests very little noble involvement in bonds of loyalty and allegiance. This is confirmed by the contents of Dudley's petition, where only nine out of eighty-four bonds concerned nobles directly, and only two of the related fifty-one bonds cancelled immediately by Henry VIII after 1509 involved nobles. This is significant, since the bonds agreed in chancery were clearly political rather than feudal or fiscal. It does not suggest that bonds were targeted directly at nobles. Henry's determination to confront abuses of lordship at varying levels meant that he targeted networks and affinities rather than individuals.[11] By compelling loyal behaviour, Henry stifled the threat without the need for fines or more serious punishment.

Bonds were directed against tenants and servants as a way of obliging affinity leaders to exercise greater control. The king was targeting the ties of lordship and mutual expectation between servants and lords: servants faced potentially massive fines that they could only pay with the help of their masters. The onus was therefore placed on lords to regulate their followers' future behaviour so that the bonds were not forfeited – made explicit after a council order in July 1486, when lords were made responsible for producing servants involved in riot 'or other excess' before the council.[12] The vast majority of bonds of allegiance do in fact relate to men of lower rank, especially tradesmen and yeomen, but the implication is that ties of affinity and service were being monitored through the imposition of a general condition of allegiance, especially as Henry addressed at the same time other abuses of lordship such as illegal retaining, maintenance, and embracery.

Henry and his council introduced bonds as stabilising tools in cases of explicit gentry violence. In December 1488, Lords Clifford and Dacre were bound following their appearance before the council for attacks on Sir Christopher Moresby. All three were committed to the Fleet on their appearance before the king himself later that month. Numerous bonds directed individuals to do no malice towards other named persons, nor commit arson against their homes and property, while some more generally required the peace to be kept towards the king's people. Some agreements resulted in banishment from a region. Thomas Wrangwash was excluded from Yorkshire as a condition of his pardon after the Yorkshire rising of 1489. Part of Lord Abergavenny's punishment in 1507 was an agreement not to enter Kent, Sussex or Surrey without permission.

Many of the bonds refer directly to appearances before the council. In July 1486 Thomas Green was obliged by the council to produce a retainer suspected of murder. Henry Mitchell was duly bound before the council on 1 August. Sir Richard Corbet agreed to a bond in December 1487 to come before the council at Hilary next, but by May the council had found against him. Thomas Cruker, master of St Bartholomew's hospital, was bound for good behaviour on 21 July 1486, and this was evidently for rioting, since he confessed before the council and was fined the following day. Other bonds signify wide council interest in the proper performance of office. Many relate to tax assessors who had failed to deliver their collections or who were blatantly guilty of embezzlement.

The council was crucial to this process, and Henry's councillors must have had an unequivocal understanding of what the king was trying to achieve. This begins to explain his reliance upon a small group of officials who were solely and directly responsible to him. Some bonds state specifically that defendants were to appear before Bray and John Mordaunt as successive chancellors of the duchy of Lancaster, Lovell, and James Hobart and Thomas Lucas as attorney general and king's solicitor in the duchy chamber, or before the king and his council on progress. A small group of professional administrators who were also Henry's closest personal servants were relied upon to push through council business long before Dudley appeared. These men were the figures singled out as bad counsellors by the Cornish rebels in 1497, and suggests that the swift and forceful justice dispensed by the council was already seen by some as unjust and inequitable even before bonds became more numerous after 1502.

Since bonds were initiated as part of council business throughout the reign, the numerous nobles who served as councillors or judges in equity must have been at least aware that bonds had a track record of success as a means of achieving compliance to the law and in enforcing loyalty. This probably meant that the expansion in the use of bonds after 1502 was not a bolt from the blue that caught the early Tudor aristocracy by surprise. Many of the bonds and recognisances imposed on peers towards the close of the reign were legitimate fines for offences against the king's rights of marriage, wardship and livery of lands. And although the pursuit of Henry's feudal rights was pressed zealously by his ministers, some of the related bonds were manipulated for political rather than financial advantage. This is where criticism of Henry's use of bonds is perhaps justified.

It was only through the process of creating stability and enforcing loyalty that the inner resilience of the Tudor regime was developed. By imposing regulation upon the relationship of the crown and representatives of regional government, Henry accomplished one of the most important feats of late medieval government. He re-established a distinctly royal dignity and an obvious gulf between his wealth and power and that of England's leading subjects. This was fundamental to the subsequent ambitions and achievements of his heirs, and the employment of bonds was crucial to this process.

# 10

## THE KING'S NATION

### HENRY VII AND THE CHURCH

The power of the English Church dominated the daily lives of Henry's subjects to a far greater extent than his laws, his royal officials, or any prescient power of the monarchy itself. The Church was the focus of community life in each parish, and attendance was expected on Sundays and the main feast days. This regulation of communities was enforced by the crown and ruling elites since it helped to maintain stability and social order. This had been the case for many years, as Church and state had worked jointly to control moral and political behaviour.

Kings were expected to assist the Church in the defence of general morality, since disobedience of God's laws would also gnaw at Henry's own power. But he was further concerned with the specific conduct of clerics in their various roles. His attack encompassed the sexual offences of the clergy (addressed in a statute of 1485),[1] and the evils of simony,[2] pluralism,[3] and absenteeism. All were to be contained since they decayed the Church, undermined respect for clerics, and deprived Tudor subjects of spiritual guidance. Unravelling moral fabric was a short step from social breakdown and rebellion.

Henry's Church can be divided into secular and monastic communities. The leading bishops and archbishops presided over their cathedrals, chapters, dioceses, and archdioceses, and controlled the lower clergy who organised parish life. The abbeys of the main religious orders and less significant friaries, priories, and nunneries probably contained no more than 10,000 nuns and monks. But they held enormous estates based upon decades accumulating and defending their ancient endowments. The Church was the major landholder after the crown. Individual houses and bishoprics possessed their own lands and private rights, perhaps controlling up to a quarter of all land in England in 1485. No major new abbeys had been built in England after Henry V endowed Syon in 1415. Although Henry VII helped his favoured order of observant Franciscans to found new houses, the fifteenth century as a whole was one of consolidation of the Church resources and influence founded earlier. Church possessions were approaching the peak level that would be ruthlessly exploited by Henry VIII in the 1530s. This made the structure of the English Church that his father inherited stable and powerful.

The integrity of the Church could only be maintained through the appointment of men most suitable for spiritual office and the crushing of heresy and heterodoxy. Henry defended the orthodoxy of the Church. Convicted heretics could expect little leniency. As many as a hundred heretics were condemned during the reign, but only a handful refused to recant and were burned. At Canterbury, during Easter 1498, Henry intervened personally to force a Lollard to return to the Church's grace. Henry's primary concern was to enforce orthodoxy, since late medieval heresy was never far away from political rebellion in the eyes of the crown. The vast majority of the population, however, were orthodox. Many might have complained at the conduct of their clergy, but few went down the route of the Lollards – bypassing priests and the Latin Bible to take direct and personal control of the connection to God.

The link between heresy and rebellion also led to the Church becoming a target for Henry's prerogative interests after 1500: a rich Church, with too much freedom from royal power, and too strong a connection to Rome, could be a source of instability for a dynasty determined to control all challengers. Henry took this role as head of the Church very seriously, and balanced his own priorities with the valuable support of Rome against his enemies. While English Church and Tudor state were natural partners in the preservation of a stable society, it was vital for Henry that the crown dominated the relationship and used the papacy to uphold his personal power.

At the start of March 1486, Innocent VIII approved Henry's marriage to Elizabeth of York, his title as king of England, and the right of his heirs to inherit the crown by virtue of military victory and the assent of parliament. The Tudor right to the crown was also backed by Innocent's threat of excommunication to any rebels against Tudor kingship. Henry went so far as to start excommunication proceedings against the Irish archbishops of Armagh and Dublin for their support of Simnel in 1487. One scornful man, who falsely reported Henry's defeat at Stoke, fell dead on the spot after denouncing the usefulness of Henry's papal backing – a clear sign that Henry's benefactor existed at the highest level.

The Milanese ambassador noted In the autumn of 1497 that God was so fully on Henry's side that the Cornish rebels were suddenly dying as if poisoned after consuming beer and bread made from that year's harvest. These reports carried weight to contemporaries, and suggest Henry's awareness that the link between papal support and divine providence helped to legitimise Tudor kinship at the parish level. The crown fed this growing demand for gossip and information through the power of the new printing presses. In 1486 the first known broadsheets were mass-produced to proclaim papal acknowledgement of Henry's right to the throne.

In securing this, John Morton, in his role as Henry's campaigner in Rome, seems to have promised the papacy the financial support of a Tudor regime in England – both for the military threat to the Papal States and against the Turks. When this failed to materialise by 1489, the warm words of support for Henry emanating from Rome ceased. Henry's heavy taxation of the clergy, when so little came directly to the curia from the English crown, might also have disappointed Innocent VIII. English neutrality in the Holy League in the 1490s was also perhaps not a sufficient demonstration of commitment to Alexander VI's papacy to secure all the favours Henry wanted. His ardent wish to sanctify Henry VI sank in a morass of prevarication and delay at Rome. Despite proposing five candidates, only Archbishop John Morton was elected to the College of Cardinals during the reign. Henry received the cap, sword of maintenance and golden rose by each of the three popes that acceded during his reign. He maintained diplomatic contacts with Rome and appointed Giovanni and Silvester de Gigli as bishops of Worcester in 1497 and 1499 as reward for their services at the curia. Westminster's relationship with Rome was carefully checked and balanced. Henry retained the upper hand in England, however, simply because his royal predecessors had secured enough concessions from Rome to create a budding Church of England.

Henry clearly benefited from the effect of the pope's distant authority, but he sidelined it without a second thought when it conflicted with his political priorities. Fourteenth-century statutes obliged the pope to seek the king's agreement to any promotions to benefices in his gift. As head of the Church, the pope was allowed to collect fees for appointments to Church livings that were his to give and from the Peter's pence.[4] England was not a wealthy or generous land and Henry ensured that much Church wealth was directed into his coffers and not to the pope's. In 1501 he did send the pope an entire clerical subsidy towards a crusade – the meagre sum of £4,000. Despite papal gifts and political backing, Henry was not at all comfortable with the ways in which his authority could be sidestepped by appeals to Rome.

Potential disagreement between pope and king caused some of Henry's clerical councillors painful moral difficulties. Bishops' oaths of obedience to the pope were sometimes hard to observe when, as councillors, they acted to enforce Tudor policy on *praemunire* and mortmain. A writ of *praemunire* charged someone with resort to a foreign jurisdiction in a matter that should have been decided at an English court. Henry's lawyers, especially his attorneys James Hobart and John Ernley, applied the statute of *praemunire* to limit papal appeals over benefices, or failure to pay papal taxes and tithes. Where action was investigated and allowed, Henry also charged for the privilege. In 1505 Robert Rede of St Paul's found 50 marks to be allowed to send a letter to Rome against Archbishop Warham. Hobart fell from office in 1507 as a result of over-zealous *praemunire* prosecutions against leading churchmen. This evidence is suggestive of friction, if not factionalism, between the lawyers and clerics of the council. Henry pocketed over £500 for Hobart's pardon. *Praemunire* prosecutions continued under Ernley, but Henry was conscious of the clerical opposition this particular policy generated.

Land in mortmain was held inalienably by an ecclesiastical corporation. The Tudor king and his officers searched hard for grants and bequests of land and property from individual subjects to ecclesiastical bodies. Edward I had outlawed this practice in 1279, but since then the crown had made money by licensing specific gifts. Fees and fines were extracted for pardons where permission was not obtained.

Cardinal Morton was in the unique position of being able to temper royal demands upon the Church by reason of his personal connection to Henry and his command of the regime's institutional power. This was not always successful. Morton's role in the 1491 benevolence damaged his reputation, and he did little to stop the hounding of clerics for their contributions while he delayed his own payment. The dean and chapter of Wells were still struggling to pay their contribution in 1506. Henry used Morton to extend new demands to the clerical sphere. Convocations of Canterbury fell in line with parliament and granted fixed-sum subsidies instead of the usual tenths in 1489 and 1497. Early Tudor Church subsidies, forced loans, and benevolences were among the most frequent and aggressive of the fifteenth century.

Other councillors faced more pointed personal problems. On the one hand, Henry's almoner Christopher Urswick championed the king's rights to the goods of suicides and deodands (objects that caused accidental death), while on the other his clerical appointments brought him into conflict with his royal master. In 1498 Urswick was dean of Windsor when the intended burial place of Henry VI at St George's chapel was challenged. Urswick naturally backed Windsor against St Peter's Westminster but objected to the right of the council to decide the matter. Urswick was also friendly with other clerics who suffered under the king's mortmain and *praemunire* policies. Despite being a royal insider, he possessed texts and held opinions that indicated his interest in upholding the rights and liberties of the Church in the face of aggressive secular power.

Henry had to guard against the personal influence of clerics involved in the political networks of secular lords. Clerics were influential in their parishes not only because of their control over the sacrament but also for their apparent education. Many priests and chaplains owed their appointments to the patronage of greater figures that held the right of presentment to a parish living (an advowson). More senior men like William Beverley, dean of Middleham, or John Sant, abbot of Abingdon, frequently acted as spokesmen for their masters, or promoters of particular causes. As intermediaries between regional politics and community life, clerics held an important responsibility in the maintenance of loyalty and good order. Evidence of bonds throughout the reign suggests that Henry considered many clerics to have been too active in secular life.

Because service in the Church and a qualification in canon or civil law were clear indicators of education and ability, churchmen always had a role in government. The guardians of Henry's ruling conscience, such as the chancellor or keeper of the privy seal, were normally senior clerics. Roles that guarded the king's private conscience, like the deans of the household Geoffrey Simeon, Thomas Savage, and James Stanley, were important as masters of poor men's causes in the early court of Requests.

Henry's bishops were also more likely to be trained civil lawyers rather than simply career churchmen. This widened their value to the king and meant that there was a strong episcopal presence on the king's council that showed a definite royal preference for the promotion of lawyers over theologians among Henry's bishops.[5] Twenty-seven bishops were appointed during his reign. Only six were theologians; sixteen were lawyers. Edward IV, in a reign of similar length to Henry's, advanced just sixteen. The numbers of early Tudor appointments imply that Henry quickly and systematically began to use the abilities of his bishops in the widest possible way, with secular service through the council and household becoming the key to a prosperous career.

Henry's bishops were often men very well experienced in the secular world. The appointment of James Stanley, warden of Manchester College, as bishop of Ely in 1506 occurred for political reasons. He was promoted despite having three illegitimate children, and the reign's largest fine for illegal retaining. It is difficult to imagine a less suitable appointment on theological grounds. Richard Fox's skill as a diplomat made him the ideal border negotiator – tough and determined. Henry also saw the value of matching the best men to suitable appointments. At the close of the reign, Thomas Routhall, Henry's secretary, was nominated as bishop of Durham. He had been heavily involved in the conduct of council business. His vast experience of government at Westminster made him ideal in the most secular bishopric of Durham.

The roles acquired by bishops in the early Tudor regime made it easier for Henry to secure allies for his attack on abuses of Church liberties – primarily sanctuary. All sanctuaries could be used as places from which to abjure the realm and avoid punishment. Henry reacted vigorously to the abbot of Abingdon's aid for the rebels of 1486 and 1487. It was decided that evidence in the form of a charter or grant had to be produced to preserve the liberty of an established sanctuary. No liberties would be allowed in cases of treason. In August 1487, Henry secured a papal bull against abuses of sanctuary.

Benefit of clergy was another ancient right that exempted clerics from trial and punishment at common law. Previous kings had chipped away at laxity that had extended the right to all men who could read. Henry ensured that high treason and misdemeanours were exempted and the courts could decide when the benefit applied. Claims could only be made after conviction, so a felon's good were already forfeited in law. Henry saw that loopholes were closed in cases of petty treason (i.e. the murder of a master by a servant) and almost all felonies. To prevent more than one claim, branding became mandatory for those who received the benefit.

Kings too were frequently guilty of the sins and abuses that they were exhorted to undermine. Henry's enforcement of his rights was mirrored by a less honourable trade in direct crown appointments, and financial pressure on the rights of others to select those presented to livings. For example, Henry charged Thomas Knolles £100 to be sub-dean at York Minster, whereas James Harrington paid 1,000 marks to become dean there in 1508. Smaller priories did not escape Henry's attention. The Cistercian order, and the abbeys of Christchurch London, and St Mary's York, paid heavily for the right to select their own abbots – effectively to secure Henry's indifference when they might have expected him to interfere.

Although most of this debt was in the form of bonds, the cash income was substantial. Observance of conditions allowed the king to gain closer control over the type of behaviour clerics had to display to prevent forfeiture of the larger sums. Close crown scrutiny became more apparent in severe fines for breakouts from Church or abbey prisons. Archbishop Warham paid £1,600 for escaped felons in 1504, and others were fined in proportion to their status. These financial penalties reminded senior clerics that they served Tudor secular society as well as the Church.

Although fines for the restitution of bishops' temporalities could be high early in the reign (the new bishop of Lincoln paid £1,000 for his rights in 1494), most payments were modest and arrived as cash sums into the chamber. In the final years of Henry's kingship, not only were the payments greater but a much larger proportion was required by obligation. In September 1507 the restoration of the temporalities of Ely cost £3,800. Steven Gunn has calculated that Edmund Dudley collected over £38,000 for the king in the four years after September 1504 for confirmation of privileges of ecclesiastical bodies.[6] Henry's relationship with the Church blended his reliance upon its authority with a need to assert dominance over its resources. It was very much in keeping with the king's approach to secular power, where Henry was adamant that the Tudor crown would be the sole dominant force.

## LONDON AND THE CROWN

The population of the capital and its near suburbs was close to 50,000 in 1377. In the mid-fifteenth century the figure was probably between 30,000 and 40,000. London dwarfed York and Bristol, the next most populous cities. The foundation of London's influence was built on the 3,000 or 4,000 inhabitants who were adult male freemen, or citizens with some degree of political status. Government was based on twenty-five wards that were dominated by the livery companies. While citizenship was acquired by apprenticeship, purchase, or patrimonial inheritance, it was active participation in the political and mercantile life of the city that sealed reputations and ensured entry to the ruling elite. Freemen took their share of the burdens of city administration, serving as alderman, sheriff, and even mayor, in return for trading privileges and tax relief. Each October several hundred of the freemen met at the Guildhall to elect the mayor. The merchant rather than artisan companies usually dominated the commonalty or body of freemen, who cooperated to form London's government – the common council. Both groups also suspended their differences to defend London's liberties from crown encroachment.

Because it was the largest of England's settlements with the greatest concentration of wealthy and politically enfranchised residents, London was at the centre of almost all national activity. London drew the ablest business and legal minds, because its commercial and financial opportunities outstripped those available elsewhere. This trend was boosted by the proximity of the crown's administrative capital at Westminster. The royal chancery, Exchequer and the king's courts attracted a regular influx of people, and meant that the country's administrative and legal focus fell there. The stability of these institutions, and regular spectacular events such as royal processions, funerals and parliaments confirmed the capital as the social and fashion centre of the realm.

The city residences of nobles and bishops kept them close to the machinery of state and the Church. Great houses like Derby House, Coldharbour, and Baynard's Castle involved prominent national figures at the very centre of London life. The use of Crosby Place as a lodging for foreign ambassadors placed them within the orbit of the city as well as Westminster. A London or Westminster base was essential in the competition for influence and patronage around the court. In November 1496, for example, the feast to admit the new sergeants-at-law was held at the bishop of Ely's palace in Holborn and attracted the king and queen, 'and many lords of this land such as were then near unto the city'.[7]

Monarchs had also reduced the scale of their journeys away from London during the fifteenth century. From Henry VI's reign onwards kings had spent much of their year at Westminster or nearby on the river at Sheen, the Tower, or Greenwich. Henry VII was little different. After excursions to the north and East Anglia during his first decade as king, Henry became firmly rooted around London and the Thames valley.

As many as one in forty of the population lived in late fifteenth-century London. A wide range of high-status people who temporarily resided in the capital gave it enormous political weight. The depth of the medieval city's population had grown rapidly through the influx of British and foreign immigrants. The frequent clashes of cultures and commercial interests this generated provided an ideal platform for political leaders to exploit the congestion and intensity of London life. The ebb and flow of the dynastic struggle between Lancaster and York in the mid-fifteenth century had attached growing importance to the opinions of Londoners of all levels.

The population of the city became the sounding board for the crown's intentions and decisions. This process was formal through the powerful trading lobby of the city merchants and their representatives in parliament. Royal appeals for loans and gifts were also negotiated directly. Manipulation of Londoners was also informal, as they became the primary target of political propaganda in proclamations, public speeches, and moralising sermons at St Paul's cross. This relationship had been honed over centuries, but during the Wars of the Roses control of rumour and propaganda reached new levels.

Attempts by London's authorities to manipulate the capital's population were frequently at odds with the mood of the people. The Commons had seized food intended for the Lancastrian army in February 1461. A decade later, the aldermen and council held out for Edward IV while the mob enthused for disorder. There was a clear economic and social distinction between the wealthy and empowered and the poor and unenfranchised. But the constancy of both groups was always calculated with their own priorities foremost.

The scope for resentment between freemen and those who were not citizens was great. The 10,000 or so adult male labourers, servants, apprentices and vagrants could cause real problems of disorder for London's authorities at times of crisis. In March 1494 the mercers' apprentices attacked the Steelyard with the help of other 'idle and ill disposed persons'. London's packed communities transmitted political and economic changes to the inhabitants of the city almost instantly. This volatile mix was at once threatening and useful to fifteenth-century authorities.

London and Westminster's gravitational pull had helped to evolve the most sophisticated and politically aware citizenry. The key to success in the Wars of the Roses was the allegiance of the men and women who made the political, financial and trading centre of the realm function. London had been the political jewel for Richard, duke of York, who cultivated his popular reputation extensively. Edward IV and Richard, earl of Warwick, sought to exploit their connections in the capital during the readeption of Henry VI, 1470–1. Richard, duke of Gloucester, despite many years away from court in the 1470s, recognised that he had to secure London's favourable opinion once he decided to depose Edward V. Richard persuaded the politically astute Londoners that he had a right to rule even after the disappearance of Edward V while under his care.

Henry probably learned much from Richard III's successful interaction with London. Once Richard's own death was confirmed, London's governors wasted no time in making contact with him. This probably shows how the institutional power of the late medieval crown had developed despite the Wars of the Roses. The crown warranted obedience, regardless of who wielded its authority. Although Henry's victory might have seemed to be yet another short-term phase in the juggling of the crown, a usurping king backed by a victorious army had to be welcomed appropriately. It was because Henry was unknown as a man that London acted to flatter him to ensure that the power of the new Tudor monarch looked favourably upon London's liberties.

Unfortunately for Henry, his army carried a virulent new disease, known at the time as 'sweating sickness',[8] which began to kill hundreds of Londoners within a month of Bosworth. The serving mayor Sir Thomas Hill, his replacement Sir William Stokker, and several aldermen all died suddenly in September 1485. Henry was immediately at a disadvantage. The violent change of ruler and the outbreak of disease were linked as an omen of disaster. Many might have considered it to be God's second thoughts about the Tudor victory. The epidemic in London tested the organisational and propaganda skills of the fledgling king. Discussion of the disease, prophesising and speculation on its significance were banned as Henry sought to control the London printing presses. This was an inauspicious start for the new king and brought misery and suspicion to his early relationship with the capital.

Henry's reign therefore began with an urgent need for command of the crown's relationship with the population – what today would be called political spin. One important method was the encouragement of public celebration. The king's almoner enforced parish participation through the ringing of bells and compulsory masses.[9] Citizens could be fined for not heeding the bells that announced royal journeys through London's parishes. The mayor and aldermen were encouraged to light bonfires and to provide wine in celebration of the various treaties and agreements made with foreign rulers. In March 1503, Henry's oath during a mass at St Paul's to observe covenants agreed with Maximilian's ambassadors was celebrated with a Te Deum in the cathedral. An order for the same was passed to all London churches. Victory in battle, like Stoke in 1487, was marked in a similar way, as was news of the birth of and death of Prince Arthur. St Paul's Cross, or the door into St Paul's churchyard, were the venues for the cursing by bell, book and candle of the king's traitors. Publication of broadsheets sped this process, and ensured that the crown had more control over gatherings of London's population and the information it received.

Like previous kings, Henry had to maintain London's central role in crown finance through income from loans, taxes, and the customs revenue. The crown could reciprocate by actively stimulating London's prosperity through tax concessions and trading privileges. Henry's previous anonymity and the strained start to his relationship with the city brought new tensions that heightened the established pattern of fluctuating mutual reliance and distrust.

The king's private connections with London certainly existed before Bosworth. In February 1486 Henry repaid money borrowed in London for military supplies towards the Bosworth campaign. The king's search for further allies in London also singled out suppliers for the provision of everyday purchases and luxury goods once Henry had a royal household to maintain. The saddler John Broughton was the preferred merchant for the queen's expensive horse equipment and also supplied to the royal stables. The king's cordwainer, Anthony Gyse, could be sure of prompt payment of his bills. Others also had a role in strengthening the working relationship between London and the crown. Men like John Flygh, yeoman of the robes in the wardrobe, John Grice, royal apothecary, and Vincent Tutellar, Henry's armourer, used their posts to determine which other merchants were appointed to supply the raw materials to the king's own artisans. Flygh's personal associations could explain why business was offered to traders like Henry Rousselyn who supplied fourteen dozen skins to the wardrobe in August 1486. In the same year the mercer Thomas Fuller provided products as diverse as Henry's brigandines, gowns for the queen, and satin for lining the king's tippets.[10]

The king's personal grooming of London's merchants was also matched by attempts to make institutional contacts at a greater scale. Early attempts to cultivate the city were made tentatively through those royal servants with London connections. The records of the common council show that Henry received at least £13,000 in loans before the close of 1491. In 1485 the London merchant Avery Cornborough served as joint under-treasurer of the Exchequer with Reginald Bray. Bray's wide contacts enabled him to become the chief negotiator for royal loans from the city during Henry's early years. Cornborough was also involved as a mediator between the lawyers who advised the royal council and London's merchants when the statutes governing the sale and export of unfinished cloth were examined in November 1487. With many London men on the inside of the Tudor regime, the city felt confident about standing up to the king's demands, and made him work for whatever it was willing to give. In 1486 the Treasurer, Lord Dinham, accompanied Bray to request a loan of 6,000 marks. A meeting of the common council offered the king £2,000, which was repaid the following year. A similar situation occurred in 1497 when Henry asked for £10,000 to help defend the realm against the Scots. After discussion London offered £4,000.

Individual merchants and the company members also suffered under Henry's 1491 benevolence and the forced loan of December 1496. The London chroniclers recorded the resentment generated by the tactics of the king's officials. In 1491, when Henry asked Mayor John Mathew for a personal contribution of £200, many aldermen and lesser officials feared a similar demand, and some of them refused payment altogether, leaving their executors to wrangle with the crown after their deaths. The king's councillors and other commissioners were assigned groups of merchants and company members. The discretion this allowed caused some to be treated harshly. Chancellor Morton, for example, charged the drapers up to £40 each, while Peter Courtenay, bishop of Winchester, extracted up to 60 marks from members of the mercers company. The whole city was reported to have raised over £9,682. The grinding and relentless pursuit of the sums assessed continued for years. An Act in the 1495 parliament allowed the crown to chase promissory notes and commissioners tracked down defaulters. In London the benevolence was renamed 'malevolence' for the charge it imposed. The double standards applied were demonstrated by the fact that Chancellor Morton did not make payment of his own assessment of £1,500 until June 1496.

The loans London offered and the availability of its wealth to royal tax assessments encouraged Henry's reliance on its financial power. Of the 1486 loan, £937 came directly from the mercers, grocers and drapers. Such impressive wealth created the leverage that fortified the city's negotiating position when changes to its liberties were proposed. Londoners were very mindful of their own authority and the city's ancient independence from direct royal control. Late fifteenth-century officials were elected time and again under the principal aim of defending the city's rights. Unlike other towns, London's sophisticated ruling structure had always clashed with the increasingly powerful royal presence down the road at Westminster. A complex relationship therefore developed that posed particular problems for an assertive but insecure monarch like Henry. Even if Henry could not control how the liberties of London were exercised, he demanded to know exactly what those rights were, and how they might conflict with crown interests.

The crown had encroached upon London's privileges in the recent past, and this made the capital wary. During the 1440s, Henry VI alienated London's elite when he began to sell the city's offices to household men as a way of raising cash. Technically, London's privileges were gifts of the crown, periodically negotiated and confirmed by the issue of a new charter. Where London offended or opposed the crown, consequences could be severe. Richard II had withdrawn the city's liberties in 1382 following the Peasant's Revolt, and only regranted them on payment of £30,000. The balance of the relationship between the king and the mayor was that both parties knew the limits of their own bargaining position. Henry VI's intervention overstepped the boundary, and deliberately challenged the rights of those mercantile companies associated with particular posts. London's council tried to negotiate limitations on these grants by arguing that they undermined the mayor's authority. Part of this process was to threaten the flow of loans to the crown.

Henry VII's pressure on London was not primarily to raise cash or to find new ways to reward crown servants, although this did occur. His insecurity made him concerned at the uncontrolled influence of the London-based merchant oligarchy, since it dominated national wealth creation and controlled access to markets for English goods. London's political decision-makers had determined who would wear the crown in 1461 and 1470–1. Henry could not prevent this self-interest from reappearing if the capital's political and economic sympathies moved against the Tudors. Neither could he allow it to threaten the regime's general security. The influence of Londoners in the Calais staple and among the merchant adventurers in the Netherlands created a dangerous connection that could transmit conspiracy as well as uncertainty. Instead of buying the favour of the mayor and aldermen, Henry sought to intimidate London's rulers into accepting the concessions he offered, with the caveat of more forceful royal scrutiny of their business.

The king's men who forged the crown's links with London also acted as Henry's chief agents in his attempts to dominate the capital. Long before Edmund Dudley began to hound London's leading figures from his house in Candlewick Street, Henry's household officers employed a network of promoters and agents. They monitored what was going on in the city and looked for lapses in behaviour or fraud that the king could exploit. In May 1495, for example, one of these men, John Baptist Grimaldi, uncovered offences against old mercantile statutes committed by the alderman Sir William Capel who was fined over £2,743. Capel used his wife's kinship with Lady Daubeney to secure a reduction of this fine, but he still paid over £730 in cash during the following three years.

Constructive personal connections were vitally important in smoothing the relationship between London and the crown. The other side of these private contacts was the personal animosities that sometimes grew from rivalries and conflicts. The crown's awareness of these clashes offered Henry the means to exert influence over London's close-knit government. In June 1488, Grimaldi was in prison on various charges of debt, trespass, and detention of goods. The originator of some of these indictments was Robert Watts, a draper associated with William Capel, who died in office as sheriff when Capel was mayor in 1504. By then, Grimaldi was working tirelessly for Empson and Dudley in the pursuit of lapsed recognisances and debts due to the crown. It was perhaps no coincidence that Capel then suffered a repeat of his 1495 charges. When the crown's officers began to rely on the information supplied by shady figures that moved throughout the social flux of London life, it was almost inevitable that grudges and old scores would play some part in the execution of the king's policies.

Dudley, like Bray, had solid links with London before he moved into direct royal service. Dudley was a brilliant student at Gray's Inn during the 1480s and was an MP in the parliaments of the early 1490s. He was under-sheriff of London from November 1496 and served on various city courts. He was also awarded a fee for life from London before he resigned his official contact with the city in 1502. When Dudley entered the king's service he had an extensive knowledge of how London was governed, of how Londoners lobbied parliament, and an expert appreciation of the ways in which the law could define the capital's relationship with the crown. With his background, Dudley was an ideal figure through whom Henry could exert greater influence. It is perhaps no coincidence that instances of crown interference in the city increase once Dudley became a royal councillor.

In a shocking case from 1505–06, Mayor Thomas Kneseworth and his two sheriffs Richard Shore and Roger Grove were accused of abusing their office and imprisoned in the Marshalsea. Trading offences similar to those alleged previously against Capel were the basis for this prosecution, and could represent a royal clampdown on the privileges that London's rulers had previously enjoyed. When Kneseworth and Grove were pardoned and released from prison in February 1508, the price of the king's forgiveness was cash payments, recognisances, and obligations totalling over £1,300.

This mentality of suspicion compounded more direct threats to London's independence, such as the manipulation of elections. In 1498 Henry sent a letter to Mayor William Purchase expressing his preference for Sir John Percival in the forthcoming mayoral election. This was a thinly veiled demand on the king's part, especially as Thomas Savage, bishop of London and president of Henry's council, had already voiced this request. The common council had blocked Percival in previous years, perhaps because he reputedly coveted the post obsessively, but the king's bullying secured his election.

Henry also employed his influence to unsettle the relationship between London's livery companies. At the start of 1503 negotiations were underway between the mayor and the crown for a new charter for the tailors' company. The tailors considered the title 'merchant tailors' to be more appropriate to how their status had developed. By November 1503 the mayor was summoned to appear in council to show why the king should not allow the tailors to change their style. In this instance the king was clearly challenging the mayor's authority, knowing perfectly well that there were few grounds on which royal wishes could be resisted.

When the other companies heard of this there was opposition and the common council voted to block the charter. The threat of violence against the tailors became so serious that the king's council issued an injunction. The mayor was made responsible for any disturbances in the city, while individual aldermen would answer for misconduct in their wards. The next master of the tailors, William Fitzwilliam, took up the task in 1505. Despite the animosity of many mercantile aldermen, Henry granted the charter. His price was £100 for his 'especial and gracious favour' in exercising his royal prerogative, and for allowing the tailors to enrol the charter – something that should have been a normal and less expensive part of the process of such grants.

Once aligned with the crown Fitzwilliam was caught between the two competing influences of king and mayor. Later in 1505, the outgoing mayor Thomas Kneseworth proposed Fitzwilliam as one of London's two sheriffs. The king expressed his wish that Fitzwilliam should serve. This was seen as a derogation of the city's liberties, and the common council swiftly rejected him in favour of their own candidate Thomas Johnson. He was prevented from being sworn in while the king's decision was awaited. Johnson returned to London and performed his office for ten days until the king forced a new election. Fitzwilliam was then imposed upon the city authorities, and the properly elected Johnson was displaced. In September 1506, Dudley extracted £100 in cash from Fitzwilliam for the king's favour in backing his election as sheriff. But London had its revenge after Henry's death. The council tried to make Fitzwilliam serve as sheriff once again. When he refused he was stripped of his citizenship and fined 1,000 marks. Only Thomas Wolsey's intervention restored his status in 1511.

At a practical level Henry's officers also interfered with the daily roles of the mayor and his colleagues. The king was not satisfied that the mayor had done enough to investigate the embracery and contempt of a jury in a London case in 1488. The throwing down of the king's bill within the mayor's court during this case also concerned Henry greatly. It was a symptom of tensions over legal jurisdiction that grew as the reign progressed. In 1491 the king's almoner Christopher Urswick clashed with the sheriffs' officers over rightful possession of the valuable goods of a tailor named Roger Shavelock who had committed suicide in his shop.

By 1496 London's rulers were surer of their ability to resist the king's intrusions. When trade was renewed between England and the Netherlands in 1496, the common council vehemently resented Henry's request that the common seal of London should be exchanged with those from the Low Countries as part of Henry's treaty with Maximilian. The mayor and several aldermen were called before the council, but not even high-powered delegations could convince the merchant adventurers to relent. The mayor was eventually obliged to submit his personal bond and seal to the king's ambassador going to Calais to meet with his Burgundian counterparts. By 1499 the council agreed with London's sentiments. Burgundy demanded that a record of English wool purchases and exports be created at Calais. The royal council felt that spies within the town would soon uncover England's trading secrets, and asked Henry's secretary to create a suitably impressive reply declining Maximilian's request.

Ill feeling resulted when Henry's intrusions sought to bypass the established democracy of city government, or simply interfered with established rights in a disruptive way. The conduct of London's rulers when exercising their right to claim the property of orphans was investigated in January 1499. William Moore, one of the sergeants-at-arms, was instructed to cause the mayor and chamberlain to appear with the records of recognisances for the safe keeping of orphan's goods. Henry's demands also had a cumulative effect. Although the mayor and common council changed with each election, the crown's impositions institutionalised a spirit of resistance among prominent Londoners that transcended individuals and crafts. Growing corporate animosity towards the Tudor crown partly explains why the king targeted the existing rivalries between certain livery companies as a way of grasping some influence. Some royal commands were obeyed but were reported in language that suggests genuine reluctance.

In May 1488 the mayor was ordered to investigate merchants who had exported goods despite the trade embargo with the Netherlands. The mayor and aldermen were given the king's version of the full facts concerning Burgundian help for Lambert Simnel's rebellion. They deliberated with the merchant companies and 'freely and gladly' offered to bear the financial cost of losing their main markets in Flanders and Brabant until trade was restored. In this case the crown had to coerce London into following royal policy. An admission by the mayor that there had been recent and widespread disregard of the embargo suggests something of the differing priorities of the city and the crown.

A relationship based on confrontation emerged more strongly as Henry's reign neared its end. Royal servants who were grudgingly respected in London for their personal qualities were replaced as they died by others who enforced the king's wishes more ruthlessly. Although Bray was not well loved by Londoners, after his death he was remembered as a straightforward man who did his best to earn his bribes. Dudley took the money but was more likely to play one suitor against another for his and the king's benefit. The latter part of Henry's reign is characterised by the rapid rise to notoriety of king's agents like the London promoters John Baptist Grimaldi and John Camby, a corrupt sheriff's sergeant. They had emerged under Bray and Empson in the search for old debts and lapsed fines, but thrived under Dudley.

Dudley's familiarity with London pushed up the price of royal favour. In 1504 the city paid 5,000 marks for confirmation of its charter. This was the culmination of over two years of negotiations, and tied the city into extensive bonds. Dudley's policy also ensured that there was a general tension between London and Westminster over how recognisances were handled. Attempts by Henry to deprive the mayor of his right to forfeited recognisances or broken sureties of the peace were resisted fiercely in 1506. The mayor and aldermen often responded to crown meddling with a forceful declaration of the ancient privileges of the city. Particularly important here were the written records of those rights and liberties. London's government resolutely defended royal requests to take over indictments for felony or trespass and to surrender original records related to offences committed within their jurisdiction. In other instances the mayor exercised his legal right to hear cases before the arrival of writs from the king's chancery, and resisted writs of *certiorari* that attempted to remove into the Westminster courts cases that had commenced in London.

By 1507 Henry's regular incapacity through illness allowed Empson and Dudley to operate without any apparent royal restraint. Henry's sanction for this policy cannot be questioned, but his direct control over its exercise was virtually absent in his final years. In the 1507–09 period, Camby and Dudley were responsible for squeezing unlawful payment of £500 from the haberdasher Thomas Sunyff for a recognisance for good behaviour that he did not forfeit. He was imprisoned as an accessory to a fabricated murder, had his lands seized on illegal grounds, was forced to make further payments to escape house arrest, and finally locked in the Tower until after Henry's death. Other persecutions continued. In 1508 Dudley threw Sir William Capel in the Tower for refusing to pay £2,000. Empson similarly locked up the previous mayor Sir Lawrence Aylmer. This year also saw Kneseworth, Shaw and Grove released on the promise to make payments and enter bonds already mentioned.[11] How times had changed from December 1488 when the council ordered that Sir Robert Pilkington be locked in the Fleet and fined 10 marks for the unjust imprisonment of a poor man. Twenty years later royal councillors were openly applying even more callous policies on the king's behalf, and seemingly with his full knowledge.

Many figures agreed to bonds simply to end the uncertainty and evasiveness of the king's councillors. When coupled with the pressure on London's institutional independence, these measures might seem like a deliberate policy to wear down the resistance of the common council to royal encroachments upon liberties. It was certainly an unscrupulous and unsubtle policy that does not sit comfortably with Henry's reliance upon London's contribution to the crown's income through taxation and customs revenue. It was also a dangerous area in which to persist. Political feeling, as voiced by the *Great Chronicle*, showed real hostility to Empson and Dudley for their devious entrapments on behalf of the king. Things were becoming so bad by 1509 that civil unrest was a possibility. Looming rebellion was all but acknowledged by the wording of Henry VIII's general pardon of 24 April 1509 of all recognisances except provable debts and accounts.

These cases indicate a deliberate attempt by Henry, Empson, and Dudley to force defaulting individuals to compound with the crown for a myriad of offences that went way beyond the normal hazards of public office. The additional punishments of imprisonment, penalties for release, and fines for pardon, were unjust and illegal impositions.

While we can understand Henry's wish to enforce security through obedience of his laws and the proper performance of officials, such aggressive attacks on the wealth and status of London's influential elite bred real resentment. Few aldermen could have doubted that when their turn came to serve as sheriff and then mayor, royal scrutiny of their conduct in office could result in personal imprisonment and near financial ruin. For many within London's inner ruling circle, Henry's death was a relief. His policies were formally abandoned, although the management of many accumulated bonds and debts to the crown was maintained. The release of the pressure that Henry's web of financial constraints had built up was very apparent in the rejoicing of London at his son's accession. Empson and Dudley became the convenient focus for London's hatred. They were sacrificed on the block in 1510 to spare the new king unpleasant facts about the persecutions of his father's last few years.

## TRADE, COMMERCE, EXPLORATION, AND THE ECONOMY

We have already seen how Henry sought to control his subjects and strengthen his kingship by manipulating their wealth. As this policy strengthened during the reign, the realm's leading subjects especially had to feel that they were becoming more prosperous if the king's biting financial measures were to be tolerated. In the long term, the regime had to ensure that the economy and trading climate remained healthy. Yet it had always been difficult for the crown actively to influence and regulate economic behaviour. Kings could put their personal economies in order relatively easily, as long as they had realistic but clear aims and recruited diligent officials. The crown set the framework for the economy through parliamentary legislation and the controlling influence of the royal council and courts. But trade was so dependent on England's established markets that economic prosperity went hand in hand with political stability and beneficial foreign policy.

Early Tudor England was a self-sufficient agricultural nation of about 2.5 million people. Natural pressure of pestilence on population and the British climate on agricultural harvests made the crown reactive to these two major factors at the heart of an essentially rural economy. Edward III and Richard II had been forced by the plague-related population disasters of 1348 and 1375 to attempt to control wages through acts such as the statutes of labourers. Skilled craftsmen placed a higher price on their labour. Landlords in their roles as employers would not be held to ransom.

Henry VII's generation of Englishmen also faced the full economic impact of the final loss of England's French lands by 1453. With the end of empire markets in Gascony and Normandy, Calais remained the sole English-controlled outlet for English exports on the European mainland. The merchants of the staple of Calais handled all the exports of English wool,[12] which gave Calais an economic prominence by 1485.

The focus of England's primary export on Calais drew the business of the cloth merchants of the Low Countries. In turn, Yorkist kingship became politically and culturally more aligned to the Burgundian Netherlands. The narrowing of economic opportunities for wool exporters and the stranglehold of the Calais staplers on the English wool trade might have been a factor in the rise of English cloth manufacture and export during Edward IV's reign. English manufacturers sought ways of bypassing the monopoly of the staplers. Figures for the customs duty on exported cloth show a rise during the 1470s that continued steadily throughout Henry's reign. This was achieved with careful direction by the crown. Towards the end of 1487, Henry investigated the existing practice for the export of unfinished cloth when the legal officers of the council examined and reported on the relevant statutes.

English merchants for goods other than wool were able to seek out markets on the basis of their trading skill, the quality of their products, and the prices they offered. This 'merchant adventuring' took traders into the lands of all England's neighbours. The merchants of cities like Coventry, York, Norwich, and Bristol were used to working within structured organisations as members of guilds and fraternities. The small ports down England's east coast had ready access to northern European markets. It was London that led the way, however. The largest port contributed the most in customs revenue and provided the basis from which most other trading activities, trends, innovations, and developments took their cue.

When late fifteenth-century kings showed renewed interest in gaining control over the capital's key contribution to national wealth, the merchants themselves responded by pooling their resources. In the Yorkist period members of the leading London livery companies of the mercers, drapers and skinners began to combine their foreign trading activities.

They also offered to the crown on an informal basis their expert knowledge of conditions and affairs in England's near neighbours. By 1486 circumstances were right for formal recognition (by London's common council, not Henry) of a court of merchant adventurers.

Henry saw this as an opportunity to foster a useful working relationship with the capital and encouraged London's companies to control the organisation of adventuring merchants in the Low Countries and the Netherlands. The circular relationship between London's rulers, Henry's financial preoccupations, and the freedom to trade of London's merchants became a driving force in the early Tudor economy. Henry's desire to influence London's government meant that the crown had to engage with the mercantile oligarchy that ran the city.[13]

It was in the activities of the merchant adventurers that Henry's backing for English traders aligned economic strategy most closely with foreign policy. For a king with many external enemies and a constantly shifting diplomatic strategy to maintain England's position, this was vital. Henry's regulation of trade therefore offers an interesting insight into how he attempted to project England's reputation around Europe. Almost all the treaties agreed with foreign powers contained clauses that looked to define or protect English trading rights. England's ports also became more focused on their most appropriate markets – Southampton dealing with Mediterranean trade; Bristol with Ireland, Spain and stockfish suppliers in Iceland.[14] Newcastle already exported coal, and ports all along the east coast linked to Scandinavia and the Baltic. The position of the Thames estuary focused London's regional hinterland on trade with the Netherlands.

The importance of this trading link was demonstrated by Henry's willingness to negotiate directly with Archduke Philip during the mid-1490s when his father refused to stop supporting Henry's nemesis Perkin Warbeck. Henry had already recognised that his maritime trading policy was also closely bound with the internal politics of England's trading partners. In July 1486 the Cinque Ports received a proclamation ordering good treatment of Burgundian ships and safe conduct for merchants from the Low Countries. Other nations and trading groups like the Hanseatic League, with which England was at truce in 1486, were to receive similar treatment.

The Yorkist kings had extended the trading presence of the Hanse within England, but English North Sea traders found their opportunities reduced by the powerful monopoly of the Hanse traders. By 1486, Henry set about asserting English trading rights. Restrictions on the type of goods the Germans could trade, complaints of protectionism, and commercial treaties with nations like Spain and Denmark, put pressure on the Hanse exclusion of England from northern waters. When some Hanse merchants acted as couriers for Warbeck in 1493, Henry placed the leading Hanse men under a massive bond not to trade with Archduke Philip the Fair's lands. By 1498 Henry had agreement from the Hanse to uphold mutual trading opportunities. An independent treaty in 1504 with Riga, the dominant Hanse town in the Baltic, did bring the League to the negotiation table. In parliament that year Henry confirmed the privileges of the Hanse because he was assured that the League would now honour English concerns. Henry's policy was dogged and clear, and he ultimately secured the rights denied to the Yorkist kings.

Where Henry acted resolutely to uphold English rights, English merchants also did their part. Burgesses from the major ports had been behind the Navigation Acts that tried to protect domestic shipping from the better-organised cartels of the Hanse and Venice. In 1485 foreign vessels were barred from importing wine from Gascony and in 1489 a statute permitted only English ships to bring woad[15] from southern France. This same act also tried to prevent Englishmen from using foreign ships to export their goods. The Act was not widely obeyed, but the king's intention to force a reliance on English shipping was still apparent in July 1504. A council decree that month ordered all customs officers to charge native-born merchants who shipped goods in foreign vessels at the higher rate as if they were foreign traders. This encouraged compliance with the Navigation Acts and shows that Henry was trying to make the English economy the main beneficiary of English trade.

This made sense to the crown because most of England's cloth trade went to the Low Countries. There was also a thriving trade for English wool and cloth with the Italian republics. Henry used his knowledge and interest in Italian affairs to advantage English trade where he could. Italian merchants dominated the import business at Southampton. The control of Venice and Genoa over the carriage of spices and wine from the eastern Mediterranean meant that England had to pay high freight charges. Attempts by the English to undercut Venice resulted in extra taxes on wine carried in foreign vessels. Henry already charged aliens higher customs and double taxation rates, but he soon looked for other outlets in Italy.

England established links with the Florentine republic by 1486. A consulate at the Florentine port of Pisa and a favourable trading treaty in 1490 supported a staple for English wool. Henry tried to limit the amount of wool supplied to Venice and in return the republic tried to stop her ships trading to Pisa. England responded with a higher duty of Mediterranean wine and a maximum sale price. A compromise was reached, but even in resisting Venice's demands, Henry showed himself willing to risk a great deal in defence of England's interests.

It was no surprise that Henry's attention to economic matters extended to over fifty out of 192 parliamentary statutes. Acts fixed the price of woollen cloth and of hats and caps, and banned the export of bullion and jewels without licence. Legislation showed a concern for the influence of population fluctuations and the knock-on effects of poor or bumper harvests on prices and wages. The infrequency of Henry's parliaments also allowed the king a greater role in regulating economic developments through proclamations and ordinances. Ensuring that economic statutes were applied and enforced was a key function of the council, and was conducted with the same rigour as political and diplomatic matters. This was something of a double-edged sword. Without frequent parliaments, Henry did not have a regular and formal indication of the priorities of the mercantile classes – if such a thing existed uniformly. The private petitions of the Commons that were discussed and presented as an agreed appeal to the king and the Lords became dissipated. An increasing number reached the crown as individual grievances in equity suits before Chancery or the council. This clouded the king's ability to gauge the mood of the trading community in response to the royal direction of policy. The type of pressure that had resulted in the Navigation Acts of 1485, 1489 and 1491 had to be channelled towards the king in different ways.

Council decrees, and obligations and recognisances, played a familiar role in controlling economic performance. Virtuous conduct in office became a pressing concern of the king as economic officials and agents were placed under the same scrutiny as the stewards and constables of crown lands and castles. Customs officers were monitored especially closely. In June 1486, letters were sent to the mayors and officers of the ports to enforce the law and customs regulations against departing ships. Any punishment would fall upon the negligent officers, rather than the masters or owners of the vessels.

Specific offenders were confronted forcefully, as Hugh Killinghall and Maurice Filiol, respective customers of Newcastle upon Tyne and Poole, found in April 1505. They were bound to abide by the statutes that governed their office, and were not to abuse their positions by bringing in goods without paying duty. Henry also required documentation of all their business activity to be presented at the Exchequer each Easter. Henry needed the skills of experienced officials, but only if crown interests were their primary concern. Towards the end of the reign the council was particularly expert at tracking customs evasion, malpractice of searchers at the ports, and accounting laxity. The Exchequer court coped with perhaps as many as 1,400 cases concerning customs evasion during the reign, with many more settled by fine or bond through the council or local commissioners.

Henry also introduced a clear way of calculating the duty due on particular types of goods, by giving them a formal value in a book of rates. The book was in use in the port of London in 1502. When the values given to imported goods were realistic and accurate reflections of the market price, the crown was guaranteed a regular rate of customs duty. When prices began to differ from the formal valuation, merchants began either to pay too much duty on their goods or the crown's income fell as prices of goods increased. During the prosperous years of Henry VII's reign this did not become a problem, but later Tudor monarchs attempted to compensate for the static nature of the rates by reissuing them for various ports in line with inflation.

Henry seems to have been particularly concerned to intervene to stimulate and direct the aspects of trade within royal control. He personally engaged in commerce, especially in bullion dealing and wool exports. Specialist royal contacts in this area made Henry keenly aware of the profits that could come the way of his officials and other individuals through mercantile activity.

Another lucrative approach exploited the early Tudor rise in production and export of worked cloth. The king became ruthless in his control of imports of alum from Italy. This mineral fixed dye to cloth. It was therefore essential because cloth and unworked wool probably accounted for more than 80 per cent of England's exports during Henry's reign. Henry supported a judicial decision to resist the pope's claim to monopoly on alum export, despite the threat of excommunication.

The king not only issued licences for the import of alum to factors and agents, such as the Bolognese merchant Ludovico de Fava, he also demanded bonds for the payment of what were effectively hiked customs duties. In December 1507 he even allowed his own vessel, the *Regent*, to be chartered to Italy to bring back 7,000 kintals (hundredweights) of the mineral. Laurence Bonvixi, from Lucca, was licensed to import alum, but by May 1508 he was obliged by indenture to pay the king 13s 4d for every kintal he sold. There is a real sense here that Henry exploited the boom in cloth trade to benefit himself as well as the wider economy.

Henry's direct links with foreign merchants were crucial to the maintenance of trade and the benefit of crown coffers. They were an obvious source of loans and, as aliens, paid higher tax revenues. They could be licensed to bypass the political barriers to free trade, such as Thomas Maungall's warrant to import madder from the lands of Maximilian in 1506. Henry also made loans from his private resources to merchants who then could generate a real return directly to royal coffers. There were many complex arrangements. In 1508 Laurence Bonvixi agreed to pay an additional £400 directly to the king over the usual custom rate of 100 marks, for as long as he held 5,000 marks lent by the king. This may have been linked to Laurence's activities as an alum importer. The same year Lukyn di Vivaldis was given £2,000 of the king's money, but had to repay it on two months' warning. The scope for personal profit must have been great since, while he was using the cash to fund his business, Lukyn had to pay the crown an additional 500 marks in annual customs.

Henry also engaged in foreign currency and rate speculation. One of the chamber books contains an inventory in his own hand of foreign coins paid to John Heron. In 1509 some merchants agreed to obligations to honour increases in the exchange rates of pennies to ducats over five quarter years. The boost to the economy was indirect, but these were considerable sums which Henry had available as cash. Henry demonstrated an economic interest, grasp of technical procedures, and flair for profit. Even at the end of the reign, when his health was in decline, Henry and his ministers continued intricate arrangements that brought thousands of pounds to the crown. Henry's concern here outlawed the establishment of money exchanges without licence, and limited moneylending.

Crown control of the coinage was something Henry established early in the reign. New coin designs were introduced soon after Lord Daubeney was made joint master of the mint in November 1485. Henry evidently saw the purity of the coinage as the vital foundation of the economy. In 1489 the forging of foreign coins was made treasonable. By 1504 Henry further defined the penalties for clipping the new coins introduced earlier. Council proclamations and statutes were used to make these new gold royals, angels, silver groats, pennies and farthings familiar as tender. Perhaps more important was the symbolism associated with new designs.

The new silver shilling of 1489 was the first English coin to have a recognisable image of the reigning monarch. The heavy gold sovereign, introduced at the same date, showed Henry wearing an imperial closed crown – an image developed by his Tudor successors. The intended symbolic impact of the coins minted for the 1492 French expedition has already been mentioned.[16] The public emphasis on royal control of the coinage was a major part of Henry's propaganda to stamp a Tudor presence on the history of English kingship. There were powerful ideological messages of legitimacy and authority, as well as economic necessity, behind Henry's development of the coins in circulation.

Henry's attention to profitable trade was also at the root of his interest in exploration. England's position on the edge of Europe, and her earlier medieval empire in south-west France, meant that English sailors were familiar with long-distance trade routes to Portugal, Spain, and Madeira. Bristol mariners had fished the cod-rich seas off Iceland for generations. By the early 1490s, the Spanish ambassadors were aware that Englishmen had been searching for the mythical Atlantic Isle of Brasil. These reports and quayside gossip might even have reached Columbus's ears.

Henry's failure to re-establish England's French empire in 1492 coincided exactly with Columbus's apparent landfall in Asia. News of his amazing discovery might have prompted Henry to sponsor a search for new lands in the west. He had missed his chance to support Columbus, who had sent his brother to England in 1489, but in 1494 the Bristol-based Genoese John Cabot successfully petitioned for authority to explore on Henry's behalf.

In March 1496 Cabot and his sons were given the right to discover and investigate lands previously unknown to Christians. They did not sail until about 20 May 1497. Cabot probably made an American landfall from his ship the *Matthew* in modern Newfoundland or Maine on 24 June 1497. He tracked the coastline before returning via Brittany by 10 August, when Henry interviewed him personally. The king was pleased enough to grant Cabot a pension of £20 per year from the Bristol customs.

There is little evidence that Henry became wildly enthusiastic for Cabot's revelations, although the Milanese ambassador reported in December that the king intended to equip a larger expedition directly. In May 1498 Cabot did again set sail westwards, perhaps because his 1497 voyage had produced concrete proof of new land. Cabot had even provided a map of his discoveries to Henry's court.

Nothing more was heard of Cabot. Expeditions to northern waters by the Portuguese in 1500 and 1501 confirmed Cabot's earlier identification of the mainland (and discovered a broken sword and people wearing European earrings). Storms or the shoal banks of Newfoundland could have claimed Cabot. Some writers have controversially argued that Spain's jealous protection of her discoveries, reinforced by the demarcating treaty of Tordesillas with Portugal in 1494, encouraged the elimination of other explorers once England and Portugal dispatched expeditions of their own.

It was a mark of Henry's image of his own kingship that he felt able to compete with his Spanish allies in the sponsorship of adventurers in search of a western route to the spice-rich lands of Asia. Henry's patronage reaped the rewards of discovery but shared none of the personal risks that captains and their crews endured when sailing into the barely known west. England looked to the sea and trade as the mainspring of wealth. That Henry tapped into this existing dependency is understandable. There are strong suggestions, however, that he recognised the immense potential of the New Found Land and offered his personal support as a further way of matching his kingship against England's European rivals. The ambassadors of Venice and Spain recognised that England was serious about establishing contacts with new overseas lands.

Bristol men certainly sensed a great opportunity. In the summer of 1502 an expedition had left the port under the control of a company of adventurers. By April 1504, chamber payments suggest some kind of fledgling settlement, perhaps connected to the production of stockfish on Newfoundland. A priest was paid 4s before his voyage to the new lands. By the end of September the first supplies of Newfoundland stockfish and fish livers were imported at Bristol. At a value of over £200 this was the start of a substantial market, especially if it could be monopolised by England.

Even at the end of his reign, there is evidence that Henry supplied John Cabot's son Sebastian with ships and 300 men for a northern voyage.

This enterprise was blocked by frozen waters in 1509, and it returned to find a new king on the English throne. Henry's death ended this particular avenue and the accession of Henry VIII put England once again into rivalry with Europe's monarchs in Europe itself. In comparison to his son's disinterest in the potentials of exploration, Henry VII displayed a healthy awareness of the potential advantages of royal involvement. Henry's reign marks the formal beginning of English involvement in North America and the very first stages of a new maritime empire based on distant trade and conquest.

Henry was quite prepared to blend England's trading prosperity with his own dynastic security. Such gambling with subjects' livelihoods during the 1490s, and after 1501, indicated that any specific trading policy was too closely tied to the confrontation of foreign sponsorship of Henry's enemies to be considered as a consistent independent initiative of the king. Even the search for favourable terms with the Hanseatic League and in Mediterranean trade responded to pressure on traditional markets brought about by political necessity.

# 11

## PROJECTING TUDOR INFLUENCE

### THE DEFENCE OF ENGLAND

Although he was one of the very few English kings to seize the throne through battle, historians have been reluctant to recognise Henry VII as a king with military ability. Henry put himself in danger in the field only at Bosworth, where he acquitted himself better than many expected, but probably contributed little as a battlefield commander. His reputation as a strategist has also taken something of a battering from historians. The clashes at Stoke (1487) and Blackheath (1497) were victories over vastly inferior rebel forces, devoid of cavalry and cannon, which should have been achieved more easily than they were. The ineffective intervention in Brittany, and abortive invasions of France (1492) and Scotland (1497) have also been undermined as serious enterprises.

Did Henry suffer military underachievement simply because he was personally more inclined to peace than to war? He knew that war placed a heavy financial and administrative burden upon the country. Late medieval armies were raised on the king's behalf only when required; there was no major permanent army or navy. The crown could only afford to provision, supply and pay troops for the length of a planned campaign if parliament was willing to make a grant of taxation. The tax burden was borne by subjects whose loyalty to the Tudor crown remained less than clear well into Henry's final decade. He could not risk excessive tax demands since the perceived injustice of taxation led to rebellions in

1487 and 1497. Warfare and violence were also uncertain and imprecise ways of achieving his political aims.

Henry did balance the costs of war against the potential benefits of battlefield glory. His campaigns were very well prepared and his decision to go to war fitted exactly with his priorities. In August 1485 boldness in battle had won him the crown when a realistic calculation of his chances would have left him kicking his heels at Charles VIII's court. Henry certainly did not fear the hazards of battle, but he was probably cautious of the other costs involved in getting his forces into the field.

Modern writers can distinguish between threats to the Tudor regime and challenges to England's sovereign rights. As a usurper, Henry faced real difficulty in equating his own security with that of England. Here Henry perhaps followed Richard III and tried to merge his own position as king with the well-being of the realm, implying that good national rule depended upon his continued personal kingship. In the conditions attached to the thousands of bonds issued between 1485 and 1509, Henry developed this theme by demanding an obligation of loyalty and acceptable behaviour, both to himself and his future heirs.

Henry also used the law to streamline state preparations for war. In 1487 acts were passed preventing the retaining of royal tenants and officers. The king reserved sole right of recruitment within the extensive and well-organised crown demesne lands. The men of the household and royal affinity, acting as crown stewards, became the king's agents in bringing royal tenants to war. This vital military role boosted Tudor security and created a semi-permanent standing force under the officers running the king's estates.[1] The same parliament acted to keep the price of longbows below 3s 4d. Henry was determined to maintain the skill and reputation of England's archers. By 1503 a property qualification banned the shooting of crossbows to all but wealthy men.

In 1491 the build-up to the invasion of France resulted in a soldiers' Act and an Act concerning war service. The first ensured that captains supplied the numbers of troops for which they had been indented and paid, and that they distributed wages to their troops within six days of receipt. The penalty was forfeiture of lands and goods, and imprisonment. On pain of execution, soldiers were to remain with their muster unless licensed to depart. The second Act gave legal protection to the lands and goods of the king's soldiers when on campaign, and offered them leave to make grants of their lands without licence.

By the mid-1490s, when the loyalty of his inherited supporters was under severe pressure, Henry's statutes tried to enforce the existing link between grants of crown patronage and service to defend the king from his enemies. By the 1494 Attendance in War Act, office holders would lose their posts if they did not perform their service to uphold the crown. This act was refined in the parliament of 1504 to specify further punishments for not joining the king on campaign. It also clarified the rates of wages of war and the periods in which they would be paid.

By 1485 the English had perhaps almost forgotten the collective military experience accumulated over long periods of campaigning earlier in the century. The French, however, had not. When 6,000 archers and infantry were sent to Brittany in April 1489, French commanders warned that the English 'of old were seasoned warriors and to be especially invincible in any battle while they are fresh'.[2] The French therefore adapted their tactics to avoid a pitched battle. Instead they harried the English with cavalry and skirmishers and wore down their effectiveness. There remained a certain level of respect for English fighting skills that was at least forty years old by 1485. Yet Henry could not instil the knowledge of veterans into the semi-feudal levies that made up his armies. Reluctance among the French to join battle in 1489 and 1492 prevented the English from reviving their experience of war against their ancient enemy. Tudor forces spent more time fighting domestic rebels than the armies of other states before 1509. God's providence aside, therefore, it was only the organisation, supply, training, and leadership of these troops that would bring military and dynastic success to Henry when battle became unavoidable.

The first step towards a stable dynasty was to protect its embodiment – the king himself. The Yeomen of the Guard were created from the examples of the *petit garde* and Scottish guard of the French monarchs. The Yeomen perhaps totalled 500 men, initially drawn from the survivors of Bosworth. They became the permanent core of the royal household and removed responsibility for royal protection from servants who might have had secondary allegiances to other powerful courtiers.

Frequently, Henry demonstrated an obvious attachment to men who had followed him 'beyond the sea and in our realm', 'at our late journey and field', or 'in subduing our rebels and traitors'.[3] Yeomen of the Guard such as Robert Baggar or Owen ap Griffith were formally appointed in September 1485 but had served Henry long before he arrived in the

English midlands. Henry trusted these men, and their sole purpose was to ensure the personal security of the royal family, especially on ceremonial occasions. The Guard was also used as a military force in its own right, usually serving under their captain Sir Charles Somerset. Household troops scattered the Richmondshire rebels in 1486, and over 156 yeomen and 100 archers of the Guard joined the French expedition in 1492.

Other household men did not have a permanent military role, but they were required to serve the king in time of war. Over eighty named officers received wages of war under Christopher Vincent, Marshal of the Hall, in 1492. In this capacity the royal household could muster several hundred men to support the king on campaign – both as part of a mobile household and as rank-and-file troops. Royal servants with a more honourable and ceremonial role, such as the knights and esquires of the body, were prominent in their own right. As part of an aristocratic class educated and trained in war they were expected to muster their own troops. This shift in household military capability occurred in response to Warbeck's conspiracy, as the crown servants with the strongest and most immediately accessible military resources became the officers managing royal estates.

The only permanent forces available to Henry were the standing garrisons at Calais and Berwick. Since 1347 the English regime had kept its major garrison at Calais. By the Yorkist period it functioned because the mayor and staple were granted the customs duty on the wool monopoly passing through the town. The town's governors provided a sum of about £10,000 to the crown to pay the wages of the military officers and troops stationed there – about 600–700 during peacetime. Calais was also important because Edward IV had used the fortresses there as the main arsenal for England's gunpowder weaponry. The garrison had been fiercely loyal to the Yorkist crown under Edward IV and the Tudors were justifiably wary of a stable group of experienced troops who had not been vetted or appointed by the new regime. A force of about two hundred men had defected from Calais after Bosworth. They ended up in Maximilian's service and fought in the Yorkist cause at Stoke in 1487.

Another of Henry VII's initiatives undermined Calais' position as the crown's repository of military expertise. Sir Giles Daubeney became lieutenant with remit to uncover disloyalty among those who survived the change of king in 1485. The Calais victualler, William Ross, found his accounts transferred to the royal chamber for the king's close scrutiny. Henry also ensured that the master of ordnance and the Tower became the centre of the manufacture and storage of artillery by 1489. That year gunners had been sent *from* London to Calais during the English intervention in Brittany. Eight years later, the king's massive artillery train for Scotland was assembled at the Tower before departing north. This concentration of skills placed England on a new footing to take advantage of technological and strategic developments in the use of such weaponry.

The English had maintained a permanent garrison at Berwick after the town was recaptured from the Scots in 1482. The normal garrison was inadequate to repel full-scale raids from the Scots, so when the earl of Northumberland became warden of the East March with Scotland in January 1486, Henry deliberately separated control of Berwick from wider responsibility for the border zone. Once Berwick's government was taken out of the warden's hands, Henry could boost the royal presence on the border through the promotion of his household officers.

At the start of 1488 the king's esquire Richard Cholmeley became chamberlain of Berwick. He was also made receiver-general of various northern manors assigned to provide over £1,800 annually for the safe keeping of the town and castle. Berwick came to be maintained by the region it protected. As early as 1488 the king's council agreed that the earl of Northumberland and bishop of Durham should arrange with the king to put a total of 500 men between them into the field for the defence of Berwick if the Scots marched against the town. By 1501, mindful of the earl of Suffolk's treason, the king called the chief officers of the town to Richmond to sort out disputes and delays over the payment of wages to the garrison.

England also kept a nominal military force in Ireland. English overlordship usually operated through the resources of the Anglo-Irish nobles and administrators who ran the Dublin pale. Even in times of crisis, little English input was needed if the resident nobles recognised that their interests were under threat. In the final months of 1494, only about 650 troops under Edward Poynings protected the English pale. This force represented the level of commitment the English king had to make to defend an extended Irish frontier. This was also a mobile army and not one laden with artillery designed for pitched battle or siege warfare. When fighting did break out in Ireland, as at the battle of

Knockdoe in 1504, the Fitzgeralds and their Gaelic allies bore the brunt of this frontier conflict on behalf of the crown.

Other much smaller English garrisons permanently protected frontier castles like those at Carlisle and Montourgill on Jersey. As few as twenty soldiers (as at Carlisle) were maintained through the complex indentures between captains and the crown, and were frequently financed out of the pockets of royal officers to be repaid from the Exchequer. When Lord Dacre was appointed keeper of Carlisle in January 1502 he had to pay his own servants, watchmen and guards, repair the castle, and make accounts of artillery and arrange for its maintenance. The permanently mobilised armed forces of Henry's regime in peacetime were probably no more than 2,000 troops. With most soldiers in Calais and around the king's person at any one time, Henry relied upon his household men and aristocratic retinue leaders to mobilise forces rapidly at times of crisis.

National defence grew from the willingness of the king's ruling partners to contribute their own resources. Henry's friends also paid twice over: once towards the taxes that bankrolled large-scale campaigns, and again through the supply of troops, weapons and leadership that made the royal army an effective force. The king not only managed the process through his own initiative and the advice of his council. He also had a broader political role to ensure lasting support for particular campaigns. In 1487 at Stoke, for example, Henry had to press the point that his nobles were fighting to uphold the Tudor right to the throne against Yorkist rebels, some of whom had been royal officials only a few weeks previously. Their willingness to stand and fight required as much royal effort to build unity of purpose and morale as it did to provide up-to-date equipment and tactics.

Tudor armies were mustered in traditional separate wards, with wings to the vanguard. The supply of each was almost independent, meaning that each self-contained force could act almost unilaterally. The vanguard in 1497 was made up of the contingents brought by many household men, royal constables, and officers of the regime. It was the core of Henry's army and totalled about 7,000 troops from forty-four separate retinues. With the largest numbers of mounted troops and foot soldiers supplied by officers like Sir Rhys ap Thomas and Sir Thomas Lovell, the regime's military security remained firmly in the hands of the survivors from 1485. Rather than expand the nature of his military resources to include vast numbers of militia raised on each county,

Henry relied ever more completely upon the retinues of the men he trusted most.

In the late 1480s, over two hundred knights were named in the muster lists of the royal army. Warbeck's influence on the Tudor elite undoubtedly contributed to a narrowing of Henry's confidence in the wider aristocracy. By 1497 it is striking that the proposed vanguard contained no forces from the senior branch of the Stanley family. The military reliance on Stanley troops was replaced by the exploitation of the official positions held by the king's own men. For the major invasions of 1492 and 1497 Henry contracted with a wider range of captains. More numerous and smaller retinues ensured that no one contingent of troops stood out.

Leaders contracted with the crown to supply an agreed number of troops for a specific period. One month's wages were paid as cash to captains in advance of embarkation. This innovation solved some of the problems of provisioning for an army of invasion. It allowed the independent groups of men from the scattered manors of their masters to buy and transport their own supplies from within England. Payment in this way also kept small contingents together and perhaps made the soldiers more confident that their lord would look after their wages. An army formed from the retinues of leading nobles and knights exploited the links of lordship and service that brought order to local communities. Henry emphasised the responsibility lying with his captains by printing ordinances for war for the first time. This novel approach ensured that there was some consistency in how the objectives of the campaign were circulated, how the invasion was to be regulated, and how the troops were to be controlled.

The military skills of his loyalists may have ensured a more disciplined and cohesive army, but it was by no means a force of professional soldiers. Nor was any early Tudor army entirely English. The expertise of foreign mercenaries was familiar to all late medieval English commanders. There was nothing exceptional in Henry's willingness to utilise the skills of mercenary troops. They were present on the 1492 campaign. In 1497 Henry's heralds bought the services of Swiss foot soldiers. The king also recruited the key officers of a mercenary army that had recently fought in Germany for René, duke of Lorraine.

Henry's interest in the expertise of foreign master armourers and gunners was more novel. In 1497, Henry's lieutenant of ordnance organised an impressive array of English artillery experts under master gunner Richard Falconer.[4] Other masters were hired from the Netherlands and Flanders. By the time the Scottish campaign started there were over 200 gunners preparing Henry's artillery. Their skill in preparing sights, constructing gun carriages, corning powder and smoothing shot ensured a major improvement in England's capacity to wage a war of technology by 1497. Many weapons were even tested on a specially built range at Mile End just outside London.

The testing of weapons was just one aspect of the advanced planning and organisation that Henry brought to the construction of his armies. Numerous warrants and accounts from the Exchequer provide the evidence of how the materials of war were purchased and assembled. For the major campaigns where preparation was in the king's hands, the machinery of war could be gathered systematically. Commissions set up small manufacturing and requisitioning teams throughout the country. In 1492 one group was given a free hand to access all materials needed to make gunpowder. By 1497 the provision of weapons and powder was an altogether more industrial process.

New guns were cast at a factory in the Duchy of Lancaster forest of Ashdown on the Kent/Sussex border. Iron shot was also manufactured there by immigrant workers from France and the Netherlands. Foundries were set up at the end of 1496 to deliver artillery in time for the campaign. The midland towns of Shrewsbury, Leicester, and Coventry were centres for the delivery of bows, while arrows were brought from as far away as the Forest of Dean. Separate programmes were set up to assemble arms, equipment and men. Weapons caches had been established at royal castles such as Kenilworth, Berwick, and Newcastle, which were also muster points.

The crown's ordnance officers established a massive train to move Henry's artillery. In 1497 it included over a thousand horses and 600 men. This force also had to be supplied with everything from hay and transport wagons, to nets, sacks, and brushes. In November 1496 three new breweries were set up at Berwick in anticipation of the army's arrival. Prefabricated building sections were also transported in Lord Willoughby's fleet to be assembled as stables and bakeries. The campaign also utilised the 1496 harvest. Over £9,000 was spent on grain to supply the sea force and the vanguard of the army under Lord Daubeney.

Henry's balancing of his private power with his embodiment of English military strength is seen in the way his soldiers were uniformed.

Since Henry appeared at Bosworth as rightful king of England it is possible that some of his household soldiers wore variants of the royal arms during the fighting. Henry's personal livery colours were green and white – the background to his red dragon standard. Later in the reign he did supply jackets in these colours to contingents of his soldiers, but a distinction must be made between occasions where they were representing the nation of England and when they acted as the king's personal troops.

The sailors on the king's own vessels the *Regent* and the *Sovereign* wore white and green coats in 1495. At the start of 1490, London tailors supplied the crown with several thousand brigandines in white cloth with the red cross of St George. These uniforms were worn by foot soldiers engaged in Brittany. Here Henry emphasised his possession of the English crown. It is debatable whether this was the first time that an entire English army wore almost the same uniform.

As with land forces, the crown in 1485 did not have the resources to maintain a permanent fleet at sea. Henry V's fleet of fourteen great ships and scores of other cogs and transports had long been laid up and sold off as the permanent war with France ended. Edward IV possessed sixteen vessels, and Richard III owned about ten ships. Both kings built up their fleets to counter overseas threats and piracy. Once Henry was crowned, the absence of immediate military campaigning outside England meant that royal ships were used mainly to conduct the monarch's private business and to escort the wool exports across the Channel.

Although the crown owned seven vessels in 1485, the external political threats Henry faced at his accession soon required a far stronger naval capacity, especially in the Channel. In February 1488 a naval flotilla and an unofficial force under Lord Scales were dispatched to aid Brittany. The small fleet provided transport and escort to an infantry force. This was the most common type of naval action Henry's sea forces engaged in, but it did not necessarily mean a programme of new royal naval shipbuilding. Henry's response was not to throw money at the widespread construction of new ships. He pursued a policy of more aggressive commandeering when required, but also began some innovations in maritime policy.

In the late 1480s Sir Richard Guildford was instructed to construct the *Regent*. It was completed by 1490, and was the first English-built vessel to have cannon on a lower gun deck behind portholes. The heavier weight carried by these ships, and the force created by a greater weight of broadside metal when the guns were fired, prompted innovation in hull design. Guildford adapted French designs, and although the ships were not as heavy as Henry V's massive vessels they were able to carry a staggering array of artillery for their day.

At about 600 tons, and with four masts, the *Regent* was one of the largest English ships of the second half of the fifteenth century. With 225 cannon and other guns, the ship was far more than a floating fighting platform for crowds of infantry. Heavier artillery augmented the arrows, handguns, and upper-deck cannon that had previously contested naval actions. Concentrations of cannon that targeted the hull of enemy ships nearer the waterline, as well as the sailors, masts, and rigging on the exposed deck, brought the possibility of greater decisiveness to sea battles. The *Sovereign* was built at Southampton under the supervision of Sir Reginald Bray. It was a smaller vessel with 141 guns, but performed a similar function to the *Regent*.

The dry dock, defences, and storage yards begun at Portsmouth during 1491–2 as part of the preparations for the invasion of France (at a cost of about £2,100) mark the beginning of a permanent association of Portsmouth and the crown's naval forces. They may not have been finished until 1497, but helped the king to maintain the hardworking ships he owned. The king's own vessels were fully committed to the invasion across the Channel in 1492, but an enormously expanded naval capacity was required to convey to France an army of about 12,000 men, its horses, equipment and provisions. The crown negotiated the hire of over 630 other ships, many from the Netherlands, and commandeered almost all suitable vessels along England's Channel coast at a rate of 1s per ton. Henry's rates for the hire of mariners ensured that occasional royal service was well rewarded.

The truce with the Scots at Ayton at the end of 1497 marked the final time that a large English army and naval force combined during Henry's reign. For the next twelve years it was not necessary for England to pay for military supply. The end of major campaigning testified to Henry's careful development of policy. In 1497 he had demanded that the Exchequer archives were searched for evidence of how Edward III, and more recently Edward IV, had prepared their armies for war with Scotland. Such meticulous planning underpinned all Henry's military preparations. The fact that Henry won all the battles he contested testifies to his skill in strategic leadership, logistics, and supply. Henry ensured that England was very well prepared for war, even if the need for mass armies did not emerge until 1513 when Henry VIII enjoyed the benefits of his father's groundwork.

## HENRY VII AND THE BRITISH ISLES

### Early Tudor relationships with Ireland

When Henry became king of England he also inherited the intractable problem of how English lordship in Ireland could be made effective. An established pattern of rule did exist. Nominal English influence was built upon an uncomfortable frontier struggle between the descendants of the Anglo-Norman settlers of the twelfth century and the Gaelic chieftains, who in 1485 ruled much of the north and west of the island. English government was most effective in an area of land known as the Pale within the east midland counties of Dublin, Meath, Louth and Kildare.

Fifteenth-century English kings had claimed to be lords of Ireland, but this level of control was impossible to realise in practice. The English had never been willing to finance massive military forces to deal with the 'problem' of the native Irish. The native Irish chiefs operated almost wholly on a war footing, with territory won and lost among themselves by raiding. Consequently, the borders of the English territory came to be defended in much the same way. The borderlands between the Pale and the Gaelic areas functioned under a form of martial law that had to be more aggressive than on England's other frontiers.

Ireland became neglected while the Lancastrian kings were occupied in France. English rule shrank back towards the Pale as the Irish chieftains forced the Anglo-Irish lords to take greater control over the defence of their own lands. Such crown reliance on the resources of the Irish landholders also drew their existing feuds into the struggle for the English throne in the period 1455–61. The Butler earls of Ormond and Wiltshire, and the Fitzgerald earls of Kildare and Desmond, came to represent the Lancastrian and Yorkist interests respectively. As Irish landowners began to be executed by the rival English factions, so Ireland's most experienced noble families suffered setbacks that further robbed the island of its most able rulers. It was only as Edward IV's reign stabilised by the 1480s that the favoured Fitzgerald connection, now headed by the young Gerald, eighth earl of Kildare, began to have a galvanising effect within the Pale.

As Kildare extended the areas under his control, so the Pale expanded and the violent frontier moved further away from the centre of Irish government. The English king's trust in Kildare was maintained by his ability to blend his own priorities with those of the crown. By the time of Edward IV's death, Kildare had several years' of consolidated authority behind him. And because his rule was self-financed and contributed towards the king's objectives, the Westminster government was prepared to allow him virtually a free hand within Ireland.

Kildare was reappointed by Richard III, but took advantage of Richard's difficulties to secure his family's position within the lordship. He considered Tudor to be a Lancastrian claimant and doubted that his own Yorkist credentials would endear him to a Tudor king. In June 1485 Kildare used his dominance of the Irish parliament to ensure that he would retain power in the event of Henry's victory. Kildare's influence beyond his own personal estates was based principally upon the power he wielded as king's representative. After August 1485 his duty was to uphold Tudor authority, a power some other members of the Irish elite did not acknowledge. In common with many nobles prominent under the Yorkists, Kildare perhaps believed Tudor's victory to be an aberration that would soon be reversed.

Henry acknowledged that Kildare was in a strong position. Removing him would have created outright enemies when Henry was struggling to assert himself within England and Wales. Kildare was careful not to appear as an opponent of the Tudor accession, and he was soon renewed in post as deputy lieutenant to Jasper, duke of Bedford. His attempt to squeeze further concessions from Henry was unrealistic, but Kildare did seek improved relations with the Butlers, now firm favourites of the king. One of his daughters married Sir Piers Butler, heir to the earldom of Ormond, in 1486.

Kildare found his personal position as a Yorkist deputy lieutenant to a rejuvenated Lancastrian regime especially difficult, as external pressures moved events beyond his control. Henry VII's enemies focused on the problem of allegiance in Ireland in May 1487 when Lambert Simnel was proclaimed in Dublin as Edward VI. Kildare seemed powerless to resist the momentum of rebellion. To avoid being sidelined he took over Irish government, showed his true colours towards the Butlers when he attainted their leaders of treason, and promptly supplied Gaelic warriors to the rebel army. The slaughter of the Irish at the battle of Stoke left Kildare once again isolated and he was forced to submit to Henry VII.

Henry's investigations indicated that the conspiracy was found to have attracted almost all the prominent Yorkists. Even then, the potential problems of managing the lordship from Westminster, or by an Englishman in Dublin castle, obliged the king to issue a general pardon. Henry sent a trusted councillor Sir Richard Edgecome to deliver it, and he was also authorised to get the Irish lords to agree to bonds for future loyalty. The Irish nobles refused to cooperate and threatened to throw in their lot with the native Irish clans should the king continue to demand too much from them. Henry was now forced to back down, primarily because the murder of James III of Scotland on 11 June 1488 again threatened England's border. Henry still did not have the resources or security to intervene forcefully on two frontiers simultaneously.

Kildare, amazingly, rapidly regained enough confidence in his own position to ignore a summons to Westminster for almost a year. His allies backed up his excuses and provided evidence of his struggles against the Gaels. Henry could do little about this, but since Ireland offered little to disturb his security at this time, the Fitzgeralds were allowed to continue their campaigning and to rule on behalf of the Tudor king.

The next challenge to Kildare's relationship with Henry came when Perkin Warbeck arrived at Dublin in November 1491. Henry sent English help to the Butlers in the southern midlands, and by promoting Sir James Ormond he was able to disrupt the dominance of the Kildare and Desmond Fitzgeralds. Kildare's regime was replaced. By exploiting the Butler feud with the Yorkist earls, Henry successfully reduced the Fitzgerald dominance and in the short term prevented Ireland from becoming a base for Warbeck.

Henry did not abandon Ireland even after the influence of the dynastically loyal Butler family was increased. He was forced to remain involved because the promotion of the Butlers simply gave them sufficient influence to renew the violent conflict with the Fitzgeralds. Rioting and murder erupted in Dublin, and Kildare allowed his Gaelic frontiers to become more disrupted. The Fitzgerald connection was so great in the Pale that no Irish government could work effectively without some degree of cooperation from Kildare and Desmond. Henry again sent troops – 300 arrived under Sir Roger Cotton in March 1493. They helped to secure territory, but it became clear to the king that growing international support for Warbeck required a new approach to ruling Ireland if a repeat of 1487 was to be avoided.

The crown offered Kildare a way to recover his position. He was pardoned of treason and persuaded to agree to the bond for his future allegiance that he had refused in 1487. He also consented to travel to England in September 1493. Kildare was still at court in the spring of 1494, actively working with the king on ways to curb the earl of Desmond's continuing hostility towards the crown. Unfortunately reports of Warbeck's imminent invasion renewed Desmond's enthusiasm for rebellion. In June 1494 Maurice, earl of Desmond, broke his oath of loyalty and began a serious rising in Munster.

In response, Sir Edward Poynings was sent to Dublin in October 1494 as deputy to the four-year-old Henry, duke of York. At first sight this whole enterprise matched Edward IV's appointment of English outsiders in the 1460s. But Henry approached the situation with a more integrated strategy. The creation and appointment in Ireland of Henry, duke of York, was designed to undermine Warbeck's credibility in the lordship, since it obscured his reputed status as the Yorkist duke of York, Richard of Shrewsbury. Also, Henry did not ignore the root cause of Irish instability: the frontier war with the Gaelic clans.

With the Butlers involved, Henry created a balanced administration under Poynings in Dublin. The new deputy arrived with a ready-drafted programme of reform for Irish government. These measures, known as 'Poynings' Law', were put to the parliament at Drogheda on 1 December 1494. They established direct royal control over the right to call parliament in Ireland. Any bills put to the assembly were also to have the approval of the English royal council as well as that of the deputy lieutenant in Dublin. Such a step was felt necessary because of the way Kildare and his followers had been able to call parliament in Ireland principally to cement their personal power. It was an essential measure to free the Pale government from the stranglehold of the Fitzgeralds.

Instead of trying to confront the Fitzgerald personalities, Henry cleverly tied the mechanics of Irish government more closely to the English crown's priorities. The king made the links between Westminster and Dublin more explicit, and created clear boundaries between what had to be referred and what could be authorised directly within the Pale. The parliament passed an act of resumption of Irish grants back to 1327.

Further controls on Irish rule made appointments conditional on Henry's goodwill, limited noble retaining, and licensed gunpowder weapons.

Poynings renewed the Statutes of Kilkenny that had been introduced in 1366. The Acts sought to preserve the literal and cultural frontier between Anglo-Irish lands and people, and what were widely thought of (at least in Westminster) as the savage clans of the Gaelic wastelands. The Statutes controlled intermarriage, dictated codes of dress, encouraged archery but discouraged hurling, and insisted on the English language and customs within the Pale. Henry's approach to the Gaelic frontier was fundamental to this process because the conflict with the clans had always been the priority to Anglo-Irish landowners. Henry realised that persistence in this area would ultimately strengthen English security.

To back up the legislative and administrative reforms, Poynings ensured that up to a thousand troops were in Ireland by the summer of 1495. The deputy saw the necessity of involving the native Irish chiefs in a new approach that acknowledged the existence, if not the claims, of all parties. This aspect of Poynings's mission brought disaster during a brutal military expedition against Warbeck's Gaelic allies in Ulster by Sir James Ormond. In November 1494, Poynings viewed Kildare's communications with the O'Hanlon clan suspiciously. By February 1495 Kildare was under arrest for treason. He was accused of helping the king's enemies and of plotting the death of Poynings. He was again sent to England. Without his far-reaching influence, the old problems of feud and overstretched resources quickly resurfaced.

Poynings used his limited troops where he could: the Butlers helped him to besiege Kildare's revolting brother James in Carlow castle. But the earl of Desmond rallied to Warbeck once more and some Gaelic clans began to waver in their submission to Henry. Warbeck headed to Ireland after his failed landing at Deal in July 1495. In combination with Desmond, he offered Poynings a severe military test at the siege of Waterford later that month. Poynings had to scrape together a force from militia and willing Gaelic chiefs, but was ultimately successful because the artillery he possessed scattered Warbeck's fleet. Warbeck and Desmond were then driven to Scotland by the thoroughness of Poynings's clampdown on the rebels during the summer. By December his commission had expired and he returned to England with most of the army.

Kildare's second enforced visit to the king in England allowed the two men further opportunities to discuss exactly how Henry wanted Ireland to be governed. Despite the fluctuations in loyalty within the lordship, both Kildare and the king knew that Poynings's mission had simply streamlined the way things were to be done. Henry was not convinced of Kildare's overt treason at the end of 1494 and soon received evidence that he had actually encouraged the O'Hanlons to ally with Poynings.

Kildare emerged from this important period of transformation as a senior and well-trusted member of the Tudor hierarchy. He married Margaret Beaufort's half-sister Elizabeth St John in the summer of 1496, and resumed his post as deputy in August under more generous terms. His son was left at court as security and he agreed a series of indentures confirming his position as defender of Tudor interests in Ireland. Kildare also carried a pardon for Maurice, earl of Desmond, who had shown himself willing to submit. In return for the loyalty of his new deputy, Henry offered Kildare land and the freedom to appoint all officers except the Irish chancellor. Under attainder at the end of 1494, eighteen months later Kildare was one of Henry's chief allies: a startling conversion considering the political upheavals during that period. Here, Henry displayed a clarity of purpose that, while risky, ultimately secured Tudor influence in the lordship.

Kildare's reappointment brought immediate submissions from many chieftains on the borders of the Pale. Now that Gerald Fitzgerald had a very clear idea of the king's expectations he also worked hard at maintaining good relations with the kinsmen of Thomas, 7th earl of Ormond, who by this time was resident at Henry's court in England. Ormond's illegitimate brother Sir James Ormond had played a crucial role for the king in 1491, but found his opportunities limited under Kildare's dominance after 1496. He caused some disruption in the Butler lordships and exasperated Kildare to the extent that he was sent to Henry VII. The irony of a Fitzgerald censuring a Butler for disrupting the hardwon harmony of Lancastrian rule in Ireland cannot have been lost on Kildare. Kildare's son-in-law eventually murdered Ormond on the pretext that he was actively seeking to usurp the earldom of Ormond with Warbeck's help. In July 1497, and a matter of days after Ormond had been killed, Warbeck did make a brief appearance in Cork. He stayed only long enough to recruit some diehard Yorkists and then made his way to Cornwall.

Increased stability improved profits in the Pale lands and allowed the collaboration among the nobles to be brought to bear on troublesome

Gaelic clans. Kildare's personal goals were now aligned with those of the wider Anglo-Irish community: chiefly to push back the Gaelic chieftains who had continued to exploit disharmony and distraction within the Pale. The king's interests were therefore protected without the need for him to contribute the costly resources of English troops. Through careful management, Henry effectively persuaded the leading nobles of Ireland to protect a vulnerable frontier of his power: because first and foremost their own territory and influence were threatened. The relationship with Kildare was also a blueprint for the type of crown–noble interaction that Henry hoped to develop throughout his kingdom.

In 1503 Kildare visited the king in celebratory circumstances for the marriage of his son Lord Offaly to Elizabeth Zouche. The following year he was elected to the Garter. Through Kildare, Henry seemed to have achieved the political solution to the problem of governing Ireland. Kildare acknowledged that his authority stemmed solely from his lieutenancy of the king's authority. The Anglo-Irish nobles knew that strong leadership defended their estates. By the start of the sixteenth century they were willing to support a regime that confirmed the dominance of the Fitzgerald connection. Kildare was both preferred by the crown and maintained by the nobility. His network extended into the Gaelic areas and, in careful balance with his other responsibilities, this also enhanced his reputation between both crown and nobles.

For most of his decade as deputy after 1496, Kildare was campaigning against native chiefs like O'Brien in Limerick or grinding out alliances such as with the O'Neils of Ulster. In 1506 he even got an initial agreement from the king to come with an army of 6,000 soldiers to tackle the continuing problem of the 'wild Irish'. Ten years of Kildare's leadership had proved to Henry that the complete reduction of Ireland to his permanent rule would still require massive military intervention. The main problem for the king was whether to attempt an expensive conquest in alliance with Kildare, or to maintain the unstable balance of smaller-scale campaigning, leverage and containment. In the end, conquest proved a step too far for Henry.

Henry would have removed Kildare in 1487 or 1494 had he the resources and political will to have set up a reliable alternative. By August 1504, Kildare's victory over the Gaelic Burkes and O'Briens at Knockdoe in Galway confirmed to the king that the Irish nobles and their growing Gaelic allies could rule Ireland and even fight pitched battles without additional help from Westminster. The situation remained largely unchanged at Henry's death.

Henry VII focused long and hard on Ireland because for the first decade of Tudor rule it was a principal source of his insecurity. Neglect of Dublin government and weak control of the powerful Anglo-Irish noble network encouraged the type of disorder that was very hard to counteract once it had seeped into the complex stew of Irish politics. As the likelihood of Irish-inspired rebellion receded, the king was content to leave the management of Ireland to resident lords. Henry's personal relationship with Gerald Fitzgerald may have been short-sighted for the longer-term stability of Ireland. He certainly deferred the quest for a lasting solution to English rule there to later monarchs. Yet where previous kings had failed, Henry succeeded in realising his own goals within the lordship. Rebellion and conspiracy were extinguished, a drain on English finances was avoided, and a key aspect of Tudor security was healthily preserved.

## Henry VII and Wales

Jasper and Edmund Tudor had been the first Welshmen to enter the English peerage. Their closeness to Henry VI gave the Tudor brothers the highest public profile of any Welshmen since Owain Glyndwr. As allies of the Lancastrian crown, this positive association was remembered long after the transition to Yorkist rule. Henry Tudor was more English than Welsh. His kinship with the Maredudd family, and his descent back to leading servants of Llewellyn the Great made much for Welsh poets and chroniclers to eulogise. The survival of Jasper Tudor to enjoy the fruits of his struggle as his nephew took the throne, obliged Henry and his family to carry many of the expectations of new Welsh prosperity within Britain.

The story of Henry's christening in Pembroke castle, as related by the bard Elis Gruffydd, is a good example of how myth and fact about Henry's Welsh origins and destiny were blended. Henry was apparently actually christened with the name Owain, but Margaret Beaufort demanded that he be called Henry. So although Henry VII did not bear the actual name of the prophetic British conqueror of England, the sixteenth-century Welsh historians ensured that he personified many of the ancient predictions of Welsh glory.

The language of Henry's proclamations and letters appealing for regional support promised a new golden age for Welsh independence on the back of a Tudor victory. Henry's personal heraldry, the greyhound and red dragon of Cadwallader, and its rapid prominence as part of the identity of the new regime, sent the message that Henry was proud of his Welsh ancestry. The extent to which any of this propaganda emerged as crown policy newly beneficial to Wales is open to question.

He was brought up in Wales and the Marches before 1471, but his personal connection to this Welsh childhood surfaced only in his immediate quest for the crown in the summer of 1485. The invader's targeting of the Pembroke peninsula exploited Jasper Tudor's former reputation. Numerous Welshmen from the Bosworth campaign found places in Henry's service in the royal household or yeoman of the guard, where there must have been some degree of Welsh flavour to the lower levels of royal service.

At higher levels, in knights like Rhys ap Thomas, Henry promoted the status of his Welsh supporters to the very heart of his regime after 1485. Rhys was an isolated example, and scarce evidence of his council attendance suggests he maintained a strong regional profile. Hugh Vaughan, on the other hand, was a Welsh household servant who worked very hard at court to drag himself up the service scale, becoming a knight by 1500 and making a good marriage with one of the earl of Northumberland's daughters.

With such a complete victory in 1485, there can be no surprise that early Tudor Wales was dominated by crown landholding. Estates of the principality of Wales, the duchy of Lancaster, and crown demesne lands (including many forfeited semi-independent Marcher lordships), made King Henry the greatest lord in Wales at the end of 1485. Control of the earldom of March and the minority of the earl of Warwick also pushed crown control into central Wales and Glamorgan. Henry made his son, Arthur, Prince of Wales and earl of Chester on 29 November 1489. The Yorkist kings had established a clear and effective structure for the patrimony of the king's heir in Wales until he took the throne. Henry made it clear that he intended to follow this precedent. Of course, the heirs of Edward IV and Richard III died before their royal training could be put into practice.

In the organisation of Arthur's council as Prince of Wales, the king had envisaged strong regional representation of his own power. Arthur was to be surrounded by prominent men of the regime while he learned the subtleties and skills of adult rule. Arthur's uncle Jasper and the king-making Sir William Stanley became chief justices of south and north Wales respectively in 1485. Jasper Tudor had probably prepared the authority of the prince's council until Arthur's appointment. It was he who was given power to oversee the prosecution of crimes in Wales and the Marches early in the reign, and he frequently remained in the region during the northern crises before 1490.

Surviving indentures between the crown and the Marcher lords show a consistent approach to the kaleidoscopic local authority of the border lords, each of which had a particular set of structures of law and lordship. Henry used these agreements to oblige the major landholders of the region to observe his demands for good lordship in return for the continuation of their liberties. This ruling structure was already in place before the Prince of Wales was 10 years old and was intended to make his role easier once he was in full command of his council at Ludlow.

Arthur's control of the lands of the earldoms of Chester and March made him the most powerful regional noble. William Smyth, bishop of Lincoln, had been president of the prince's council for six years when Arthur went to live at Ludlow in 1501. The fact that Arthur was married and was accompanied by his young wife Catherine further boosted the strength of his lordship. It allowed him to develop a court and household, and master the practical and political roles of supervising both. Government in Wales suffered the least after Arthur's death. The prince's council continued to function without a leader until Prince Henry took over the principality in February 1504. The successful jurisdiction of the council and good relations with the Marcher lordships without the direct presence of the prince suggested a growing independence of government that would be further developed by Henry VIII in the 1530s.

Can Henry VII be credited with trying to fulfil the promise he made at his landfall in August 1485 to throw off English rule and restore the ancient rights of the Welsh? In response to Arthur's death, Henry heeded advice from the prince's council to seek some uniformity in the way the Marcher lords upheld the law. Brynmore Pugh has shown that the agreement was easier to achieve than enforcement of the king's intentions.[5] This development can be seen in the same light as Henry's struggle to keep control over the practitioners of local law and lordship in England.

Henry did go further than other medieval English kings in addressing the laws passed against Welsh freedoms during the Glyndwr rising against Henry IV. Henry was the first king to attempt a change in the structure of lordship and law in Wales that had existed for most of the fifteenth century. In October 1504 Henry seems personally to have pushed through a charter for the inhabitants of the northern counties of Caernarvon and Merioneth that relaxed the restrictions on property ownership on both sides of the border, and tried to introduce English forms of land inheritance.[6] Other grants in 1505 and 1506 extended similar rights to other northern and border counties, chiefly within the principality and Marcher lordships that had come into the king's hands, such as Bromfield and Yale. Other provisions brought liberty to men previously the king's bondmen (a diluted form of serfdom).

Historians have questioned why Henry did not extend these rights to other areas under crown control, and have looked for money-making opportunities in the fees that could be charged in the exercise of new liberties. Despite the claim that the grants were given freely, the charter cost the lordship of Denbigh 1,000 marks in 1506. The legal capacity of Henry to override earlier statutes by his prerogative power alone has also been challenged. Henry was granting exemptions, and they could be challenged at law, which fortified towns like Beaumaris and Conway did in 1509, although Henry's death prevented legal judgement.

Late sixteenth-century Welsh antiquarians praised these charters as grants of liberties that threw off oppressive English laws and rid the Welsh of archaic customary practices. These commentaries can be viewed in the same light as Elis Gruffydd's romanticising of Henry's Welshness. Henry probably viewed the Welsh part of his realm in the same way as the rest of it: his lands could supply loyal servants but needed to be administered securely to prevent unrest and disorder. The Tudor reinvention of Welsh imagery emphasised the novelty of Henry's rule but could do little to support his claim to the throne. Henry was very conscious of his lineage, and used it constructively to boost his support. The condition of Wales was not a priority for most of his reign because it offered few challenges to his authority, and Henry never again visited the principality once he entered England on 17 August 1485.

# 12

## CONCLUSION

### HENRY'S POSTHUMOUS REPUTATION

The roots of the modern image of Henry VII are found in near-contemporary accounts of his life, especially the work of Polydore Vergil. Here is the real basis of many subsequent works, including those by Shakespeare, and the first important history of Henry by Francis Bacon in 1622. Vergil was an Italian humanist scholar who came to England with the pope's representative in 1502. In 1506 Henry VII asked Vergil to start a history of England – the *Anglica Historia*, but he had already been in contact with the people involved in Henry's quest for the throne. After his arrival in England Vergil probably wrote concurrently, and the compilation of a manuscript in 1512/13 gives his work a contemporary character. Some of this changed by the time the first printed version of the *Historia* appeared in 1534.

Henry's employment of Vergil and his continued service after 1509 make it unlikely that he would have written anything to offend his royal patrons. In terms of his description of events from 1480 onwards, Vergil's work is very much official Tudor history – an authentic, contemporary view of early Tudor England, but one that was authorised by Henry VII and his son.

The authenticity of Vergil's work is also apparent from the use he made of the memories and recollections of the key figures in the events of the first half of Henry's reign. The value of this hearsay evidence is less easy to assess. Although Vergil was probably trying to be objective when describing English events within his own lifetime, he was at the mercy of his contacts and of the more direct propaganda the Tudor crown wished to project.

Vergil had no access to the opinions of men who had opposed Henry before 1485, or who subsequently rebelled or otherwise fell from royal favour. He relied upon contacts with Henry's fellow exiles like Urswick and Fox, who were close friends of Vergil. Crucial also were the recollections of Thomas More, brought up in the household of Chancellor Morton. The *Historia* is full of comments citing Vergil's conversations with people personally involved in the events he described. Vergil's contacts have given his work the stamp of Tudor propaganda. Even if the awareness of this is only apparent from detailed studies of Vergil, notably by Denis Hay in the 1950s,[1] modern historians have done little to challenge the view of Henry VII as adapted from Vergil by other writers.

Vergil's view has persisted because it was the incestuous source material for many of the earliest printed histories of England. These works included Edward Hall's *Chronicle*, Thomas More's *History of King Richard III*, John Stowe's *Annals*, and Richard Grafton's *Chronicle*. In terms of popular opinion, Vergil's influence is most strongly felt in Shakespeare's history plays, and his version of English history can be said to have entered the national consciousness through Shakespeare's *Richard II*, *Henry V* and *Richard III*.

How did Vergil influence other writers? Firstly, Thomas More's prose *History of King Richard III* was written by 1513 – the year of Vergil's manuscript – but not published in English until 1557. This was the direct origin of Shakespeare's play, and More undoubtedly knew Vergil well. He was influenced by Vergil's humanism, especially in exploring the moral content of history. The fact that both Vergil and More did not publish their works until the mid-sixteenth century also had a profound effect on the perpetuation of Vergil's influence. Edward Hall's *Chronicle*, published in 1548, paraphrased Vergil and even lifted entire passages. He followed Vergil's lead in attempting to treat written history as a properly sourced record of the past, designed to celebrate fame and glory, and based upon a theme or argument. Hall's transmission of Vergil's groundwork in preparing the first humanist history of England was very popular with sixteenth-century audiences, and is a strong factor in the modern image of Henry VII.

The theme all of these sixteenth-century humanist sources repeated was that English history, from the deposition of Richard II in 1399 to the accession of Henry VIII in 1509, charted a degeneration of the nation from harmony to discord, followed by a slow and bloody recovery back to harmony, through civil war. This is obvious in the broad progression of Shakespeare's history plays. The framework provides the basic material for our modern representation of Henry as the nation's saviour from tyranny and civil war.

The image of Henry VII as the unifier of a discordant kingdom is most clearly found in Francis Bacon's *History of the Reign of King Henry VII*, written from 1621 to 1622 and dedicated to Charles, Prince of Wales, later Charles I.[2] Bacon used Hall extensively, and perhaps the versions of Vergil's *Historia*, printed by 1555. By adapting these works, he emphasised to Prince Charles the virtues of stability and sound finance through enforcement of the royal prerogative. Charles, as heir of James I, could expect to continue the Stuart dynasty if he followed this model. Bacon's work shows him to have been very interested in personalities, and history as a mirror for human motivation and ambition. In using his sources to investigate how and why the Tudors succeeded, he established the familiar image of Henry as a cautious and preoccupied manipulator.

John Ford also transformed Bacon's characterisation of Henry into popular entertainment in his play *The Chronicle History of Perkin Warbeck*, printed in 1632. This play is in itself interesting in that it is effectively a continuation of Shakespeare's history cycle. Ford absorbs Bacon's interest in the deduction of motives from events. He tried to portray the past as it actually was, and not as the moral attitudes of Charles I's reign would have interpreted it. This play is one of the few literary works to give Henry any colour or human quality, and as such illuminates how Henry has been judged in the past.

Along with much other historical literature consumed in a similar way, the characters and events depicted in Vergil and Bacon have become firmly rooted in a modern view of the Tudor past. Yet voices of caution were heard, even in the sixteenth century. The poet Sir Philip Sidney stated in *An Apologie for Poetrie* in 1595: 'the historian ... authorizing himself upon other histories, whose greatest authorities are built upon hearsay, has much ado to pick truth out of partiality'.[3] This neatly sums up the difficulty faced by modern historians in trying to untangle possible bias and half-truth from history based on historical literature or memoir.

The combined effects of these works persisted into the modern age. Even James Gairdner, a great Victorian records scholar, who published the first modern biography of Henry in 1892, did not deviate too far from the standard portrait built up since 1500. Historians have started to use the documentary sources for the late fifteenth and early sixteenth centuries only relatively recently. Collections of documents relevant to Henry VII's reign have been in print many years. Sir Henry Ellis's *Letters Illustrative of English History*, completed by 1846, and Willhelm Busch's *England under the Tudors*, from 1892, both contain transcripts of interest to early Tudor scholars.

These works tended to highlight the themes contained in the older authorities without providing any more modern analysis. Busch's work was a major attempt to reinterpret the reign through a focus on Henry's diplomacy and external links. Its departure from Bacon stands in contrast to Gairdner's biography of 1892. A.F. Pollard's *Reign of Henry VII from Contemporary Sources*, published in 1913, was a massive work. Although it tended to confirm the view of Henry as a hardworking administrator, it has perhaps not made the impression on modern studies it deserved.

It was only with the studies made by K.B. McFarlane in the 1940s and later that analytical writing began fully to investigate the fifteenth century. McFarlane broke away from the Whig interpretation of history as constitutional development, and put some human and political dynamic into our understanding of events. The late medieval period had been largely neglected, perhaps because the institutional foundations of the English state that were laid in the thirteenth century did not change substantially until the creation of the State Paper Office in the first half of the sixteenth century. Study of Henry VII arrived relatively recently in this post-war study, with deep investigation deterred by Stanley Chrimes's detailed but colourless 1972 biography. Fortunately the baton has now passed to a new generation of historians once again curious about Henry's reign.

## MODERN OPINIONS OF HENRY VII

This is an exciting time to be studying Henry VII. Several scholars are focusing on the reign in an expanding debate about Henry's place in the development of crown power. None of the works cited in the Selected

Further Reading section is without its criticism. There is no school of unquestioning apologists for the first Tudor king, nor any one writer who would not acknowledge his success in avoiding deposition. Henry's reign is currently fertile ground for researchers, as ideas and concepts about kingship merge with extensive archival research on the copious sources for the reign.

What follows demonstrates almost a new beginning for studies of Henry VII. We might look to the 1993 Harlaxton symposium on Henry's reign as a key turning point. Publication of the proceedings in 1995, and of Christine Carpenter's 'self consciously polemical piece' on Henry and the English polity, threw down the challenge to see Henry not as an innovative new monarch but as an ignorant outsider, struggling to keep the throne within a long-term trend of growing central crown power in England. This was a radical reworking of Bacon's view of Henry as the clear-sighted administrator-king, and one that historians are still responding to. Carpenter remains a self-confessed 'unrepentant critic of the king',[4] but this consistent criticism makes objective analysis of Henry's reign all the more interesting.

Some new analysis was already in place, but during the late 1970s and 1980s it was not part of a linked corpus of study. The publication of Dudley's petition by C.J. Harrison in 1972 would have made a major impact had Henry then been as controversial a monarch as he has now become. Margaret Condon's seminal article on Henry's ruling elites remains the essential starting point for modern understanding of his achievements and weaknesses as king. It was written over twenty-five years ago, and gives a clearer understanding of Henry's interactions with his ruling partners, and the problems of political control, than can be found in S.B. Chrimes's far longer biography. Nevertheless, Chrimes's work was a major turning point in studies of Henry VII. His focus on administrative change and its development of his early work on English constitutional ideas is now reviving through the work of Watts and Cavill, mentioned on pp. 124, 279 and 280.

Condon's article was not joined by other focused new work on the substance of Henry's reign until Steven Gunn's article on Henry's courtiers in 1993. Sandy Grant's short book on Henry VII in 1985 successfully revisited the idea that his reign was a turning point. Ralph Griffiths and Roger Thomas produced their long view of the Tudor family's route to the throne in 1985. This does provide a clear and comprehensive summary of how Henry vanquished Richard III. Two books by Michael Bennett on the battles of Bosworth and Stoke also appeared in 1985 and 1987 respectively. Although concentrating on the conflicts, there is also much of substance here for an understanding of Henry's motivations and concerns during those years.

Margaret Condon and Steven Gunn head the list of current experts on Henry's government and its chief personalities. Condon's other work on Reginald Bray and on Henry's council only scratches the surface of an immense understanding of Henry's reign gleaned from surviving crown records. Gunn has offered a masterful overview of early Tudor government, and has produced several essential pieces on the power and personnel of Henry's regime. The position of Gunn and Condon as scholars of Henry's reign allows them to look forward and back from 1485 to 1509, and to place their analysis of the substantive themes of Henry's reign in a broader context than many other medieval or Tudor scholars have so far been able to achieve. Both of these writers are primarily masters of archival research, but have also synthesised a wide range of other evidence to offer the most rounded understanding of Henry VII.

John Watts is bringing his powerful grasp of concepts of monarchical rule to bear on Henry's ruling ideology and ideas of governance put into practice after 1485. Close analysis of constitutional theory and practice, which Watts is impressively equipped to achieve, will create a vital foundation for our understanding the type of kingship Henry put into practice. Michael K. Jones has blended his expert knowledge of the Beaufort family, especially Margaret Beaufort, onto a strong interest in the confrontation between Richard III and Henry Tudor to produce several expert works. While many of his pieces have advanced the depth of our knowledge of Henry's reign, his recent book relocating the battle of Bosworth shows how bold strokes can thrust the late fifteenth century firmly and unexpectedly into modern popular culture.

In the field of Henry's early foreign policy only John Currin has offered systematic new interpretations of England's difficulties and successes. His analysis of England's involvement in Brittany, and the reinterpretation of the objectives of the 1492 French campaign, has used a range of European sources and pulls into focus the absence of modern analysis of foreign policies towards the close of Henry's reign. Michael C.E. Jones has also scoured the Breton and French sources he knows so expertly for evidence of Henry Tudor's exile. The work of Stephen Ellis on early

Tudor frontiers, and Ireland in particular, is unparalleled and is relied upon by all other scholars of the period. Ian Arthurson has also contributed a great deal to our understanding of the intricacies of Henry's relations with Europe's rulers during the 1490s in his immensely detailed and rewarding work on Perkin Warbeck. His articles on espionage and Henry's military response to internal and external threats have stemmed from his major research on the Scottish war and Western rising of 1497. We await publication of this important analysis.

A glance at the publications of Cliff Davies shows an immense knowledge that is by no means limited to early Tudor England. But students of Henry Tudor, France, and the end of the Wars of the Roses have much to be grateful for in his regular forays into Henry's reign. Dominic Luckett keeps a low profile but has contributed essential work on Henry's relationship with and control of the officers that represented the crown in England's regions. David Grummitt, also, has broad interests. His work on Henry VII's finances is one of the more important articles of recent years. We await the publication of his extensive work on Tudor Calais for a fuller understanding of political manoeuvring in England's last continental outpost.

Paul Cavill's recent thesis on Henry VII and parliament demonstrates a tremendous understanding of the reign. Publication of this important work will boost studies of the early Tudor period considerably. There is also much hope among scholars that DeLloyd J. Guth will also soon return to his important work on the role of Henry's Exchequer in penal law enforcement, so far largely unpublished. This present author is also working on an analysis of Henry's adoption of bonds as mainsprings of his ruling policy. This is a key theme of Henry's reign that must be addressed in its proper context.

The very recent debate on Henry VII is therefore attracting new scholars to the early Tudor period. Consensus about the king and his reign has not yet formed, nor is it likely to until more investigation and analysis is published. Nevertheless, Henry VII is now rapidly emerging from the shadows of misrepresentation and misunderstanding as his intriguing reign begins to receive the attention it deserves.

## HENRY VII'S PLACE IN HISTORY

In *1066 And All That* Henry VII is the victim of absurdly confusing waves of pretenders. He was a miser who was very good at statecraft.[5] Beneath this cutting satire is an accurate generalisation of how historians have assessed the main difficulties and achievements of Henry VII – a struggle to establish solid government in the face of chronic conspiracy growing from the nature of his own accession, and bred by the political legacy of a century of noble-led civil conflict.

Henry was very successful at borrowing the initiatives of previous rulers, at innovating beyond existing practices, and at focusing doggedly upon specific policies or problems until he achieved his goals. These characteristics can be seen in his reliance on existing legal skills and the enforcement of the process of the law on his terms. Henry stands out as a ruler who controlled the political application of the law for the preservation of his dynastic power. In the area of finance the function of the Exchequer remained unaltered. Even the prominence of the royal chamber as the clearing house for crown income was a revival of the way Edward IV and Richard III had developed their finances.

In the ruthless search for dynastic security, it is possible that Henry also strove for something more personal – the stability his life had always lacked. A secure throne allowed the roots of a strong dynasty to grow as the Tudor royal family expanded. Henry was the only child of his mother, Margaret. She was the last surviving child of her father Henry, duke of Somerset. Jasper Tudor died in 1495 without fathering any children. For the House of Tudor to prosper, Henry had to create the circumstances in which his children could flourish. The political environment of their upbringing would be vastly different from that Henry had faced.

Henry IV, Henry V, Edward IV, and Richard III had all passed through a phase of their lives where they were the sons of peers who shared the royal blood, and attended court as companions of the royal family. Henry IV and Richard III, especially, had enjoyed prominent independent status as noblemen before they seized the crown. During this period valuable education was received in practical skills of estate management, appropriate social graces, military arts, and grammar and literature. Only Henry VI became king at such a young age that his experience of dealing in the political world of capricious nobles was based on an entirely royal perspective. Fifteenth-century kings, dukes and earls were royal cousins with a common descent from Edward III (1327–77). They held a shared elite outlook. Rather than misunderstanding what was required of a medieval English monarch, Henry Tudor had virtually no personal understanding.

Henry's permanent adult exile separated him entirely from England's ruling elite, both literally and in terms of his outlook and experiences. On the one hand, this gave him an opportunity to unlock the closed network of personal service that had surrounded medieval princes of Wales or nobles of the royal blood; on the other, it created a disproportionate dependence upon the advice and skills of the few people who had helped him before Bosworth. Henry's base of support did cut across existing and inherited allegiances. This was an advantage if it could be transformed into Tudor loyalty; it would be disastrous to Henry's authority if it fragmented and reverted into separate and competing constituencies. As a result its control was fundamentally important to Henry's dynastic success.

He arrived from relative obscurity in 1485 and began to rule more like a landlord than the first among aristocratic equals. His management of the crown lands, royal patronage, the creation of peers, and the punishment of offenders, began to elevate the position of the king above the ruling elite from which previous English rulers had emerged. This change allowed Henry to dominate the structures of the state rather than to share in their development as part of the ruling class. But it did not force the king to rule personally. Henry managed strategically while well-trained and closely allied bureaucrats projected royal power under his watchful eye.

Henry's chosen way of ruling required him to possess immense clarity about his goals. It also needed constant personal vigilance and a ruthless determination to intervene when decisions went wrong or officials performed unacceptably. The dangers of kingship constructed on the strength of the king's ability to manage it must have been obvious from the ways that Edward IV and Francis, duke of Brittany, had developed similar systems. Any king who encouraged specialists to run his institutions had to have the right kind of controls in place.

The strongest, but least accessible development of Henry's reign was his apparent attempt to create and enforce a new ideology of service and loyalty to the crown that enhanced the medieval concept of allegiance to an immediate lord, the king, and the nation. This stood alongside Tudor restructuring of existing institutions, to transform the mentality of the ruling elites. It is also a practical example of what Philip Corrigan and Derek Sayer identified as the state's moral regulation of relationships.[6] We see in the conditions attached to bonds, a demonstration of Henry's authority and his control over the legal definition of acceptable behaviour, loyalty, and personal governance. This attitude was universal: it was applied against pardoned political suspects as well as allies commanding important castles or occupying official posts.

As more people within a community became bound for their own collective loyalty, the links of marriage, service, and landholding that created that community soon forced it to remain loyal or risk devastation. Even then, Henry scaled down forfeitures to ensure that offenders were restored under strict royal control. He did not want their destruction, only their cooperation in upholding the law and local rule. This system was therefore self-perpetuating; if people were provoked into rebellion they did so in increasing isolation. Since many bonds were never cancelled the crown's hold over aristocratic behaviour stretched across generations.

Henry's fear of a resurgence of noble-led treason caused him to downplay the role of the noble class within his regime – best seen in his failure to call a Great Council after 1496. This was reversed by Henry VIII, who remoulded noble power and prestige for a new level of rivalry among Europe's rulers. His father had pushed the aristocracy close to rebellion, but Henry VII did fragment the unified influence that the aristocracy had wielded over the crown for most of the fifteenth century. Henry's focus in this area was essential if Tudor power was to continue after his death. Henry VIII inherited a bruised and uncertain peerage. Once the bitter taste of his father's final years had cleared, the second Tudor could contemplate an entirely different type of kingship in partnership with nobles ready for a return to magnificence and glory. As a class, however, they were far less of a threat to the crown after 1509 than they had been before 1485.

Despite Henry's instability he passed his crown to a natural heir who was of adult age. Henry was the first king since Henry IV in 1413 to achieve this. He was also the first ruler since 1422 to avoid deposition. Whilst he did encounter threats that warranted severe action, Henry did not face serious and organised rebellion from the nobility. After the first attainders of 1485, only the earls of Lincoln, Warwick and Suffolk, and Lord Audley among the peerage suffered forfeiture for treason. Henry was lucky that many of the great noble titles were in minority for much of his reign (Northumberland, Buckingham, Warwick). He also kept other estates and titles in abeyance or within the royal family. In elevating the Tudor crown to a position of supremacy, Henry inevitably demoted the status of the nobility in the eyes of the crown. They were no longer partners but chief subjects.

Towards the end of Henry's reign, members of the elite were competing for office and influence within a clearly defined structure of crown service. They were not challenging independently for resources of land and men that could threaten Henry's stability. Nobles were still great landowners, courtiers, or commissioners, but they were obliged – literally – to be the king's men. They were powerful because Henry allowed them a degree of power suitable for the role he expected of them. By about 1506, noble title, status, or inherited rights were no longer enough to command major influence within a region. The king's control of this system of lordship became more centralised, formal, and structured than it had been.

To Henry's domestic struggles we must also add the potentially more risky attempts to manipulate England's foreign relations. He started his diplomatic policies with a lavish gesture of honour over Brittany. He was also perhaps unrealistic about his ability to revive England's claims to parts of France in 1492. Foreign policy was a far harder skill to master than internal politics for a king without previous involvement in elite court culture. Yet this is the area where Henry's achievements are perhaps most impressive. Simnel, Warbeck, and Margaret of Burgundy ensured that England's internal politics were welded to large-scale relations between Europe's rulers. The problems arising in one arena could not be resolved without engaging fully with the other.

Henry did make England a valid player in European diplomacy. By the time of his death he had reversed the erosion of England's status that had started in the 1440s. He set the foundations for Henry VIII's more dynamic involvement in European politics. By restricting himself to diplomatic manoeuvring and, unlike most other powers, avoiding the heavy financial cost of permanent war, Henry probably gave his son the financial ability and political security to impose himself so forcefully on the affairs of Europe after 1509.

It is unlikely that Henry VII enjoyed more than nine of his twenty-four years as king without a real threat of rebellion or conspiracy. These interludes were scattered throughout the reign. There was no gradual conquest of his enemies to leave him with several golden years of security and prosperity at the end of his reign. Henry's successes in reforming domestic government and recovering England's influence in Europe were hard earned by effort and vigilance within a clear political programme. The peace he achieved may have been 'smooth-faced' but it required constant awareness, a vast personal knowledge of landholders and their connections, and a mastery of archived documents. This book has only been able to suggest how the personal and regal qualities of Henry Tudor merged to create his role as king between 1485 and 1509. It was entirely Henry VII's personality that shaped and directed the course of his reign. Yet a true understanding of the man is lost along with the key evidence that might have brought this book closer to a true biographical picture of him. The balance of domestic security, excellent financial management of the crown's resources, and realistic aspirations in foreign affairs made Henry's reign the important transition between the political disorder of the Wars of the Roses and the strident, confident Tudor monarchies that followed him.

# NOTES

## 1 INTRODUCTION

1 William Shakespeare, *King Richard III*, ed. Anthony Hammond, (Arden edn, London, 1987), p. 331.

2 The debate is summarised in M.C. Carpenter, 'Henry VII and the English Polity', in B. Thompson (ed.), *The Reign of Henry VII* (Stamford, 1995), pp. 11–30, and restated in M.C. Carpenter, *The Wars of the Roses: Politics and the Constitution in England, c.1437–1509* (Cambridge, 1997), pp. 219–221.

3 S.B. Chrimes, *Henry VII* (London, 1972), p. 332.

4 Sir H. Ellis (ed.), *Original Letters Illustrative of English History, etc* (1st series, 1825), 46.

## 2 GAINING THE CROWN

1 The legal guardianship and right to determine how an underage heir would be brought up and whom he would eventually marry – frequently a child of the guardian.

2 *Three Books of Polydore Vergil's English History*, ed. Sir Henry Ellis, Camden Society, original series, 29 (London, 1844), p. 194.

3 R.A. Griffiths and R.S. Thomas, *The Making of the Tudor Dynasty* (Gloucester, 1987), p. 96.

4 British Library, Harleian Manuscript 787, fol. 2; R. Horrox, 'Henry Tudor's Letters to England during Richard III's Reign', *The Ricardian*, 80 (1983), 155–158.

5 M.K. Jones, 'The Myth of 1485 – did France really put Henry Tudor on the Throne?', in D. Grummitt (ed.), *The English Experience on France, c.1450–1558: War Diplomacy and Cultural Exchange* (Aldershot, 2002).

6 M.K. Jones, *Bosworth 1485, Psychology of a Battle* (Stroud, 2002), pp. 132, 165–166.

7 Livia Visser-Fuchs, 'Phantom Bastardy and Ghostly Pikemen', *The Ricardian*, XIV (2004), 117–118.

8 C.S.L. Davies, 'The Wars of the Roses in European Context', in *The Wars of the Roses*, ed. A.J. Pollard (London, 1995), p. 244.

9 Henry's possession of a battle standard of the Dun Cow (a mythical beast associated with the Coventry area) showed his focus on this region as key to his strategy.

10 John D. Austin, *Merevale and Atherstone: 1485, Recent Bosworth Discoveries* (Atherstone, 2004).

11 Peter Foss, *The Field of Redemore: The Battle of Bosworth 1485*, 2nd edn (Leicester, 1998). Jones and Foss summarised their viewpoints in *Ricardian Bulletin*, summer 2003, pp. 25–31.

12 For a discussion of the traditional site, see C.D. Ross, *Richard III* (London, 1981); M.J. Bennett, *The Battle of Bosworth* (Gloucester, 1985).

13 Ian Arthurson and Nicholas Kingwell, 'The Proclamation of Henry Tudor as King of England, 3 November 1483', *Historical Research*, 63 (1990), 104.

## 3 FORGING THE DYNASTY

1 *The Parliament Rolls of Medieval England, 1275–1504*, general ed. Chris Given-Wilson, (Woodbridge/London, 2005), vol. XV, *Richard III, 1484–85 and Henry VII, 1485–87* (ed. Rosemary Horrox), pp. 107–112; *Rotuli Parliamentorum*, VI, 275–278.

2 *The Parliament Rolls of Medieval England, 1275–1504*, vol. XV, p. 97; *Rotuli Parliamentorum*, VI, 268–270.

3 Bonds, obligations and recognisances were legally binding agreements whereby a person, group, or organisation agreed to perform some act (such as payment of a debt) or condition (to stay loyal to the king), under penalty of forfeiture of a large sum of money, goods, or land. Agreements often involved others who stood as pledges for the compliance of the main people involved. See pp. 215–23.

4 See pp. 157–8.

## 4 PERKIN WARBECK

1 I. Arthurson, 'Perkin Warbeck and the Princes in the Tower', in. M. Aston and R. Horrox (eds), *Much Heaving and Shoving: Essays for Colin Richmond* (Lavenham, 2005), pp. 158–170.

2 A. Wroe, *Perkin: A Story of Deception* (London, 2004), pp. 516–518.

3 John M. Currin, ' "To Traffic with War"?: Henry VII and the French Campaign of 1492', in D.A. Grummitt (ed.), *The English Experience on France, c.1450–1558: War, Diplomacy and Cultural Exchange* (Aldershot, 2002).

4    Francis Bacon, *The History of the Reign of King Henry VII*, ed. R. Lockyer (London, 1971), p. 137.

5    The Hansa or Hanseatic League was an economic federation of north German and Baltic towns, ports, and regions that combined to defend mutual trading rights and interests. Their English headquarters were at the Steelyard in the city of London.

6    The Cinque Ports – originally Dover, Sandwich, Hythe, Romney, and Hastings on the Kent-Sussex coast – associated together to provide ships for the king's navy in return for special legal rights and the profits of justice in their courts.

7    See p. 182.

8    The Great Council was a formal gathering of those lords normally summoned to parliament (i.e. noblemen, bishops and abbots), without the representatives of the Commons. It was an extension of the king's smaller executive council that met regularly to discuss the crown's affairs.

9    See pp. 268–9.

10   Arthurson, 'Perkin Warbeck', p. 161.

11   *Calendar of State Papers, Spanish, I, Henry VII, 1485–1509*, ed. G.A. Bergenroth (London, 1862), pp. 177–178.

## 5   THE RIGOURS OF KINGSHIP

1    The royal household had a customary legal jurisdiction within a radius of 12 miles of wherever it was based.

2    Arthur and Catherine were 'married' by agreement (with diplomats taking their places) three times. The final two – in May 1499 and November 1500 – were agreed to cement England's friendship with Spain as Warbeck's conspiracy was finally unravelled.

3    See pp. 271–2.

4    John Leland, *De rebus Brittanicis collectanea*, ed. T Hearne 6 vols, (1715), V, 373–374.

5    See the sections on royal prerogative rights (pp.135–7), bonds and recognisances (pp. 215–23), the Church (pp. 230–31), ideology (pp. 129–30), and London (pp. 241–3).

6    See pp. 155–9.

7    C.J. Harrison, 'The Petition of Edmund Dudley' *English Historical Review*, lxxxvii (1972), 86–90.

8    M.C. Carpenter, *The Wars of the Roses: Politics and the Constitution in England, c.1437–1509* (Cambridge, 1997), p. 248.

9   J. Gairdner (ed.), *Memorials of King Henry VII*, Rolls Series (1858), pp. 223–239.

10  S. Anglo, 'Image Making: The Means and the Limitations', in J. Guy (ed.), *The Tudor Monarchy* (London, 1997), pp. 16–42.

11  TNA, PRO E 23/3, fols 1–1v.

12  BL Harley 433, fols 273v–274.

# 6 TUDOR GOVERNMENT AT WORK

1   TNA, PRO C 53/198, m. 1

2   Sir John Fortescue, *De Laudibus Legum Anglie*, ed. S.B. Chrimes (Cambridge, 1942), p. 33.

3   John Watts, '"A New Ffundacion of is Crowne": Monarchy in the Age of Henry VII', in B. Thompson (ed.), *The Reign of Henry VII*, Harlaxton Medieval Studies, V, Proceedings of the 1993 Symposium (Stamford, 1995), pp. 31–53.

4   A.R. Myers (ed.), *The Household of Edward IV: The Black Book and the Ordinance of 1478* (Manchester, 1959).

5   For Sunyff, see p. 242.

6   N. Pronay, 'The Chancellor, the Chancery and the Council at the End of the Fifteenth Century', in H. Hearder and H.R. Lyon (eds), *British Government and Administration: Studies Presented to S.B. Chrimes* (Cardiff, 1974).

7   Figures from B.P. Wolffe, *The Crown Lands, 1461–1536* (London, 1970), p. 69.

8   BL Lansdowne 127, fol. 53.

9   Extracts from lost books relating to 1491 were made by the antiquarian Craven Ord around 1800 and survive as British Library, Additional MS 7099.

10  D. Grummitt, 'Henry VII, Chamber Finance and the "New Monarchy": Some New Evidence', *Historical Research*, 72 (October 1999), pp. 229–243.

11  Tallies were small sticks carved with notches to represent sums of money accounted at the Exchequer: the thicker the notch, the higher the value. Once carved, the hazel stick was split, so that when debt was settled the two halves could be rejoined as proof that the transaction 'tallied'.

12  Retaining is defined on p. 209. Maintenance was the action of wrongfully aiding and abetting litigation: more specifically the support of a suit or suitor at law by a party who has no legally recognised interest in the proceedings.

13  Paul Cavill, 'Henry VII and Parliament', Unpublished Oxford University, D.Phil. thesis, 2005, pp. 66–69. See also p. 44.

14  The first book of receipts is TNA, PRO, E 101/413/2(i) (4 July 1487–29 September 1489). The first payment from Thomas Lucas, Henry's solicitor, is on fol. 14 (3 March

1488). Where money was received upon a pardon or fine it was noted specifically in this document.

15 Embracery was the offence of influencing a jury illegally and corruptly. In this sense, livery was the distinctive uniform, badge, collar or hood, bestowed by a lord upon his retainers or servants. It was a token by which they might be recognised, in a wider sense, as a follower of that lord.

16 See pp. 229–30.

17 M.C. Carpenter, *The Wars of the Roses: Politics and the Constitution in England, c.1437–1509* (Cambridge, 1997), p. 240.

18 The quorum was originally the number of JPs, usually of experience or ability, whose presence was necessary to form the bench to hear cases at quarter sessions.

19 J.R. Lander, *English Justices of the Peace, 1461–1509* (Gloucester, 1989), pp. 112–119, 139–140.

20 1488 (4 Hen VII, cap. 12).

21 See pp. 173–93.

# 7 LORDSHIP, THE CROWN, AND THE REGIONS

1 Oyer and terminer commissioners empowered specially selected judges to 'hear and judge' specific local crimes such as riots or uprisings that could not await the regular sessions of the assizes.

2 See p. 88.

3 Enfeoffment was the investment of possession of freehold land to another individual or group.

4 Hundreds (or wapentakes in many areas of the English midlands and north) were ancient administrative divisions of counties.

5 Francis Bacon, *The History of the Reign of Henry VII*, ed. R. Lockyer (London, 1971), p. 203.

6 *CPR, 1494–1509*, p. 287.

7 M.E. James, *A Tudor Magnate and the Tudor State: Henry Fifth Earl of Northumberland* (York, 1966), pp. 17–18.

8 For the intrusive nature of crown lordship in the west midlands, see p. 63.

# 8 ROYAL POWER AND PERSONNEL

1 See pp. 128–9, for examples from 1502.

2   *Plumpton Correspondence*, ed. T. Stapleton, Camden Society, IV (London, 1839), cxiii, 117–118.

3   For example, Sir John Conyers (see p. 53) and Gerald, earl of Kildare (see p. 74).

4   College of Arms, Arundel MS, XVII, ii; D.R. Starkey, 'Intimacy and Innovation: The Rise of the Privy Chamber, 1485–1547', in D.R. Starkey (ed.), *The English Court: From the Wars of the Roses to the Civil War* (London, 1987), pp. 73–74.

5   Dyed wool of different colours, mixed before spinning.

## 9   THE PRESERVATION OF POWER

1   *The Parliament Rolls of Medieval England, 1275–1504*, general ed. Chris Given-Wilson – (Woodbridge/London, 2005), vol. XVI, *Henry VII, 1487–1504* (ed. Rosemary Horrox), pp. 330–331; *Rotuli Parliamentorum*, VI, 525.

2   D. Luckett 'Crown Office and Licensed Retinues in the Reign of Henry VII', in R.E. Archer and S. Walker (eds), *Rulers and Ruled in Late Medieval England* (London, 1995), pp. 223–238.

3   A. Cameron, 'The Giving of Livery and Retaining in Henry VII's Reign', *Renaissance and Modern Studies*, 18 (1974), 28.

4   P.M. Barnes, 'The Chancery Corpus Cum Causa File, 10–11 Edward IV', in *Medieval Legal Records*, ed. R.F. Hunnisett and J.B. Post (1978), pp. 430–476.

5   BL Lansdowne 127.

6   C.J. Harrison, 'The Petition of Edmund Dudley', *English Historical Review*, lxxxvii (1972), 86–90. See p. 111.

7   J.R. Lander, 'Bonds, Coercion and Fear: Henry VII and the Peerage', in *Crown and Nobility, 1450–1509* (London, 1976); T.B. Pugh, 'Henry VII and the English Nobility', in G.W. Bernard (ed.), *The Tudor Nobility* (Manchester, 1992), pp. 49–110.

8   Harrison, 'Petition of Edmund Dudley', p. 87.

9   See pp. 136–7.

10  TNA: PRO, C 54/376. An edition by the present author is forthcoming.

11  For use of bonds against the Stanley and de la Pole affinity members after 1500, see pp. 185 and 190.

12  Huntington Library, Ellesmere MS 2654, fol. 3d; C.G. Bayne and W.H. Dunham (eds), *Select Cases in the Council of Henry VII*, Selden Society, lxxv (London, 1958), p. 11.

## 10 THE KING'S NATION

1 HenVII, cap. 4; *The Parliament Rolls of Medieval England, 1275–1504*, eds C. Given-Wilson, P. Brand, S. Phillips, W.M. Ormrod, G. Martin, A.E. Curry and R. Harrox (Leicester, 2005), vol. XV, pp. 226–227.

2 Buying and selling of spiritual and Church benefits such as pardons, appointments, or relics.

3 Holding more than one Church living or office.

4 An annual tax, originally of one penny, paid for the maintenance of the pope in Rome.

5 R.J. Knecht, 'The Episcopate and the Wars of the Roses', *University of Birmingham. Historical Journal*, 6 (1957–8), 108–131; M.M. Condon, 'Ruling Elites in the Reign of Henry VII', in Charles Ross (ed.), *Patronage, Pedigree and Power in Later Medieval England* (Gloucester, 1979), pp. 110–111.

6 S.J. Gunn, 'Edmund Dudley and the Church', *Journal of Ecclesiastical History*, 51, 3 (2002), 509–526.

7 A.H. Thomas and I.D. Thornley (eds), *The Great Chronicle of London* (London, 1938), p. 261.

8 The infection was probably miliary fever – a highly contagious disease causing great sweating and the formation of fluid-filled sacs on the skin.

9 S.J. Gunn, 'War, Dynasty and Public Opinion in Early Tudor England', in G.W. Bernard and S.J. Gunn (eds), *Authority and Consent in Tudor England* (Aldershot, 2002), pp. 131–149.

10 Garments, usually of fur or wool, covering the shoulders, or the neck and shoulders; a cape or short cloak, often with hanging ends.

11 See p. 238.

12 A staple was an exclusive marketplace.

13 See p. 236.

14 Stockfish was dried and salted cod eaten in vast quantities during Lent.

15 This plant was the source of blue dye to clothiers.

16 See p. 69.

## 11 PROJECTING TUDOR INFLUENCE

1 This development is discussed on pp. 211–12, and fully in D. Luckett, 'Crown Office and Licensed Retinues in the Reign of Henry VII', in R.E. Archer and Simon Walker (eds), *Rulers and Ruled in Late Medieval England* (London, 1995), pp. 223–238.

2   *The Anglica Historia of Polydore Vergil, A.D. 1485–1537*, ed. D. Hay, Camden Society, vol. lxxiv (London, 1950), p. 37.

3   The forms of words in various appointments in TNA: PRO, PSO 2/1

4   Falcons were light cannon.

5   T.B. Pugh, *The Marcher Lordships of South Wales, 1415–1536* (Cardiff, 1963), pp. 438–439.

6   J.B. Smith, 'Crown and Community in the Principality of North Wales in the Reign of Henry Tudor', *Welsh History Review*, 3 (1966), 145–171; S.B. Chrimes, *Henry VII* (London, 1972), pp. 254–257.

## 12  CONCLUSION

1   *The Anglica Historia of Polydore Vergil, A.D. 1485–1537*, ed. D. Hay, Camden Society, 3rd series, lxxiv (London, 1950); D. Hay, *Polydore Vergil* (Oxford, 1952).

2   Francis Bacon, *The History of the Reign of King Henry VII*, ed. R. Lockyer, (London, 1971).

3   Philip Sidney, *An Apologie for Poetry* in E. Rhys, *Prelude to Poetry* (London, 1971), p. 20; quoted in Vergil, *Anglica Historia*, p. xxxix.

4   M.C. Carpenter, *The Wars of the Roses: Politics and the Constitution in England, c.1437–1509* (Cambridge, 1997), p. 248.

5   W.C. Sellar and R.J. Yeatman, *1066 And All That* (London, 2005), pp. 73–77.

6   P. Corrigan and D. Sayer, *The Great Arch: English State Formation as Cultural Revolution* (Oxford, 1986), pp. 4–7, 43–45.

# SELECT FURTHER READING

Restrictions of space prevent the publication of a fully comprehensive list of works used in the preparation of this book. This section omits relevant entries in H.C.G. Matthew and Brian Harrison (eds), *The Oxford Dictionary of National Biography* (60 vols, Oxford, 2004).

## 1 INTRODUCTION

### *Printed primary sources*

*The Anglica Historia of Polydore Vergil, A.D. 1485–1537*, ed. D. Hay, Camden Society, 3rd series, lxxiv (London, 1950).

Bacon, Francis, *The History of the Reign of King Henry VII*, ed. R. Lockyer (London, 1971).

Hall, E., *The Union of the Two Noble and Illustrious Families of Lancaster and York* (London, 1550; facsimile reprint, Menston, 1970).

*Letters and Papers, Foreign and Domestic, of the Reign of Henry VIII*, ed. J.S. Brewer, J. Gairdner, and R.H. Brodie, 21 vols, with 2 vols of addenda (London, 1862–1932).

*Letters and Papers Illustrative of the Reigns of Richard III and Henry VII*, ed. J. Gairdner, 2 vols, Rolls Series, xxiv (London, 1861–3).

*Letters of the King's of England*, ed. J.O. Halliwell (London, 1848).

*Materials for a History of the Reign of Henry VII*, ed. W. Campbell, 2 vols (London, 1873).

*Memorials of King Henry VII*, ed. J. Gairdner, Rolls Series, x (London, 1858).

*Original Letters and Papers Illustrative of English History*, ed. Sir H. Ellis, 2 vols (London, 1824–7).

*The Paston Letters*, ed. J. Gairdner, 6 vols, (London, 1904; facsimile reprint, Gloucester, 1983).

*The Reign of Henry VII from Contemporary Sources*, ed. A.F. Pollard, 3 vols (London, 1913–14).

*Three Books of Polydore Vergil's English History*, ed. Sir H. Ellis, Camden Society, 29 (London, 1844).

*Tudor Royal Proclamations*, eds P.L. Hughes and J.F. Larkin, 3 vols (New Haven, 1964–9).

## Secondary works

Busch, W., England Unter den Tudors I (Stuttgart, 1892). English translation by A.M. Todd, *England Under the Tudors*, I, *Henry VII* (London, 1895).

Carpenter, M.C., *The Wars of the Roses: Politics and the Constitution in England, c. 1437–1509* (Cambridge, 1997).

Chrimes, S.B., *Henry VII* (London, 1972).

Condon, M.M., 'Ruling Elites in the Reign of Henry VII', in Charles Ross (ed.), *Patronage, Pedigree and Power in Later Medieval England* (Gloucester, 1979), pp. 109–142.

Cunningham, S., 'The Establishment of the Tudor Regime: Henry VII, Rebellion, and the Financial Control of the Aristocracy, 1485–1509' (Unpublished Lancaster University Ph.D. thesis, 1995).

Davies, C.S.L., 'The Wars of the Roses in a European Context' in A.J. Pollard (ed.), *The Wars of the Roses* (London, 1995), pp. 162–185.

Dobson, R.B., 'General Survey, 1300–1540', in D.M. Palliser (ed.), *The Cambridge Urban History of Britain, 600–1540* (Cambridge, 2000), pp. 273–290.

Elton, G.R., *England under the Tudors*, 2nd edn (London, 1974).

Gairdner, J., *Henry VII* (London, 1892).

Grant, A., *Henry VII* (London, 1985).

Griffiths, R.A., *The Reign of Henry VI* (Berkeley, 1981).

Gunn, S.J., *Early Tudor Government, 1485–1558* (London, 1995).

Guy, J.A., *Tudor England* (Oxford, 1988).

Harriss, G.L., *Shaping the Nation, 1360–1461* (Oxford, 2005).

Hicks, M.A., *English Political Culture in the Fifteenth Century* (London, 2002).

Jones, M.K. and Underwood, M.G., *The King's Mother: Lady Margaret Beaufort, Countess of Richmond and Derby* (Cambridge, 1992).

Lander, J.R., *Government and Community: England 1450–1509* (London, 1980).

MacDougall, N., *James IV* (Edinburgh, 1989).

Mackie, J.D., *The Earlier Tudors* (Oxford, 1972).

McFarlane, K.B., *The Nobility of Later Medieval England* (Oxford, 1973).

McFarlane, K.B., *England in the Fifteenth Century* (London, 1981).

Pugh, T.B., 'Henry VII and the English Nobility', in G.W. Bernard (ed.), *The Tudor Nobility* (Manchester, 1992), pp. 49–110.

Pugh, T.B., 'The Magnates, Knights and Gentry' in S.B. Chrimes, C.D. Ross and R.S. Griffiths (eds), *Fifteenth Century England, 1399–1509*, 2nd edn (Stroud, 1995).

Ross, C.D., *Edward IV* (London, 1974).

Scarisbrick, J.J., *Henry VIII* (London, 1968).

Storey, R.L., *The Reign of Henry VII* (London, 1968).

Storey, R.L., *The End of the House of Lancaster* (Gloucester, 1986).

Wedgwood, J.C. (ed.), *History of Parliament, Biographies of the Members of the Commons House, 1439–1509* (London, 1936).

Weightman, C., *Margaret of York, Duchess of Burgundy, 1446–1503* (Stroud, 1989).

Wernham, R.B., *Before the Armada* (London, 1968).

Williams, P., *The Tudor Regime* (Oxford, 1979).

Wolffe, B.P., *Henry VI* (London, 1981).

## 2 GAINING THE CROWN

Antonovics, A.V., 'Henry the VII, King of England "by the grace of Charles VII king of France"', in R.A. Griffiths and J. Sherborne (eds), *Kings and Nobles in the Later Middle Ages* (Gloucester, 1986), pp. 169–184.

Austin, J.D., *Merevale and Atherstone: 1485, Recent Bosworth Discoveries* (Atherstone, 2004).

Bennett, M.J., *The Battle of Bosworth* (Gloucester, 1985).

Commynes, Philippe de, *Memoirs: The Reign of Louis XI, 1461–83*, trans. M.C.E. Jones (Harmondsworth, 1972).

Conway, A.E., 'The Maidstone Sector of Buckingham's Rebellion', *Archaeologia Cantiana*, 38 (1909), 97–120.

Davies, C.S.L., 'Richard III, Brittany and Henry Tudor, 1483–85', *Nottingham Medieval Studies*, xxxviii (1993), 110–126.

Foss, P., *The Field of Redemore: The Battle of Bosworth 1485*, 2nd edn (Leicester, 1998).

Griffiths, R.A. and Thomas, R.S., *The Making of the Tudor Dynasty* (Stroud, 1985).

Horrox, R., *Richard III: A Study of Service* (Cambridge, 1989).

Horrox, R. and Hammond, P.W. (eds), *British Library Harleian Manuscript 433*, 4 vols (Gloucester, 1979–83).

Jones, M.K., *Bosworth 1485, Psychology of a Battle* (Stroud, 2002).

Mancini, Dominic, *The Usurpation of Richard III*, ed. C.A.J. Armstrong (Oxford, 1969).

More, Sir Thomas, *The History of King Richard III*, ed. R.S. Sylvester (New Haven, 1963).

Pronay, N. and Cox, J. (eds), *The Crowland Chronicle Continuations: 1459–1486* (London, 1986).

Richmond, C.F., '1485 And All That, or What was Going on at the Battle of Bosworth', in P.W. Hammond (ed.), *Richard III, Loyalty, Lordship and Law* (Gloucester, 1986).

Ross, C.D., *Richard III* (London, 1981).

## 3 FORGING THE DYNASTY

Anglo, S., 'The Foundation of the Tudor Dynasty: The Coronation and Marriage of Henry VII', *Guildhall Miscellanea*, 2 (1960), 3–11.

Bennett, M.J., *Lambert Simnel and the Battle of Stoke* (Gloucester, 1987).

Bennett, M.J., 'Henry VII and the Northern Rising of 1489', *English Historical Review*, 105 (1990), 34–59.

Cavell, E., 'Henry VII, the North of England, and the First Provincial Progress of 1486', *Northern History*, 39 (2002), 187–207.

Cunningham, S., 'Henry VII and Rebellion in North-Eastern England, 1485–1492: Bonds of Allegiance and the Establishment of Tudor Authority', *Northern History*, XXXII (1996), 42–74.

Currin, J.M., 'Henry VII and the Treaty of Redon (1489): Plantagenet Ambitions and Early Tudor Foreign Policy', *History*, 81 (1996), 343–358.

Dockray, K., 'The Political Legacy of Richard III in Northern England', in R.A. Griffiths and J. Sherborne (eds), *Kings and Nobles in the Later Middle Ages* (Gloucester, 1982), pp. 205–227.

Hicks, M.A., 'The Yorkshire Rebellion of 1489 Reconsidered', *Northern History*, 22 (1986), 39–62.

Williams, C.H., 'The Rebellion of Humphrey Stafford in 1486', *English Historical Review*, 43 (1928), 181–189.

## 4 PERKIN WARBECK

Archbold, W.A.J., 'Sir William Stanley and Perkin Warbeck, *English Historical Review*, 14 (1899).

Arthurson, I., '1497 and the Western Rising', 2 vols (Unpublished Keele University Ph.D. thesis, 1981).

Arthurson, I., 'The King's Voyage into Scotland: The War that Never Was', in Daniel Williams (ed.), *England in the Fifteenth Century* (Woodbridge, 1987), pp. 1–22.

Arthurson, I., 'The Rising of 1497: A Revolt of the Peasantry?', in J. Rosenthal and C. Richmond (eds), *People, Politics and Community in the Later Middle Ages* (Gloucester, 1987), pp. 1–18.

Arthurson, I., *The Perkin Warbeck Conspiracy, 1491–1499* (Stroud, 1994).

Bain, J. (ed.), *Calendar of Documents Relating to Scotland* (Edinburgh, 1881).

Conway, A.E., *Henry VII's Relations with Scotland and Ireland, 1485–1498* (Cambridge, 1932).

Currin, J.M., '"To Traffic with War"? Henry VII and the French Campaign of 1492', in D.A. Grummitt (ed.), *The English Experience in France, c. 1450–1558: War, Diplomacy and Cultural Exchange* (Aldershot, 2002), pp. 106–131.

Wroe, A., *Perkin: A Story of Deception* (London, 2004).

## 5 THE RIGOURS OF KINGSHIP

Condon, M.M., 'God Save the King! Piety, Propaganda and the Perpetual Memorial', in T. Tatton-Brown and R. Mortimer (eds), *Westminster Abbey: The Lady Chapel of Henry VII* (Woodbridge, 2003), pp. 59–97.

Condon, M.M., 'The Last Will of Henry VII: Document and Text', in T. Tatton-Brown and R. Mortimer (eds), *Westminster Abbey: The Lady Chapel of Henry VII* (Woodbridge, 2003), pp. 99–140.

Cooper, J.P., 'Henry VII's Last Years Reconsidered', *Historical Journal*, 2 (1959), 103–129.

Elton, G.R., 'Henry VII: Rapacity and Remorse', in *Studies in Tudor and Stuart Politics and Government*, 4 vols (Cambridge, 1974–92), i. 45–65.

Elton, G.R., 'Henry VII: A Restatement', in *Studies in Tudor and Stuart Politics and Government*, 4 vols (Cambridge, 1974–92), i. 66–97.

Harrison, C.J. (ed.) 'The Petition of Edmund Dudley', *English Historical Review*, 87 (1972), pp. 82–99.

Harrison, C.J., (ed.) 'The Petition of Edmund Dudley', *English Historical Review*, lxxxvii (1972), 86–90.

Lindley, P., *Gothic to Renaissance: Essays on Sculpture in England* (Stamford, 1995), pp. 170–187.

## 6 TUDOR GOVERNMENT AT WORK

### Ideology of kingship

Anglo, S., *Images of Kingship* (Seaby, 1992).

Carpenter, M.C., 'Political and Constitutional History: Before and After McFarlane', in R.H. Britnell and A.J. Pollard (eds), *The McFarlane Legacy: Studies in Late Medieval Politics and Society* (Stroud, 1995), pp. 175–206.

Chrimes, S.B., *English Constitutional Ideas in the Fifteenth Century* (Cambridge, 1936).

Dudley, Edmund, *The Tree of Commonwealth*, ed. D.M. Brodie (Cambridge, 1948).

Elton, G.R. (ed.) *The Tudor Constitution*, 2nd edn (Cambridge, 1982).

Goodman, A., *The New Monarchy: England 1471–1534* (Oxford, 1988).

Gunn, S.J., 'Sir Thomas Lovell (*c.* 1449–1524): A New Man in a New Monarchy?', in J.L. Watts (ed.), *The End of the Middle Ages? England in the Fifteenth and Sixteenth Centuries* (Stroud, 1998), pp. 117–153.

Gunn, S.J., '"New Men" and "New Monarchy" in England, 1485–1524', in Robert Stein (ed.), *Powerbrokers in the Late Middle Ages: The Burgundian Low Countries in a European Context* (Turnhout, 2001), pp. 153–163.

Harriss, G.L., 'The Dimensions of Politics', in R.H. Britnell and A.J. Pollard (eds), *The McFarlane Legacy: Studies in Late Medieval Politics and Society* (Stroud, 1995), pp. 1–20.

Richmond, C.F., 'After McFarlane', *History*, 68 (1983), 46–60.

Stubbs, W., *The Constitutional History of England in its Origin and Development*, 5th edn, 3 vols (Oxford, 1891–8; reprinted Oxford, 1926–9).

Watts, J.L., 'The Pressure of the Public on Later Medieval Politics', in L. Clark and C. Carpenter (eds), *The Fifteenth Century IV: Political Culture in Late Medieval Britain* (Woodbridge, 2004), pp. 159–180.

## Finance and tax

Grummitt, D.A., 'Henry VII, Chamber Finance and the "New Monarchy": Some New Evidence', *Historical Research*, 72 (1999), 229–243.

Guth, D.J., 'Exchequer Penal Law Enforcement, 1485–1509' (Unpublished Pittsburgh University Ph.D. thesis, 1967).

Harriss, G.L., *King, Parliament, and Public Finance in Medieval England to 1369* (Oxford, 1975).

Jurkowski, M., Smith, C.L. and Crook, D., *Lay Taxes in England and Wales, 1188–1688* (Kew, 1998).

Kleineke, H., '"Morton's Fork"? – Henry VII's "Forced Loan" of 1496', *Ricardian*, 13 (2003), 315–327.

Richardson, W.C., *Tudor Chamber Administration, 1485–1547* (Baton Rouge, 1952).

Schofield, R., *Taxation under the Early Tudors, 1485–1547* (Oxford, 2004).

Wolffe, B.P., 'Henry VII's Land Revenues and Chamber Finance', *English Historical Review*, 79 (1964), 225–254.

Wolffe, B.P., The Crown Lands, 1461–1536: An Aspect of Yorkist and Early Tudor Government (London, 1970).

Wolffe, B.P., *The Royal Demesne in English History: The Crown Estate in the Governance of the Realm from the Conquest to 1509* (London, 1971).

## Prerogative powers

Maitland, F.W., 'The "Praerogativa Regis"', in *The Collected Papers*, ed. H.A.L. Fisher, 3 vols (Cambridge, 1911), ii. 182–189.

McGlynn, M., *The Royal Prerogative and the Learning of the Inns of Court* (Cambridge, 2003).

Richardson, W.C., 'The Surveyor of the King's Prerogative', *English Historical Review*, 56 (1941), 52–75.

Thorne, S.E. (ed.), *Prerogativa Regis: Tertia Lectura Roberti Constable de Lyncolnis Inne Anno 11 H.7* (New Haven, 1949).

## Law

Baker, J.H., *The Oxford History of the Laws of England, 1483–1558* (Oxford, 2003).

Bellamy, J.G., *Bastard Feudalism and the Law* (London, 1989).

Blatcher, M., *The Court of King's Bench, 1450–1550: A Study in Self-Help* (London, 1978).

Campbell, L.B. (ed.), *The Mirror for Magistrates* (Cambridge, 1938).

Fortescue, Sir John, *The Governance of England*, ed. C. Plummer (Oxford, 1885).

Fortescue, Sir John, *On the Laws and Governance of England*, ed. Shelley Lockwood (Cambridge, 1997).

Guth, D.J., 'Enforcing Late-Medieval Law: Patterns in Litigation during Henry VII's Reign', in J.H. Baker (ed.), *Legal Records and the Historian* (London, 1978), pp. 80–96.

Ives, E.W., '"Agaynst Taking Awaye of Women": The Inception and Operation of the Abduction Act of 1487', in E.W. Ives, R.J. Knecht and J.J. Scarisbrick (eds), *Wealth and Power in Tudor England* (London, 1978), pp. 21–44.

Ives, E.W., *The Common Lawyers of Pre-Reformation England: Thomas Kebell: A Case Study* (Cambridge, 1983).

Lander, J.R., *English Justices of the Peace, 1461–1509* (Gloucester, 1989).

Thorne, S.E. (ed.), *Bracton on the Laws and Customs of England*, 4 vols (Cambridge, Mass., 1968–77).

## Parliament

Cavill, P., 'Henry VII and Parliament' (Unpublished Oxford University D.Phil. thesis, 2005).

Gwen-Wilson, C., Brand, P., Phillips, S., Ormrod, W.M., Martin, G., Curry, A.E., and Horrox, R. (eds), *The Parliament Rolls of Medieval England, 1275–1504* (Leicester, 2005).

Harriss, G.L., 'The Medieval Parliament', *Parliamentary History*, 13 (1994), 206–226.

Hicks, M.A., 'Attainder, Resumption and Coercion, 1461–1529', *Parliamentary History*, 3 (1984), 15–31.

Lander, J.R., 'Attainder and Forfeiture, 1453–1509', in *Crown and Nobility, 1450–1509* (London, 1976), pp. 127–158.

McFarlane, K.B., 'Parliament and "Bastard Feudalism"', in *England in the Fifteenth Century* (London, 1981), pp. 1–21.

Powell, J.E. and Wallis, K., *The House of Lords in the Middle Ages: A History of the English House of Lords to 1540* (London, 1968).

Strachey, J. *et al.* (eds) *Rotuli Parliamentorum*, 7 vols (London, 1767–1832).

# 7 LORDSHIP, THE CROWN, AND THE REGIONS

Bernard, G.W., *The Power of the Early Tudor Nobility* (Brighton, 1985).

Carpenter, M.C., *Locality and Polity: A Study of Warwickshire Landed Society, 1401–1499* (Cambridge, 1992).

Cunningham, S., 'Henry VII, Sir Thomas Butler and the Stanley Family: Regional Politics and the Assertion of Royal Influence in North-Western England, 1471–1521', in T. Thornton (ed.), *Social Attitudes and Political Structures in the Fifteenth Century* (Stroud, 2000).

Gunn, S.J., 'Henry Bourchier, Earl of Essex (1472–1540)', in G.W. Bernard (ed.), *The Tudor Nobility* (Manchester, 1992), pp. 134–179.

Hicks, M.A., 'Dynastic Change and Northern Society: The Career of the Fourth Earl of Northumberland, 1470–1489', *Northern History*, 14 (1978), 78–107.

Hicks, M.A., *Bastard Feudalism* (London, 1995).

James, M.E., *A Tudor Magnate and the Tudor State: Henry, Fifth Earl of Northumberland*, Borthwick Paper 30 (York, 1966).

Jones, M.K., 'Sir William Stanley of Holt: Politics and Family Allegiance in the Late Fifteenth Century', *Welsh History Review*, 14 (1988), 1–22.

Luckett, D., 'Crown Office and Licensed Retinues in the Reign of Henry VII', in R.E. Archer and S. Walker (eds), *Rulers and Ruled in Late Medieval England* (London, 1995), pp. 223–238.

Luckett, D., 'Crown Patronage and Political Morality in Early Tudor England: The Case of Giles, Lord Daubeney', *English Historical Review*, 110 (1995), 578–595.

McFarlane, K.B., 'Bastard Feudalism', *Bulletin of the Institute of Historical Research*, 20 (1943–5), 161–180.

Pollard, A.J., 'The Richmondshire Community of Gentry during the Wars of the Roses', in C.D. Ross (ed.), *Patronage, Pedigree and Power in Later Medieval England* (Gloucester, 1986).

Pollard, A.J., *North-Eastern England During the Wars of the Roses* (Oxford, 1990).

Rawcliffe, C., *The Staffords, Earls of Stafford and Dukes of Buckingham, 1394–1521* (Cambridge, 1978).

Virgoe, R., 'The Recovery of the Howards in East Anglia, 1485–1529', in E.W. Ives, R.J. Knecht and J.J. Scarisbrick (eds), *Wealth and Power in Tudor and Stuart England* (London, 1978), pp. 1–20.

# 8 ROYAL POWER AND PERSONNEL

## The court and household

Gunn, S.J., 'The Courtiers of Henry VII', *English Historical Review*, 108 (1993), 23–49.

Harriss, G.L., 'The Court of the Lancastrian Kings', in J. Stratford (ed.), *The Lancastrian Court* (Donington, 2003), pp. 1–18.

Morgan, D.A.L., 'The King's Affinity in the Polity of Yorkist England', *Transactions of the Royal Historical Society*, 5th series, 23 (1973), 1–25.

Morgan, D.A.L., 'The House of Policy: The Political Role of the Late Plantagenet Household, 1422–1485', in D.R. Starkey (ed.), *The English Court: From the Wars of the Roses to the Civil War* (London, 1987), pp. 25–70.

Myers, A.R. (ed.) *The Household of Edward IV, the Black Book of the Ordinances of 1478* (Manchester, 1959).

Starkey, D.R., 'The King's Privy Chamber, 1485–1547' (Unpublished Cambridge University Ph.D. thesis, 1973).

Starkey, D.R., 'Intimacy and Innovation: The Rise of the Privy Chamber, 1485–1547', in D.R. Starkey (ed.), *The English Court: From the Wars of the Roses to the Civil War* (London, 1987), pp. 71–118.

## The royal council

Bayne, C.G. and Dunham, W.H. (eds), *Select Cases in the Council of Henry VII* Selden Society, lxxv (London, 1958).

Condon, M.M., 'An Anachronism with Intent? Henry VII's Council Ordinance of 1491/2', in R.A. Griffiths and J. Sherborne (eds), *Kings and Nobles in the Later Middle Ages* (Gloucester, 1986), pp. 228–253.

Ford, L.L., 'Conciliar Politics and Administration in the Reign of Henry VII' (Unpublished St Andrews University Ph.D. thesis, 2001).

Holmes, P., 'The Great Council in the Reign of Henry VII', *English Historical Review*, 101 (1986), 840–862.

Pronay, N., 'The Chancellor, the Chancery, and the Council at the End of the Fifteenth Century', in H. Hearder and H.R. Loyn (eds), *British Government and Administration* (Cardiff, 1974), pp. 87–103.

Somerville, R., 'Henry VII's "Council Learned in the Law" ', *English Historical Review*, 54 (1939), 427–442.

# 9 THE PRESERVATION OF POWER

## *Retaining*

Cameron, A., 'The Giving of Livery and Retaining in Henry VII's Reign', *Renaissance and Modern Studies*, 18 (1974), 17–35.

Cameron, A., 'Complaint and Reform in Henry VII's Reign: The Origins of the Statute of 3 Henry VII, c. 2?', *Bulletin of the Institute of Historical Research*, 51 (1978), 83–89.

Dunham, W.H., *'Lord Hastings' Indentured Retainers, 1461–1483'*, *Transactions of the Connecticut Academy of Arts and Sciences*, 39 (1955).

Hicks, M.A., 'The 1468 Statute of Livery', *Historical Research*, 64 (1991), 15–28.

## *Bonds and recognisances*

Clayton, D.L., 'Peace Bonds and the Maintenance of Law and Order in Later Medieval England: The Example of Cheshire', *Bulletin of the Institute of Historical Research*, 58 (1985), 133–148.

Lander, J.R., 'Bonds, Coercion and Fear: Henry VII and the Peerage', in *Crown and Nobility, 1450–1509* (London, 1976), pp. 267–300.

# 10 THE KING'S NATION

## *London*

Barron, C., *London in the Later Middle Ages: Government and People, 1200–1500* (Oxford, 2004).

Green, R.F. (ed.), 'Historical Notes of a London Citizen, 1483–1488', *English Historical Review,* 96 (1981), 585–590.

Gunn, S.J., 'War, Dynasty and Public Opinion in Early Tudor England', in G.W. Bernard and S.J. Gunn (eds), *Authority and Consent in Early Tudor England* (Aldershot, 2002), pp. 131–149.

Guth, D.J., 'Richard III, Henry VII, and the City: London Politics and the "Dun Cowe"' in R.A. Griffiths and J. Sherborne (eds), *Kings and Nobles in the Later Middle Ages* (Gloucester, 1986), pp. 185–204.

Thomas, A.H. and Thornley, I.D. (eds), *The Great Chronicle of London* (London, 1938).

## Trade, commerce, exploration and the economy

Britnell, R.H., 'The English Economy and Government, 1450–1550', in J.L. Watts (ed.), *The End of the Middle Ages? England in the Fifteenth and Sixteenth Centuries* (Stroud, 1998), pp. 89–116.

Farmer, D.L., 'Prices and Wages, 1350–1500', in E. Miller (ed.), *The Agrarian History of England and Wales, 1348–1500* (Cambridge, 1991), pp. 431–525.

Lloyd, T.H., *The English Wool Trade in the Middle Ages* (Cambridge, 1977).

Potter, W.J.W., and Winstanley, E.J., 'The Coinage of Henry VII', *British Numismatic Journal*, 30 (1962), 262–301; 31 (1963), 109–24; 32 (1964), 140–60.

Williamson, J.A., *The Cabot Voyages and Bristol Discovery under Henry VII*, Hakluyt Society, second series, 120 (Cambridge, 1962).

## The Church

Davies, C.S.L., 'Bishop John Morton, the Holy See and the Accession of Henry VII', *English Historical Review*, 102 (1987), 2–30.

Goodman, A., 'Henry VII and Christian Renewal', in K. Robbins (ed.), *Religion and Humanism*, Studies in Church History, 17 (Oxford, 1981), pp. 115–126.

Gunn, S.J., 'Edmund Dudley and the Church', *Journal of Ecclesiastical History*, 51, 3 (2002), 509–526.

Kaufman, P.I., 'Henry VII and Sanctuary', *Church History*, 53 (1984), 465–476.

Knecht, R.J., 'The Episcopate and the Wars of the Roses', *University of Birmingham. Historical Journal*, 6 (1957–8), 108–131.

# 11 PROJECTING TUDOR INFLUENCE

Bryan, D., *Gerald Fitzgerald, the Great Earl of Kildare, 1456–1513* (Dublin, 1933).

Currin, J.M., ' "The King's Army into the Partes of Bretaigne": Henry VII and the Breton Wars, 1489–91', *War in History*, 7 (2000), 379–412.

Ellis, S.G., *Tudor Ireland* (London, 1985).

Griffiths, R.A., *Sir Rhys ap Thomas and his Family: Study in the Wars of the Roses and Early Tudor Politics* (Cardiff, 1993).

Grummitt, D.A., ' "For the Surety of the Towne and Marches": Early Tudor Policy Towards Calais, 1485–1509', *Nottingham Medieval Studies*, 44 (2000), 184–203.

Hooker, J.R., 'Notes on the Organization and Supply of the Tudor Military Under Henry VII', *Huntingdon Library Quarterly*, 23 (1959–60), 19–31.

Lacey, K.E., 'The Military Organization of Henry VII', in M. Strickland (ed.), *Armies, Chivalry and Warfare in Medieval Britain and France: Proceedings of the 1995 Harlaxton Symposium* (Stamford, 1998), pp. 234–255.

Pugh, T.B., 'The Indentures of the Marches between Henry VII and Edward Stafford, Duke of Buckingham, 1477–1521', *English Historical Review*, 71 (1956), 436–441.

Smith, J.B., 'Crown and Community in the Principality of North Wales in the Reign of Henry Tudor', *Welsh History Review*, 3 (1966), 145–171.

## 12 CONCLUSION

Anglo, S., 'Ill of the Dead. The Posthumous Reputation of Henry VII', *Renaissance Studies*, 1 (1987), 27–47.

Carpenter, M.C., 'Henry VII and the English Polity', in B. Thompson (ed.), *The Reign of Henry VII* (Stamford, 1995), pp. 11–30.

Currin, J.M., 'England's International Relations, 1485–1509: Continuities Amidst Change', in S. Doran and G. Richardson (eds), *Tudor England and its Neighbours* (Basingstoke, 2005), pp. 14–43.

Gunn, S.J., 'The Accession of Henry VIII', *Historical Research*, 64 (1991), 278–288.

# Index